Praise for M

## *Confessions of the Flesh*

"Required reading for those who cling to stereotyped ideas about our difference from the Greeks in terms of pagan license versus Christian austerity, or their hedonism versus our anxiety."　　　　—*Los Angeles Times Book Review*

"A brilliant, challenging contribution to the history of ideas."
　　　　　　　　　　　—*Kirkus Reviews* (starred review)

"Carefully constructed, exquisitely reasoned and internally cogent."　　　　　—*The New York Times Book Review*

Michel Foucault

# *Confessions of the Flesh*

One of the leading philosophical thinkers of the twentieth century, Michel Foucault was born in Poitiers, France,
in 1926. He lectured in universities throughout the world;
served as director at the Institut Français in Hamburg, Ger-
many, and at the Institut de Philosophie at the Faculté des
Lettres and the University of Clermont-Ferrand, France;
and wrote frequently for French newspapers and periodi-
cals. His influence on generations of thinkers in the areas of
sociology, queer theory, cultural studies, and critical thinking
was profound. Among his many books are *The Archaeology of
Knowledge, The Birth of the Clinic, Discipline and Punish, The
Foucault Reader, Madness and Civilization, The Order of Things,*
and *Power/Knowledge*. At the time of his death in 1984, Foucault held a chair at the Collège de France, one of France's
most prestigious institutions.

Frédéric Gros (editor) is a professor of philosophy at the
University Paris-Est Créteil and the Paris Institute of Political Studies. He was the editor of Foucault's last published
collection of lectures at the Collège de France. He has written books on psychiatry, law, and war, as well as the inter-
national bestseller *A Philosophy of Walking*. He lives in Paris.

ALSO BY MICHEL FOUCAULT

*Confessions of the Flesh*

# Confessions of the Flesh

## The History of Sexuality

### VOLUME 4

## MICHEL FOUCAULT

*Translated by Robert Hurley*

EDITED AND WITH A FOREWORD
BY FRÉDÉRIC GROS

VINTAGE BOOKS
A DIVISION OF PENGUIN RANDOM HOUSE LLC
NEW YORK

FIRST VINTAGE BOOKS EDITION, JANUARY 2022

*English translation copyright © 2021 by Penguin Random House LLC*

The Library of Congress has cataloged
the Pantheon edition as follows:
Names: Foucault, Michel, 1926–1984, author. | Hurley, Robert,
translator. | Gros, Frédéric, editor.
Title: Confessions of the flesh / Michel Foucault ; translated by
Robert Hurley ; edited and with a foreword by Frédéric Gros.
Other titles: Les aveux de la chair. English.
Series: The history of sexuality ; volume 4.
Description: First United States edition. | New York : Pantheon
Books, 2021. | Includes bibliographical references.
Classification: LCC HQ12 .F68 2021 | DDC 306.709—dc23
LC record available at https://lccn.loc.gov/2020024533

Vintage Books Trade Paperback ISBN: 978-0-525-56541-3
eBook ISBN: 978-1-5247-4804-3

www.vintagebooks.com

Printed in the United States of America

# Contents

# Foreword

In 1976, Michel Foucault publishes—under the title *La volonté de savoir*[1] [The Will to Know]—the first volume of a *Histoire de la sexualité* the back cover of which announces a coming series in five volumes, entitled respectively 2. *La chair et le corps* [The Flesh and the Body]; 3. *La croisade des enfants* [The Children's Crusade]; 4. *La femme, la mère et l'hystérique* [The Wife, the Mother, and the Hysteric]; 5. *Les pervers* [The Perverts]; 6. *Population et races* [Population and Races]. None of these works will see the light of day. The Foucault archives[2] deposited in the Bibliothèque nationale de France (Département des manuscrits) reveal, however, that at least two titles (*La chair et le corps*[3] and *La croisade des enfants*[4]) had already been the object of substantial first drafts. In 1984, shortly before Foucault's death, volumes 2 and 3[5] of this *History of Sexuality*, begun eight years before,[6] were published, but their content is very far from the initial project, as is announced both in the chapter "Modifications" of *The Use of Pleasure* ("This series of investigations is appearing later than I had anticipated and in a completely different form . . ."[7]) and a "Please insert" slipped into the volumes at the time of their publication. The plan to study the modern biopolitical *dispositif* of sexuality (sixteenth through nineteenth century)—partially treated in Foucault's courses at the Collège de France—was dropped in favor of the problematization—through a rereading of the philosophers, physicians, and orators of Greco-Roman antiquity—of sexual pleasure from the historical perspective of a genealogy of the desiring subject and under the conceptual horizon of the arts of existence. Volume 4, devoted to the problematization of the flesh by the Christian Fathers of the early centuries (from Justin to Saint Augustine), forms part of this new *History of Sexuality*, displaced by a full dozen centuries from the initial project and finding its point of gravitation in the construction of an ethic of the subject. The "Please insert" of 1984 concludes as follows:

> Hence, finally, a general recentering of this vast study on the genealogy of desiring man, from classical antiquity to the first centuries of Christianity. And its distribution into three volumes, which form a whole:
>
> • *The Use of Pleasure* studies the way in which sexual behavior was reflected by Greek thought [. . .]. Also how medical and philosophical thought elaborated this "use of pleasure"—*krêsis aphrodision*—and formulated several themes of austerity that would become recurrent on four major axes of experience: the relation to the body, to the wife, to boys, and to truth.
>
> • *The Care of the Self* analyzes this problematization in the Greek and Latin texts of the first two centuries of our era, and the inflection it undergoes in an art of living dominated by the preoccupation with oneself.
>
> • *Confessions of the Flesh* will deal, finally, with the experience of the flesh in the first centuries of Christianity, and with the role played in it by the hermeneutic, and purifying decipherment, of desire.

The genesis of this ultimate work is complex. One needs to recall that in the *Histoire de la sexualité*, "plan one," the Christian practices and doctrines of confession of the flesh were to form the object of a historical examination in a volume titled *The Flesh and the Body*.[8] It was then a matter of studying "the evolution of the Catholic pastoral and of the sacrament of penance after the

Council of Trent."[9] A first overview of this research had been presented during the lecture of February 19, 1975, at the Collège
de France.[10] Rather quickly, though, Foucault decided to go back
to the very beginning of the age to recapture the point of origin in Christian history, the moment of emergence of a ritualized
truth obligation, of an injunction of verbalization by the subject,
of truth-telling about oneself. In this way, as early as the years
1976–1977, there accumulated a certain number of reading notes
about Tertullian, Cassian, and others.[11] Daniel Defert writes concerning the month of August 1977: "Foucault is at Vendeuvre.
He's writing about the Church Fathers and attempting to shift his
history of sexuality by several centuries."[12] In the framework of a
study of "governmentalities" at the Collège de France (lectures
of February 15 and 22, 1978[13]), he takes advantage of these first
readings of the Fathers to characterize the Christian moment of
"pastoral governmentality":[14] "truth acts" (telling the truth about
oneself) hinging on practices of obedience. These results will be
taken up and synthesized in October 1979 in preparation for the
first of two presentations in the framework of the Tanner Lectures
at Stanford University.[15]

The year 1980 constitutes a decisive moment in the development of studies leading to the manuscript of the *Confessions*. Foucault presents at the Collège de France, in February and March
1980, without ever indicating that they have their place in a history
of sexuality, a series of precise and documented historical inquiries
relative to the Christian truth obligations in the preparation for
baptism, the rites of penance, and monastic direction between the
second and fourth centuries of our era.[16] In autumn of the same
year, in the United States, he gives, at the University of California,
Berkeley, and at Dartmouth College, two lectures setting out these
same themes in their grand conceptual generality,[17] and above all,
in the context of a seminar in New York with Richard Sennett, he
presents, again in a schematic way of course, many of the articulations of what will become the *Confessions of the Flesh*.[18] Indeed
in this seminar one finds expositions on Clement of Alexandria's
doctrine of marriage, the Christian art of virginity (its evolution
from Saint Cyprian to Basil of Ancyra, going by way of Methodius
of Olympus), as well as Foucault's examination of the basic mean-

ing that, with Saint Augustine, the concept of *libido*—after the fall and in marriage—has assumed in our culture.[19] So one can say not only that, as early as the end of 1980, Foucault has a strong intuition of the architecture and the main arguments of the *Confessions of the Flesh*, but also that he has already accomplished a substantial investigation of the sources, at least for the study of the rituals of penance and the principles of monastic direction.

The definitive drafting of the text of the *Confessions* can be situated in the years 1981 and 1982. In an issue of the journal *Communications*,[20] Foucault offers in May 1982 what he presents as "an excerpt from the third volume of *The History of Sexuality*."[21] However, in parallel fashion, in his courses at the Collège de France, Foucault carries out, in an ever more massive way, his "turn" to antiquity. To be sure, the Greco-Latin moment had not been completely neglected up to then, but from 1978 to 1980, it was reduced to the role of a counterpoint, invaluable above all for determining the points of irreducibility of the Christian practices of veridiction and governmentality (that is, the differences between the government of the city-state and pastoral governmentality, the direction of existence in the Greco-Roman philosophical sects and that practiced in the first monasteries, the Stoic and Christian examination of conscience, and so on). Thus, what was only a simple counterpoint will become more and more its own consistent and insistent object of research. The tendency is marked as early as 1981: the course at the Collège de France offered that year is completely dominated by classical references (problems of marriage and the love of boys in antiquity[22]), whereas the cycle of lectures given at the University of Louvain in the month of May still tries to maintain a balance between the ancient and Christian references.[23] In 1982, the specifically Christian style of truth obligations and other austerities is no longer foregrounded in his great cycles of lectures in North America ("Telling the Truth About Oneself" at the University of Toronto in June;[24] "Techniques of the Self" at the University of Vermont in October[25]), while in his courses at the Collège de France, it is evoked only in a marginal way, as a simple vanishing point.[26]

One can say, then, concerning the process since *La volonté de savoir* (1976), that as early as 1977–1978 the project of a history of modern sexuality (sixteenth through nineteenth centuries) is abandoned for the sake, in a first phase (1979–1982), of a recentering in the direction of a historical problematization of the Christian flesh—through the principal "truth acts" (exomologesis and *exagoreusis*), the arts of virginity, and the doctrine of marriage in the Christian Fathers of the first centuries—and then, in a second phase (1982–1984), of a decentering toward the Greco-Roman arts of living and the place occupied by the *aphrodisia* within them.

It must have been in the autumn of 1982 that the manuscript on the Christian conception of the flesh—along with the corresponding typescript—was delivered to Gallimard.[27] Pierre Nora recalls that on this occasion Foucault lets him know that this doesn't mean the publication of the *Aveux de la chair* will be imminent, however, because he's decided, encouraged by Paul Veyne, that this book that he's just had transcribed will be preceded by a volume devoted to the Greco-Roman experience of the *aphrodisia*. The extent of the investigations that we've just noted will be such that Foucault will add to that book the two volumes that we are familiar with: *The Use of Pleasure* and *The Care of the Self*. The work on and drafting of these two volumes—ongoing even as he is launching yet another new field of research at the Collège de France: a study of *parrêsia*[28]—will delay him in his rereading of the *Confessions of the Flesh* and will possibly dissuade him from undertaking a rewrite. From March to May 1984, as he is finishing the editorial work around volumes 2 and 3, exhausted and gravely ill, he takes up the correction of the typescript of the *Confessions of the Flesh*. Hospitalized on June 3 following a physical breakdown, he dies at the Salpêtrière on June 25, 1984.

To establish this edition, we have therefore drawn on the manuscript written in Foucault's hand, together with the typescript.[29] This typescript, which was established in turn by Éditions Gallimard on the basis of the manuscript, then conveyed to Michel Foucault for correction,[30] is rather faulty—it could not be entrusted, for reasons of unavailability, to the secretary who usually typed his texts and was very familiar with his handwriting.

We thus returned to and prioritized the original text,[31] while taking into account the corrections to the typescript that Foucault had had the time to make, at least within the first two parts of the text.[32] We altered the punctuation to make reading of the text more fluid, we homogenized the modalities of referencing and applied the editing codes established for volumes 2 and 3 of *The History of Sexuality* (*The Use of Pleasure, The Care of the Self*). We have verified (and corrected where necessary) the citations. The brackets that appear in the printed text refer to interventions on our part.[33] These interventions are of several types: drafting notes when the manuscript carries only a simple footnote number without any content;[34] adding notes and numbers when citations are given without referencing; supplying missing words, rectifying grammatically shaky, incorrect, or obviously faulty phrases; correcting errors of proper names; adding a translation to passages cited directly in Greek, Latin, or German;[35] adding chapter titles when they are missing. For the titles, we have opted for descriptive restraint, except perhaps for the chapter "The Libidinization of Sex," but Foucault himself speaks in the body of the text of a "libidinization of the sexual act." For the chapters, we have preserved the divisions present in the manuscript. The titles "The Laborious Baptism" and "The Art of Arts" are Foucault's. One finds them in a projected plan (box 90, second page of folder 1).

For this editing work, we sought assistance from the archive boxes containing his own reading notes relating to the first Christian Fathers of the first centuries.[36] The quality of Michel Senellart's work[37] rendered us immense service, as did Philippe Chevallier's thesis.[38] I am grateful to Daniel Defert and Henri-Paul Fruchard for their patient and productive rereading of the text. The final bibliography was fashioned according to the editorial principles of *The Use of Pleasure* and *The Care of the Self*: it contains only works mentioned in the body of the text. It must be emphasized, however, as the archive boxes of Michel Foucault's reading notes regarding the Christian Fathers show,[39] that the works cited represent only a small part (especially for modern writers) of the read and processed references.[40] At the request of the rights holders, the text does not include any editor's notes that would consist of commentary, references internal to Foucault's work, or erudition. Our work is limited to the editing of the text.

We have added to the end of the text four appendices, which have a different status than the main text. The first three correspond to pages held in separate folders and physically placed in Foucault's manuscript, at the end of the first part of the *Confessions*.[41] Appendix 1 is a simple and brief reminder of general objectives ("What is to be demonstrated . . .") and may correspond to a projected introduction or perhaps to a clarification for personal use.[42] Appendix 2 consists of a critical examination of the relations between *exomologesis* and *exagoreusis*. This study fits into the strict continuity of the last developments of the first part of the text, but it's not possible to know if Foucault wrote these pages and ultimately decided not to include them or if he drafted them after his manuscript was transcribed. Appendix 3 is an expansion on an evaluation that appears in a tighter form in chapter 3 ("The Second Penance") of Part I, concerning Cain's curse, which would be tied above all to his refusal to acknowledge the crime. Appendix 4 corresponds to the last exposition of the manuscript and the typescript. We've chosen to place it among the appendices because it announces thematics that are in fact developed earlier. One notes that the book's closing paragraphs, once this shift has been made, have a conclusive look and feel.

Michel Foucault's heirs agreed that the moment and the conditions were right for the publication of this major unpublished text. Like the preceding volumes, it is appearing in the Bibliothèque des Histoires series edited by Pierre Nora.

The "Please insert" of 1984 indicated

Volume 1: *La Volonté de savoir*, 224 pages
Volume 2: *L'Usage des plaisirs*, 296 pages
Volume 3: *Le Souci de soi*, 288 pages
Volume 4: *Les Aveux de la chair* (forthcoming)

This has now been accomplished.

*Frédéric Gros*

# PART I

*The Formation of
a New Experience*

# 1

# Creation, Procreation

The *aphrodisia* regime, defined in terms of marriage, procreation, a disqualification of pleasure, and a respectful and intense bond of sympathy between spouses, was formulated, it seems, by non-Christian philosophers and teachers, and their "pagan" society thought of it as an acceptable code of conduct for everyone—which doesn't mean it was actually followed by everyone; far from it.

One finds this same regime, essentially unmodified, in the doctrine of the second-century Fathers. Those theologians, in the view of most historians, would not have found their basic principles in the early Christian communities nor in the apostolic texts—with the exception of the markedly Hellenizing letters of Saint Paul. These principles would have migrated, as it were, into Christian thought and practice, from pagan milieus whose hostility Christians needed to disarm by displaying forms of conduct that pagans already recognized and valued highly. It is a fact that apologists like Justin or Athenagoras assure the emperors they are addressing that in regard to marriage, procreation, and the *aphrodisia*, Christians base their practice on the same principles as the philosophers. And to emphasize this sameness, they employ, with scant alterations, those aphoristic precepts whose words and formulations readily indicate their origin. "For our part," says Justin, "if we marry, it is only that we may bring up children; or if we decline marriage, we live in perfect continence."[1]

Speaking to Marcus Aurelius, Athenagoras uses references of

a Stoic sort: control of desire*—"for us procreation is the measure of desire";[2] rejection of any second marriage—"whoever repudiates his wife to marry another is an adulterer," "every remarriage is an honorable adultery";[3] negativity toward pleasure—"we despise the things of this life, even to the pleasures of the soul."[4] Athenagoras doesn't make use of these themes to indicate traits of Christianity that are distinct from paganism. It's a matter of showing instead how Christians don't deserve the reproaches of immorality that have been aimed at them, and how their life is the very realization of a moral ideal that the wisdom of the pagans has long recognized.[5] Above all, he underscores the fact that the Christians' belief in eternal life and their desire to unite with God constitute a strong and profound reason for them to truly follow these precepts in their actions—and better still, to keep their intentions pure and to banish the very thought of the actions they condemn.[6]

The work of Clement of Alexandria, at the end of the second century, offers a much ampler testimony concerning the *aphrodisia* regime as it seems to have been incorporated into Christian thought. Clement evokes the problems of marriage, sexual relations, procreation, and continence in several texts, primarily in the *Paedagogus*, chapter 10 of book 2, and also (though in a more cursory way) chapters 6 and 7 of the same book and [chapter 8] of book 3; and in the second *Stromata* book, chapter 32 and the whole third book. I will analyze the first of these texts here, clarifying it when necessary by the others. There is a reason for this: the large text of the third book of the *Stromata* is devoted essentially to a polemic against different gnostic themes. It is developed on two fronts: first, Clement wanted to refute those for whom the disqualification of the material world, its identification with evil, and the certainty of salvation for the chosen ones made obedience to the laws of this world irrelevant, when they did not make such transgressions obligatory and customary; second, he also sought to distance himself from the numerous Encratist tendencies that, aligning themselves more or less closely with Valentinus or Basilides, wished to deny marriage and sexual relations to all the faithful, or at least to those who intended to lead a truly saintly life.

---

* Typescript: childbirth as desire's reason for being.

These texts are obviously crucial for understanding, through the question of marriage and self-restraint, the theology of Clement, his conception of matter, of evil and sin. The *Paedagogus*, though, has a very different purpose: it is addressed to Christians after their conversion and their baptism—and not, as has sometimes been said, to pagans still making their way toward the Church. And it offers these new Christians a precise, concrete code for daily living.[7] It is a text whose objectives are comparable to the advice on behavior that the Hellenistic philosophers might give and consequently the comparison between them should be worthwhile.

Doubtless these life precepts don't cover all the obligations of Christians and will not lead them to the end of the road. Just as, before the *Paedagogus*, Clement's *Protrepticus* had the purpose of exhorting the soul to choose the right path, after the *Paedagogus*, the teacher will still need to initiate the disciple into the higher truths. In the *Paedagogus*, then, one has a book of exercise and advancement—the guide for an ascension toward God, which subsequent instruction will have to carry to completion. But the intermediary role of this art of living in the Christian manner doesn't warrant relativizing it: if it is far from saying everything, what it says never becomes inoperative. The more perfect life, taught by another tutor, will reveal more truths, but it will not obey different moral laws. To be very precise, the precepts dispensed by the *Paedagogus* concerning marriage, sexual relations, and pleasure do not constitute an intermediate stage appropriate to a middling life, and which might be followed by a more rigorous and purer stage, suited to the existence of the true gnostic. The latter, who does see what the simple "student" is not able to, does not have to apply different rules in these matters of everyday life.

This is something one can see in the *Stromata*, in fact, where, apropos of marriage, Clement never suggests different precepts for the "true gnostic" and the *Paedagogus*. If he absolutely refuses to condemn marriage—to see a *porneia*, a fornication, in it as some do, and even to regard it as a difficult obstacle impeding a genuinely religious life—he doesn't make an obligation of it either: he leaves the two paths open, recognizing that each of them, marriage and chastity, has its burdens and obligations,[8] and in the course of reflection or discussion he in turn underscores

the greater merit of those who meet the responsibility of having a
wife and children, or points out the value of a life without sexual
relations.[9] What one reads in the *Paedagogus* regarding the life of
a man with his wife does not therefore constitute a provisional
condition: these are common precepts that hold for all who are
married, whatever their degree of progress toward the gnosis
of God.* And moreover, what the *Paedagogus* says about its own
teaching reflects the same idea. The "Educator" is not a temporary and imperfect instructor: "He resembles his Father, God [. . .]
He is without sin, without blame, without passion of soul, God
immaculate in the form of man, accomplishing His Father's will,
God the Logos, who is seated at the right hand of His Father,
with even the nature of God."[10] The Educator is therefore Christ
himself; and what he teaches, or more precisely what is taught
through him and what is taught by him, is the *Logos*. As the Word,
it teaches God's law; and the commandments it formulates are the
universal and living reason. It is the second and third parts of the
*Paedagogus* that are devoted to this art of conducting oneself in a
Christian manner, but in the last lines of chapter 13 of the first
part, Clement explains the meaning he gives to these lessons to
come: "Man's duty, consequently, is to cultivate a will that is in
conformity with and united throughout his life to God and Christ,
properly directed to eternal life. The life of the Christian, which
we are learning from our Educator, is a unified whole made up
of deeds in accordance with the Logos; that is, it is the unfailing
practical application of the truths taught by the Logos, an accomplishment which we call fidelity. The whole is constituted by the
Lord's precepts, which have been prescribed as spiritual commandments, useful both for ourselves and for those near to us."
And among these necessary things, Clement distinguishes those
concerning life here below—which one will find in the subsequent
chapters of the *Paedagogus*—and those concerning heavenly life,
which can be deciphered from the Scriptures. An esoteric teaching? Perhaps.[11] But it remains clear that in these laws of every-

---

* Translator's note: To clarify, Clement was not himself a gnostic, but apparently
that brand of dualism was popular in his day and he used some of its vocabulary
to appeal to its adherents.

day existence, we must see a teaching of the *Logos* itself; in the behavior that submits to it we must recognize *the right action* that leads to *eternal life,* and in these right actions which are in keeping with the *Logos,* we must recognize *a will united with God* and with Christ. These words that Clement uses as he is about to present his rules for living are quite significant. They clearly indicate the double register to which they must be referred: according to the Stoic vocabulary, these rules for living do define right behavior (*kathêkonta*), but also those rationally justified actions in which the man who performs them merges with universal reason (*katorthô-mata*); and according to the Christian thematic, they define not only the negative precepts that allow one to be accepted in the community, but the form of existence that leads to eternal life and constitutes their faith.[12] In sum, what Clement offers in the teaching of the *Paedagogus* is a prescriptive corpus in which the level of "right actions" is only the visible aspect of the virtuous life, which in turn is the journey toward salvation. The omnipresence of the *Logos,* which commands right actions, manifests right reason, and saves souls by uniting them with God, ensures the cohesiveness of these three levels.[13] The "practical" books of the *Paedagogus,* which begin immediately after this passage, teem with minor precautions whose concern with pure and simple propriety may be surprising. But they must be placed within the overall intention, and the details of the *kathêkonta,* where Clement's recommendations often seem to get lost, should be deciphered in terms of this *Logos* which is at the same time the principle of right action and the movement toward salvation, the rationality of the real world and the word of God calling one to eternity.

A reading of the *Paedagogus,* II, X, calls then for a number of preliminary remarks.

1. The common practice is to pick out explicit or implicit citations of pagan moralists found in that text, Stoics in particular. Musonius Rufus is undoubtedly one of those used most often, although he is never named there. And it's a fact that on four or five occasions at least, Clement transcribes sentences of the Roman Stoic, and on essential points, almost word for word. Thus, Musonius is cited on the principle that a legitimate union

must desire procreation;[14] on the principle that seeking pleasure by itself, even in marriage, is contrary to reason;[15] on the principle that one must spare one's wife any form of indecent relations;[16] and on the principle that if one is ashamed of an action it's because one knows it is wrongful.[17] But it would be a mistake to conclude that in this chapter Clement has only interpolated a teaching he has borrowed from a philosophical school without really trying to give it a Christian meaning. In the first place, it should be noted that here, as in many other texts by Clement, the references to pagan philosophers are very numerous. One can discover silent borrowings from Antipater, from Hierocles, and no doubt sentences by Sextus as well. Aristotle, who is not cited either, is used often, as are naturalists and physicians. Finally—and again, this is not unusual in Clement—Plato is one of the rare authors cited by name and the only one to be cited widely.[18] But it should also be noted that none of the great prescriptive themes evoked by Clement are presented without the accompaniment of scriptural citations: Moses, Leviticus, Ezekiel, Isaiah, Sirach. Rather than a massive, barely altered borrowing from late Stoicism, we must see in this chapter the attempt to integrate the precepts prescribed by the moralists of the era into a triple reference: that of the naturalists and physicians, which shows how nature grounds them and manifests their rationality, testifying in this way to presence of the *Logos* as this world's organizing principle; that of the philosophers, especially Plato, the philosopher par excellence, who shows how human reason can recognize and justify the precepts, attesting that the *Logos* inhabits the soul of every man; and lastly that of the Scriptures, which show that God has explicitly given men these commandments, these *entolai*, affirming in this way that those who obey him will unite with him, will be of the same will: either in the form of the Mosaic law, or in the form of the Christian gospel.[19]

Each of these major precepts, which this chapter 10 of the second book formulates, comes under a principle of "triple determination," therefore: by nature, by philosophical reason, by the word of God. Of course, the content of the teaching, the codification, as to what it permits, forbids, or recommends is absolutely consistent, apart from a few details, with what was taught in the philosophical schools, the Stoic ones in particular, starting in the

preceding centuries. But all of Clement's efforts involve insert-
ing these well-known and current aphorisms in a complex web of
citations, references, or examples that gives them the appearance
of prescriptions of the *Logos*, as it declares itself in nature, human
reason, or the word of God.

2. The second and third books of the *Paedagogus* are thus
a code for living. Underneath the apparent disorder of the
chapters—after the matter of drinking, it is a question of luxury
in furnishings; between the precepts for living together and the
correct use of sleep, there is talk about perfumes and crowns, then
shoes (which should be simple white sandals for women), then dia-
monds, with which one must avoid being fascinated, and so on—
one can recognize a depiction of "regimen." In the medical-moral
literature of the epoch, these models were presented in different
forms. For example in the form of an *agenda*, following almost
hour by hour the course of the day as it unfolds: thus the regimen
of Diocles, who takes up a man from the very first gestures to be
performed upon waking and leads him to the moment of falling
asleep, then indicates the modifications to be applied according to
the season, and finally gives opinions about sexual relations.[20] Or
also the enumeration of Hippocrates, which for some constitutes
a canonical table: exercises, then food, then drink, then sleep, and
lastly sexual relations.[21]

Quatember[22] has suggested that Clement, in his rules of daily
life, follows the cycle of daily activities, but starting with the evening meal, and hence with advice about food, drink, conversations, and table manners; then he goes to the nighttime, to sleep
and the precepts having to do with sexual relations. The views
concerning clothing and appearance that follow would relate to
the morning toilette, and most of the chapters of book 3 would
correspond to daytime life, to domestic servants, the baths, physical exercise, and so on.

As to chapter 10, concerning marital relations, despite the
apparent disorder of the text, which more than one commenta-
tor has noted, here too Quatember suggests a simple and logical
design. In his view, after having determined the goal of marriage—
namely procreation—Clement condemns unnatural relations;

then, proceeding to relations internal to marriage, he considers in turn pregnancy, unfruitful relations, and abortion, before setting out the principles of moderation and propriety to be observed in marriage relations. Through many detours and interlacings, one does find approximately this succession of themes. But at the same time one can recognize another concatenation that in no way excludes this first schema.

The type of explicit or implicit citations that Clement foregrounds by turns can serve here as a guiding thread. Not that he isn't careful, throughout the text, to interweave the authority of the Scripture, the testimony of philosophers, and the claims of physicians and naturalists, following the principle of triple reference. But in a noticeable way, the accent constantly shifts, the coloration of the references changes. First the lessons of farming and natural history are invoked (the right way to sow seeds, the "metamorphoses" of the hyena, the bad morals of the hare) to explain Mosaic law.[23] Then there are borrowings above all from the medical and philosophical literature, regarding the human body, its natural impulses, and the need to maintain control of the desires and avoid the excesses that exhaust the body and disturb the soul.[24] Finally, in the last pages of the chapter, the citations from the Scripture, which had never been absent from the text and served as a counterpoint to the other references, become predominant (not without one or two explicit returns to Plato and implicit ones to Musonius).

Let us say that in this complex text, there is, superimposed on one another, a "thematic" composition (which goes from condemnation of unnatural relations to recommendations of reserve in the use of marriage) and a "referential" composition that gives another dimension to these prescriptions of "regimen." This shifting of references allows one to hear in turn the different voices through which the *Logos* speaks: that of the figures of nature, that of the reason which must preside over the human configuration, that of God speaking directly to men in order to save them (it being understood that the first two are also the *Logos* of God but in a different form). This succession thus makes it possible to establish the same prescriptions and the same prohibitions (which are repeated several times in the text) at three different levels: that of the order of the world, as it has been set by the Creator, and to which certain "unnatural" animals bear witness; that of human moderation, as taught by the wisdom of the body itself and by the principles of a reason that desires to remain master of itself;[25] and that of a purity that gives access to incorruptible existence beyond this life. Perhaps here one should recognize, albeit in a shrouded way, the tripartition, important in Clement's anthropology, between the animal, the psychical, and the pneumatic. Even if this is not the underlying schema, the chapter clearly follows an upward movement that goes from examples deposited in nature as lessons to appeals that assign Christians the objective of a "Godlike" existence. And it's over the whole length of this road that the economy of sexual relations will be determined.

3. The leading question raised by the pagan philosophers' moral treatises or diatribes concerned the advisability of marriage: *Ei gamêteon* (Should one marry?). Chapter 10 of the *Paedagogus* deals with this question elliptically: Clement indicates within the first lines that he will speak for married people; then, after an exposition in which there is the question of sexual relations during pregnancy and the illnesses that may be caused by their excess, he again elides the question, saying that this theme is discussed in the treatise *On Continence*. Is this a separate work? Or texts that appear in the *Stromata*? Two sections in the *Stromata* can be supposed to constitute this treatise, or at least to reproduce its content: book 3 in its entirety, which as we've seen is a long discussion around Encratism, common to several gnostic tendencies, or about certain "licentious" forms of dualist morality; and more probably the thirteenth and final chapter of book 2 of the *Stromata*, which introduces the reader to book 3 and in fact presents itself as being an answer to the traditional question in traditional debates of practical philosophy: should one get married?[26] And it's precisely to the analysis of this question that the *Paedagogus* refers.

The answer given by this passage of the second book of the *Stromata* doesn't present any departures from the philosophical morality of the time. If it tries to set itself apart, this is not relative to the philosophers' general principles but rather to their real attitude, whose laxity is not corrected by the theory. In the *Stromata* and the *Paedagogus*, Clement declares the purpose of marriage to be the procreation of children.[27]* On the basis of this link between the value of marriage and the procreative finality, Clement can define the major ethical rules that should govern relations between spouses: the bond between them must not be owing to pleasure and sensuality but to the *"Logos"*,[28] one mustn't treat one's wife like a mistress,[29] or scatter seed to the winds;[30] and the principles of restraint must be observed—rules that the animals themselves respect.[31] This bond must not be broken; if it is, one must forgo remarriage as long as the partner is still living.[32] Finally, adultery is forbidden and should be punished.[33]

Most of these points—and particularly those concerning relations between spouses—are also found in the *Paedagogus*, but treated much more fully there. The continuity and homogeneity between the two texts is obvious, with this difference: that the *Stromata* texts speak of marriage and its value in terms of procreation, whereas the *Paedagogus* speaks of procreation as a principle of discrimination for sexual relations. In one case it's a matter of procreation as the ultimate aim of marriage; in the other it is a matter of this same procreation in the economy of relations and sexual acts. The main interest of this chapter 10 and its novelty—at least in the Christian literature, if not in all the moral literature of antiquity—is its interweaving of two types of questions, two traditional debates: that concerning the right economy of pleasures—the *aphrodisia* theme—and that of marriage, of its

---

* Passage crossed out by Foucault in the typescript: "And according to a completely Stoic type of procedure, starting from this definition by finality, Clement considers in turn: the question whether one should marry, in general, and the conditions that may modulate this obligation, preventing one from giving it one answer valid for everyone all the time; the opinions of the different philosophers on this subject; what makes a marriage a good: namely that by giving man descendants, it perfects and completes his existence; it provides citizens for his homeland; in the event of illness, it ensures the solicitude and care of his wife; it provides help when old age comes. To which is added, as a negative proof, the fact of not having children is either penalized by the laws or condemned by morality. Clement's reasoning consists in deducing the positive value from what perfection or utility there may be in having offspring. Which shows very clearly that the latter are *the* end of marriage in the strong sense of the expression—its raison d'être and justification; but also that procreation can constitute a good worthy of being pursued as an end only if it occurs within marriage."

value and of how to conduct oneself within it, given that marriage is justified by procreation and on that basis one can define in what sense it can be a good (a thesis developed in the second book of the *Stromata* and recalled in the *Paedagogus*). Of course, this was not the first attempt at defining the kind of sexual conduct spouses should practice, but it appears to be the first regimen of sexual acts developed not in terms of wisdom or individual health but from the standpoint of rules intrinsic to marriage. There had been a regimen of sex and an ethics of marriage: they overlapped, quite obviously. But here, in this text by Clement, one has a merger of the two points of view. What goes on between spouses, and what the moralists of antiquity treated, if not obliquely, then at least briefly and from some distance—they were content simply to enumerate rules of decency and carefulness—is becoming an object of concern, intervention, and analysis.

Under the somewhat enigmatic title "What must be distinguished regarding procreation," chapter 10 of the second book of the *Paedagogus* deals in fact with a relatively precise question. It is the one that's formulated as early as the first line of the text and that reappears in the last line: the question of the right moment, the right occasion, the opportuneness—*kairos*—for sex between married persons.[34] Insofar as it applies to a regulation of days and nights, this term *kairos* does have the narrow meaning of "opportune time." But that is far from being the only meaning. In the philosophical and above all the Stoic vocabulary, *kairos* refers to a set of conditions that can make a merely permitted action into an action that effectively has a positive value. *Kairos* doesn't characterize an exercise of caution, avoiding the risks and dangers that might make a neutral action a bad one; it defines the criteria that a concrete action will need to satisfy in order to be good. Whereas law separates the permitted from the prohibited among all the positive actions, *kairos* establishes the positive value of a real action.

So the question that will be addressed in this chapter of the *Paedagogus* is that of setting the conditions that give a positive value to sexual relations between married people. The fact that it is *this* question that is given such attention in this book of conduct has its importance: in it one sees that, relative to a process that we have noted in the pagan authors of the preceding epochs, the question of sexual relations, of the *aphrodisia*, is now very much subordinated to the question of marriage; it has lost its independence to such a point that the term *aphrodisia* doesn't appear in this text by Clement. It is procreation, or rather the procreative union, that constitutes the general theme under which the whole chapter will be placed. Further, we have here undoubtedly the first text in which marital sexual relations are themselves considered in detail, and as a specific and important element of conduct. Once again, the philosophers had already formulated most of the precepts that Clement spells out, but they had situated those precepts within an overall ethics of relations between spouses, in a regulation of the way to live together when one is married. Plutarch's *Conjugalia praecepta* gives advice for the proper general functioning of that community of two which the couple constitutes; views concerning sexual relations are only one element for this life, which marriage should not prevent from being philosophically sound. The *Paedagogus* says little about the couple, but it treats sexual relations between marriage partners as an important and relatively autonomous object. We can say that, in this, it offers the first example of a genre, or rather of a practice that will have a considerable importance in the history of Western societies—the examination and analysis of sexual relations between spouses.

Finally, the question of the *kairos* of marital relations allows one to see how Clement integrates a code that he has effectively received from the Hellenistic philosophies (and no doubt also from a whole social movement) into a religious conception of nature, the *Logos*, and salvation. His is a very different solution, as we shall see, from that proposed by Saint Augustine—and it is Augustine's that will be retained by the institutions and doctrine of the Western Church. In Clement's reflection on the *kairos*, it would be a mistake to see simply a graft, more or less skillful, of elements borrowed from the prevailing morality and merely rendered a little more demanding or austere. The *kairos* of the sexual relationship is defined by its connection to the *Logos*. Let us not forget that for Clement the *Logos* is called Savior, because this *Logos* has invented for men "the remedies that give them a just moral sense and lead them to salvation," and this by seizing the right "occasion."[35]

. . .

Clement starts from the proposition that sexual relations have procreation as their end. A completely ordinary thesis for his time. One finds it in the physicians.[36] One finds it in the philosophers, either in the form of a linkage among three terms—no sexual relations outside of marriage and no marriage that shouldn't find its end in its offspring[37]—or in the form of a direct condemnation of any sexual act that doesn't have procreation as its object.[38]

In this, then, there's nothing peculiar in Clement of Alexandria. Just as there's nothing new about his general distinction between the "goal" or "objective" (*skopos*) of an action and its "end" (*telos*). On the other hand, it does seem that his application of this difference to the domain of sexual relations—while in the "spirit" of the Stoics and within the logic of their analyses—had not been frequently done before, to say the least. And in fact the use of this distinction in Clement's text leads to a result that at first glance may appear to lack any fertile meaning. The "objective" would be *paidopoiia*: making children, progeny in the strict sense. The end, on the other hand, would be *euteknia*, which is sometimes translated as "fine children" or "a large family." Actually, though, the word should be given a broader sense: it refers to finding a plenitude and a satisfaction in the descendants one has, in their life and happy fortune.[39] So the objective (*skopos*) of the sexual relation would thus be the existence of the progeny; the end (*telos*) the positive relation to this progeny, the accomplishment they constitute. Two considerations that Clement immediately adds may allow us to clarify the value of this distinction.

Clement first compares the sexual act to sowing seeds. A traditional metaphor. One finds it in Athenagoras and in the Apologists. It seems to have been common in the philosophical diatribes, where it served to illustrate the rule that seeds must be deposited in the furrow where they could germinate. But Clement also uses it to better mark the distinction between what the "goal" of sexual relations should be and what their "end" should be. The goal of the grower, when he sows: to procure something to eat. His end: "to have a harvest," says Clement's text simply—meaning, no doubt, to see the seeds through to their point of natural accomplishment, when an abundance of fruits is produced. This comparison with sowing remains rather elliptical; but presumably it allows one to consider as the "goal" this procreation of children, which was so often shown by the philosophers to be useful to parents—for ensuring their status or securing support in their old age—and to consider as "ends" something much more general and less utilitarian—namely the human accomplishment that having descendants constitutes.[40] And since it's this end that Clement wants to bring out in this chapter, by analyzing the *kairos* of sexual relations, it is understandable that he would devote little attention to the personal advantages and social benefits that might come of having children.[41]

That this non-utilitarian end is indeed Clement's theme here is shown by the idea that he immediately links to the metaphor of the sower. Man doesn't plant "because of himself"; man must plant "because of God." By this, Clement doesn't mean the end that directs the action, but rather the principle that permeates and sustains it throughout.[42] The act of [pro]creation must be performed "because of" God, in the sense that, first of all, it is God who prescribes it by saying "Increase and multiply," but also because by procreating, man is the "image of God," and he "collaborates," for his part, "in the birth of man."[43]

This proposition is important for Clement's whole analysis, since it establishes in human procreation a relation to God that is close and complex at the same time. That by procreating, man is the "image of God" should not be interpreted on the assumption of an immediate likeness between the creation of Adam and procreation by his descendants. Doubtless, as Clement explains elsewhere,[44] God, who was content to give an order to make the animals appear on earth, had molded the first man with his hands, thus marking an essential difference and a greater proximity between him and that being who was created in his image. But this doesn't mean for Clement that the Creation transmitted to man something of the essence of the nature or power of God: there is nothing in us that "matches up" with God.[45] And yet one can speak of a "resemblance" to God—the resemblance evoked in the Genesis narrative. This resemblance was that of man before the fall, and it can, it must become his again. It is realized not through the body, but through the spirit and through reasoning;[46]

it is ensured by obedience to the law: "The law says [. . .]: Walk behind the Lord [. . .] The law, in fact, calls it a walking after; and this makes them similar, as much as it is possible."[47] So it is not procreation in itself and as a natural process that is "in the likeness" of Creation—it is procreation insofar as it is accomplished in the right way and by "following" the law. And if the law prescribes conformity with nature, this is because nature obeys God.[48]

In this progression toward resemblance, a "synergy" of man and God thus finds its possibility. In fact, God created man because he was "worthy of his choice," worthy consequently of being loved by him. If there had to be a reason for man's creation, it consists in the condition that without man, "the Demiurge would not have been able to prove his goodness."[49] So the creation of man is as much a manifestation of God's goodness as it is of his presence. Man, in return and as a result, offers, by being worthy of being loved, the possibility of demonstrating his goodness. By procreating, man thus does something much more and altogether different than "imitating," as some might imagine, the capacities of the demiurgic act. For all his humanness, he partakes in the power and "philanthropy" of God. Man procreates, along with God, human beings who are worthy of being loved with a love whose manifestation was the "cause" of the Creation, and later the Incarnation. The "synergy" of man with God in the procreative act[50] doesn't just consist in the support of God in human generation—it's a matter of fulfilling what a formula predating Clement said: "God receives from man that which he had created: man."[51]

Chapter 10 of the second book of the *Paedagogus* thus devotes its analysis of "the distinctions to be made regarding procreation" to the complex and fundamental relations between Creator and creatures. The content of the very "quotidian" precepts that Clement offers on the subject may be nearly identical to the teaching of the pagan philosophers, but this doesn't imply a relinquishment of the regulation of sexual relations to a Stoic or Platonic wisdom that is accepted and certified by a rather broad consensus. Undoubtedly, Clement has taken up the codification and the rules of conduct that were formulated moreover by the philosophy that was contemporaneous with him, but he has rethought them and integrated them into a conception that he is careful to recall in a few sentences at the beginning of this chapter, and that brings into play, in procreation, the relations of man to his Creator, of God to his creatures. But a word of caution: Clement does not in any way attribute, by this means, a spiritual value to the sexual act (even in the framework of marriage, even if it is for procreative ends alone). What is meaningful, according to him, for the relationship between man and God, is not the sexual act in itself, but the condition that in performing it one follows the teaching, the "pedagogy," of the *Logos* itself. It's the observance of the "commandments" that God has prescribed through nature, its examples, its forms, and its arrangements, through the organization of bodies and the rules of human reason, through the teaching of the philosophers and the words of the Scripture. Obedience to these different lessons can give the procreative conjugal relationship the value of a "synergy" with God.

One can better understand the seemingly rather arbitrary distinction that Clement introduces between the generation of progeny, which must be the "goal" of sexual relations, and the value of having descendants, which must be its "end." The latter definitely constitutes a completion—*teleiôtes*—for the procreator, as the Stoics said: it completes what nature has made and what connects him, through time, to other men and to the order of the world. But Clement shows that this "beautiful posterity" which with God's help man has given birth to, constitutes for God an object worthy of love and an opportunity to manifest his goodness. Subordinated to the "goal" of "making children," and, beyond that, to a purpose that accords with that of the whole Creation, sexual relations must be subject to a "reason," a *Logos* that, present in all of nature and even in its material organization, is also the word of God. Placed at the head of his analysis, the distinction and articulation between goal and end allow Clement to firmly inscribe the rule of sexual relations in a great "lesson of nature": "We must learn from nature and observe the wise precepts of its pedagogy for the right time of union."[52] A lesson of nature that is in the very teaching of the *Logos*. The "logic," one could say, of a nature that should be understood in the very broad sense, and in its different guises: the "logic" of animal nature, the "logic" of human nature and of the relationship of the rational soul with the body, and the "logic" of Creation and of the relationship with the Creator. These are the three logics that Clement develops in turn.

1.  The lessons that Clement borrows from the logic of animals are negative ones.[53] The hyena and the hare teach what mustn't be done. The hyena's bad reputation stemmed from an ancient belief—one found it in Herodorus of Heroclea*—that every animal of this species had two sexes and played the role alternately of male and female, from one year to the next. As for the hare, it was thought to acquire an extra anus every year and to make the worst use of these added orifices.[54] Aristotle had rejected these speculations and subsequently few naturalists gave them any credence. This doesn't mean, however, that people had stopped seeking moral lessons from the natural history of these animals. In the Hellenistic and Roman age, natural history was effectively subjected to two apparently contradictory processes: a screening of knowledge in terms of the strictest observational rules; and the increasingly pronounced interest in drawing lessons from this nature into which, according to the philosophers, the human individual has a duty to integrate. But an increased concern with exactness and the search for moral lessons could go hand in hand. Thus, the alternating hermaphroditism of the hyena and the yearly perforations of the hare became mere legends, but the naturalists could still read lessons of conduct into the behavior of these animals. As Aelian said, the hyena "shows," not through speech [but] through actions, "how contemptible Tiresias was."[55]

The manner in which Clement, in his turn, refutes the legend but gleans the moral lesson is interesting for his conception of the relations of nature with what is contrary to nature. The hyena, he says, doesn't change sexes from one year to the next, because once nature determines what an animal is, it cannot be changed. To be sure, there are many animals with traits that change with the seasons. The hot and cold seasons modify the voices of the birds or the coloring of their plumage,[56] but this is the effect of physical and external actions. The nature of the animal is not transformed for all

---

* Cf. infra, n. 4, p. 17. Foucault notes: IV, 192, without one's knowing what this corresponds to.

that. What about the sex, then? An individual cannot change sexes, or have two of them, or a third one that would be intermediary between male and female: these are chimera that men imagine but that nature doesn't allow. Here Clement is referring, in an implicit but clear enough way, to a discussion that was "classic" at the time. In the eyes of the Epicureans, the possibility of metamorphoses— maggots born out of cadavers, little worms materializing in the mud, or bees formed on a steer carcass—constituted proof that these bodies were not of divine origin; as they saw it, these transformations were the result of "autonomous" mechanisms.[57] By carefully differentiating between species' "stability" and the mechanical alteration of certain traits, Clement joins with the position of all those—Aristotelians, Stoics, Platonists—who wanted to maintain the stamp of a creative reason, or the continuous presence of a *Logos*, in the specifications of the animal world.[58] But it is very likely, too, that Clement is thinking of the problem he evokes in chapter 4 of the first book of the *Paedagogus*: namely the status of the difference of the sexes with regard both to eternal life and to life on earth. The solution proposed by Clement is simple, even if it presents a certain difficulty: in the world to come, there will be no differences of sex. "It is only here on earth that the feminine sex is distinguished from the masculine." It is a difference based consequently on the *Logos* that governs the order of this world, but one that does not prevent us from applying the name *human beings* to men and women alike. The same prescriptions hold for both sexes, and the same form of life: "one assembly, one morality, and one modesty; shared nourishment, a shared conjugal bond; everything is the same: respiration, sight, hearing, knowledge, hope, obedience, love."[59] It is to this "life in common," this common kind, beyond the differences of the sexes but not nullifying them, that grace is directed; it is this humankind that will be saved and will meet again in eternity, all differences of sex erased. In rejecting the idea of the hyena's alternation of sexes, Clement reiterates this principle of the "naturalness" of the male-female difference within the framework of specific entities. Man and woman are, and hence must remain, according to the *Logos* of nature, distinct from one another, which does not prevent them from belonging to the same humankind, nor from waiting for the next world to liberate them from the "duality of their desire."[60]

There does exist, however, a peculiar trait in the hyena that is not found in any other animal. Clement describes it by following Aristotle, almost word for word.[61] It involves an outgrowth of flesh that traces a form below the tail very similar to a female sex, but a quick inspection will show that this cavity does not open into any canal leading toward the womb or the intestine. But Clement doesn't treat this anatomical feature as Aristotle does. The latter uses it to explain how hasty observers let themselves be misled by the ambiguity of appearance: they thought they saw two sexes on the same animal; he sees this only as a case of human error of interpretation. But Clement sees in this anatomical peculiarity an element that has a relation of both effect and instrument to a moral fault. If hyenas have a body that's arranged in such an odd way, this is because of a defect. A defect "of nature," taking "nature" to mean the characteristic traits of a species, but a defect that is nonetheless utterly similar to a moral fault found in men: lasciviousness. And it's in view of this defect that "nature" has devised a supplementary cavity in these animals for them to use for their equally supplementary sallies. In sum, to the "excessive" natural propensity for pleasure that characterizes the hyena, nature has responded with an excessive anatomy that enables "excessive" relations. But, in this, nature shows that it's not only in terms of quantity that one must speak of excess: since the hyenas' surplus pouch is not connected by any channel to the organs of generation, the excess is "useless," or more precisely cut off from the end that nature has assigned to the organs of generation, to sexual relations, to semen and its emission—that is, procreation. And since this finality is disrespected in this way, it is a counter-natural activity that this tendency to misbehavior, both natural and excessive, permits and encourages. So we have a whole cycle that goes from nature to contrary-to-nature, or rather a constant intertwining of nature and counter-nature that gives hyenas a blameworthy trait, excessive inclinations, extra organs, and the means to use them "for nothing."[62]

The example of the hare is analyzed by Clement in the same manner. This time, however, it has to do with an excess not in connection with sterility, but with fertilization itself. Clement moves on from the fable of the hare with the annual anus, replacing it with the idea of superfetation. So licentious are these animals that they tend to copulate constantly, not even respecting the period of gestation and nursing. Nature has given the female a womb with two branches that allows it to conceive with more than one male even before giving birth. The natural cycle of the womb—which, according to physicians, calls for fertilization when it is empty and refuses sexual coupling when it is full—is thus disturbed by a disposition of nature that makes it possible to juxtapose pregnancy and heat in a completely "counter-natural" way.

Clement's long detour through the lessons of the naturalists may appear enigmatic, if one compares it for example with the *Epistle* of Barnabas. The latter does also evoke the cases of the hare and of the hyena—to which he adds other animals such as the kite, the crow, the moray eel, the polyp, the cow, and the weasel, but only in connection with the dietary prohibitions of Leviticus. He gives an immediate exegesis of those prohibitions, one that was common in that period.[63] The behavior that these animals manifest or symbolize is what is in fact condemned: the birds of prey signify the eagerness to despoil others, the hare signifies the corruption of children, the hyena adultery, the weasel oral relations. Clement, too, recalls the dietary prohibitions of Leviticus; he too claims to see in these dietary prescriptions the symbolism of laws dealing with conduct. Yet he doesn't confine himself to that exegesis, invoking it only at the beginning and end of his long excursion through natural history.[64] But he makes sure, first, to challenge the explanation that he himself calls "symbolic"[65] and replace it with a serious anatomical analysis. And he emphasizes, at the end of the exposition, that only these considerations of natural history can account for the prophet's "enigmatic" prohibitions.[66] For Clement, it's a matter of showing that the same *Logos* that Moses transmitted succinctly as law is manifested in detail by nature, in figures that one can analyze. By placing before his eyes the example of all these blameworthy animals, nature shows man that as a rational individual he need not model himself on beings that have but an animal soul. It also shows him the counter-natural point to which every excess can lead, according to a law which comes from nature itself. Finally, it makes it possible to base general prohibitions, which one finds in pagan philosophers and Christians alike—no adultery, no fornication, no corruption of children—on considerations of nature. For this is undoubtedly one of the most remarkable features of Clement's entire chapter, and of this passage about the hare and the hyena in particular. The philosophers had never ceased to remind people that the law governing the use of the *aphrodisia* was nature's law. But most of the considerations they put forward concerned the nature of man as a rational and social being (the need to have children for the day when one would be old, the usefulness of a family for one's personal status, the obligation to provide citizens to the state, and men to mankind). In this text, Clement eliminates everything having to do with man's social being; he instead develops naturalist points to bring out what is undoubtedly the core of his argumentation:

*a*. Nature indicates that the procreative intention and the sexual act must be exactly coextensive.

*b*. Through the counter-natural games that it organizes, nature shows that this principle of coextension is a fact that can be read in the anatomy of the animals and a requirement that condemns those who fail to observe it.

*c*. So this principle forbids, first, any act that would be committed outside the organs of fertilization—"principle of the hyena"—and, second, any act that would be added on to the accomplished fertilization—"principle of the hare."

Though the philosophers had sought to place the *aphrodisia* under the law of nature and to exclude what was contrary to nature, never had they placed their analysis under the sign of nature to this degree—nature understood as what naturalists read in the animal world.

2.   Clement also places his next exposition under the sign of nature, but this time of man's nature as a rational being. And this time he will stitch together, through the voice of Moses[67] and the example of Sodom,[68] the teaching of the masters of pagan wisdom, all those who endeavored to regulate the relations of the soul and the body—the Stoic philosophers, the physicians, and

Plato above all: Plato, who is even assumed to have read Jeremiah and his imprecations against men "resembling lusty stallions," since he also speaks of the soul's unruly steeds.[69]

What Clement submits here is the principle, familiar to the philosophers, of "temperance," with its two correlative aspects: the soul's control over the body, which is a natural prescription, since it is the nature of the soul to be superior and the nature of the body to be inferior as indicated by the location of the belly, which is like the body of the body ("one must dominate the pleasures and also command the belly, as well as what is below it"[70]); and the restraint, the moderation with which one must satisfy one's appetites after becoming their master. Quite logically, he correlates the adjective *aidoios* (shameful), which is applied to the sex organs, with the noun *aidôs*, to which he gives the meaning of restraint and right measure: "it seems to me that if this organ has been called a shameful part (*aidoion*), this is above all because one must use this organ with restraint (*aidôs*)."[71] This restraint is therefore the rule that should govern the exercise of the soul's control over the body. Now, in what does this consist? "Doing in the order of lawful unions only what is fitting, what is useful and decent."[72] The first of these adjectives refers to what belongs by nature to this kind of relation, the second to its outcome, and the third to a quality that is moral and aesthetic at the same time. And what is thus designated is what is recommended by nature itself. So it gives exactly the same lesson here as before with the animal figures: positively, to "desire" procreation; negatively, to avoid the fruitless sowing of seeds.[73] Thus, Clement restates exactly the basic propositions that he had selected and justified in the terms of natural history. But this time, the spiral of exposition having done a spin around itself, he takes them up again at the level of the human order. He repeats them nearly element for element, but in a context where the terms *Nomos* (law), *Nominos* (lawful), *Paranomos* (unlawful), *Themis* (justice), *Dikaios* (just), and *Adikos* (unjust) are utilized.[74] It's not that it's a matter here of counterposing the human order to that of nature, but rather of showing how nature is manifested therein. "Our entire lives can be lived in observance of nature's laws, if we master our desires."[75] The mastery that reason prescribes and that defines the lawful forms of behavior is yet another way of attending to the *Logos* that rules nature.

To this restraint, which demonstrates reason's control of the appetites, Clement gives four principal forms.

*a.* The first restricts sexual relations to the woman to whom one is joined by marriage. Plato said it ("refrain from plowing in every female field"), borrowing, says Clement, from Leviticus ("You shall not have intercourse with your neighbor's wife to defile yourself with her," 18:20). But the *Paedagogus* gives a different justification for this rule than Plato: in monogamy, the *Laws* found a means of limiting the ardor of the passions and the humiliating servitude in which they could keep men;[76] as for Clement, he sees in it the assurance that semen—which he said contained the "ideas of nature,"[77] making fertilization part of the relations between God and his creatures—will not be wasted someplace without honor. A certain value of semen in itself—what it contains and what it promises, the synergy that it calls for, between God and man, in order to attain its natural end—makes it unlawful and "unjust" to bestow it on anyone other than the wife with whom one is united.

*b.* Another principle of restriction: abstaining from sexual relations during menstruation. "It is not in keeping with reason to defile with the impurities of the body the most fertile part of the sperm, which may soon become a human being, to drown it in the murky and impure flow of matter: this is to steal the possible germ of a blessed birth from the furrows of the womb."[78] Here we have a prescription of Hebraic origin. But Clement situates the prohibition within both a set of implicit medical references and his general conception of semen. For him, the menses are indeed an impure substance.[79] But further, as the physician Soranus said, "semen is diluted in the blood and expelled by it."[80] So it carries away the semen that is intermixed with it, separating it from its goal, which is the womb, and from its end, which is procreation. Since "for reasons of nature" semen constitutes a material receptacle and since it has potentials that, developed in their rational

order, will give birth to a human being, it does not deserve
to be exposed to contact with defilements or delivered
over to a brutal expulsion.

*c.* The prohibition of relations during pregnancy constitutes the reciprocal of the preceding principle. For if
it's necessary to protect semen from any impure evacua-
tion, it is likewise necessary to protect the womb once it
has received the semen and undertaken its activity. One
must respect the rhythm that Clement evokes thus: when
empty, the womb desires to procreate, it seeks to welcome
the semen and therefore the mating cannot be considered
a sin, since it responds to that legitimate desire.[81] Here
again Clement is echoing a current medical teaching:
"every moment is not favorable to the semen projected
into the uterus by sexual coupling"; it's once the menstrual flow stops and the womb is empty that "women are
inclined to the venereal act and desire it."[82] This alternation in the body's dispositions shows very clearly, according to Clement, the reason that presides over its nature,
defining the correct limits of moderate conduct. But the
*Paedagogus* shifts the meaning of both this rhythm and the
rule of moderation that is derived from it. The physicians
advised against sexual relations during pregnancy, the last
months especially, for such relations "set the whole body
in motion" and "are dangerous during the entire pregnancy" due to the shocks they give to the uterus.[83] Clement himself appeals to the fact that if the womb closes up
during pregnancy this is because it "is busy making the
child," and it is accomplishing this labor "in synergy with
the Demiurge."[84] As long as this elaboration and collaboration is in progress, any new delivery of semen will appear
excessive: a "violence" that cannot "rightly" be imposed
on it. During pregnancy, anything coming in addition will
be "in excess."

*d.* But if the woman's "nature" dictates such a strict
economy, how do things stand with the man? Position-

ing himself, no doubt, within the historical development
of this question, Clement evokes a medical theme that is
completely traditional: the long series of medical ailments,
diseases, and weaknesses to which the too frequent use of
love's pleasures can lead. Clement alludes to the direct
proofs that were ordinarily given, along with the indirect
ones, which were no less customary: the vigor of all those,
men or animals, who abstain as much as possible from
sexual relations. Clement links this banal idea to Democritus's proposition, often repeated as well, that orgasm
is "a little epilepsy."[85] While not endorsed by all the physicians, this related notion turns up rather frequently in
the medical literature: in its literal form as in Galen,[86] or
in a broader form as in Rufus of Ephesus, who places the
"violent movements" that accompany coitus in the "family of spasms."[87] Now, Clement gives a precise meaning
to this connection between epilepsy and the sexual act, a
meaning which he supports moreover with a double reference that allows him to interweave a text by Democritus—"a man is born of a man and is torn from him" [fr. 32
Diels]—with a verse from Genesis: "this is the bone of my
bones and the flesh of my flesh" (2:23). If the body is so
violently shaken in the emission of semen, it's because the
substance that is detached from it and projected contains
the material reasons for forming another man like the one
it comes from. Here one perceives the tendency, which
was frequent in antiquity, to make ejaculation the symmetrical analog of childbirth. But by citing Adam, from
whom God has extracted a rib in his sleep with which to
make his companion, Clement is clearly evoking God's
"collaboration" in this work of a purely masculine flesh.
So the prescription not to overindulge doesn't just relate
to the prudence of bodies. The necessarily costly tremors
of the emission of semen are a reminder of the indispensable gravity of this synergy.

From these great principles of restriction in sexual relations,
one can deduce a whole series of diverse prescriptions that Clem-

ent piles up without much apparent order. Some forbid abortion; others advise against sexual relations during the day, or after leaving church or a meeting, or at the hour of prayer, permitting relations only in the evening; others prescribe not treating one's wife like a "harlot"; others exclude the marriage of youths and of old people. All this clearly defines a code of self-control whose conclusions, even if they are more severe, are of the same type that can be found in the pagan philosophers. And it's this rule of temperance that Clement repeatedly recalls: man must remain in control of his desires, not letting himself be carried away by their violence, nor surrendering, without the control of reason, to the drives of the body.[88] It's the ideal of what he calls elsewhere the "temperate marriage."[89] But it seems that for Clement this principle is not the final principle. If one needs to remain "master of oneself," this is not so much in order to maintain the correct balance and the necessary hierarchy between the faculties, but to ensure the respect, the modesty, the self-restraint demanded by a semen that forms the receptacle of "reasons" inherent in nature and the opportunity for a cooperation between God and man. A union in which the rational being respects the soul that must prevail over the body and the conscience that must keep the involuntary impulses in check? Yes, undoubtedly. But Clement's "temperate marriage" is respectful, above all, of that which radiates out from the eternal Creator to the multiplicity of future creatures, and finds an important material moment in semen and fertilization. It's the "economy" of this movement, more than the structure of the human configuration, that defines the *kairos* of sexual relations.

3.   The last section of the text is much shorter than the others. It opens with the final recommendations concerning temperate marriage: the more tenuous, more demanding ones that surround the major prohibitions. No obscene remarks, refrain from licentious gestures, no relations with prostitutes, and also remember—here Clement repeats almost verbatim an aphorism already found in the philosophers—that one commits an adultery when one acts with one's wife as if she were a courtesan. With these prescriptions, one enters the domain of transgressions that elude the gaze of others and that are committed above all in the eyes of one's conscience. Sins of the shadows. It should be noted that here it's not

a matter of wrongs of intention, of bad thoughts, or of lusts and temptations that will be, in a slightly later Christianity, the key component of the sins of the flesh. Clement speaks only of sins that don't have a public character. Darkness and silence envelop them; they apparently have no other witness or judge than the conscience of the one committing them—here the partner's conscience seems to have no importance. The problem of the sin without any witness other than the conscience is again a very frequent theme in the philosophical literature, and Clement treats it using an argumentation that was also very classic. By trying to conceal a sin in shadows and solitude, one doesn't lessen its gravity—one shows how conscious one is of its importance. Secrecy reveals the shame, which constitutes a judgment that conscience itself renders. And if a sin of this kind does no harm to anyone, conscience is still there as an accuser and a judge: it is oneself that one has wronged, and it's for one's own good that one must condemn oneself. One finds the same reasoning in Musonius[90] and in Seneca.[91] Clement goes over it again briefly.

And yet his analysis—or rather the themes that he varies, quite freely—will have a different focus concerning the question of the secret transgression. He first evokes the theme of darkness and light. However deep the shadows surrounding the transgression may be, there is always a light that dwells there, illuminating what they hide. The gaze of God from which nothing escapes, a spiritual light, always present in the world? Yes, undoubtedly, and the pagan philosophers recognized the self-evidence of this.

But it's also the light that dwells in us and constitutes our conscience. It is a fragment of the *Logos* that reigns over the world, that deposits an element of purity inside us. In relation to it, the sin that one commits constitutes not just a disobedience, an infringement of the principles of reason, but also a defilement. And temperance is not simply compliance with the natural order, but a pure parcel of this light: let us not seek "to conceal ourselves in darkness, because thought dwells within us; [. . .] the dark illuminates virtuous thoughts: and it is to the thoughts of good men that Scripture has given the name 'lamps that never go out.' "[92]

As the pure can have contact only with the pure, if we defile the purity of his *Logos* within us God can only turn away from us. He then abandons us to our life of "corruption." And by this, Clement means both in the metaphorical sense—the life of sin—and in the strict sense—a life that is bound toward death. Intemperance corrupts: not because it would extinguish the light, which in itself is inaccessible and cannot be darkened, but because it obliges the light to abandon the body to its mortal destiny. The intemperate body will rot because in abandoning it, God leaves it in its corpse state,[93] whereas he who remains temperate will cloak himself in an "incorruptibility," that of the *Logos* which dwells within him and will give him access to eternal life.

There is in this conception of "temperance" in Clement more than just the requirement of a well-maintained balance between the body and reason. But it's not, in the dualist manner, a radical rejection of the body as a substantial principle of evil. It speaks not of an imprisonment, but of a dwelling of the *Logos* in the body, and "temperance" consists in making sure that this body becomes or remains "God's temple" and that its members are and remain "Christ's members." Temperance is not a tearing away from the body, but an action of the incorruptible *Logos* in the body itself, a movement that transports it all the way into that other life where, there and only there, the angelic life can be lived, where the completely purified flesh will no longer know the difference of the sexes nor the relations that unite them. This is how Clement interprets the passage in the Gospel of Luke concerning the remarriage of widows,[94] which was the object of so many controversies: he doesn't see in it, as some do, the idea of a distinction between "children of the world," who would take a husband or wife, and those who, taking neither husband nor wife, would have a share in the resurrection; but the idea that on the basis of marriage, which is the law of this world, the abandonment of the acts of the flesh and the incorruptibility we take on thus enable us to "pursue a life like that of the angels."[95] In this way, then, "the works of the Educator" can be accomplished, and the Word, "according to the image and resemblance,"[96] fulfilled.

It's certain that, with these themes of the inner light, of the pure and the impure, of the body as Christ's temple, and of this ascension toward incorruptibility, Clement touches on themes that in the third and especially the fourth century would assume a very great importance—particularly under the influence of monastic asceticism: the theme of strict purity of thought and the theme of virginity of the heart as essential conditions of the angelic life. But it should immediately be noted that the requirement of a purity of thought, with a renunciation that even includes the desires themselves, is not mentioned till the very end of the chapter, in a single sentence. With all this, Clement does not allude to, as will be done later, the vigilant, constant, and prior withdrawal from the slightest desires that may form in the heart, but affirms the resolve not to be defeated by them.[97] It should be noted that immediately after this final recommendation, he contrasts the blame for this defeat with the principle of good conduct, the principle he had evoked at the beginning of the chapter and to which he returns at the end: the necessity of sowing seeds only at the right moment, when the *kairos* calls for it. He doesn't place the work of the flesh in opposition to a total renunciation, but appeals—in regard to the defeat one suffers versus the *aphrodisia*—to the principle of good and effective sowing. The very structure of this last paragraph presents a face-off between the fact of being "subjected to the *aphrodisia*" and the fact of consenting only to the planting of seeds.[98] Finally and most importantly, one should note that the word employed by Clement—not only at the beginning of the text when he defines the natural reason that presides over good sexual relations, but at the end of this chapter concerning the body as God's temple, and the cloak of incorruptibility—is still the same word with which the philosophers designated temperance: *sôphrosunê*. Doubtless, he gives this term a meaning different from self-control alone, control of one's passions and one's body. But he doesn't give it the sense of a renunciation of sexual relations—for which he regularly uses (in the third book of the *Stromata*) the term *eunoukhia*. With this "temperance," it is clearly a matter of an economy of procreation. The latter must be determined by the natural reason of "human sowing," but it is also and at the same time a collaboration of God and man. The "crown of life" and the robe of immortality cannot be the prize of a rupture of this economy—it can even be said that celibacy is an impious act insofar as it does away with this "generation."[99] They will be the prize of a strict adherence to what the *Logos* requires in order for this economy to attain the ends that are set for it: namely making children in accordance with a "wise and holy will."[100]

In a passage of the third book of *Stromata*, Clement comments

on the Genesis passage about the fall of the first human couple:
did the wrong committed consist of the sexual act? A long-debated
question[101] to which Clement gives a subtle answer: it was not the
sexual relation that constituted the sin, but the fact of not having
had it at the right time, "when it was appropriate." Against the
orders that had been given to them, Adam and Eve had sex too
young.[102] They disrespected the economy of the *kairos* and failed
to heed the law of timeliness. Precocious and willful children,
they evaded that reason which now the *Paedagogus*, the Educator,
must teach a humanity that can be regenerated only if it sees that
it's still a "child." Such was the fall, as the *Protrepticus* explains it:
Adam the child, by "succumbing to sensuality" and letting himself
be "seduced by his desires" lost his childhood state; his disobedience made him a "man," deprived of all the support of the educa-
tive *logos*.[103] This fall due to early indulgence shows very clearly
that generation is not bad in itself, but that only the condition in
which it occurs can be bad. It is innocent of Adam's wrongdoing,
and this is why it is not only exonerated, but celebrated in this
same passage of book 3 of the *Stromata*; Clement plays on the
word *genesis*, which refers to both Creation and procreation. Even
after the first sin, "genesis remains holy," the genesis by which
"were constituted the world, the natural essences and beings, the
angels and the powers and the souls, the commandments, the laws
and the Gospel, and the gnosis of God."[104]

The act of human procreation is linked therefore to the power
of Creation within which it is inscribed and from which it draws its
own power. But Clement also conceives of it in relation to what,
in the history of the world, constitutes the replica of the Creation
by the Father: the regeneration through Christ, by means of his
Incarnation, his sacrifice, and his teaching. In the long chapter 6
of the first book, devoted to the use of the word "children," the
*Paedagogus* develops the theme of Christ's teaching as nurturing
milk.[105] He sketches a whole "physiology" of blood in its metamorphoses: a substance that contains within itself all the powers of
the body, the *Logos*-blood also appears in two other forms. Heated
and agitated, it froths and becomes sperm, thus transmitting to
the wetness of the womb the principles from which another body
can develop and be born; but, when cooled and suffused with air,
blood becomes milk within the mother and, in this form, continues

to transmit to the child the forces that dwell within the bodies of the parents; breastfeeding is the continuation of the act by which life was given to the child through fertilization; the same blood and the same powers, in a different guise, are transmitted to the child. Thus, after having given his blood, Christ gives human children the milk of his *Logos*. He teaches them, he is their educator. Between the blood spilled in the past, in the Passion, and the milk that flows indefinitely from his Word, procreation gives rise to this people of "little ones" that the *Logos* engenders and regenerates.

This passage of the *Paedagogus*, in which Clement lays out the theory of teaching that he will give in the following books, only mentions the sperm, between blood and milk, very much in passing. The essence of the text deals with regeneration and not with genesis. But Clement does clearly indicate the place of procreation in the great "physiology" of the *Logos*. He emphasizes the kinship and hence the resemblance that connects us to God: the "kinship" through blood, the "sympathy" through the education[106] described in this passage will be completed by the synergy in the procreation discussed in chapter 10 of the next book. The cycle of blood, sperm, and milk—with the *Logos* that dwells in them, and is transmitted by them—ties us firmly to God's parenthood.

And when the *Paedagogus*—as a teaching from Christ, as milk with which he feeds our childhood—tells us the right moment, the *kairos*, for procreation, it places the economy of generation squarely within the great movement from Creation to Deliverance, from Genesis to Regeneration.

So the *Paedagogus*, as it's very often been said, shows a great continuity with the texts of pagan philosophy and morality of the same epoch, or the period immediately preceding it. There is the same form of prescription: a "regimen" of life that defines the value of acts according to their rational ends and the "occasions" that make it possible to perform them in a lawful manner. And it features a "classic" codification, since the same prohibitions appear in it (adultery, debauchery, defilement of children, relations between men), and the same obligations (having procreation in mind when one marries and when one has sexual relations), with the same reference to nature and its lessons.

But this visible continuity must not lead one to believe that Clement simply inserted a fragment of traditional morality, supplemented with Hebraic add-ons, into his religious concepts. For one thing, he combined into one prescriptive ensemble an ethics of marriage and a detailed economy of sexual relations. He defined a sexual regimen for marriage itself—whereas the "pagan" moralists, even as they accepted sexual relations only within marriage and only with a view to procreation, analyzed separately the economy of pleasures necessary to the well-advised subject and the rules of prudence and decency appropriate to marital relations. And, further, he gave a religious meaning to that set of prescriptions, reshaping it globally according to his conception of the *Logos*. He did not slip into his Christianity an ethics that was alien to him. Out of an already formed code, he constructed a Christian way of thinking and an ethics in regard to sexual relations, thus showing that more than one way of understanding these matters was possible, and hence that it would be completely wrong to imagine that it was *the* Christian faith that—by itself and by the strength of its internal demands—inevitably imposed that strange and singular set of practices, notions, and rules that is simply called Christian sexual morality.

In any event, Clement's analysis is far removed from the themes that will be found later in Saint Augustine and that will play a much more determining role in the crystallization of "that" morality. From Clement to Saint Augustine, there is obviously all the difference between a Hellenizing, Stoicizing Christianity, inclined to "naturalize" the ethics of sexual relations, and a more austere, more pessimistic Christianity, conceiving of human nature only by way of the fall, and consequently giving sexual relations a negative cast. But one can't be satisfied with merely noting this difference. And above all one cannot assess the changes produced in terms of "severity," or austerity, or a greater strictness in the prohibitions. For, if one considers only the code itself and the system of prohibitions, Clement's morality is scarcely more "tolerant" than what will be found subsequently: the *kairos* that legitimizes the sexual act only within marriage, only with a view to fertilization, never during menstruation or pregnancy, and at no other time of the day than the evening, doesn't offer it a wide range of possibilities.[107] And in any event, the great dividing lines between the permitted and the forbidden, essentially and in their general design, stayed the same between the second and the fifth century.[108] On the other hand, in this same time span, crucial transformations will be produced: in the general system of values, with the ethical and religious preeminence of virginity and absolute chastity; in the interplay of the notions employed with the growing importance of "temptation," of "concupiscence," of the flesh and of "first movements"—notions that show not only a certain modification of the conceptual apparatus, but a shift of the domain of analysis. It's not so much that the code has been reinforced, or sexual relations more strictly repressed; it's a different type of experience that is being formed little by little.

Obviously, this change needs to be linked to the entire very complex evolution of the Christian Churches that led to the creation of the Christian Empire. But more specifically, it can be correlated to the establishment of two new elements in Christianity: penitential discipline, starting in the second half of the second century; and monastic asceticism, starting at the end of the third. These two types of practice didn't simply produce a reinforcement of prohibitions or call for a greater strictness in morals. They defined and developed a certain mode of relation of oneself with oneself, and a certain relation between the wrongful and the true—let us say, more precisely, between the remission of sins, the purification of the heart, and the revealing of hidden transgressions, secrets, and mysteries of the individual in the examination of oneself, in confession, in the direction of conscience or the different forms of penance.

The practice of penance and the exercises of the ascetic life organize relations between "wrong-doing" and "truth-telling"; they bundle together relations to oneself, to evil and to truth, in a way that is doubtless much more innovative and much more determinant than this or that degree of severity added or subtracted from the code. What is at issue, in fact, is the form of subjectivity: the exercise of oneself upon oneself, knowledge of oneself, the constitution of oneself as an object of investigation and discourse, the liberation or purification of oneself and salvation by means of operations that carry light to one's innermost being, and drive one's deepest secrets up to the light of redemptive exposure. It is a form of experience—understood both as a mode of presence to oneself and a program for self-transformation—that was developed in that period. And it is this form that gradually placed the problem of the "flesh" at the center of its apparatus (*dispositif*). And instead of having a regimen of sexual relations, or *aphrodisia*, that blends into the general rule of a righteous life, one will have a fundamental relationship with the flesh that runs through one's whole life and serves as a ground for the rules that are imposed on it.

The "flesh" should be understood as a mode of experience— that is, as a mode of knowledge and transformation of oneself by oneself, depending on a certain relationship between a nullification of evil and a manifestation of truth. With Christianity, one didn't go from a code that was tolerant of sexual acts to a code that was severe, restrictive, and repressive. We need to think differently about the processes and their articulations: the construction of a sexual code, organized around marriage and procreation, was largely begun before Christianity: outside it, then alongside it. Christianity essentially took charge of it. And during the course of its later developments and through the formation of certain technologies of the individual—penitential discipline, monastic asceticism—a form of experience was constituted that activated a new modality of the code and caused it to be embodied, in a totally different way, in the behavior of individuals.[*]

And in order to write the history of this formation, it's necessary to analyze the practices that established it. Not that the aim here is to retrace the genesis of these extremely complex institutions. It's a matter of attempting to bring out the relations that developed between the forgiveness of wrongdoing, the manifestation of truth, and the "discovery" of the self.

---

[*] Passage crossed out by Foucault on the typescript: "In short, the schema of the code, repression, and the internalization of prohibitions is not able to account for these processes that are precisely what enables the codes to become behaviors or behaviors to take the form of codes—namely the processes of 'subjectification.' The flesh is a mode of subjectification."

# 2

# The Laborious Baptism

"Let each one of you be baptized for the forgiveness of your sins."[1] Until the second century, baptism was "the only ecclesiastical act that could ensure the remission of sins."[2]

The authors of the second century generally associate this remission with the four effects produced by the very act of baptism. It *cleanses*, erases, purifies: immersion carries the stains away. "We go down in the water laden with filth, and rise up from it bearing fruit."[3] It also stamps a *sign:* "the baptismal water" is "the seal of the son of God";[4] those who receive it are thus dedicated to God; they bear within them the sign of their belonging and the commitment they have taken on: like a seal at the bottom of a document, the brand on livestock, or the tattoo on a soldier's arm.[5] Baptism, moreover, constitutes a *new birth:* it restores life. This palingenesis is sometimes represented as a second birth. After the first birth—which, according to Justin, occurred out of "necessity" and in "ignorance," starting from a "moist semen," in the "coupling of our parents"—baptism "rejuvenates" us by causing us to be born again, but this time by "free choice" and in "knowledge": in this way we become the children of a Father who is the "Father and Lord of all things."[6] In a similar vein, Saint Irenaeus spoke of the "new generation" that God grants us and that, through faith, causes us to be born from the Virgin.[7] This rebirth is also described as access to life beyond death. In our first existence, says Hermas, we had received but a mortal nature; man lived there only in death and as if dead himself: from the ritual water into which he descends, he will rise a living being.[8] Finally, baptism *illuminates:* it pours into the soul a light that comes from God and fills it completely; the shadows are dispelled, and all at once the soul is opened to the light and occupies it: "This ablution is called illumination because those who receive this doctrine have spirits filled with light."[9]

Beneath these different aspects, baptismal remission is linked to an access to truth. First of all, because baptism is administered at the end of a teaching: one learns the doctrine and the sum of rules that define the "path of life" as opposed to that of death.[10] Baptism will be given only to those who "believe that the things they have been taught are true."[11] But there is more: each of the effects attributed to baptism is at once a mechanism of forgiveness and a procedure for accessing the truth. Purification: it erases the defilements and removes the stains that darken the soul and block the light. The seal: it marks one's commitment and belonging, but it also engraves the name of Christ—his name, which is to say his image present henceforth in the soul.[12] Regeneration: it gives one access to a life which is free of evil and which is both a "true" life and a life of truth. And illumination, finally: it dispels the dark-nesses which are both of evil and of ignorance. While the teach-ings received in the catechesis prepared the mind by transmitting those truths that must be accepted, baptism itself coincides with the coming of the light.

The link, in baptism, between the remission of sins and access to truth is therefore, in the age of the Apostolic Fathers and the Apologists, quite strong. It is a direct link, since the same effects of baptism erase sins and bring the light. It is an immediate link, since it is not once the sins are forgiven that the light is then addi-tionally granted, nor after faith has been completely formed and the truth acquired that the sins are pardoned as a reward. Is it also an "unreflected" link—I mean, is it a link such that forgiveness of sins and knowledge of the truth are produced in the soul without the soul having to know the truth about the sins it has committed and for which it asks forgiveness? Are remission of sins and access to the truth linked in one way or another to knowledge of the sins themselves and by the subject himself?

The answer has to be nuanced. It depends on the meaning we

should give to the term *metanoia*, which the Latin authors trans-
late as *paenitentia*, and which is used regularly in connection with
baptism. "Those," says Justin, "who believe that what we teach
and say is true, undertake to live accordingly. We teach them to
pray and to entreat God, in the fast, for the remission of their
sins, and we ourselves pray and fast with them"; then, when the
moment of baptism comes, "over he who chooses to be born again
and has repented of his sins, we pronounce in the water the name
of God the father"—and this is done so that they don't remain
children of ignorance and necessity, but rather of choice and science.[13] The text is clear: he who receives baptism, who becomes
a child of choice and science, and whose sins are pardoned, is one
who has not only received the teaching and desires rebirth, but
also repents. *Metanoia* and *paenitentia* are central in baptism.

But this *metanoia* is not organized as a developed and regulated
penitential practice—it is not a set of acts obliging the subject to
take precise stock of the sins he may have committed—exploring
the roots of evil deep in his soul, its hidden forms, his forgotten
transgressions—to undertake, in order to cure himself of these
things, a long labor combining constant vigilance and gradual
renunciation, and to impose punitive rigors upon himself proportional to the gravity of the offenses in the hope that God's wrath
will be appeased. The penitence that is required in baptism—at
least the kind described in the era of the Apostolic Fathers and the
Apologists—is not characterized by a long discipline, an exercise
of oneself upon oneself, nor an apprehension of oneself by oneself. A passage from Hermas on this point is significant. The angel
of repentance is speaking: "To all who repent, I give understanding. Do you not think that this very act of repentance is understanding? [. . .] For the sinner understands that he has done evil
before the Lord, and the deed he has done enters into his heart,
and he repents, and does no more evil; on the contrary, he puts all
his zeal into doing good, humbling his own soul and putting it to
the test because it has sinned. You see then that repentance is an
act of great understanding."[14] Penitence is clearly linked to an act
of understanding, *sunesis*, but this is not knowledge in the sense
of something learned or of a discovered truth; what is involved
is a comprehension, a realization that enables one to reach an

"epiphany."[15] This realization comprises three aspects: one must, in allowing formerly committed acts to rise to the surface of the heart, convince oneself that they were bad—bad "vis-à-vis" God,[16] which is to say at once in relation to him, against him, and under his gaze; one must understand the need now to turn away from evil and adhere to the opposite, to the good; and finally, one must authenticate the change, "humble" the soul that has sinned, "put it to the test" now that it has been renewed—that is, give to oneself and to God the signs that testify to this change.[17] Around this turning point and this renunciation-promise that the candidate must make at the moment of baptism, around this *metanoia*, Hermas's *Shepherd* does make room for acts of truth. They are in the category of recognition rather than knowledge: by allowing it to surface in the heart, recognizing the evil one has done and giving signs showing that one is no longer the person one was, that one has indeed changed one's life—that one is cleansed, marked by the seal, regenerated, filled with light.

It seems then that in this conception of baptism, the relation between remission of sins and access to truth—as strong, direct, and immediate as it is—does not simply consist in a conversion of the soul, pivoting on itself, turning away from darkness, evil, and death in order to orient itself and open itself toward the light, which inundates it. It's not a question simply of a break, a transition, or a movement of the soul in which the soul would be simultaneously the agent of its own conversion and be acted upon by the goodness of God who erases the sins that it turns away from and grants it the light that it turns toward. The remission of sins and the access to truth require a third element: *metanoia*, penitence. But the latter must not be understood as the calculated exercise of a discipline. It is not linked to an objectification of the self, but rather to a manifestation of the self—a manifestation that is both awareness and confirmation of that which one is ceasing to be, and of the regenerated existence according to which one is already living. It is the awareness-confirmation of a transition that is not simply a transformation but a renunciation and a commitment. *Metanoia* doesn't split the soul into one part that knows and another that must be known. It holds together, in the order of time, that which one no longer is and that which one is already;

in the order of being, death and life, the death that is dead in life and the life that is new life; in the order of will, detachment with regard to evil and commitment with regard to good; in the order of truth, the awareness that one has truly sinned and the confirmation that one is truly converted. The role of *metanoia* in baptism is not to go deep into the soul to see what it may contain and bring its secrets into the light of consciousness or into the view of others. It is to manifest the "passage"—the wrenching-away, the movement, the transformation, the access—and to manifest it both as a real process in the soul and as an effective commitment of the soul. *Metanoia* thus constitutes a complex act that is the soul's movement acceding to truth, and the manifested truth of this movement.

The texts that Tertullian devoted to baptism, at the turn of the third century, are evidence of a number of significant changes. These have to do with the preparation for baptism and the meaning given to the ritual and to its efficacy.

Chapter 6 of Tertullian's *De paenitentia* seems to give this period of preparation an importance and operational value much greater than those attributed to it in the past. "Are we purified for the reason that we are absolved? By no means! Rather we are purified when approaching forgiveness; the debt of the sentence is acquitted [. . .] when God threatens, not when he pardons." And a little further on, he adds: "We are not baptized so that we may cease sinning but because [. . .] we are already clean of heart."[18] Relative to the theme of a baptismal act that would be both a purification and a remission, Tertullian appears to perform a triple displacement: in time, since the purification procedure now seems to need to precede both the pardon and the very ritual of immersion; in the purifying operation whose agent now seems to be man himself acting upon himself; in the very nature of this operation, where the role of the moral exercise seems to outweigh the force of the illumination. In short, the purification, instead of being integrated into the very movement that carries the soul to the light and ensures its remission, takes the form of a precondition. And further, at the beginning of this same passage, does Tertullian not say that man must "pay for" his salvation at the price of penitence, and that this penitence is what God receives in exchange for the pardon?

This text merits some commentary. Tertullian—and he returns to this often[19]—doesn't mean to contest the efficacy of the rite, nor to pass the crux of the operation over to man purifying himself. *De baptismo* is explicitly directed against a sect of Cainites who refused to accept that "a little water could wash away death."[20] Tertullian replies to them with a "eulogy of water" in which he recalls its spiritual values, manifested in the Scripture: water that was the seat of the Spirit before the Creation; water that God used to mix the clay to fashion man in his image; water that purified the earth in the Flood, freed the Hebrews from their Egyptian pursuers, slaked the thirst of the chosen people, healed the sick ones in the pool of Bethsaida.[21] Endowed with such powers in the ancient law, how could this water not still have them, now that the Holy Spirit, inaugurating another law, has descended upon it to baptize Christ?[22] The water of baptism assumes all the functions that the Scripture had prefigured: it heals, it nurtures, it liberates, it purifies, it makes it possible to refashion man, and it makes the soul of the baptized the throne of God. But these functions are now integrated into the economy of salvation. Tertullian can therefore recall, in the first lines of *De baptismo*, the principle that the baptismal water washes away sin, in a formula that follows the second-century wording very closely: "Happy is our sacrament of water that, in washing away the defilements of our former blindness, liberates us into eternal life."[23]

The problem, then, is to determine the place and meaning of this prior purification, of which *De paenitentia* speaks, if it is true, as *De baptismo* says, that it is the water of baptism that has the power to cleanse us of our defilements.

There is a reproach that Tertullian addresses to those who ask for a baptism that can put them on the right path. He criticizes the candidates for baptism who are content to regret some of the wrongs they have committed—thinking that this is quite sufficient for God to forgive all the others—and then hasten to request baptism. Others, on the contrary, seek to delay it as long as possible; knowing that they won't have the right to sin after receiving the sacrament, but knowing that this sacrament will erase all their sins, whatever they may be, they postpone the moment of baptism so they can sin.[24] Now, in these two attitudes there is both presumption and pride. And behind that, two serious mistakes.

The presumption consists in imagining that, by means of the sacrament, one can constrain God; that man thereby has a hold on him and that it suffices to go through baptism to obtain a certain, total, and definitive pardon. Such a misconception would make a "servitude" out of God's grace. Tertullian does not assume that those who come to baptism with these deficient or bad dispositions are not actually redeemed; he does not call into question the efficacy of the rite. But he does assume that those one later sees relapsing, breaking the commitment they have made and returning to the sins that were forgiven, are precisely the ones who thus "slipped into baptism." They were able to "fool men," but they don't escape the one who sees all: they will fall again. The redemption that man obtains in baptism must be seen as the effect of God's *liberalitas*—both the generosity that forgives and the freedom to forgive. Right at the beginning of *De paenitentia*, Tertullian gives the fall and the forgiveness a very significant interpretation: God, having seen all the crimes of human recklessness, exemplified by Adam, had delivered a judgment against man, had expelled him from paradise and subjected him to death. But he had come around to mercy and had himself "repented."[25] The pardon that God grants men should be understood as a kind of *metanoia* in which God decides, freely, to suspend the effects of his wrath. Taking this pardon as the necessary effect of a rite to which man would decide to submit—this constitutes the presumption in question.

As for pride, for the sinner who requests baptism, it consists in trusting in himself. He doesn't realize that he could always fall or fall back—before baptism or after. He who goes toward the light doesn't follow a straight and easy path. He's like a newborn animal, nearly blind, constantly stumbling and crawling on the ground.[26] He should also bear in mind that Satan, who took possession of men's souls after the fall and made each of them into his church,[27] so to speak, doesn't see without anger that through baptism he will be dispossessed of them. He thus redoubles his efforts, either to prevent this defeat, or later to reconquer that lost place.[28] Hence the period preceding baptism must not be one of arrogant self-reliance. It is, rather, the time "of danger and fear."[29] Tertullian attaches a great importance to this need for "fear" in the path that leads to baptism and in the very life of the Christian. Of course, he is taking up a theme that predates him, but he gives it a particular modulation. It's no longer simply the fear of God, in the sense that, in the Old Testament, one must fear God's wrath if his commandments have not been respected. By the need for *metus* as a constant dimension of Christian existence, he means both the fear of God and the fear of oneself—that is, the fear of one's own weakness, of the failures of which one is capable, of the Enemy's insinuations into the soul, of the obliviousness or indulgence that will allow us to be surprised by him. One who must have a baptism must have confidence, but not in himself, in God. Uncertainty— not as to the power of God, but as to one's own nature, weakness, powerlessness—must always be present.

One can understand therefore the importance of a time of preparation for baptism, which is not simply initiation into truth or learning the rules of living. It is a time that enables the candidate not to expect, in pride and presumptuousness, a total pardon that God would be constrained to grant. The preparation for baptism is a time when one learns respect for God's *liberalitas*, thanks to the awareness one gains of the seriousness of one's wrongdoing, of the fact that God could have chosen not to forgive, and that if God forgives sins, it's only because he truly wants to. But it's also the time for acquiring the feeling of "fear," of *metus*—that is, the recognition that one is never master of oneself, that one never knows oneself completely, and that since one can't know what fall one is capable of, the commitment that one makes is all the more difficult, all the more dangerous. In insisting on the need to prepare for baptism, and in evoking the purification that will occur therein, Tertullian doesn't tamper with the basic principle of remission through the sacrament itself, but he restructures a relation to God and to oneself in this procedure of redemption. God is at once all-powerful and entirely free when he pardons: the man who undergoes the procedure of redemption must never be completely sure of himself. The preparation for baptism purifies:

not in the sense that it can in itself assure redemption, but—on the contrary—in the sense that it leads one to depend on God's free generosity to efface sins from which one detaches oneself, not only through repentance, but through the relation of fear that one permanently establishes with oneself. Such a preparation is not simply limited to breaking from what one had once been; it should teach one to continually detach oneself, as it were, from oneself.

Considering these elements, one understands Tertullian's construal, new in part, of the preparation for baptism. He couples the catechesis, and the teaching of truths and rules, with a labor of moral purification. And conversely, he tends to organize the movement of *metanoia* in a regulated form from the start of the preparation. This period should be thought of as a time when one learns not only the truths that must be believed, but the penance that must be practiced. "A sinner must weep for his faults before the moment of pardon, because the time of penitence is also a time of danger and dread. I do not deny to those who will enter the water the assurance of divine benediction; but to get there, one must do the work." *Elaborandum est.*[30] A labor that has its form, its rules, its tools, its *ratio.*[31] This is what Tertullian calls the *discipline of penitence*, to which the candidate for baptism must submit before plunging into the water: "Grant, Lord Christ, that thy servants may know or learn from my words the discipline of penitence, in that it is forbidden for the Auditors themselves to sin."[32]

Tertullian finds the model for this discipline—its necessary, regulated, but merely anticipatory nature—in the Johannic baptism. There have been countless discussions, of course, concerning the extremely difficult problems raised by the existence of this baptism prior to the Savior (which consequently could not ensure salvation), but to which the Savior himself submitted. A purely human baptism, since it doesn't cause the Holy Spirit to descend into the soul of those receiving it, a baptism given by a Precursor whose role is to herald the One who is coming as promised, it must be understood as the "baptism of penance."[33] And if Christ receives it, it's not that he himself has to practice penance; it's to show that henceforth, in the new age, baptism will mark the coming of the Holy Spirit, hence the light and salvation; but it's also to show that the baptism of the Spirit must be preceded by the baptism of penance, as the sacrament of Christians was preceded by the mission of John. The Precursor "preached repentance as a prerequisite for the cleansing of souls, so that whatever the filth resulting from ancient error, whatever the defilement of the human heart resulting from ignorance, repentance might sweep it up and scrape it away and throw it out of the house, making ready the heart as a clean dwelling place for the coming visitation of the Holy Spirit, in order that He might gladly there take up his abode."[34] Thus, what John's baptism teaches us in a word is that, as *De baptismo* says, "repentance is antecedent, remission subsequent."[35]

On this penitential discipline prior to baptism, Tertullian gives very few details. A few negative rules: Don't give baptism too soon, for there is always more danger in rushing it than in delaying it; don't grant it to just anyone, which is like offering holy things to dogs, or pearls to swine; don't give it to children or to unmarried persons whose continence is not certain. A few general prescriptions: "The sinner must lament his wrongs before the time of pardon";[36] and when the moment of baptism is near, those about to receive it "must invoke God with fervent prayers, fasts, genuflections, and vigils all night through."[37] But what is significant is the two kinds of effects that Tertullian expects from this discipline, in addition to purification of the soul as such. If it is rigorous and demanding, this is because for one who aspires to the Christian life it must constitute an "exercise." Against the Christian, the Enemy doesn't relent—on the contrary: he will do his utmost to defeat him, and the baptized must be accustomed to his attacks, his traps, his enticements so as to be able to resist him. He must have learned to recognize the Enemy's ways and trained his soul to resist. Since it's so serious a matter to fall away after being absolved a first time, the baptized must be armed and ready to triumph over the Enemy. Penance is this preparation—a training of forces and an acquisition of vigilance—that will enable him no longer to fall away. If the penance, the *metanoia*, must be of a piece with baptism from the start, this is because it is not just a purification, but also an exercise and an exercise that, if indispensable for redemption, must be useful afterward, and throughout the Christian life. As early as its pre-baptismal forms, penance appears as that form of exercise of one on oneself which must be coextensive with the Christian's entire life.

But it also has another meaning that we've already noted: it is the price one pays for redemption. "What folly it is, as insensible as it is unjust, to practice an imperfect penitence and then to expect a pardon for sin! This is to stretch forth one's hand for merchandise and not pay the price. And the price which the Lord has set on the purchase of pardon is this: He offers impunity to be bought in exchange for penitence."[38] It may seem that in this passage Tertullian is reverting to the idea of an equal exchange, hence of a restrictive mechanism: man having paid the necessary price, God would then be obliged to grant him the pardon. This is not the meaning of the text, however. The coins that one gives in penitence will never be worth what God grants in return— eternal life. And so God's generosity will never be constrained. The money of penance doesn't measure the value of the remission obtained, it attests to the authenticity of that which is given in payment. It is not envisaged as a countable quantity, but as evidence, or rather proof. The rest of the passage shows this clearly: when one buys, the merchant "first examines the coin, which they have stipulated as their price, to see that it has not been clipped or plated or counterfeit; do we not believe that the Lord, also, preexamines our penitence?" In speaking of penitence-retribution, Tertullian doesn't imagine a purchase that one would make from God, but an examination, before him, to which one submits. *Probatio paenitentiae*. It's a matter of solid, tangible, genuine proofs of the change that takes place in the soul, of the work that one carries out upon oneself, of the commitment that one makes, of the faith that is formed. As it's said a bit further on, in a compact formula, "the faith commences and is recommended by the faith in penance." The word *penitence* thus designates two things: change of the soul, and manifestation of this change in the acts that allow it to be certified. It must be a proof of oneself.

These analyses of Tertullian are neither isolated nor premonitory, even if they have a different tone than those of his contemporary, Clement of Alexandria, and are more elaborate than those of Justin.

During the same era in which Tertullian wrote, a new institution was developing that had the role of organizing, regulating, and controlling this purification prior to baptism. Doubtless this did not involve a radical innovation so much as an institutionalization, according to a model that tends to give a general form to the practices of catechesis and preparation for baptism. Historians recognize several reasons for this establishment of a catechumenate, which, in the third century, came more and more to resemble an "order," alongside that of the baptized believers. There was the influx of candidates, which threatened to weaken the intensity of religious life; the existence of persecutions, causing the insufficiently prepared to abandon their faith; and the struggle against heresies, implying a more rigorous instruction in the rules of living and in doctrinal content. To which the model of the mystery religions should perhaps be added, with the care that was taken in training their initiates.[39] The catechumenate constitutes a very long period of preparation (it can last three years), in which the catechesis and the teaching of the truths and the rules are combined with a set of moral prescriptions, ritual and practical obligations, and duties. In addition—and this is what should be retained here—this preparation is punctuated with procedures designed to "test" the candidate: that is, to show what he is made of, attest to the "labor" he is engaged in, testify to his transformation and to the genuineness of his purification. These procedures correspond to the *probatio*, which for Tertullian was one of the meanings of the discipline of penitence that he considered indispensable to baptismal preparation. And they show that *metanoia* must not be understood only as the movement by which the soul turns toward the truth in detaching itself from the world, from errors and sins, but also as an exercise in which the soul must reveal itself, its qualities and its will. In short, it's the institutional aspect of the principle that the soul's access to truth cannot be gained without the soul manifesting its own truth. This is the "price," in a sense—to take up Tertullian's metaphor with its quite particular interpretation— that the soul must pay for entry into the light that will fill it.

The *Apostolic Tradition* of Hippolytus offers the most detailed evidence of what these probation procedures must have been, at least as they were practiced in the Western catechumenate.[40] It describes several of them before the terminal moment of the "profession of faith," when the baptized would solemnly affirm, in response to a triple interrogation, that he believed in the Father, the Son, and the Holy Spirit: in this manner, the catechumen himself manifested the authenticity of his belief with a proclamation that would be answered, via the epiclesis of God's names and the laying on of hands, by the coming of the Holy Spirit and the illumination. Access to truth and the manifestation of the soul in its truth are thus brought together in the very act of baptism. But the *Apostolic Tradition* indicates and describes in some detail other acts of probation, which are spread over the entire preparation for baptism. They can be grouped into three major forms.

1. The interrogatory investigation. This involved a relatively simple procedure, unfolding as a round of questions and responses. It took place, if not in secret, at least with limited participation: the "doctors" in charge of the catechumenate, the candidate himself, and those who "had brought him," playing the role of witnesses and sponsors.[41] The investigation appears to have focused on external particulars: the candidate's status, his occupation—this because of a certain number of incompatibilities—and his lifestyle. But it also focused on interior elements, mainly on the candidate's relation to his former religion and the reasons that may have led him toward the Christian faith. "Let them first be brought before the teachers before the people enter. Let those who bring them bear witness concerning them so that we know whether they are able to listen. Let them be questioned concerning their manner of living: have they a wife, are they a slave? [. . .] Let us inquire into the works and occupations of those brought to instruct them."[42]

After being admitted as auditors, the catechumens led, for a period as long as three years, a life in which instruction in the fundamental truths was combined with religious obligations, but also with rules of conduct, tasks, and charitable deeds. At the end of this period, a second inquiry took place, in forms that seemed very much like the first. The witnesses-sponsors are also questioned. But the examination focuses this time on the period of the catechumenate itself: "When we choose those who are to receive baptism, we examine their lives: have they lived righteously while they were catechumens? Did they honor the widows? Did they visit the sick?

Have they done all kinds of good works? If those who brought them bear witness for each one: he has acted thus, let him hear the Gospel."[43] It is then that the catechumens were accepted for baptism. They were then subjected for several weeks—generally those preceding Easter—to a more intense preparation: prayers, fasts, night vigils whose rigor was meant to prove their faith. It's this period that Chrysostom would call "the time of palestra."[44]

2. The tests of exorcism. The laying on of hands and blowing on the face are ancient rites for driving out the spirits that have taken hold of man's body and soul. They were very anciently linked with baptism.[45] But perhaps they were never so widespread and frequent as they were in the fourth century, when they were employed right at the beginning of the candidate's entry into the order of the catechumens,[46] and several times more during his stint as an auditor. On the other hand, the *Apostolic Tradition* indicates, by the end of the second century, the requirement of a solemn exorcism before the baptism is given: "When the day approaches on which they are to be baptized, the bishop exorcises each one of them, so that he will be certain if they are pure (*ut possit cognoscere si mundi sunt*). If there are any who are not pure, let them be set apart. They have not heard the Word of faith."[47] In Saint Augustine's era, the same type of ritual is conducted just before baptism.[48] The candidate strips off the sackcloth and places his feet on it—a gesture that shows one shedding the old self and that forms part of the traditional practices of exorcism. The bishop pronounces the imprecations and, hearing them without flinching, the catechumen shows that he has been freed of impure spirits. The bishop then pronounces the words: "*Vos nunc immunes esse probavimus.*"

These exorcisms doubtless don't refer to a form of possession like that of the energumens.[49] The laying on of hands would signify a transfer of power: replacing the power of the malevolent spirit, which has reigned over man's soul since the fall, with the power of the Holy Spirit. The former is dethroned, dispossessed, driven out of that soul and that body where he has established his seat, and this by the power of the one who is stronger than he, but who cannot coexist with him, nor descend therefore into a soul from which the Other has not already been expelled.[50] But the exorcism is also a proof of truth: by evicting the spirit of evil, it separates within the soul the pure from the impure, it subjects the soul to an authentication procedure like that to which a metal is exposed when one passes it through fire:[51] one drives out the elements that degrade it, one measures its degree of purity. The expressions used by tradition and the formula cited by Saint Augustine indicate clearly that the exorcism "tests," "shows," and enables one to "recognize." It constitutes in its way an examination of the soul.

Hence the expressions that are regularly employed in the fourth century, and later, to designate these practices of exorcism. In his *Explanatio symboli*, where Ambrose explains to those coming to receive baptism the meaning of the rites to which they have been subjected, the author places exorcism among the "*mysteria scrutaminum*": "One has sought to know if there is some impurity in the body of man; through exorcism, we inquired into the sanctification of not only the body but also the soul."[52] And the bishop Quodvultdeus, addressing those who will receive the sacrament, gives the same meaning to exorcism: "We celebrate the examination upon you and the devil is extricated from your body, while Christ, at once very humble and very high, is invoked. You will ask then: test me, Lord, and know my heart."[53]

3. Finally, the confession of sins—which neither the *Didache* nor Justin's *Apology* evoked as mandatory prior to baptism—is regularly spoken of as such from Tertullian's *De baptismo* onward. "They who are about to enter baptism must invoke God with repeated prayers, fasts, genuflections, and vigils. They will also prepare for it with the confession of all past sins. And this in memory of the baptism of John, who is said to have received it *confessing his own sins*."[54] This "confession" is thus completely different from the questioning that opened and concluded the period in which the catechumen was an auditor. It is not information that those in charge ask for concerning the past life and conduct of a candidate—it's an act that the latter performs himself, among the other exercises of piety and asceticism. Did it involve a detailed confession to a priest of "all sins" committed in the past? Tertul-

lian says only that Christians today should rejoice that they don't
have to "publicly confess our iniquities and turpitudes"[55] as in the
time of John. Are we to understand, then, that the catechumen
had to review his past life, recall the memory of his transgressions,
and confide them either to the bishop or to the person responsible
for guiding him? Possibly so. And the later texts do make it clear
that during this epoch, prior to baptism, the one requesting it had
to perform a particular act with the bishop or priest[56] in which he
"confessed" his sins.

In any case, one must bear in mind that the term *confession*
had a very broad meaning—equivalent to the Greek word *exomologesis:*[57] a general act by which one recognized being a sinner.
And clearly the *confessio peccatorum* expected of the aspiring Christian cannot compare to the detailed, exhaustive recollection and
disclosure of all one's wrongdoings according to their respective
categories, circumstances, and gravity: but [it's necessary] rather
[to think of] an act*—or several acts—by which one recognizes
oneself as a sinner, before God and eventually before a priest. It's
essentially a matter of manifesting one's awareness that one has
sinned, that one is a sinner, and the desire to free oneself from
that state. It is a testimony of oneself concerning oneself, a certification of change rather than a recounting of "all sins" actually
committed.

This is the meaning that seems to emerge from a passage in
Saint Ambrose's *De sacramentis:* "When you gave your name [to
be baptized], the priest took mud and smeared it over your eyes.
What does this signify? That you confessed your sin (*fatereris*),
that you examined your conscience (*conscientiam recognoscere*), that
you performed penance for your sins, that is, that you recognized
(*agnoscere*) the lot of human generation. For, even if he who comes
to baptism does not confess sin, nevertheless by this very fact he
fulfills the confession of all sins, in that he seeks to be baptized so
as to be justified, that is, so as to pass from fault to grace [. . .] No
man is without sin. He who takes refuge in the baptism of Christ
recognizes himself as human."[58]

An important text. First, because it allows us to see the breadth

---

* Manuscript: "but rather an act."

of meaning that the word *confession* conveys: from the act by which one actually confesses a specific sin to the recognition of the fact that as a human being one cannot help but be a sinner. But also in its pointing out that the passage from sinfulness to grace—which is the purpose of baptism—cannot be accomplished without a certain "truth act." A "deliberate" act in the sense that the catechumen is urged to explicitly manifest, in the form of an avowal, his recognition of being a sinner. There is no remission, no saving access to the light, without an act in which he affirms the truth of his sinning soul, an act that also serves as a veridical mark of his determination to stop being a sinner. Telling-the-truth-about-oneself is essential in this game of purification and salvation.

In a general way, from the end of the second century onward one sees the growing place occupied, in the economy of every soul's salvation, by the manifestation of one's own truth: in the form of an "investigation" where the individual is the respondent of a questionnaire or the object of testimony; in the form of a purificatory trial where he is the target of an exorcism; in the form, finally, of a "confession," where he is both the subject who speaks and the object of which he speaks, but where it's a matter of attesting that one knows oneself to be a sinner rather than drawing up an exact list of sins to be forgiven. But it is clear that the form and evolution of baptismal confession can be understood only in relation to the extremely important development of the "second penance"—starting in this same close of the second century.

The institution of the catechumenate, the decision to submit candidates to rigorous rules of living, the implementation of procedures of verification and certification, cannot be separated from the new developments in the theology of baptism that one observes starting in the third century. All of this forms a whole ensemble in which the liturgy, the institutions, the pastoral practice, and the theoretical elements entail and reinforce one another. It's not a matter, however, of a new baptismal theology, but rather of a new emphasis. This is noticeable on two points in particular: the theme of death and that of spiritual combat.

From the moment that baptism was seen as a regeneration and a second birth, it included a connection to death—at least in the sense that after a first generation destined to die, it allowed one

to be "born again" into a life that was the true life. Baptism had
a connection to death insofar as it was a delivery from it. Thus
Hermas, apropos of souls as stones with which the tower of the
Church is built: "It was necessary for them to ascend from water
that they might receive life. For they could not otherwise enter
into the kingdom of God, but by rejecting the death that was
their former life."[59] But starting at the end of the second century, one sees a development of the theme that baptism, even as it
opens one's access to life, must itself be a death; and while Christ,
through his resurrection, announced this "new birth," with his
own death he showed what baptism is. It is a way of dying with
and in Christ. There thus occurred in baptismal theology, beginning at the end of this era, a return to the Epistle to the Romans
and to the Pauline conception of baptism as a death: "We were
dead and buried with him in baptism, so that just as he was raised
from the dead [. . .] we were walking into new life."[60]

Tertullian, in *De resurrectione carnis*, referred to a text of Saint
Paul: he stated the principle that we die in baptism *per simula-
crum*, but that *per veritatem* we come back to life in the flesh, "like
Christ."[61] But for the most part it's after Tertullian—who doesn't
allude to the principle in his treatises either on penitence or on
baptism—that this association of baptism with death through
the passion of Christ will be developed. It is all argued through a
series of analogies: between immersion and burial,[62] between the
pool and the "shape of the tomb,"[63] between the triple plunge that
follows the triple profession of faith and the three days that pass
from the Crucifixion to the Resurrection.[64] Through these analogies, several themes emerge. In the first rank, one finds the idea
that baptism must be accompanied by the killing of the old self:
one must, according to the Epistle to the Romans, "crucify it so
that the body of sin is destroyed."[65]

An "unpleasant and bitter" baptism whose prefiguration Origen sees in the crossing of the desert that must precede the return
to the Promised Land.[66] But since the former life that is shed by
crucifying it was only death itself, one must therefore conceive
of baptism as the death of death. This is what Saint Ambrose
explains in an important passage of *De sacramentis*: after Adam's
sin, God condemned man to die. A formidable and irremediable

punishment? No, and for two reasons: because God has allowed man to come back from the dead; but also because death, as the end of mortal life, is also the end of sin: "When we die, we cease to sin." Thus death, an instrument of punishment, when it is associated with resurrection, becomes an instrument of salvation: "the condemnation serves as a blessing"; "the two things are in our favor": "death is the end of sins and resurrection is the reparation of nature."[67] So baptism constitutes a kind of inversion of the meaning of death, a dying to sin and to death itself that should therefore be fervently desired.

But there is more: this death in baptism should not only bury, once and for all, the remains of the life that the Christian has abandoned, it should mark him always and throughout his life as a Christian. He has in fact received, with the seal of baptism, the sign of the Crucifixion. Such is the "resemblance" to which he must subordinate his life. The *homoisis tô theô* that promised, to those capable of it, a life of light and eternity, tends to be replaced by the principle of a resemblance to Christ in his passion, and hence of a Christian life placed under the sign of mortification.

1.  This recentering of baptism around death, or at least the death-resurrection association, has three consequences concerning the notion of *metanoia* as indispensable to baptism. The first is that this conversion of the soul, this disengagement by which one renounces the world of sin and turns away from the path of death, increasingly takes the form of an exercise of oneself upon oneself, consisting of a mortification—of a deliberate, diligent, and continuous elimination of everything in the body or soul that might be attached to sin. The second is that this mortification must not be localized in the moment of baptism alone, but demands a long and slow preparation. It must not come to an end with the redemptive immersion, but must be pursued in a life of mortification that will end only in death itself. Baptism, conceptualized as a death and a resurrection, no longer simply marks one's entry into Christian life; it is a permanent matrix for this life. Finally, another consequence—the requirement of a *probatio*, which had to verify both the desire and the ability of the candidate to reach the truth—will tend, while keeping that function, to give more and

more prominence to a set of "tests" that are at once exercises of
mortification and confirmation of this death to sin—of this death
"to the death of sin." The relation of self to self, understood as a
labor of oneself upon oneself and as a coming to awareness of oneself by oneself, thus assumes a more and more distinct and salient
role in the overall process of conversion-penance designated by
the word *metanoia*.

2. But another factor intervenes, with convergent effects.
It's the development, in the theology of sin and baptism, of the
theme of the Enemy present in the soul and reigning over it. One
mustn't be misled, however: the specification and multiplication
of exorcism practices in the catechumenate period, and in the rites
that immediately precede baptism, don't signal the triumph of a
demonological conception of evil. What one sees rather is a whole
series of efforts to articulate on the new idea of original sin the
omnipotence of a God who agrees to save and the principle that
every person is responsible for their salvation. Tertullian's conception was a response to this exigency: he saw the effect of the fall
not only in man's mortality, not only in his corrupted soul and his
life given over to evil, but more precisely in the fact that Satan had
managed to establish his dominion over men, down to the bottom
of their hearts. As a jurist, it seems that Tertullian imagined possession more as a matter of "jurisdiction" and an exercise of power
than as an insinuation of alien entities. So baptism had the effect
of producing a "dispossession" that had two aspects: the Holy
Spirit could establish its seat in the soul liberated by purification;
and man acquired a force stronger than that of the demons—he
could resist them, he could command them. From the fall to salvation, there was a whole relation of forces that came into play
and was overturned: man was not absolutely constrained to do evil
before the coming of the Savior, nor was anyone unconditionally
redeemed after his sacrifice. Everything was a battle. But this battle
did not pit God against the principle of evil: it unfolded between
man and the one who had rebelled against God, who intended to
seize control of man's soul and could not accept "without groan-
ing" that it might be snatched away from him.

It is this theme of spiritual combat that, beginning in the third century, will give a particular significance both to the preparation for baptism and the effects expected of it. The preparation must be a struggle against the Enemy, a constantly renewed effort to defeat him, a call to Christ to lend his support and compensate for the weakness of man. But baptism will give neither security nor rest: the Enemy will be all the more determined because he feels dispossessed; and since he no longer reigns in the soul, he will try to make his way back in. The Christian, if he is not as prepared as he should be, will fall again.[*]

It's clear, then: just as the theme of death—implied by that of regeneration, of the second birth, of resurrection—shifted toward mortification, the theme of the purification that detaches the soul from its defilements likewise shifted toward the idea of a spiritual combat. And each of these two shifts gives the subject a larger and larger role: baptism must be prepared, accompanied, and extended by operations that the subject brings to bear on himself in the form of mortification, or within himself in the form of spiritual combat. He establishes a complex, strenuous, and changeable relationship with himself. Doubtless the doctrine doesn't in any way allow that God's omnipotence can be undercut or limited as a result (even if it was extremely difficult to construct theoretically the system of this omnipotence in the face of human freedom). But, staying within the boundaries of the present study, one sees how these self-to-self relations became indispensable in the subject's progress toward light and salvation.

3. Now, all this points to another change of accent in the doctrine of baptism: that having to do with the effect of the sacrament. On this point, I will be very brief, simply recalling, for the beginning of the third century, the indications of Origen, and for the end of the fourth the theses of Saint Augustine.

---

[*] Here Foucault scribbles: "—Le baptême rachète / mais il y faut la *remissio cordis* / Cf. Histoire des dogmes /—Tout cela convergeant vers le problème de la connaissance de soi." ("—Baptism redeems / But it requires the *remissio cordis* / Cf. History of tenets / All that converging on the problem of self-knowledge.")

# 3

# The Second Penance

The fourth Precept of Hermas's *Shepherd* is well known: "I have been told by some teachers that there is no repentance except that of the day [that was vouchsafed us] we descended into the water." To which the angel of repentance replies: "'What you have heard is correct; such is the case. The person who has received remission of sins must no longer sin, but remain in purity. However, since you are inquiring accurately into everything, I shall also clarify the matter for you, without giving pretext to sin either to those who will believe or now believe in the Lord, for neither have to make repentance for sins: they have absolution from their previous sins. It is therefore only for those who have been called before these very last days that the Lord has instituted a penance. For, the Lord has knowledge of hearts and knows all things in advance, the weakness of men and the multiple intrigues of the Devil, the evil he will do to the servants of God and his wickedness against them. In his great mercy, the Lord took pity on His creatures and prescribed this penance and has appointed me to direct it. But this I say to you,' he continued, 'if, after this solemn and holy call, someone, seduced by the devil, commits a sin, he has one chance of repentance; but if he sins again and again, even if he repents, penance is useless to such a man.'"[1]

This text has long passed as proof that, in early Christianity, no other repentance existed than that of baptism, and as evidence that in the middle of the second century a second recourse was established for already-baptized sinners: a single, solemn, unrepeatable recourse, from which would arise, through successive transformations, the penitential institution. My intent is not to evoke, even from afar, the discussions raised by this passage from Hermas: Does it manifest the first important softening of an early rigorism? Does it form a criticism of the overly strict lesson of "some teachers" who would need to be identified? Is it based on the distinction between two teachings: the instruction given before baptism and that which is reserved for the baptized, to whom one can announce the possibility of a second penance? Was the latter, in Hermas's view, a jubilee that would take place only once, or a recourse that Christ's imminent return made urgent, indispensable, and necessarily unique?[2]

Let us keep in mind only that the obligation of a *metanoia*, a repentance-penance, is endlessly repeated to Christians in the texts of the apostolic period. To be sure, it is said in the Epistle to the Hebrews that it is "impossible, for those who were once enlightened and tasted of the heavenly gift, and became partakers of the Holy Spirit and tasted the good word of God and the powers of the age to come and nonetheless fell, to renew them a second time unto repentance."[3] But the text is referring to the uniqueness of baptism as an act of total "renewal" of the individual. It excludes neither the hatred of sins nor the supplication of forgiveness on the part of those who have received baptism: "For whatsoever we have done wrong, and for whatsoever we have done at the instigation of the Enemy's henchmen, let us beg forgiveness."[4] A supplication that takes ritual and collective forms: "In the assembly, you shall confess your offenses, and shall not come forward to your prayer with an impure conscience";[5] just as when one meets on the dominical day, one breaks bread, one gives thanks "after first having confessed the sins, so that the sacrifice may be pure."[6] The whole community is called to take part in this repentance that everyone must experience and manifest. It may take the form of a mutual correction: "the admonition which we give to one another is good and most beneficial, for it unites us to the will of God."[7] It may take the form of intercessions for one another, addressed to the one who forgives.[8] Or the form of fasts and supplications that should be done with those who have sinned.[9] And it's the role of the presbyters to show themselves to be "compassionate, merciful to all" and to "guide back the wanderers."[10]

Repentance and supplication for forgiveness were thus an

integral part of the existence of the faithful and of the life of the community before Hermas had the angel, to whom he had been entrusted, announce the establishment of another penance. It shouldn't be forgotten that *metanoia* is not just a change of attitude necessary to baptism—it is not simply a conversion of the soul that the Holy Spirit produces at the moment it descends into it. Through baptism, one is called "to metanoia,"[11] which is both a starting point and a general form of Christian life. The repentance to which the texts of the *Didache*, and those of Clement or Barnabas, call Christians is the same repentance that had accompanied baptism: its prolongation, its sustained movement. So the problem posed by *The Shepherd* is not that of a Church of perfect practitioners transitioning to a community recognizing the existence of sinners within it and adjusting to that. And it's doubtless not even the transition from a rigorism accepting only baptismal penance to a more indulgent practice. What is involved, rather, is a mode of institutionalization of this repentance after baptism and the possibility of re-enacting—fully or partially—the procedure of purification (and even redemption) that baptism had occasioned a first time. In fact, it concerns nothing more or less than the problem of repetition, in an economy of salvation, of illumination, of access to the true life, which by definition only knows one axis of irreversible time informed by a decisive and singular event.

I will leave aside the history of this institutionalization itself, and the theoretical and pastoral debates to which it gave rise. I will limit myself to considering the forms taken, starting in the third century, by "canonical" penance; that is, by the ritual measures arranged under the authority of the Churches for those who have committed serious sins and for which forgiveness cannot be obtained by their repentance and prayers alone. How can baptized persons obtain anew their forgiveness if they have violated the commitments they have made and turned away from the grace they received?

This reconciliation was defined in relation to baptism. Not that it was a repetition of it, because baptism could not be repeated. The grace that was bestowed then was granted once and for all, and the sins remitted were remitted definitively—we can be reborn only once.[12] But the "penitence" that accompanies baptism and to which it is an introduction—the movement by which the spirit frees itself of its sins and becomes dead to that death, and the pardon that God grants in his benevolence—that can be renewed. No second baptism, then;[13] and yet, as Tertullian already said, a "second hope," a "different door," on which the sinner can knock after God has closed that of baptism—"a repeated beneficence," or rather "an increased beneficence," for "giving back is greater than giving"—a *paenitentia secunda*.[14] Against the Novatians, it was said to be necessary in order not to drive to despair all those who had fallen away and not lead those who were not yet Christian to delay the moment of baptism.[15]

The relation of the second penance to baptism is marked in different ways. First of all, by the principle that in both instances it's the Holy Spirit that operates and pardons sins: "Men implore and the Divinity forgives [. . .] it's the supreme Power that bestows his favors."[16] The same mystery and the same ministry, the authority exercised by the priests is the same whether they baptize or reconcile: "What difference does it make whether it is through penance or through baptism that the priests claim this right given to them?"[17] Just as the water of baptism washed away former sins, one asks the tears of repentance to wash away the failures that have occurred since baptism.[18] And despite the desire to reserve to baptism the power of bringing about a rebirth—of regenerating— one finds the theme[19] that penance causes one to pass [from death to life].* Saint Ambrose's *De paenitentia* is significant in this regard. The text first connects penance with the episode of the Samaritan in the Gospel of Luke: like the man injured on the road to Jericho, the sinner can be saved because he is still "half alive"; if he were fully dead, what could be done for him? Must penance be required of those who can no longer be healed?[20] But in book 2 of the same text, penance is linked to the resurrection of Lazarus: "If you have confessed at the call of Christ the bars will be broken, and every chain loosed, even if the stench of bodily corruption be grievous [. . .] you see that the dead come to life again in the Church, and to be raised again by receiving forgiveness of their sins."[21]

In sum, salvation can be obtained through baptism only when

---

* Manuscript: "from life to death."

one is not yet a Christian; penance alone will make it possible for Christians who have lapsed after baptism.[22] Two ways, then, to be saved. This is what Saint Leo will repeat after Ambrose.[23]

This notable analogy with baptism explains the paradox that penance, while being in a certain sense the "repetition" of baptism (at least in some of its effects), is not itself repeatable. Like baptism, it occurs but once: "There is but one baptism; just as there is one penance."[24] So there is nothing surprising in its being organized—at least to a certain extent—on the model of baptism and its preparation.

Canonical penance gradually took the form of a "second novitiate."[25] The expression *paenitentiam agere*—employed to designate any form of repentance (even interior repentance) to which a sinner applies himself in order to obtain forgiveness of his sins (even minor ones)—is also used to designate the regular form according to which the penitential procedure should unfold: under the authority of priests, with a certain number of defined practices, at the right moment and during a specified time period.[26] Penance practiced in this manner is not simply an act, or a series of actions: it is a status.[27] One becomes a penitent according to rules to which not only sinners must submit, but also the priests who regulate this penance.[28]

Ecclesiastical penance is "requested," "granted," "received." The Christian who has committed a grave sin—and of course the lapsed one who has sacrificed or signed a certificate of sacrifice—asks the bishop for the possibility of becoming a penitent, or he is exhorted to become one by the priest who knows about his sin.[29] And it's in response to this request that the bishop "grants" penance—an act that should be considered, in a fundamental sense, less as punishment imposed than as a recourse whose access and unfolding are carefully controlled. Penance commences with a ritual that includes the laying on of hands—a gesture that refers to exorcism and implores God's blessing on the penitential exercises. These exercises last a long time: months, years. And when they are finished, the penitent is admitted into reconciliation in the course of a ceremony that constitutes a kind of copy of the first one: the bishop again lays on his hands and the penitent is readmitted into the *communicatio*. The penitential status, for as long as it lasts, entails ascetic practices (fasts, vigils, numerous prayers) and charitable acts (alms, aid to the sick); it also comprises prohibitions (for example, regarding sexual relations between spouses) and a partial exclusion from community ceremonies (the eucharist in particular).[30] However, even after reconciliation, the former penitent does not return to the status he previously held. He remains marked, as it were: he cannot become a priest; public responsibilities are forbidden him, as are certain professions; he is advised to avoid disputes.[31]

Relative to baptism, the carefully regulated practice of the "second" penance is not any less demanding. On the contrary—penance is a matter of soliciting what had once been granted and of obtaining through exception the effect of a grace already offered to the baptized. Penance is stricter than baptism. God offers baptism to every person who recognizes it, and so he offers the remission of sins as a *gratuita donatio;* by contrast, he concedes forgiveness to the penitent as a fruit of the long labor he has exerted on himself.[32] The authors of the third and fourth centuries don't revisit the principle that preparation for baptism cannot dispense with discipline, but they do stress that in penance the sinner who has already received grace must take responsibility for his own sins. This is Origen's principle: *apolambanein tas hamartias.*[33] And in spite of the principle that there is no second baptism, penance is occasionally spoken of as the "laborious baptism."[34]

One can say—without going into the problems of sacramentary theology and its history—that starting in the third century, a difference of accent becomes noticeable in the way the authors describe the *metanoia* connected with baptism and the *metanoia* that is indispensable to ecclesiastical penance. Doubtless in both cases it always involves a repentance by which the soul frees itself from the sins that defile it. But in connection with baptism it is liberation, *aphesis*, that is underscored; for the *metanoia* necessary to reconciliation, it's above all the labor that the soul exerts on itself and on the offenses it has committed.

In the unfolding of canonical penance, the procedures for manifesting the truth of the penitent soul are numerous. And they present appreciable differences compared to those employed for baptism and its preparation.

I

We can put aside the recourse to testimonies or inquiries that make it possible to be sure of the repentance and good dispositions of those requesting reconciliation. In the period following the great persecutions, Saint Cyprian's letters show the importance of the problem: the difficulty of finding the right balance between rigor and indulgence, the dogged efforts of some *lapsi* to regain the peace of the Church, and the mulishness with which it was sometimes refused them—in any case, the painfulness of the discussions. Saint Cyprian comes back to the matter several times: in a way, between the two dangers of reconciling too quickly or of leaving the sinners without hope, the decision will always be blind: "It being given to us to see and to judge, we only see the exterior of everyone; as to plumbing the depths of the heart, and penetrating the soul, we cannot."[35] An argument that inclines him not to a severity, but to a leniency for which he reproaches himself at times.[36] He fears, like everyone else, that "incorrigible minds," "men defiled by adulteries or the contagion of sacrifices," will come back and corrupt righteous souls—yet he thinks the task is not so much to exclude those whose sincerity is not certain, but rather to work toward their healing.[37] Besides, the reconciliation that is granted here below is not binding to God. He who sees everything, even into the secrets of the heart that elude us, is not committed to pardon when someone has taken advantage of his people's indulgence: "God will judge of those things which we have looked upon imperfectly and will correct the judgment of his servants."[38]

It's still true that one can't welcome everyone back without precaution; one must reflect and examine. The testimonies of those who had accepted facing martyrdom, in support of those who had "fallen"—either they had sacrificed, or they had signed certificates of sacrifice—cannot suffice, especially when they take the form of a sort of collective recommendation covering a whole family or household. More or less spontaneously, Cyprian—while maintaining his position of indulgence in principle—comes round to a practice that had been established and seems to have been codified into a written prescription of the procedures to be followed:[39] examine, one by one, the situations of those asking to be admitted as penitents; consider the intentions and circumstances of the deed (*causae, voluntates, necessitates*); differentiate between "the one who rushed in immediately, of his own free will, to take part in the abominable sacrifice and the one who, having long struggled and delayed, finally came by compulsion to the disastrous deed; the one who betrayed both himself and his own people and the one who, approaching the crisis for all, protected his wife and children and whole household."[40] It seems that another examination was in order—this time involving not the circumstances of the sin but the sinner's behavior since then:[41] that is, in the period when, either spontaneously or following the canonical forms, he does his penance, manifests his remorse, and shows his determination to live as a believer: "Let them watch at the gates of the heavenly camp, but armed with the modesty by which they recognize they have been deserters";[42] to whomever does not profess his sorrow (*nec dolorum [. . .] manifesta lamentationis suae professione testantes*), one must refuse the hope of communion and peace.[43]

Given the difficulty of such an examination, the communities' expressed opposition to the return of the *lapsi*, and the hostility that personal decisions could arouse, the decisions often had to be made collectively, under the direction of and in the presence of the faithful. This is shown by a letter of the Roman priests to Cyprian: it is "extremely unpopular and burdensome to us not to examine through many what seems to have been committed by many and for one to give a judgment [. . .] since that cannot be a firm decree which will not seem to have the agreement of the majority."[44]

The importance of these examination practices was linked to a particular conjuncture that explains the scale they attained at a given moment. Doubtless they disappeared with the end of the persecutions. But the external control of penitents—which calls to mind the control that, through interrogation, investigation, and testimony, was brought to bear on catechumens—played a relatively small role compared to another truth procedure that was

much more central to penance: the procedure by which the sinner
himself recognized his own sins.

II

There is a strong correlation between these "well-thought-
out" procedures and the Latin terms *confessio* and *exomologesis*—
commonly employed from the second to the fourth century,[45]
with an equivalent meaning. In any case, what each of them designates exactly is subject to discussion. According to the references chosen, some historians insist on the existence of a definite
act by which the penitent would confess to offenses committed;[46]
others stress that often these terms—and particularly that of
exomologesis—are a way of designating the ensemble of penitential acts the sinner is expected to perform.[47] It seems that in fact
we can distinguish three elements.

1. There first had to be an expression of the request. The
sinner who solicited penance would confide to the bishop or pres-
byter both his desire to become a penitent and the reasons he had
for becoming one. A detailed statement? We have seen, in regard
to the apostasies and the practice of the *examinatio*, that this sometimes must have been the case. The sinner could even make use
of testimonies and all sorts of inquiries: it's to this approach that
the juridical type of expression one finds in Saint Cyprian applies:
*exposita causa apud episcopum.*[48] But, except for these particular
situations, the penance request must have been much more discreet. Did it involve only an oral confession expressed in general
terms—perhaps simply by means of the recitation of a repentance
psalm?[49] One imagines that a succinct exposition was necessary
to indicate the nature of the sin, allow its gravity to be assessed,
and perhaps set the time, the *justum tempus*, that needed to elapse
before the reconciliation could be envisaged.[50] It was then no
doubt that it was decided whether the sin merited the recourse
to penance, or whether forgiveness could be obtained in other,
less rigorous ways. Apparently, Cyprian is referring to this practice in *De lapsis* when he distinguishes those who must "do penance" because they have sacrificed or signed the certificates from

those who did nothing more than entertain that idea: the latter group should "confess this to the priests of God simply and contritely."[51] It's of this practice as well that Saint Ambrose's biographer is thinking when he praises his subject for the indulgence with which he listened to sinners: often, instead of playing the part of public accuser, he chose to weep with the guilty one over his transgressions "without saying a word to anyone" and to intercede with God so that he might grant his pardon.[52] Between the sinner and the one who granted the penance there was room, therefore, for a private interview—which doesn't mean that it took place every time and necessarily. Here it is certain that we approach, up to a certain point, the form of the *confessio oris* as it will be found later at the heart of the penitential rite and as one of its essential components. But there is this fundamental difference: the verbal confession is here a simple preliminary to confession, and one that is not even absolutely necessary. It doesn't constitute an integral or essential part of the practice.

2. At the other end of the penitential procedure, when the moment of reconciliation came, it does seem that provision was made for a well-defined episode of exomologesis. At least this is what seems to be indicated by several passages of Cyprian's correspondence where, in regard to what is necessary for reconciliation of the *lapsi*, he regularly suggests the series: *paenitentiam agere, exomologesim facere*, and *imposition manus*.[53] After he has led the life of a penitent during the required time span, and before the rite of laying on of hands has marked his reconciliation, the sinner would then need to do exomologesis. Is this a verbal confession of sins? It seems not. It's true that Saint Cyprian doesn't give information about this episode of the penitential rite: at the most he evokes, in a partly symbolic way no doubt, the penitent at the threshold, knocking on the door and asking to enter. But other texts, earlier or later, enable one to form a more exact idea of this exomologesis.

In *De pudicitia*, after becoming a Montanist, Tertullian describes positively the sinner who leads the penitent's life all the way to the end without ever being reconciled: "he stands before the doors, warning others by his exemplary shame; he calls to his assistance the tears of the brethren."[54] On the other hand, he

evokes in a critical way the penitent who is led into the church
to receive reconciliation: he wears the sackcloth and ashes; he is
clothed miserably; he is taken by the hand and introduced into the
church; he publicly prostrates himself before the widows and the
priests, he clings to their coattails, he kisses the imprints of their
footsteps; he hugs their knees.[55] This undoubtedly gives one a
notion of that phase of exomologesis that completes the life of
penance and precedes the return to communion. It is a description
whose emphasis may be explained by Tertullian's hostility. But this
hostility is directed at the fact of reconciliation, not at the abjec-
tion that the penitent is made to undergo. And much more recent
texts don't give a very different image of that moment when,
before being reconciled, the sinner is asked to publicly recognize
his or her wrongdoing. "In the presence of all Rome," recounts
Saint Jerome, concerning Fabiola who, divorced, had remarried
before the death of her first husband, "during the days preceding
Easter, she stood in the ranks of the penitents and exposed before
bishop, presbyters, and people—all of whom wept when they saw
her weep—her dishevelled hair, pale features, soiled hands and
unwashed neck [. . .] She laid bare her wound to the gaze of all,
and Rome beheld with tears the disfiguring scar that marred her
beauty. She uncovered her limbs, bowed her head and closed her
mouth."[56] In a much less explicit way, and without using the term
*exomologesis*, Saint Ambrose is presumably referring to this type of
ritual when he mentions the necessity of the penitent to entreat
God, at church and in the presence of the faithful, according to
forms that recall the ancient supplication: "Can anyone endure
that you should blush to entreat God, when you do not blush to
entreat a man? That you should be ashamed to entreat Him who
knows you fully, when you are not ashamed to confess your sins
to a man who knows you not? Do you shrink from witnesses and
sympathizers in your prayers, when, if you have to satisfy a man,
you must visit many and entreat them to be kind enough to intervene; when you throw yourself at a man's knees, kiss his feet, bring
your children, still unconscious of guilt, to entreat also for your
father's pardon? And you disdain to do this in the church?"[57] Or
again when he evokes, after the Gospel of Luke, the sinful woman
who kissed Christ's feet, washed them and dried them with her

hair: "What is the meaning of the hair, but that you may learn that, having laid aside all the pomp of worldly trappings, you must implore pardon, throw yourself on the earth with tears, and prostrate on the ground move people to pity."[58]

3. But the terms *exomologesis* or *confession* don't just designate this terminal episode of penance. Often, too, they relate to the whole unfolding of the penitential procedure. It's in this sense that Saint Irenaeus spoke of a woman who, after having espoused gnostic ideas, returned to the Church and spent the rest of her days "doing exomologesis"; or of a heretic who alternated between professing his errors and doing exomologesis.[59] And when Tertullian evokes God's establishment of "exomologesis in order to restore the sinner to grace," and of that king of Babylon who for seven years running had done exomologesis, he's thinking in fact of the whole penitential enterprise.[60]

If penance in its entirety can be called exomologesis, this is because the public and ostentatious expressions of repentance, which are required in a particularly solemn manner and with a very marked intensity in the moments preceding reconciliation, also form part of the penitential action during the time the latter unfolds. Penance—and this is one of its essential aspects—must constitute a kind of demonstration, of renewed "confession," attesting that one has committed a sin, that one knows one is a sinner, and that one repents. Such is the meaning that Tertullian, in chapters 9 and 10 of *De paenitentia*, gives to exomologesis as a permanent dimension of penance. Repentance must not be accomplished "solely within one's conscience but it must be shown forth in some external act." It is to this act—which is not so much an episode of penance but its external side, its visible and manifest face—that the word *exomologesis* should be applied. And thereby a "discipline," a way of being and of living, a regimen that involves *habitus atque victus*, is designated: "It bids you to lie in sackcloth and ashes, to cover your body with filthy rags, to plunge your soul into sorrow, to exchange sin for suffering. Moreover, it demands that you know only such food as is plain; this means it is taken for the sake of your soul, not your belly. It requires that you habitually nourish prayer by fasting, that you sigh and weep and groan day and night to the Lord your God, that you prostrate yourself at the feet of the priests and kneel before the beloved of God, making all the brethren commissioned ambassadors of your prayer for pardon. Exomologesis does all this to render penitence acceptable."[61] The obligation to do penance and the status in which it takes form imply, throughout its unfolding, these acts of exomologesis that manifest and attest it. Texts more recent than Tertullian's *De paenitentia* or *De pudicitia* show this. And they emphasize the demonstrative value of these practices. Through them it's a matter not only of exhibiting penitence, but of proving it. A cleric of the Church of Rome wrote to Saint Cyprian, apropos of the apostates: "It is time that they should do penance for the sin, that they should prove sorrow for their lapse, that they should show reserve."[62] Saint Cyprian himself, calling the lapsed to penance, exhorts them to these manifestations in which the groanings of those who have sinned should be mixed with the tears of the faithful.[63] And at the end of the fourth century, it is still by these acts for the purpose of testing and proving that the practice of the penitent life is being characterized: groanings and tears, says Saint Ambrose at the beginning of *De paenitentia*,[64] groanings, *lamentations*, and tears, he adds a little further on, stressing that these are a freely consented-to expression, a sort of voluntary confession— but in the sense of a profession of faith—by which the apostates try to gain pardon for the involuntary disavowal, which they may have declared under torture.[65] And Pacian, in his *Paraenesis*, notes that the true life of penance—the life that is led not just in a nominal way—finds its instruments in the sackcloth, ashes, fasting, and affliction and the participation of many people in prayers asking for forgiveness of the sinner.[66]

The historians who contested the existence of a defined ritual of exomologesis, between the acts of penance and the reconciliation, were mistaken, no doubt, in light of testimonies such as those of Saint Cyprian. But they were not wrong when they emphasized that the entire life of the penitent—through the different obligations they were under—must have played a confessional role. The penitent must "profess" his repentance. No penance without acts that had the dual function of constituting punishments that one inflicts on oneself and of manifesting the truth of this repentance.

Tertullian employed a meaningful expression to designate this exomologesis that was inherent in the penitential process: *publicatio sui.*[67]

One sees, then, that forgiveness of serious sins committed after baptism and the return to communion of those who fell away cannot be obtained without the implementation of a whole set of truth procedures. Procedures more numerous and more complex than those prescribed in connection with baptism. Their range is wide, since they go from declarations the sinner may make when soliciting penance to great expressions of humility and supplication that take place at the threshold of the church, before the final reconciliation. All these procedures can be distributed along different axes.

• The axis of the public and the private. On the private side we must place the secret things the sinner confides to the bishop or the priest when he asks to be granted the status of penitent; on the public side, all the acts by which the penitent must show himself to others in sackcloth and ashes, prostrate in tears begging their intercession on his behalf, and calling the faithful to weep and moan with him. Thus understood, penance is a public and collective rite.

• The axis of the verbal and the non-verbal. On one side there is the necessarily oral disclosure which the penitent must make to the one who will admit him into penance; and on the other the series of gestures, attitudes, tears, garments, and cries by which the one who has sinned shows his repentance. Perhaps he proclaims the nature of his sin—but this utterance itself belongs to a whole ensemble of expressions in which the entire body is the main element.

• The axis of the juridical and the dramatic. On one side, the penance must begin with an account, albeit brief, of the wrong committed—of what characterizes it and of the circumstances that may alter its seriousness; in this way it can be determined whether penance is called for, and how long it should last before the reconciliation. But at the other pole there are dramatic and intense manifestations that don't obey any calculation of economy and don't seek an adjustment, made in the strictest possible way, to the gravity of the sin committed; they obey on the contrary a principle of emphasis; they must be as vigorous as possible.

• The axis of the objective and the subjective. On one side one finds the designation of the sin, at least in its essential elements; on the other, what the major practices of exomologesis have to manifest is not so much the sin itself in its particularity as the state of the sinner himself, or rather the states that in him are superimposed, intertwined, and in competition. He does have to display himself as a sinner, symbolically covered with filth and the defilement of sin, sunk into this life of sin that is the way of death. But the visible intensity of penitential acts also has the goal of certifying that he is already freeing himself from that life and that he renounces it; the tears he sheds onto his breast are washing it away; he purifies himself by means of the filth he covers himself with; by humiliating himself he shows that he is raising himself back up and is worthy of being raised.[68] The manifestations of exomologesis don't aim to make [the sin] appear in the form that it was truly committed: their purpose is to make the penitent himself emerge into the light and just as he is: at once truly a sinner and already no longer truly one.

We can say, then, that truth procedures in the ecclesiastical penance of the first centuries are grouped around two poles: one is that of the verbal and private formulation, which has the role of defining the sin with the characteristics by which it can be assessed, making it possible to determine how its forgiveness can be granted; the other, which is that of general and public expression, has the role of manifesting, as dramatically as possible, both the sinfulness of the sinner and the movement that delivers him from his sin. Of course, these are the two poles between which the different ways, in penance, of manifesting the truth of the sinner and of his sin are distributed. They are not two independent institutions, or two practices utterly foreign to each other; they coexist, interfere with each other, and sometimes merge together: it's clear that there were extreme fasts and exomologesis conducted in private;[69] and we also have accounts of public and verbal declarations of wrongs committed by this or that member of the community.[70] But nevertheless, one can recognize the existence of [two] types of practice, two ways of making the truth appear: telling the truth about the sin and manifesting the being-true of the sinner.

And between these two modalities the distribution is not even: the verbal enunciation of the sin is seldom required except when it's a matter of determining the penance, examining whether the sinner can be admitted into it and merits being reconciled. "Telling the sin"—bringing into play, in the verbal dimension, the confession and the examination, demanding of the sinner a "veridiction" of his sins—is necessary only prior to the penitential procedure and so, in a way, is outside it. On the other hand, the ostentatious, gestural, corporeal demonstration of what the sinner is in his being forms an intrinsic part of penance. It forms an essential and constant dimension of it. The penitent is expected not so much to "tell the truth" [*"dire le vrai"*] concerning what he did as to "do the truth" [*"faire vrai"*] by manifesting what he is.

This necessity of penitential practice—that it be carried out only through manifestations designed to bring the penitent's truth to light—raises a problem: when one has sinned, why must one not only repent—imposing rigors and macerations upon himself—but also show these acts and show oneself as one is? Why does the manifestation of the truth constitute an intrinsic part of the procedure that enables one to redeem the sin? When one has "done wrong," why is it necessary to make the truth shine forth, not only the truth about what one did, but about what one is? The answer is obvious: once the Christian religion was formed into a Church endowed with a strong communitarian structure and a hierarchical organization, no serious infraction could be pardoned without a certain number of proofs and guarantees. Just as a candidate for baptism couldn't be accepted without having been tested beforehand through the catechumenate—*probatio animae*—the Church

couldn't reconcile those who hadn't clearly manifested their
repentance through discipline and exercises that stood for punishment in relation to the past and showed commitment to the
future. They had to practice the *publicatio sui.*

But what is more enigmatic—from the standpoint of the history of the experience of the self—is the way one thought of and
justified the sinner's obligation to speak the truth—or rather to
manifest himself in his truth—in order to obtain forgiveness for
his sins. This obligation is affirmed, in fact, over and over again.
No pardon if there was no exomologesis, no recognition by the
sinner of his sin, no outward, explicit, visible manifestation of
that recognition: "He that confesses his sin is released from servitude [. . .] not only free but also just, for justice is in liberty and liberty in confession. As soon as a man shall confess he is absolved."[71]
And Saint John Chrysostom, in short: "Declare your sin: you will
destroy your sin."[72] This is the general principle underlying the
exegeses that Saint Ambrose and Saint John Chrysostom make of
the curse of Cain. His sin, as grave as it was, was not unpardonable.
When God [asked him] what he had done with his brother, it was
not that God didn't know, of course; it was to give him the possibility of confessing. And what made it unpardonable was that he
replied: I don't know. This is the principle of eternal damnation.
Graver than the fratricide was this lie, which Saint Ambrose calls
a "sacrilege."[73] The "I don't know" of the criminal, the refusal of
truth is, on the part of the sinner, the gravest possible offense:
it cannot be atoned for. In contrast to Cain, David confesses his
sins spontaneously; he-who-was-just is the image of the penitent:
the truth he professes saves him.[74] And if Adam and Eve are not
damned for Eternity, it's because they, too, confessed; according
to Chrysostom, they even confessed to their crimes twice: verbally, by replying to God; and in their gestures and their bodies,
by hiding their nakedness.[75]

Long before the institution of sacramental penance and the
organization of auricular confession, the Christian Church posited
the fundamental character of the truth obligation for anyone who
has sinned and as a precondition for possible redemption. Speaking the truth about one's sin—or rather manifesting in its truth
one's state as a sinner—is indispensable if the sin is to be forgiven.

Manifestation of what is true is a necessary condition for what is true to be erased. To think this relation through and to explain this necessity, ancient Christianity had recourse to several models.

1.   The medical model is used quite frequently: sins are represented as injuries or wounds, penance as a remedy. A theme all the more common as it could take support from both the Hebraic tradition of sin-as-wound and the Greek notion of sicknesses of the soul. The idea of a penitential medicine is a commonplace feature in the Christian pastoral as early as the first centuries,[76] and would remain so thereafter. A difference should be noted, however. When the penitential institution assumes the form of the sacrament by which it will be definitively recognized in the twelfth century, the priest, having the power to absolve, will occupy the place of the physician. The necessity of confession in the form of an individual, secret, and detailed avowal of sins will then be justified by the principle that every sick person has an obligation to reveal to his caregiver the infirmities he is hiding, the pains he feels, the illnesses he has suffered. From this viewpoint, the manifestation of what the sinner is in his truth and of the secrets of his soul constitutes a technical necessity.[77] But in early Christianity it's not the priest who treats wounds but Christ—that is, God himself: "But for their former sins, God who has the power of healing that will give a remedy; for he has the power of all things."[78] But is it necessary that the sinner show his wounds and his hidden ailments to such a physician? What needs to be made known to the one who knows everything? One can't even conceal the faults that one may have committed in the secrecy of one's heart.[79] This is the paradox of that healing through penance: it demands that one manifest, through an explicit and rigorous exomologesis, sins that are already known by that one who is expected to heal them. One must spread out before him things that in any case can never be hidden from him. The truth is owed to him, not as a necessity in order for him to choose the appropriate remedies, but as an obligation on the part of the one he intends to heal. For the sick person it is not a matter of making the therapy possible by informing the physician of his ailment, but of deserving the healing, at the price of truth.

2.  Recourse to the judicial model, very frequent as well,[80] reveals basically the same paradox. When the sacramental penance becomes clearly defined as a tribunal in which the priest must play the role of judge (a judge who represents God but whose sentences have their effects in heaven), the exact confession by the sinner of the wrongs he has committed becomes an essential part of the procedure: based on it—and given the threat that lying or willful omission may invalidate the sacrament—the confessor will be able to render his judgment and determine the conditions of the penance. In ancient Christianity, the priest doesn't play the role of judge: the penitent deals directly with God—a judge who cannot be informed of anything since he sees everything.[81] And yet he must be shown the sins committed with nothing hidden.[82] The authors of the third and fourth centuries offer several justifications for this obligation. One is completely traditional: it's that the spontaneous and sincere confession is favorable to the accused in the mind of the judge.[83] Another refers to the idea that the devil will one day be man's accuser before God, so man will be in a more advantageous position if he preempts his enemy's denunciation, if he speaks first and sets out himself the crimes for which he may be reproached.[84] Further, since Christ is man's advocate with God and serves as intercessor, the sinner must normally confide his case and confess his sins to Christ.[85] Finally, another argument, a stranger one for us perhaps: he that confesses his wrongs not only justifies himself before God, but justifies God himself and his wrath against the weakness of men: to deny one's own sins would be to try to make God a liar.[86]

3.  But truth be told, these two models—of medicine and of the tribunal, which will later become so important for organizing the penitential confession and giving it its form—seem to play only an accessory role as part of the required exomologesis. The penitent's obligation to manifest himself in the truth of his sinful condition is more deeply grounded in martyrdom. There are two reasons for this. First, the martyr is promised forgiveness of his sins: the blood he sheds washes them away. And if he professes his Christian belief, which he has affirmed a first time in baptism, a second time under torture, the ordeal will constitute a second bap-

tism, with the same effects of remission of sins.[87] Moreover, the benefits of penance—that "second baptism"—were granted, not without serious discussions, to those who had fallen away, those who chose to deny their faith rather than undergo the torture: for them, penance was a way of inflicting martyrdom on themselves to reaffirm their faith—the martyrdom they had tried, out of weakness, to escape. This theme, which appears in the wake of the great persecutions, remains in use later. Penance appears then as the substitute for martyrdom for the generation that no longer finds in this peril the occasion for proving its faith. "The martyrs have been killed," says Saint Augustine, and asks, "Who are the children of those that were killed, if not ourselves? And how are we freed, if not by saying to the Lord: you have broken my chains, I will offer you a victim's sacrifice in the form of praise?"[88]

Now, as we know, martyrdom is a conveyor of truth: evidence of the belief for which one dies, a manifestation that life here below is nothing but a death, but that death gives access to true life, a testimony by which this truth enables one to face suffering without collapsing. The martyr, without even having to speak, and by his very conduct, makes a truth shine forth that, in destroying life, makes one live beyond death. In the complex economy of the martyr's conduct, truth is affirmed in a belief, is shown to everyone's eyes as a force, and inverts the values of life and death. It constitutes a "test" [*épreuve*] in the triple sense that it expresses the sincerity of a man's belief, it confirms the all-powerful force of that which one believes, and it dispels the deceptive appearances of this world to reveal the reality of the beyond. If exomologesis is so important in penance, if it is synonymous with it in public and ostentatious rites, this is because the penitent must testify like the martyr: express his repentance, show the strength his faith gives him, and make it clear that this body that he humiliates is only dust and death, and that true life is elsewhere. By reproducing the martyrdom that he hasn't had the courage (or the opportunity) to endure, the penitent places himself at the threshold of a death that hides beneath the deceptive appearances of life, of a genuine life that is promised by death. This threshold is that of *metanoia*, or conversion, when the soul does a complete turnaround, inverts all its values, and changes in every respect. Exomologesis as a mani-

festation by the penitent himself of that death which his life has
been, and of the life he will access through death, constitutes the
evidential and exemplary expression—the proof—of his *metanoia*.

One can say that, in the practice of ancient penance, the part
played by the "confession" is both vague and essential. Vague
because it's not a matter of a specific rite localized within the whole
procedure, even if at certain moments the verbal declaration of the
sin is no doubt required (as when one asks the bishop for the status
of penitent). Essential because it is part of a constant dimension
of the penitential exercise. This exercise, in the course of its pro-
ceedings, must manifest the truth. Later, in medieval penance, the
confession will take the form of a "truth-telling" that will be the
enumeration of sins committed: here it's the entire penance that
must constitute a "truth-telling"—or rather, since in it the role of
verbal utterance is peculiarly limited in favor of gestures, behaviors, and ways of living, this will be a "truth-doing": truly doing
*metanoia*—repentance, mortification, resurrection to the true life.
But this "truth-doing" essential to penance doesn't have the role
of reconstructing the sins committed by reliving them in memory.
It doesn't seek to establish the subjects' identity or responsibility,
it doesn't constitute a mode of knowledge of oneself and one's
past, but rather the manifestation of a rupture: a temporal break, a
renunciation of the world, and an inversion of life and death. The
penitent, says Saint Ambrose, must be that young man who comes
back home, and the girl he had loved presents herself and says:
Here I am, *ego sum*. To which he replies: *Sed ego non sum ego*. A day
will come, in the history of penitential practice, when the sinner
will have to present himself to the priest and verbally itemize his
sins: *ego sum*. But in its early form, penance, at the same time an
exercise and a manifestation, a mortification and a veridiction, is a
way of affirming *ego non sum ego*. The rites of exomologesis ensure
that this rupture of identity is produced.

# 4

# The Art of Arts

Spiritual direction, self-examination, careful control by the subject of his acts and his thoughts, confiding what he has done to another, asking a guide for advice, and accepting the rules of conduct he suggests: all this is a very ancient tradition. The Christian authors didn't conceal this antecedence or deny the kinship between these older practices and the exercises they themselves prescribed. Saint John Chrysostom recommends soul-searching by referring to the example of the pagan philosophers and by citing Pythagoras.[1] Apparently, Epictetus's *Manual* was copied by Saint Nilus as if it were a Christian text offering a code of existence capable of properly shaping the souls of the faithful and leading them to salvation. There is a certain continuity from the teachers of conduct in antiquity to the guides of ascetic life—referred to, moreover, as the philosophical life. The differences, however, must not be overlooked.

Among the Greeks and the Romans, the practice of life guidance included a fairly wide range of different procedures. One finds it in the form of discontinuous and circumstantial relations: Antiphon the Sophist maintained a consulting office where he would sell advice to those facing difficult situations,[2] and the physicians would respond to requests concerning not only physical ailments but also moral illnesses: just as much as preventive methods or guidelines for health, the regimens they prescribed were rules for living, for controlling the passions, gaining self-control, managing the economy of pleasures, and ensuring fairness in relations with others.[3] But the consultations could also be acts of friendship and kindness, without remuneration: conversations, exchanges of correspondence, drafting of a little treatise addressed to a friend in distress. In general, these episodic forms of direction responded to a specific situation: a stroke of bad luck, exile, a spell of mourning could trigger them, but also a crisis, a period of difficulty, a moment of uncertainty. This was the case with Serenus when he explained his condition to Seneca, requesting the aid of his diagnosis and his counsel.[4] He felt he was no longer progressing on the path of Stoic wisdom: opposite impulses were agitating his soul, not to the point of provoking a "storm," but with enough force to give him "something like seasickness."[5]

But there also existed much more continuous and much more institutionalized forms of direction. They functioned in the schools of philosophy in particular. There the discipline of collective life that was imposed on everyone was completed by much more individualized relations. The teacher was a constant guide for the disciple: he taught him the truth little by little, helped him progress on the path of virtue, self-control, and tranquility of the soul, tested his progress, and, day by day, gave him advice on living. Thus, among the Epicureans, individual interviews were set up, a rule of frankness was imposed on members of the school, encouraging everyone to reveal their soul and not to hide anything, so that they might be guided effectively; only the wisest teachers could take charge of this individual direction of students, while the others had the collective responsibility for a group.[6]

To ensure its proper functioning, the direction called upon a whole ensemble of diverse practices.[7] One of the most important was the spiritual examination. Starting with the Pythagoreans, it figures as a key element in a large number of codes for living. But it didn't always have the same form, it didn't always focus on the same objects, and the same results were not always expected from it.[8] Little is known about the Pythagorean examination beyond the famous verses of the *Carmen aureum*, only the first two of which are thought to represent the oldest tradition: "Don't allow gentle sleep to slip in like fog before you've examined each action of your day."[9] Other than its role as a test of moral progress, this examination was perhaps one of those mnemonic exercises that the Pythagoreans cultivated. It also served, no doubt, as a purifying ritual to induce favorable dreams and prepare for a sleep in which the school saw a prefiguration of death.[10]

In the great development of Hellenistic philosophy as spiritual direction, examination of the soul plays a major role. It constitutes a kind of exchange: a relay between the one directed and the director, a transition between the period when one is being directed and the moment when that will cease to be the case. Through the examination the disciple or patient will be able to reveal the condition of his soul to his director, so that the latter can render a judgment and determine the appropriate remedy. This is how Serenus's examination begins after asking for Seneca's aid: "It is easier to give you details about the infirmity of my soul than it is to summarize [. . .] I'll describe the disturbances I experience and it will be up to you to name the disease."[11] It's also through the examination that the directee can see how his director's recommendations are acting upon his soul and helping him to improve; through it he can constantly verify that he is following them correctly and that he is thus capable of achieving his autonomy. And it's the exam that, once the period of direction is ended, allows him to prolong its effects and conduct a permanent direction of his own soul. This quadruple role of the examination as an opening of the soul to others, an internalization of the rules of direction, a testing of their success, and an exercise of self-control once autonomy is acquired appears clearly in a treatise that Galen devoted to the "passions of the soul": "First, we must not leave the diagnosis of these passions to ourselves but must entrust it to others; second, we must not leave this task to just anyone but to older men who are commonly considered to be good and noble—men to whom we ourselves have given full approval because on many occasions, we have found them free from these passions [. . .] Then, too, a man must remind himself of these things each day—if he does so more frequently it will be all the better, but if not, at least let him do so at dawn, before he begins his daily tasks, and toward evening before he is about to rest. You can be sure that I have grown accustomed to pondering twice a day the exhortations attributed to Pythagoras, for it is not enough for us to practice self-control; we must also cleanse ourselves of voluptuous eating and carnal lust [. . .] While we are novices in all these matters, we must ask others to watch over us and inform us of any error into which we fall; later on let us, without our tutors' help, keep watch over ourselves."[12]

In this role as relay and hinge, the spiritual examination is oriented toward a goal and privileges one issue: self-control. If the directee examines himself, if he takes up each of his weaknesses in turn, this is so that he might become fully in control of himself and no longer need to resort to another's help at a difficult time. This aim of self-examination appears clearly when one compares two texts connected with Stoic practice: the first shows what the examination can be within the context of direction, and the second what it is for someone who has achieved philosophical autonomy.

Representing the first situation is the letter from Serenus to Seneca. Advancing step by step, Serenus requests the philosopher's help at a time when he is experiencing a malaise involving the sensation of no longer making progress, the fear that his attachment to what is bad and what is good may be embedded in a definitive way, and the feeling that he's immobilized in a state that is not exactly deliverance and not exactly enslavement. In short, he is neither sick nor healthy.[13] So the examination that Serenus is undertaking—and for which he's asking Seneca to intervene, diagnose, and suggest remedies—consists in establishing a kind of appraisal of forces: which ones ensure the soul's stability, its serenity, its independence? Which ones, on the contrary, expose it to external trouble and make it dependent on things that are foreign to its purpose? The examination focuses successively on the problem of wealth, public duties, and the preoccupation with posthumous glory. In regard to these three points he draws a dividing line: on one side, what marks the soul's ability to be satisfied with what it has at its disposal (an adequate standard of living, a simple cuisine, furniture one has inherited), to fully carry out one's public duties (serving friends, fellow citizens, humanity), to take real and present things into consideration when one speaks; but on the other side, there is the pleasure one experiences in the spectacle of luxury on display, the enthusiasm that is sometimes aroused in one, the words that swell as if one wished above all for posterity to speak of him.

Serenus's examination doesn't focus therefore on specific acts, or on a relatively distant past; it's not a matter of tabulating what good and bad was done, or of singling out the wrongs that were committed and that called for repentance. The gaze of consciousness is fixated on the present, a present that is seen as a "state,"[14] on the play of forces that push Serenus either to stay at home satisfied with his lot, or to rush off to the forum and speak in a voice that no longer belongs to him. But the examination doesn't try to search out the causes of this state: it doesn't descend toward the hidden roots of the sickness—it tries to reconstitute it as it presents itself to consciousness, in the form of the satisfactions the latter experiences or the impulses it feels within itself. The systematic repetition of the word *placet* (it pleases) is significant: the feeling the soul has about what it does or sees forms the specific object of the examination. Thus, the examination traces the way in which the impulses that trouble the soul are manifested to it—and which, in the particular case of Serenus, pull it in opposite directions at once, immobilize it on the path of progress, and make it vacillate to the point of giving him seasickness. One thus arrives at an image of the *infirmitas* of the soul through the awareness that it maintains of itself.

In book 3 of *De ira*, Seneca offers the example of another type of examination: the one that he conducts every evening, before going to sleep, once all the lights are put out. This time it's a matter of looking back on the day and "scanning" its entire unfolding. He reviews his acts and words and assesses them: he recalls that he wasted his time trying to instruct ignorant people, or that, in attempting to correct one of his friends, he spoke to him with so much force that the friend was offended rather than corrected. In this instance, we have a clearly retrospective examination: it is oriented toward definite actions and it has the goal, in "taking their measure again,"[15] of separating the bad acts from the good ones. In this way, each deed must receive "its share of praise and blame." Here the judicial model is present (and no longer the medical one); the words say it without ambiguity: *cognoscit de moribus suis; apud me causam dico.* But it should be noted that this inquiry doesn't lead to condemnation or punishment or remorse. The self-examiner merely tells himself "I forgive you now" and "see that you don't repeat it." So the model is perhaps more administrative than judicial: the latent image in the text puts one more in mind of an inspection than a tribunal. One scrutinizes, one examines, one detects, one reassesses.[16]

Now, Seneca gives two examples that do suggest the actions for which one should reproach oneself: having tried to instruct people who were incapable of understanding, and having hurt someone he'd intended to correct—hence not having attained the goal that he had set. According to a characteristic principle of Stoicism, an action is to be evaluated and declared good or bad according to its ends or goals.[17] And it's for having disregarded certain rational principles of actions—it is useless to teach those who've never been able to learn anything; or again, it's necessary when one speaks to consider the interlocutor's ability to receive the truth—that Seneca committed "errors" relative to the objectives he was aiming for. These are consequently seen as so many "mistakes."[18] And the role of the examination is to allow one to correct them for the future, by naming the rules of conduct that were not acknowledged. It's not a matter of reproaching oneself for what was done, but of constituting patterns of rational behavior for future circumstances, and of establishing one's autonomy so that it coincides with the order of the world, by applying the principles of universal reason. One can say that in *De ira* the examination—retrospective and centered on past faults as it may be—has a "programming" function: to recognize, through the "errors" and the missed objectives, the rules that will make it possible to control the actions that one undertakes, and hence to control oneself.

These practices were not immediately incorporated into Christianity. One doesn't really see the obligation and rules of spiritual examination defined,[19] or the techniques for directing souls developed, before the fourth century. The themes of ancient philosophy spread through Christian thought long before the procedures connected with that philosophical life.

It's true that, as early as the second and third centuries, there are numerous texts that underline the importance of knowing oneself or reflecting on the acts to be done or on those one has already performed. Clement of Alexandria, at the beginning of the third book of the *Paedagogus*, reminds everyone that "the greatest knowledge is the knowledge of oneself (*to gnônai hauton*)." But there it is not a matter of an investigation of oneself, nor a retrospection of the past or the reactualization in memory of the wrongful acts one may have been guilty of. It's a matter of recognizing in oneself the element by which one can know God—the reality for which God is the guide, which consequently can lead men to him and, freeing man from the external world with its material adornments, clothe him in a pure beauty that makes him resemble God himself.[20] Here self-knowledge is not in any way a spiritual examination, or a plunge into the depths of oneself; it involves an ascent toward God, at the urging of a soul that is able to rise toward him. In a very different spirit, Saint Hilary advises the Christian to reflect carefully on his acts,[21] but he is thinking above all of a vigilance that enables one not to engage in an action casually, to foresee its dangers and to carry it out only when it has reached the necessary moment of maturity; a prospective reflection, therefore, that is in keeping with what was demanded by the philosophy of the day, and the Stoics in particular,[22] but that doesn't take the form of a systematic examination of oneself.

The same thing can be said about direction. The theme of the shepherd who must guide the flock and each sheep to the meadows of salvation is present in the oldest forms of Christianity. But it doesn't coincide with the idea of a "direction" that would take charge of an individual's life, guiding it step by step, prescribing it a specific regimen, giving it advice about everyday conduct, constantly informing itself about his progress and requiring a continuous and unfailing obedience. A text by Clement of Alexandria is meaningful on this point:[23] it stresses the necessity for a rich and powerful person (for whom, consequently, entry into paradise is especially difficult) to have someone who comes to his assistance, and he employs the traditional metaphors of direction (a "pilot," a "gymnastics instructor"); this guide will speak freely and bluntly; he must be listened to with all the more fear and respect. But this counseling activity is only one aspect of a more complex role, where the one who "directs" must pray, fast, engage in vigils, and subject himself to macerations for the benefit of the one he is directing. He is thus the directee's intercessor before God, his representative, his sponsor, just as for the sinner he is an angel sent by God. So what is involved here is a substitution or at least a sacrificial participation that goes well beyond the technique of direction. The example that Clement cites confirms this: one sees the apostle John baptize a young man, then entrust him, during his

absence, to the local bishop; and when upon his return he learns
that the neophyte has fallen back into sin, he scolds the bishop
for the bad guardianship he's exercised[24] and goes and finds the
offender: "I will defend you before Christ; if need be, I will die
in your place, and willingly, following the Lord's example. I will
sacrifice my life to yours."[25] In this way he brings the young man
back to the Church, weeping with him and sharing his fasts. The
model, as you can see, is not that of the instructor teaching his
student how to live and to conduct himself: it's that of Christ who
sacrifices himself for men after they have fallen, and who inter-
cedes for them with God. The exchange of sacrifice for redemption is the most important of these means for leading a soul and
getting it to progress little by little.[26]

In reality, the practices of direction and spiritual examination—
elaborated by ancient philosophy—were accepted into Christianity, where they saw a development of new forms and effects, only
with monasticism, within and based on those institutions. That
these ways and means of the philosophical life were put into practice there is not surprising in the least. Designed to lead to the
perfect life—"an existence in which purity of conduct is associated with the true knowledge of what is"[27]—monasticism was able
to present itself as the philosophical life par excellence: philosophy according to Christ,[28] philosophy through works.[29] And the
monasteries were able to be defined as schools of philosophy.[30]
So it was there—either in the semi-reclusion practiced in Lower
Egypt, for example, where a few disciples would come to initiate
themselves into desert life in the company of renowned ascetics,
or in the cenobia where the communitarian life would be developed according to general and strict rules—that the conduct of
individuals would be organized according to complex procedures.
These gave rise to reflection and elaboration and the creation of
an art, which, Gregory of Nazianzus would say—taking up the
expression ordinarily used to designate philosophy—was *tekhnê*
[*tekhnôn**], the art of arts: "But granted that a man is free from

---

* Manuscript: *tekhnê tekhnês*, but the text by Gregory of Nazianzus has "*tô onti
gar autê moi phainetai tekhnê tis einai tekhnôn kai epistêmê epistêmôn, to polutropôta-
ton tôn zôôn kai poikilôtaton.*"

vice, and has reached the greatest heights of virtue: I do not see what knowledge or power would justify him in venturing upon this office. For the guiding of man, the most variable and manifold of creatures, seems to me in very deed to be the art of arts and science of sciences."[31] Constantly, and up to the present age, the direction of individuals, the management of their souls, the guidance, step by step, of their progress, the exploration, together with them, of the secret impulses of their hearts, would be placed under this rubric of *ars artium.*[32]

For my comments on these practices of direction and examination, I will rely—not exclusively but in a privileged way—on the information given by Cassian. Doubtless he doesn't represent the highest forms of ascetic thought, but he was, with Saint Jerome, one of the main vehicles of Eastern experiences in the West; and he is also not content, either in the *Institutes* or in the *Conferences*, merely to cite the exploits of the most famous monks or to convey their rules of existence. Based on his own experience, he sets out "the simple life of the saints"; to his outline of the institutions and the rules, he adds an assessment "of the causes of the principal faults" and "how to be cured of them." It's less a matter of celebrating "God's marvels" than of instructing the brethren in "the correction of behavior and how to live the perfect life."[33]

A testimony, therefore, that, between the institutional rules and the most edifying examples, seeks to communicate a way of doing things, a practice with its methods and reasons. In short, to repeat a statement he makes at the beginning of the *Conferences*, the life of the monks is treated as an "art" and studied as a link between means and particular objectives and an end that is appropriate to it.[34]

## I. THE PRINCIPLE OF DIRECTION

"Those who are not directed fall like dead leaves." This saying from Proverbs[35] was regularly cited in the monastic literature in support of the principle that the monk's life cannot do without a "direction." The monk can't do without it if he undertakes to lead, in solitude, the anchorite's existence. And he can't even be exempted from direction if that life unfolds in a monastery under the yoke of a communal rule. In all cases the singular relation binding a disciple to a master—placing him under the latter's continuous control, obliging him to comply with the least of his orders and confide his soul to him without any hesitation—is mandatory. Direction is indispensable for anyone wanting to advance toward the perfect life: neither the individual ardor of the ascesis nor the general application of the code can replace it.

In the eighteenth *Conference*, Cassian, following the abbot Piamun, places the monks into three or rather four categories.[36] He essentially reproaches the two he condemns—the Sarabaites and the newly emergent anchorites—for having refused the practice of direction. The Sarabaites "have no interest in monastic discipline" and refuse to "submit to the authority of elders"; they "don't learn their instructions," "don't accept any of the rules deriving from sensible guidance," "the last thing they want is to be governed . . . ," they insist on "being free of the yoke of elders, free to do what takes their fancy."[37] The same goes for the false anchorites who, because they have no humility or patience, can't stand being "exercised" (*lacessiti*) by anyone.[38] The bad monk is one who is not directed: it's because he comes to monasticism with bad intentions—he wants to give himself the appearance, but not the reality, of monastic life—that he refuses to let himself be directed; and because he refuses this direction, the faults within him only grow worse.[39]

So one enters into the reality of monastic existence through direction. Those who choose the "high peaks of asceticism" are advised by Cassian to test themselves first in a regular cenobitic community,[40] and then to look for a teacher with whom one can learn solitude. He recalls a piece of advice given by Abbot Antony: for so difficult an apprenticeship, a single teacher will not suffice; with several, one must draw from the virtues that each of them possesses—"And therefore the monk who desires to gather spiritual honey ought, like a most careful bee, to suck out virtue from those who specially possess it, and should diligently store it up in the vessel of his own breast."[41]

Someone wishing to join the cenobium is first subjected to the big threshold test: he's made to wait at the gate of the monastery, where he begs to enter; but, pretending to suspect nothing but selfish motives on his part, the monks rebuff him for ten days, "cover him with insults and reproaches," to test his intention and his steadfastness. If he is accepted, his instruction unfolds in two phases. In the first, he's assigned an elder, who "dwells apart, not far from the entrance to the monastery, in charge of strangers and guests": there, he's trained in service (*famulatus*), humility, and patience. After a whole year, if there have been no complaints about him, he's incorporated into the community and placed with another elder, who is responsible for teaching and governing (*instituere et gubernare*) a group of ten young people. Cassian says nothing about the existence of a relationship of direction between the elders.[42] On the one hand, nothing clearly suggests that the elders were expected to have recourse, whether regularly or occasionally, to a director. However, Cassian, like all the authors of his era, insists on the principle that every soul, without exception, needs direction[43]—that even after long exercises, even when one has a reputation for saintliness, there are still cases where one lapses,[44] and that monks need to be directed till the end of their lives. On two occasions—in the *Institutes* and in the *Conferences*—Cassian recalls the great saintliness of Pinufius: the respect that surrounded him in his monastery deprived him of "the possibility of progressing in the virtue of submission to the degree that he aspired"; twice he flees in secret to take up the life of a novice again and is crestfallen when he's discovered, lamenting that he can't end his life in the submission he has acquired.[45] The fact remains, for Cassian, that only one who has learned to obey and has acquired "through the education received from the elders, that which he will have to impart to the younger ones" can be called to command; but also the highest wisdom or, better, "the highest gift" of the Holy Spirit consists in the possibility of "directing others well" and "getting directed oneself."[46] The saint is not one who "self-directs"; it's one who allows himself to be directed by God.

A universality, therefore, of the relationship of direction. Even if there's a phase of initiation into the monastic life where direction must take a dense, institutional form, organized by rules applying to all novices in common, the willingness to accept a direction, the readiness to be directed, is a constant that must character-

ize monastic life from beginning to end.[47] Cassian indicates the
two main aspects of this direction, and the way in which direction
must be exercised.

• The direction consists in an obedience training, understood as a renunciation of one's own wishes through submission to another's will: "And his concern and the chief
part of his instruction [referring to the teacher of the
novices]—through which the juniors brought to him may
be able, in due course, to mount to the greatest heights of
perfection—will be to teach them first to conquer their
own wishes; and, anxiously and diligently practicing them
in this, he will of set purpose contrive to give them such
orders as he knows to be contrary to their liking."[48]

• And to achieve this perfect and exhaustive obedience,
so that this game of nullification-replacement (nullification of one's own will, substitution of another's will) can
take place, an exercise is essential: constant examination
of oneself and perpetual confession. "And, that they may
easily arrive at this [perfect obedience and humility of the
heart], they are next taught not to conceal by a false shame
any itching thoughts in their hearts, but, as soon as ever
such arise, to lay them bare to the senior, and, in forming
a judgment about them, not to trust anything to their own
discretion, but to take it on trust that that is good or bad
which is considered and pronounced so by the examination of the senior."[49]

## II. THE RULE OF OBEDIENCE

That direction presupposes the disciple's exact obedience to the
master is obviously not a principle peculiar to Christian monasticism. In the philosophical life of antiquity, the master had to be
listened to faithfully. But that obedience was instrumental, targeted, and limited. It had a definite object: it was meant to help one
break free of a passion, overcome a mourning or a sorrow, escape
a phase of uncertainty (this was the case with Serenus consulting

Seneca), or attain a certain state (of tranquility, of self-control, of independence with respect to external events). To achieve this end, the director would utilize tailored means, and the obedience required of the disciple was limited to those necessary forms. Moreover, it was a temporary submission that would cease as soon as the goal was reached. It was just one of the tools employed by the direction, according to a strict economy that limited it solely to the moment and the objectives for which it could be useful.

Monastic obedience is of a different type altogether.

a) First of all, it is comprehensive: one is expected to obey not only insofar as this submission would enable one to obtain a result—one must obey in every case and in general. No aspect of life, no moment of existence, must escape the form of obedience. The one being directed must make sure that the least of his actions—even an action that seems clearly to fall outside the control of his own will—is subjected to the will of the one directing him. The obedience relation must permeate existence down to its smallest manifestations. This is the *subdito*, which implies that in all his behaviors the monk must ensure that he is commandable. Commanded by the rule, by the abbot's directives, by the orders of one's director, possibly even according to the wishes of one's brethren[50]—while it's true that the brethren's wishes don't emanate from a superior or an elder, they have the privilege of being the wishes of another. So there is no distinction to be made between what one does for oneself and what one does at the behest of another. Everything must be done in compliance with an order.

The *officium* of the monk, says Saint Jerome, is to obey.[51] So he must do everything by express command, or at least according to a granted permission—"Every act that is done without the order or permission of a superior is a theft and a sacrifice leading to death and not to any benefit, even if it seems so to you."[52] "The juniors not only do not dare to leave their cell without permission but do not venture to satisfy their common and natural needs."[53] And later Dorotheus of Gaza will recount the exploit of one of Barsanuphe's disciples who, exhausted by illness, kept himself from dying so long as his master had not given the authorization.[54]

b) Further, the value of this obedience doesn't lie in the content of the prescribed or permitted act. It resides above all in its form—in the fact that one is subjected to the will of another and yields to it, attaching no importance to what is wanted, but clinging to the fact that it's another who wants it. The essential thing is not to put anything in opposition to this obedience: neither one's own will, nor one's reason, nor some self-interest (even if it appears legitimate), nor the least reluctance. One must fully accept "undergoing" that other's will—being, in relation to it, ductile and transparent. This is the principle of *patientia*, which makes one accept what the director wants and tolerate everything from him. Cassian, like the other exponents of monastic life, reports the most famous tests of this patience: tests of *absurdity*—even if an order makes no sense, it has to be fully executed. Such was the case with the abbey John, hero of obedience, whose master sent him to water a dried-out stick planted in the middle of the desert for a whole year.[55] Tests of *immediacy*—once given, an order must be carried out right away, without the slightest delay: scarcely uttered, it takes precedence over any other obligation whatsoever; there is nothing that shouldn't yield to the urgency of the command. Witness that monk busy copying out the holiest Scriptures, who breaks off the moment he's called to prayer; his stylus lifts up abruptly and the letter it was shaping remains unfinished.[56] Tests of *non-rebellion*—the injustice of a command, be it contrary either to the truth or to nature, must never prevent one from executing it. It's there, rather, that obedience assumes its greatest value. Pafnutius, unjustly accused of a wrong that another committed against him, accepts his condemnation and can't wait to begin the penance imposed on him.[57] Patermutus, having joined the monastery with his young son, patiently bears seeing the bad treatment the child is made to undergo, and as soon as the order is given, he hurries to throw the little boy in the river.[58] Understood as non-resistance to everything the other wants and imposes, *patientia* turns the monk into a kind of inert material in the hands of the one directing him. "Not differing in any respect from an inanimate body or from the material employed by an artist [. . .], just as the artist shows his skill without the material hindering him to any degree in the pursuit of his goal."[59]

c) Finally, monastic obedience has no other end than itself. It is not a momentary dependence—it is not a stage that is finally crowned by the right to move freely. If the monk must obey, it's in order to attain the state of obedience. Why is it so important, in spiritual direction, to train the novice to obey someone? It's because the aim is to make him "be obedient" in the absolute sense. Obedience is not simply a relation to this or that—it's a general and permanent structure of existence. And hence a form of relationship with oneself. But this relationship doesn't consist in internalizing the mechanism of direction, as it were—in becoming one's own director and in making sure that no part of ourselves escapes our sovereign will. On the contrary: the state of obedience finds its expression in *humilitas*. The latter, instead of being a closed structure—as in someone who by obeying has learned to become his own master—is an "open figure": it ensures that the subject gives others the power over him. In humility, I see myself as such a lowly creature that I am inferior to anyone—and consequently I feel obliged to prefer their will to mine and I feel prepared to obey them in everything, as insignificant as it may be—but, moreover, I grant no legitimacy to my own will nor any justification for willing. The obedience imposed on monks promises them no dominion over themselves, but rather a humility that is nothing other than obedience as a definitive state, a permanent availability to all others, and an unending relation of oneself to oneself. Humility is both the effect of a

long exercise of obedience and the root—even in the most
solitary practitioner—of any possible obedience. It's not
surprising that in listing the marks of humility, Cassian
confines himself almost exclusively to the forms of "being
obedient": mortifying one's own will, hiding nothing from
one's elder, not relying on one's own discernment, obeying without resentment and practicing patience, not being
upset about the insults one suffers, doing nothing other
than what the rule and the examples command, being satisfied with the basest things and regarding oneself as being
without any worth whatever, declaring oneself to be the
lowest of men from the bottom of one's heart, and never
raising one's voice.[60]

Considering these three aspects, it's clear that obedience
constitutes an exercise of the will upon itself and against itself.
Willing what others will—by virtue of the intrinsic and express
privilege held by the will of others—is what is meant by *subdito*.
Willing an absence of will—intending not to oppose or resist,
willing that one's own will not get in the way of the other's will—is
what is meant by *patientia*. Refraining from willing—renouncing
the least of one's own desires—is the meaning of *humilitas*. And
this exercise of obedience, instead of being simply an instrument
for direction, forms an indivisible circle with it. Obedience is the
initial condition that enables direction to do its work—which
explains the tests of submission to which the candidate is exposed
even before he passes through the monastery gate. It is the essential
form of the director's action; it is the general form of the relation
between the director and the directee; it is, finally, the outcome
to which the direction leads, an outcome that puts the directee in
a position to accept indefinitely a different will, instead of and in
place of his own. Consequently, it is ranked first among the virtues. First, since it is with obedience that the monastic institution
and the training of novices must begin. First, too, because it is the
basis of all the virtues that direction can cultivate in anyone aiming to progress toward perfection. The monks prefer it, says Cassian, "putting it not merely before manual labor and reading and
silence and quietness in the cell, but even before all other virtues,

so that they consider that everything else should be postponed for it, and are content to undergo any amount of inconvenience if only it may be seen that they have in no way neglected this virtue."[61]

In the progression toward perfection, one can understand the place that Cassian assigns to humility, understood as a permanent state of obedience, an acceptance of every submission, a determination not to will, and a renunciation of all of one's wishes. This progression has a negative feeling as its point of departure: the "fear of God," the fear of punishments, the fear that by offending him they will provoke his wrath. The point of arrival is "charity"— that is, the possibility of acting "from love of goodness itself, and delighting in virtue."[62] Now, the transition from fear to charity is accomplished through humility inasmuch as humility—by requiring one to renounce all of one's own wishes (including the wish to avoid punishment)—leads one to accept the will of the other as a principle of all action (and in charity, it is God's will that is the principle of action).[63] Shedding fear through charity presupposes, as a preparation and an intermediate step, the exercise of obedience and the practice of the virtue of humility. Of course, there is more to the asceticism demanded of the monk than the mere fact of obeying: the fasts, the vigils, the prayers, the labor, the works of charity are required as well. But if it is to lead to a humility in which the individual will has disappeared, all asceticism must be practiced in the general form of obedience.

One can thus measure the distance separating Christian direction from the kind practiced, for example, among the Stoics. The aim of Stoic direction was essentially to establish the conditions for a sovereign exercise of the will upon oneself. It involved leading the directee to the turning point where he became master of himself. Which implied that he learn to distinguish what pertained to his will from what was outside its domain; and it armed that will with a reason that had the triple role of establishing this division, defining one's congruity with the world's order, and clearing away the errors of opinion that produce the disorder of the passions or the excess of desires.[64]

Christian direction, on the other hand, is aimed at a renunciation of the will. It rests on the paradox of a determination not to will. Submission to the master, which is its necessary instrument, never leads one to the point where one can establish sovereignty over oneself, but to the point where, forbidden any mastery, the ascetic can no longer will anything but what God wills. And tranquility of the soul, which in Cassian's vocabulary is the equivalent of the Greek *apatheia*, doesn't consist in having established a rule over involuntary impulses so complete that nothing can shake it against one's will. It consists in the state where, having abjured willing autonomously, one owes one's strength only to that of God, one is in its presence. The contemplative life can then begin.

### III. THE RECOURSE TO GOD

To justify the necessity of a direction and the obligation to obey, Cassian offers a reason that has nothing new or unexpected about it. Throughout one's monastic existence, one aspiring to perfection must avoid two dangers: first, laxity with regard to the tasks of ascetic life—the little, scarcely perceptible indulgences that lead the soul to the greatest weaknesses; and second, an excess of zeal that, by different paths, often causes the same effects as laxity. "Excesses meet. Too much fasting and too much eating come to the same end. Keeping too long a vigil brings the same disastrous cost as the sluggishness that plunges a monk into the longest sleep. Too much self-denial brings weakness and induces the same condition as carelessness and apathy."[65] The age-old theme of the peril of the two excesses, with the principle that in his conduct a man must avoid the too-little and the too-much. Classical wisdom philosophy had invoked this principle quite frequently. To designate the ability to find one's way between the two extremes, Cassian employs the term *discretio*, as an equivalent of the Greek *diakrisis* (which is, all at once, the ability to discern differences, an aptitude for deciding between two sides, and an act of measured judgment). "Avoiding extremes, discernment teaches the monk to walk always on the royal road. It keeps him from veering to the right—that is, from going with stupid presumption and excessive fervor beyond the boundary of reasonable restraint. It keeps him from going to the left to carelessness and sin."[66]

Cassian, like the theoreticians of monastic life of the same period, gives this classic notion a fundamental importance. He devotes the second of his *Conferences* to it, immediately after having explained, in the first, the goal and end of monastic life and before considering, in the following ones, the different aspects of that existence—its struggles and its duties. The notion appears therefore as the primary instrument for progressing toward perfection. "Lamp of the body," sun that must never set on our anger, counsel to which we must submit even when we drink the wine of the soul—in it "lies wisdom, intelligence, and sound judgment, without which the house of our interior life cannot be built nor can spiritual riches be amassed."[67] Now, this praise of discernment, which will be echoed by many other passages of the *Conferences*, has a particular slant to it. It is directed more against overzealousness than against sluggishness. Exaggeration emerges as the major danger.[68] All the examples invoked are those of monks who overestimated their capabilities and, too confident of their own judgment, fell at the moment their zeal pushed them too far.[69] Cassian credits Saint Anthony with this warning about immoderate asceticism: "For very often we have seen people who have been most zealous in their fasts and vigils, who have lived wondrously solitary lives, who have endured such total privation of everything that they would not allow themselves to hold on to even a day's food or even a single coin of the lowest value [. . .] then suddenly fall prey to illusion with the result that they could not give a fitting end to the work they had undertaken, but rather brought an abominable conclusion to that high zeal and praiseworthy mode of life."[70] And Cassian presents the combat against excess asceticism as tougher and more dangerous than the other one, against sluggishness. A different battle: "Often I have seen those who could not be snared by gluttony fall nevertheless through immoderate fasting and tumble in weakness into the very urge they had overcome."[71] And defeat is especially to be feared: "Each battle is raised by the devil. Yet too much restraint can be more harmful than a satisfied appetite. Where the latter is concerned, one may, as a result of saving compunction, move on to a measured austerity. But with the former this is impossible."[72]

There is a well-known historical reason for this anti-ascetic animus that accompanies all the praise of discernment: in the

fourth century, the discipline of monastic life—the cenobic rules
that were formulated, but also the prescriptions and advice surrounding desert solitude or semi-reclusion—were, especially in
Lower Egypt, where Cassian garnered most of his lessons and
examples, elaborated in reaction against unauthorized, anarchic,
individual, and competitive forms of asceticism. Faced with those
isolated hermits or vagabond monks who were competing in thau-
maturgic marvels and exploits of self-mortification, the regulation
of monastic life had the goal of defining a middle way, accessible
to the majority of monks and capable of being incorporated into
communitarian institutions. What was demanded of discernment
was to determine this middle path between the too-much and
the too-little; but it was also, in a particular way, to perceive any
dangerous excess that might lurk in the ascetic urge, in the drive
toward perfection; to distinguish what might be mixed with weakness, with indulgence, with attachment to oneself in the desire
to taste the extremes of one's exercises; and to recognize the elements of its contrary in the guise of the greatest saintliness. In this
preoccupation with a correct measure, a suitably regulated *modus*
of monastic life, there was concern with avoiding the weakness
and excess of rigor, but also and perhaps above all with detecting
the weakness hidden in every excess of mortification.

    This same historical situation explains another inflection of
the theme of discernment. In the ancient conception, the ability
to distinguish between the too-much and the too-little and to be
moderate in one's conduct was tied to each person's use of their
own reason. For a theoretician of monastic life like Cassian,[73] the
principle of right measure cannot come from man himself. If the
monk must observe himself constantly and attentively, this is not
in the hope of discovering a principle of correct equilibrium there:
it's rather to discover all the reasons for finding his bearings outside his own consciousness. The Christian monk can never be the
measure of himself, however advanced he may be on the road to
sainthood. A story told by Cassian, about the recitation of psalms,
attests to this.[74] In the exalted times of earliest Christianity, zeal
pushed everyone to chant as many psalms as their strength permitted. But it was soon realized that "disharmony" and even just
sheer variety could in the future germinate the seeds of "error,

jealousy, and schism." So the venerable Fathers got together to set the correct number, but an unknown brother, slipping in among them, and chanting only twelve psalms before suddenly disappearing, showed both what the proper limit was and that it was God himself who set it.

A banal story of the divine and miraculous establishment of rules. But here it assumes a precise meaning. Man's heteronomy is fundamental and it's never himself that he should rely on to define the standards of his behavior. There is a reason for that: since the fall, the spirit of evil has established its empire over man. It has not exactly penetrated his soul or intermixed their two substances, which would deprive man of his freedom. But the spirit of evil has both an originary kinship and a resemblance to the human soul; it can therefore set up shop in the body, occupy it in competition with the soul, and, taking advantage of this likeness, trouble the body, give it urges, disturb its economy; in this way it weakens the soul, sending it suggestions, images, thoughts, whose origin is hard to determine; the tricked soul may receive them without recognizing that they are inspired by the Other who cohabits with it in the body. The Other is thus in a position to disguise the thoughts that come from him, to get them taken for divine inspirations and to conceal, under the cloak of goodness, the evil they actually carry. Satan is therefore an agent of illusion within thought.[75] And whereas the ancient sage could appeal to his own reason against the involuntary pressure of his passions, the Christian monk can't expect to find a reliable recourse in the ideas within him that appear the truest or the most saintly. In the very workings of his thought, he always risks being fooled. And discernment, which ought to allow him to find the right path between two dangers, mustn't consist of the exercise of a reason controlling the passions that trouble the body, but of a labor of thought on itself endeavoring to escape the illusions and tricks that traverse it.

This is to say that *discretio*, which is indispensable for staying on the right path of conduct, cannot be demanded of the individual himself. He needs an external recourse against the traps that haunt his thought, that mask the origin and purpose of the ideas that come to him. This recourse is first of all divine grace.

Without God's intervention, man is not capable of discernment: discernment "is no minor virtue, nor one which can be seized anywhere by human effort. It is ours only as a gift from God [. . .] So you see that the gift of discernment is neither earthly nor of little account, but is, rather, a very great boon of divine grace. And if a monk does not do his utmost to acquire it [. . .] he will surely stray like someone in a dark night and not only will he stumble into dangerous pits and down steep slopes but he will often fall even in the level, straightforward places."[76] But if discernment is grace, it must also be virtue,[77] a virtue that one learns. And Cassian defines this necessary apprenticeship by two exercises, or rather by the permanent coupling of two exercises. First, one must practice a constant examination of oneself—one must carefully observe all the movements that unfold in thought: the "inner eye" by which we explore what is happening inside us must never be shut.[78] But, second and simultaneously, one must open one's soul to another—to the director, to one's appointed elder—and make sure that nothing remains hidden from him. "Let there be no falsely modest veil. Everything must be told openly to the elders. From them must come the cure of injury and the example of a life lived in all faith."[79]

This "discretion"—which, as an art of discernment and measure, is indispensable for advancing toward saintliness, and yet which we lack, not only owing to our passions, but owing to the power of illusion that perpetually threatens our thought—will be granted us only by divine grace. But what will teach it to us is the combination of observation and opening of the soul—the exercise of examination inseparably combined with confession. In sum, what justifies the permanence of a relation of direction is the necessity of staying on the middle path between the extremes that always may attract and seduce us. This proper progression can be assured only by the use of a discernment whose operation does not reside naturally in man. He will have to receive it from God, but also obtain it through a constant exercise of his gaze and from a truth-telling in regard to himself. In the general form of obedience and the renunciation of one's own will, direction has as its major tool the continuous practice of "the examination-confession," what is called in Eastern Christianity *exagoreusis:* "Every subordinate must on the one hand avoid keeping hidden in his innermost being any of the soul's urges; and on the other, he must take care not to say anything uncontrollably and must disclose the secrets of his soul to those of his brothers who have been assigned to tend to their patients with sympathy and understanding."[80]

## IV. THE EXAMINATION-CONFESSION

This technique—in spite of a number of traits in common— differs rather radically from the review of past acts that one finds, for example, in Seneca's *De ira*. Not that this reflection on the day gone by, prior to sleeping, was unknown in Christian spirituality. One finds it recommended by Saint John Chrysostom and in terms much like those of the ancient philosophers: "The morning is when we review our monetary expenditures. It's at night—after our meal, when we are in bed, and no one is there to distract and bother us—that we need to bring our own conduct to account."[81] But it should be noted that Cassian never mentions any such bed-time accounting among the obligations of monastic life. It's likely that this practice remained minor compared to *exagoreusis* as such.

The most salient aspect of *exagoreusis* is that it focuses not on past *acts* but on the *thoughts* that occur—which may happen to be the memory of an act committed or an act to be carried out.[82] But thought itself, *cogitatio*, is the object of the examination. That the practice of examination in monastic life is centered in this way on the thought process, rather than what was done, is not at all surprising. First of all, the strict system of obedience implies that nothing be done, that nothing be undertaken without the order or at least the permission of the director; so it's a matter of considering and examining, of bringing under control, the idea of the act before the act takes place. And more fundamentally, since the goal of monastic existence is a contemplative life in which God will be accessible thanks to one's purity of heart,[83] and since one advances toward this end through prayer, meditation, quiet reflection, and turning one's mind toward God, the *cogitatio* constitutes the main problem. It forms as it were the raw material of the monk's labor on himself. And if it's true that the macerations of the body, with a strict regimen of food, sleep, and manual work, play a capital role, this is insofar as it is a means for ensuring that the stream of *cogitationes* is as orderly and pure as possible. As Evagrius said, "The demons prefer to fight worldly people by means of things, but monks for the most part they attack by means of thoughts."[84] The term *logismoi*, used by the Greek spiritual teachers, is translated in Cassian as *cogitationes* and there it retains the same negative values that were found in Evagrius. Cassian's *cogitatio* is not simply one "thought" among others—it is what risks, in the soul straining toward contemplation, bringing trouble at any moment. Understood in this way, it is less the act of a thinking soul than a disturbance in the soul that seeks to grasp God. It is the interior danger. It must be countered by a constant mistrust that views it with suspicion.

## 1. *The battle within*

The trouble *cogitatio* can introduce has two main aspects. The first is that of multiplicity, of mobility, of disorder where the soul is in need of order, of stability, of unity without movement. Engaging in single-minded contemplation of the One Being demands that one's thought stay focused on that end alone and never stray from it. An extremely difficult task. "For who, even if he be the chief of all righteous and holy men, can we ever think could, while bound in the chains of this life, so acquire this chief good—never to cease from divine contemplation, or be drawn away by earthly thoughts even for a short time."[85] The problem is that the mind is always agitated; never of its own accord does it come to rest on a single object; "it is ever shifting and very shifting."[86] To the nuncio Germanus who asked why, in the effort to rise to contemplation, "idle thoughts steal upon us so subtly and secretly that it is fearfully hard not merely to drive them away, but even to grasp and seize them," the old man Moses gives a repetition of the question itself in reply: "It is impossible, I admit, for the mind not to be approached by thoughts."[87] And in the whole beginning of the lecture that Serenus devotes to the mobility of thought, the theme of the mind's perpetual motion keeps returning: the *nous* (mind) is always and in various forms "kinetic."[88]

But there is another danger that combines with the danger

of instability and is its consequence: profiting from this disorder and in the swiftness of the stream, thoughts occur that one barely has the time to register and that one receives without mistrust. Now, under this innocent appearance, these thoughts could well be dangerous without one's realizing it. They might convey harmful suggestions to the soul or even introduce impurities. Thoughts flutter around in the mind like a feather moved by the wind, but certain ones are stained and, like a moistened feather, are heavier than the others and tend to weigh the soul down.[89]

So one can understand the role that Cassian attributes to the exercise of examination. He explains it, or rather he has it explained by the Fathers whose lectures he is reporting, by three metaphors. That of the mill:[90] just as water makes a mill turn independently of the miller, the soul is moved by "a headlong rush of whirling thoughts." It can't interrupt this movement that assails it, but just as the miller can grind good and bad grain, wheat, barley, or rye, so the soul must separate the useful thoughts from those that are "culpable." The centurion of the Gospel is also a good comparison:[91] the officer supervises the movement of the soldiers, telling some to go and others to come; in the same manner, the examination must oversee the movement of thoughts, dismissing those we don't want, and keeping and properly arranging those that can fight the enemy. Lastly, a comparison with the money changer who inspects the coins before accepting them is another way of showing the function of the examination.[92] It's clear: the examination consists in a constant oversight of the constant and uncontrollable stream of all the competing thoughts that present themselves to the soul, and in a selection mechanism that makes it possible to separate those to be accepted from those to be rejected.

Cassian's development of the money-changer metaphor is helpful for grasping the specific task of the examination. When he is presented with coins, the banker has the job of "verification": he verifies the stamped effigy and the metal. Several cases can present themselves. The coins may shine as if they were made of gold (this is the case, for example, with philosophical maxims), but it's an illusion—the metal is not what one thought. Sometimes, on the other hand, the metal is pure—as with a maxim drawn from the Scripture—but the seducer inside us has superimposed a false

interpretation on it, as if a usurper had minted the money and
stamped the metal with an effigy without legitimacy or value. It
can also happen that the coin is of the right metal and the effigy is
as it should be, but in fact it comes from a bad workshop. This is
the case when Satan suggests to us a line of action that, while good
in itself, would be used for a harmful end: he can suggest fasting,
not in order to perfect our soul, but to weaken our body.[93] Finally,
a coin can be completely legitimate in terms of its metal, effigy, and
origin, but it may be worn down by time or degraded by rust:
some bad feeling has been able to blend into a valuable idea and
alter its value in this way (vanity can be mixed with the desire to
do an act of charity).

So in fact it's a search for truth that is directed, through the
examination, at the *cogitationes* coming to buffet the soul in their
unbroken stream. But it's not a matter of knowing if one's idea is
true or false, if one's judgment is correct or not—which was the
task of the Stoic examination.[94] In short, it's not a matter of knowing if one is mistaken or not, but of sorting between those ideas
that are indeed as they appear to be and those that are illusory.
The problem is knowing if one is being fooled. The examination
doesn't consist in determining if fasting is good or not. The monk
knows it is good. But he doesn't know whether the arrival of this
idea is owing to the Deceiver, who, hiding beneath a salutary principle, is secretly preparing his downfall.

The examination, then, does have the effect of producing a *discretio*, a differentiation that enables one to follow the straight path.
But it doesn't separate true opinions from false opinions. It seeks
the origin of the idea, its mark, that which might alter its value.
One tests "the quality of the thoughts"—*qualitas cogitationum*[95]—
by interrogating oneself on the secret depths from which they
issued, the ruses whose instruments and illusions they may be,
and that cause one to be deluded not so much, or not only, about
the things of which they are the idea—about their objective reality as people will say later—but about them: their nature, their
substance, their author. By carefully examining his thoughts, by
constantly deciding between those that should be welcomed and
those that should be rejected, the obedient and well-directed monk
doesn't consider the content of these thoughts, but the action of

the thought within the thinker: What Cassian calls the *arcana con-scientiae*. A problem of the thinking subject and the relation of the subject to his own thought (who is thinking in my thought? am I not being deceived in a certain way?), and no longer a question of the object that's thought or the relation of thought to its object. When one considers the Stoic type of examination—in which it was necessary to verify the rightness of opinions as a way of ensuring reason's hold on the movement of the passions—one sees the distance separating it from this questioning of the movement of thought, of its origin in the subject, and of one's illusions about oneself that the thought may give rise to.

## 2. *The necessity of confession*

If this continuous sorting and verification of thoughts took the form of only an interior examination, there would be a paradox: how in fact could the one examining himself be completely certain of the origin of his thoughts? How could he be sure he is not mistaken in the value he attributes to them, that the danger of being fooled—and of being fooled about himself—is averted? What would make the thought formed in the examination more certain than the thought that is examined? It's here that the necessity of confession is established. This confession shouldn't be imagined as the result of an examination first conducted in the form of strict interiority, and then offered in the form of confidential disclosure. The confession in this instance must be as close as possible to the examination—as the examination's exterior aspect, its verbal face turned toward the other. One's self-observation and the verbalization of such should be one and the same. Seeing and saying in a single act—such is the ideal to which the novice must aspire: "they are taught not to conceal by a false shame any itching thoughts in their hearts, but, as soon as ever such arise, to lay them bare to the senior."[96]

But how can the confession clear away illusions, ruses, and deceptions? How can the verbalization play a role of verification? Undoubtedly this is because the elder in whom one confides—making use of his experience, the discernment he has acquired, and the grace he has received—can see what eludes the subject himself and offer him advice and remedies. The Enemy, who is able to dupe the inexperienced and the ignorant, will fail when faced with the discernment of the elder.[97] Cassian assigns a major role to this counsel on the part of the director, and he even shows the negative outcomes that can result from an unskillful direction.[98] And yet he also attributes an effect of elimination and purification to the simple act of verbal externalization. Forming words, pronouncing them, addressing them to someone else—and, up to a certain point, to anyone else—has the power to scatter the illusions and foil the internal seducer's trickery.[99] Cassian gives several reasons for this power of confession, as an operator of discrimination.

First, there's shame. If one has trouble disclosing a thought, if the thought refuses to be told, if it tries to remain secret, this is the sign that it is bad. "The devil, subtle as he is, cannot ruin or destroy a junior unless he has enticed him either through pride or through shame to conceal his thoughts. For the elders lay it down as a universal and clear proof that a thought is from the devil if we are ashamed to disclose it to the elder."[100] The more a thought resists, the more it tends to elude the words that try to capture it, the harder, consequently, one must strive to chase it down and disclose it exactly. Shame, which should act as a brake when one commits an act, must be defied when it's a matter of manifesting in words that which lies hidden in the recesses of the heart: such shame is a clear indication of evil. If the idea that comes from the evil spirit always wants to remain buried in consciousness, this is for a cosmo-theological reason. An angel of light, Satan was condemned to darkness; the light of day was forbidden him, and he could no longer leave the folds of the heart where he hid himself. The confession, exposing him to the light, tears him away from his kingdom and makes him powerless. He can reign only in the dark of night. "For a wrong thought is enfeebled the moment it is discovered: and even before the sentence of discretion has been given, the foul serpent is by the power of confession dragged out, so to speak, from his dark underground cavern, and in some sense shown up and sent away in disgrace."[101] The bad idea loses its seductive force and its power of deception from the mere fact that it is said, that it is spoken out loud, and in this way it leaves the secret interiority of consciousness.

Cassian goes even further. The verbalization is sometimes a material eviction. With the confessional disclosure, it's the devil himself that is expelled from the body. This is the lesson that Cassian draws from a memory shared by the abbot Serapion. As a child, he was inhabited by the spirit of gluttony and every evening he would steal a biscuit; but he "was ashamed to disclose the secret theft" to the saintly old man who directed him. Finally, one day, stricken by an exhortation from the abbot Theonas, he couldn't keep from bursting into sobs: "He produced from the folds of his robe which shared his theft and received it, the biscuit which he had carried off in his bad habit to eat on the sly; and he laid it in their midst and, lying on the ground and begging for forgiveness, confessed how he used to eat one every day in secret, and with copious tears implored them to entreat the Lord to free him from that dreadful slavery." And forthwith "a burning lamp proceeding from the folds of his robe filled the cell with a sulfurous smell so that the pungency of the odor scarcely allowed them to stay there." Now, according to Cassian, the words that the abbot Theonas speaks during this scene are important. Theonas first of all stresses the fact that the deliverance is not directly due to the words spoken by the director,[102] but to the words of the sinner who confesses: "Without any words of mine, your confession frees you from this slavery." This confession has the effect of bringing into broad daylight the thing that lay hidden in the darkness of secrecy: it is an intervention of light. And at the same time, by that very fact, it is an inversion of power. "You have today triumphed over your victorious adversary, laying him low by your confession in a manner that more than makes up for the way in which he overthrew you through your former silence [. . .] and therefore after being exposed, that evil spirit will no longer be able to vex you." And this power inversion is manifested in a material eviction. In a strict sense, the confession that brings the evil spirit to light causes it to vacate the premises: "The Lord [. . .] wanted you to see with your eyes how he who was the author of this passion has been driven out from your heart by your life-giving confession, and know that the enemy who has been exposed will certainly no longer find a home in you, as his expulsion is made manifest."[103]

So in the very form of the confession, in the fact that the secret is formulated in words and these words are addressed to another, there is a specific power: what Cassian calls—using a word that will be found over and over in the vocabulary of penance and the direction of souls—*virtus confessionis*. The confession has a performative force that is peculiar to it: it tells, it shows, it expels, it frees.

This explains why discernment—that practice by which one clears up confusions, sorts mixtures, dispels illusions, differentiates in the subject what comes from himself and what is inspired by the Other—cannot operate solely through examination of the self by the self, but also requires, at the same time, a continual confession. The examination must commence without delay ("as soon as the thoughts arise") in an actual discourse addressed to another. Can the latter, in a position of exteriority, be a better judge? Undoubtedly. But more importantly, the speech act that is addressed to him, across the barrier of shame, precipitates the play of light and shade, and the material expulsion. The indispensable *discretio*—which enables one to trace the right path to perfection between the two dangers of the too-much and the too-little, this *discretio*, which is not a natural endowment of man, haunted as he is by the Enemy's power of seduction—can be practiced only with the grace of God by means of this process of examination-confession: this game in which one's focus on oneself must always be combined with "truth-telling" regarding oneself. It is then, after this discrimination focused on the origin, quality, and texture of the *cogitationes*, that the soul will no longer accept any but pure thoughts, thoughts leading to God alone since they come only from him. Such is the *puritas cordis*, a requisite condition of that contemplation that is the end of monastic life. At the beginning of book 5 of the *Institutes*, Cassian bases himself on a text from Isaiah where God the Almighty promises Cyrus, his instrument, that he will "subdue the nations before him," "break down the brass gates," "cut through the iron bars," and give him "hidden treasures, buried riches" (45, 1–3). In an odd inflection of his commentary, Cassian interprets these smashed gates and these severed bars as the work one must do on "the foul darkness of vices" to "drag them forth to light." As a result of this investigation (*indagini*) and explanation (*expositioni*), the "secrets of darkness" will be revealed, everything separating us from the true science will be struck down, and "we will be found worthy of being brought in purity of heart to the place of perfect refreshment."[104]

The *exagoreusis* that was developed in monasticism—a practice of continual examination of the self linked with an endless confession to the other—is far removed, therefore, despite certain shared traits, from the consultation found in the ancient practice, and from the trust the philosopher's disciple needed to place in the master of truth and wisdom. First of all, the examination-confession is, in its permanent nature, connected to the duty—also permanent—of obedience. If everything going on in the soul, down to its least stirrings, [must be revealed to the other], this is to ensure a perfect obedience. Neither the seemingly most insignificant act nor the most fleeting thought must escape the power of the other. And in return, unquestioning obedience in all things has the purpose of preventing the inner being from closing back on itself and, basking in its autonomy, letting itself be seduced by the deceiving powers that inhabit it. The general form of obedience and the constant obligation of the examination-confession necessarily go hand in hand.

Moreover, this examination-confession doesn't focus on a specific category of elements (such as acts or infractions). It has an indefinite task in front of it: to delve more deeply into the secrets of the soul; to always seize, as soon as possible, even the most tenuous of thoughts; to take hold of the secrets, and of the secrets lurking behind those secrets, to go as deeply as possible toward the root. In this labor nothing is insignificant—there is no pre-established limit. The practice of examination-confession must follow a slope that inclines it indefinitely toward the almost imperceptible part of oneself.

So this involves something different from the verbal recognition of offenses committed. *Exagoreusis* is not like an admission in court. It does not take place within an apparatus of juridiction; it is not a way for someone who has violated a law to recognize his responsibility in order to lessen the punishment. It is an effort to disclose not only to the other, but also to oneself, what is happening in the mysteries of the heart and in its vague shadows. It's a matter of exposing as a truth something that was not yet known to anyone. And this in two ways: by bringing to light that which was so dim that no one could grasp it; and by dispelling the illusions that caused counterfeit currency to be taken for the real thing— a suggestion by the devil mistaken for a true inspiration from God. And deliverance itself is the expected outcome of this passage from darkness to light, from the enticing mélange to the rigorous discrimination. Here, one is not in the order of the "juridiction" of acts to which one admits, but that of the "veridiction" of inner secrets that are unclear to oneself.

Finally, if *exagoreusis* recommends that one examine oneself without respite, this is not so that one might establish oneself in one's own sovereignty, or even that one might recognize oneself in one's identity. It is always conducted in relation to the other: in the general form of a direction that submits the subject's will to that of the other; with the aim of detecting the presence of the Other, the Enemy, deep within oneself; and having as its final end the contemplation of God, in a complete purity of heart. This purity itself should not be understood as a restoration of oneself, or an emancipation of the subject. On the contrary, it is the definitive relinquishment of any will of one's own: a way not to be oneself, or attached to oneself by any tie. A paradox essential to these practices of Christian spirituality: the veridiction of oneself is fundamentally bound together with self-renunciation. The endless effort to see and tell the truth about oneself is an exercise of mortification. So in *exagoreusis* one has a complex apparatus in which the duty to constantly dig down into the soul is coupled with the obligation of a continual externalization in a discourse addressed to the other; and in which one's search for the truth about oneself must constitute a certain way of dying to oneself.

# PART II

*Being Virgin*

The fact that there is an abundance of fourth-century texts devoted to virginity is well known. Among the Eastern Christians, we have the treatise *On the True Purity of Chastity* by Basil of Ancyra; the one by Gregory of Nyssa, *On Virginity*; several texts by John Chrysostom—*Of Virginity, On Suspect Cohabitations, How to Observe Virginity*; the seventh *Homily* of Esebius of Emesa; and the *Exhortation* that Evagrius Ponticus addresses to a virgin; to which one can add, among many other texts, a treatise attributed to Athanasius, poems by Gregory of Niazanzus, or another *Homily* addressed to a paterfamilias, whose author is still unknown.[1] Among the Latins, one has to mention Saint Ambrose (*De virginibus, De virginitate, De institutione virginis, De exhortatione virginitatis, De lapsu virginis consecratae*), Saint Jerome (*Adversus Helvidium, Adversus Jovinianum,* the letter to Eustochium), and Saint Augustine (*De continentia, De sancta virginitate*).

This multiplicity of texts does not indicate the emergence of an imperative in this era or a practice of total and definitive abstinence from sexual relations. In fact the valorization of virginity is attested long before, according to a tradition that refers to that famous text from the Epistle to the Corinthians (7:1) which for nearly two millennia would be at the center of any discussion of the matter: "It is good for a man not to touch a woman." There are many statements in support of this voluntary renunciation. Some come from the Christians themselves. This is Athenagoras: "Each of us reckons to be his wife she who he has married according to the laws we have laid down [. . .] You would find many among us, both men and women, growing old unmarried, in hope of living in closer communion with God. But if remaining in virginity or in the state of a eunuch brings one nearer to God, while the indulgence of carnal thought and desire leads away from Him, in those cases in which we shun the thoughts, much more do we reject the deeds."[2] Tertullian alludes to so many "voluntary eunuchs," so many "virgins married to Christ,"[3] that Saint Ambrose will be able to compare the poor seven Vestals of pagan Rome unfavorably with the "people of integrity," "the plebs of decency," and the whole "assembly of virginity":[4] a multitude that, [says Saint Cyprian], amply manifests the fertility of the Mother Church.[5] But there are also statements by outsiders. Galen's is interesting in that, while noting the fact, he doesn't really see it as anything new; at most he is surprised that so many people can practice an abstinence that used to be associated only with genuine philosophers. "The Christians observe a conduct worthy of the true philosophers. We see in fact that they despise death and that, motivated by a certain prudishness, they consider acts of the flesh to be abhorrent. There are men and women among them who abstain from the marital act all their lives. There are also those who have gone as far as the true philosophers in the governing and control of the soul."[6]

Virginity and definitive continence appear, then, to be a widespread practice among Christians in the second century, but nothing about their practice seems to set it apart. At most there was an expansion of a type of behavior that was already known, at least in its exterior form, and already valorized. Recall that the great prohibitions cited in the texts of the Apostolic Fathers or the Apologists are the same ones that were prescribed by pagan morality: adultery, fornication, corruption of children.[7] One sees then that Christianity, during the first century of its existence, seems to carry the same system of sexual morality as the ancient culture that precedes or surrounds it: the same sexual faults, equally blameworthy in all people; the same "elitist" recommendation— for certain individuals—of total abstinence.

However, the history of the practice of virginity, in the first two centuries of Christianity, doesn't consist simply in the expansion of a "philosophical" recommendation of abstinence. The Christian practice did in fact distinguish itself in its treatment of two types of conduct. It gave a different meaning to the principle of continence than the one found in pagan wisdom. It projected different results or different promises for it; it also gave it a different scope, and especially different instruments. But it also had to disengage the principle from a tendency present in Christianity itself, one that was continuously reactivated by the dualist temptation: what was called Encratism. This tendency to forbid every Christian any sexual relation as a necessary condition for their salvation was, with varying intensities and in different forms, constantly present in the first Christian centuries. It was destined to take on, with Tatian and Julius Cassianus, the appearance of a sect; to constitute one of the fundamental traits of certain heresies (as in the gnosis of Marcion or among the Manicheans); to mark the practice of certain communities as shown by the second, apocryphal, Epistle of Clement to the Corinthians, or again by the reproaches directed, according to Eusebius, at Pinytos, bishop of Knossis, who, without considering the "weakness of the great number," wanted to impose "on the brethren the heavy burden of chastity";[8] or, further, to be the implication of thoughts recognized as orthodox in other respects: witness the scandal and the debates set off by Saint Jerome's *Adversus Jovinianum*. Now, the critique of Encratism didn't question whether or not virginity should be a law imposed on anyone looking to secure their salvation; abstinence from any sexual relation was not an unconditional law. Rather, it was a matter of determining what sort of privileged, relatively "rare," and positive experience virginity should be.

Two important things are to be noted, then. What Christian thought will develop, up to the end of the fifth and the beginning of the sixth centuries—what will be the major focus of reflection and the locus of transformations—is not the table of the great prohibitions, but the question of virginity (and, as we'll see further on, the internal economy of marriage). The basic prohibitions remain what they were. It's much later that one will see the system redistribute itself, with the emergence of huge domains such as incest, bestiality, and the "counter-natural." But during the first centuries, the theoretical focus, as well as the practical question, will have to do with the value and meaning to be given

to a strict, definitive abstinence from any sexual relation whatsoever (and even to the possible thoughts about and desire for
them). But moreover, this question of virginity should not be
regarded simply as a principle of abstinence that would satisfy, as
it were, particular prohibitions by means of a general recommendation of continence. The fervor with which virginity is exalted
and recommended must not be understood as an extension of the
old prohibitions of the general domain of sexual relations: a kind
of maximization that would prohibit not just this thing or that,
and that and that, but in the end, everything. The valorization of
virginity, between the partial abstinence recommended by certain
ancient sages and the strict continence of the Encratists, gradually led to the definition of a whole relation of the individual to
himself, his thought, his soul, and his body. In short, the prohibition of adultery and the corruption of children on the one hand,
and the recommendation of virginity on the other, does not constitute a case of one prohibition feeding into another. They are
dissymmetrical and of a different nature. Interestingly, it's in the
elaboration of virginity that the Christian concept of the flesh was
formed.

Let us say, in a word, that alongside a moral code of sexual
prohibitions that remained more or less stable, there developed,
in a different register, a singular *practice:* that of virginity.

# 1

# Virginity and Continence

Relatively little is known about the form and content of this practice before the fourth century. We know the extent of it. We also know that it didn't take an institutional form through vows or in a monastic type of existence. However, it did exist, especially among women, in circles that dedicated themselves to a particularly intense religious life and refused marriage or, in the case of widows, a second wedding. But sometimes, more or less encouraged by their families,[1] young women would lead a life of virginity in their parents' milieu. This is doubtless the reason the documents we have for the third century concern the virginity of women in particular and present two situations: the young woman in her home and the circle of virgins.

I will dwell for a moment on two texts of this kind. The first is Latin. It deals with the life of a virgin in the midst of her family; it is short and essentially delivers practical recommendations. The second is Greek. It portrays an imaginary group of women who sing the praises of their virginity together. It is the first developed testimony of a Christian doctrine of virginity. While the first text, written by Saint Cyprian, dates from the first half of the third century, it is thought that the *Banquet* of Methodius of Olympus was written around 271. We will see that, in its content, it is transitional to the great texts of the fourth century.

Saint Cyprian's *De habitu virginum* constitutes, for Latin Christianity in the first half of the third century, the largest treatise devoted to the practice of virginity. To be sure, Tertullian had touched on this theme of virginity many times, but each of his various texts always concerns itself with a single aspect: the customary clothing of young people and married women in *De virginus velandis*; the problem of the remarriage of widows in the treatise *Ad uxorem* and of widowers in the *Exhortatio ad castitatem*; the penance and reintegration of adulterers in *De pudicitia*, written in the Montanist period. It's easy to see that many of the ideas developed by Tertullian turn up again later: for example, the theme of marriage with Christ, or virginity as an opening to spiritual realities.[2] But one should note his reluctance to attribute a special status to virginity in the strict sense of the term. The little treatise *On the Veiling of Virgins* is meaningful in this regard. The thesis is that virgins and married women alike should wear the veil. Three sets of arguments are advanced. The first ones base themselves on the Scripture: it's as a woman that Eve was created; it's from a woman's womb that the Savior was born; it's as women that the "daughters of men" seduced the angels. Other arguments, more singular and not repeated in later treatises on virginity, are drawn from nature: after showing that according to the Scripture women are women before being virgin, Tertullian explains, in effect, that every woman becomes a wife spontaneously and even before marriage. She becomes a wife through her awareness of being a woman, by the fact that she becomes an object for "the concupiscence of men" and can "undergo marriage": she ceases to be a virgin "from the time it becomes possible for her not to be one"; from the fact that corruption enters into the eyes and the heart; the ostensible virgin is "already married: her soul is such by expectancy, her flesh by transformation"; finally, through the very movement of nature: development of the body, voice change, and monthly "tributes": "Do you deny her to be a woman whom you assert to be undergoing womanly experiences?"[3] The last series of arguments is derived by Tertullian from the demands of discipline: married women must be protected from the dangers surrounding them. The veil ensures and symbolizes this protection. But shouldn't virginity be protected likewise against the attacks of temptation, against the javelins of scandal, against suspicions, whispers, jealousy?[4]

The *Exhortation to Chastity*, a text addressed by Tertullian to a recently widowed brother, seems, on the contrary, to absorb into virginity an ensemble of different behaviors or statuses. But there again, virginity in the strict sense is not isolated as a mode of living or a particular experience. Virginity in general is defined as a "sanctification," a sanctification as God's will, and what that will wills is that, being created in his image, we resemble him. So there are three degrees of virginity: the one bestowed on us at birth which, if we preserve it, allows us to be unaware of its own confinement, which we will later wish to be liberated from; the one that a person receives from second birth in baptism and practices either in marriage or in widowhood; and lastly the one that Tertullian calls "monogamy" and that, after the interruption constituted by marriage, renounces sex. Tertullian ascribes a specific quality to each of these three degrees. *Felicitas* to the first; *virtus* to the second; and to the third this same *virtus* plus *modestia.*[5] Now the meaning to be given to these qualifications and their hierarchy is made very clear by a passage from the *Veiling of Virgins.*[6] There Tertullian asks himself whether "continence is superior to virginity"—be it continence practiced in widowhood or exercised by joint agreement in marriage. On virginity's side of things, there is the grace that one receives; on the side of continence, virtue. Here, the difficulty of fighting concupiscence; there, the ease of not desiring what one doesn't know.

One can see the two tendencies that emerge from these texts: giving abstinence a general value, as a means for approaching a sanctified existence, a prelude to that time when the resurrected flesh will no longer know gender difference;[7] and, in the general framework of this abstinence, not granting any privileged status or preeminent position to virginity in the strict sense, even if one does indicate its place and its specificity. In reality, it's a strict morality of continence—much more than a spiritual valorization of virginity—that runs through these texts by Tertullian. In these texts, one can even recognize a resistance to any practice that would impart a special meaning or a particular status to the virginity of women.[8]

Cyprian's *De habitu virginum,* however, written in the middle of the third century, is addressed to women who have and must have the status and conduct of virgins, without it [resembling] a monastic institution. The text deals with a category of women believers sufficiently defined that Cyprian addresses them as such,[9] and sufficiently advanced in saintliness for him to ask them to remember others (himself included) at that moment when the honor will be theirs.[10] Neither praise of virginity in general, nor censure of what is taking place, the text presents itself, in the form of an exhortation, as a practical treatise: what should the "apparel" of virgins be? Significantly, it opens by praising discipline in general, more precisely with an often-repeated formula by Livy.[11] Modified, however. "Discipline, the guardian of weakness," said the Roman historian; "discipline, the guardian of hope," replies Cyprian, which clearly shows the positive function of discipline in one's ascent to divine rewards. It is "the guardian of hope, the bond of faith, the guide of the way of salvation, the stimulus and nourishment of good dispositions, the teacher of virtue, which causes us to abide always in Christ, and to live continually for God."[12]

Cyprian defines virginity in relation to baptism's purification. Baptism makes us, our body and our members, the temple of God. So we are obliged to make sure that nothing impure or even profane can penetrate this sanctified place. It behooves us to be its priests, as it were: a task required of everyone, "men and women, boys and girls, irrespective of age or sex."[13] Within this general obligation, virginity occupies a privileged place. Much more markedly than Tertullian, Cyprian singles out the state of virginity, showers it with singular praises, and gives it a fitting role. It is "the flower of the Church's seed, the grace and ornament of spiritual endowment, a joyous disposition, the wholesome and uncorrupted work . . ."[14] If virginity occupies such an eminent place for Cyprian, this is for two reasons. It preserves intact the purification effected by the water of baptism. It extends and completes what happened at that moment, when the neophyte shed the former person. The virgin's renunciation was more total than the others, since she extinguished "all the fleshly desires" within her.[15] Keeping this purity intact all her life, the virgin commences here on earth the existence that will be reserved, after death, for those who will be saved: the incorruptible life. "That which we shall be, you have already begun to be. You possess already in this world the glory of the resurrection. You pass through the world without the contagion of the world; in that you continue chaste and virgins, you are equal to the angels of God."[16] In this way, from baptism to resurrection, virginity passes through life without being touched by its defilements. It is at the same time as close as possible to the state of birth—to the state of the soul when it is born to Christian existence—and as close as possible to what the other life will be in the glory of resurrection. Its privilege of purity is also a privilege in relation to the world and to time: in a sense, it is already beyond. In virgins' lives, the initial purity and the final incorruptibility join together.[17]

This precious life is represented by Cyprian as both precarious—it is exposed to the attacks of the devil[18]—and difficult, a tough ascent, toil and pain: "Immortality is given to the persevering, eternal life is set before them; the Lord promises his kingdom."[19] So the virgin's existence is in need of assistance, encouragement, warnings, exhortations.[20] Cyprian doesn't suggest anything like a systematic direction. It's clearly not a code of living that he proposes. He indicates only that he is speaking as a parent.[21] But he also emphasizes that virginity cannot consist solely in an integrity of the body.[22]

The content of the text may strike one as odd. The recommendations given are presented in a successive series: the first concerns richness (one should not prefer the richness of jewelry, ornaments, and sumptuous clothing to the richness that is God); the second concerns the care of the body and undue attractiveness; the third the baths, and the places one shouldn't frequent. In sum, as the text says expressly, with these precepts it's a question of "apparel," "care and attention," and "ornaments."[23]

But the nearly exclusive focus on these themes is easily explained by Cyprian's general notion of the state of virginity. If, as he says, that state consists of maintaining baptismal purity until the incorruptibility of the other world is attained, then the principle to be followed is to preserve it as it was at the origin and as it should be at the end of time. A series of expressions scattered through the text are worth noting: "Do not be afraid," says Cyprian to the virgin, "to be such as you are, lest when the day of resurrection comes your creator (*artifex tuus*) does not recognize

you";[24] or further: "Be such as your creator made you; be such
as the hand of your Father ordained you. Let your countenance
remain in you incorrupt";[25] or finally: "Remain what you have
started to be, remain what you will be."[26] Essentially, then, for
the virgin it's a matter of preserving that resemblance that is the
seal of Creation, which sin had effaced and baptism has restored.
The state of virginity must be stripped of all those "ornaments,"
"adornments," treatments, and embellishments by which the
creature, in altering God's work, attempts to mask it. The virgin
must live just as she was when she left the hand that molded her,
and as she will be "recognized" on the final day. In this world, she
must be the manifestation and affirmation of that state. Hence
this recommendation by Saint Cyprian, which is not in any way
divergent from the text as a whole, but is rather its central point:
"A virgin ought not only to be so, but also to be perceived to be so:
no one on seeing a virgin should be in any doubt as to whether she
is one."[27] By renouncing all the artificial luster that richness, ornaments, and treatments can radiate, the life of the virgin should
make what she is shine forth to everyone, so that all see the uncorrupted figure that comes from the hand of the Creator only to
return there just as she is—that is, as he made her.

So we shouldn't be misled: in this brief set of admonitions
addressed to virgins (which look superficial at first glance), in these
simple precepts concerning "apparel," we should see evidence of
the special importance that feminine virginity had assumed; the
spiritual significance accorded to virginity understood as a total
integrity of existence and not simply as a strict continence; and
finally the value attributed to it as an absolutely privileged relationship to God. The significations are implicit, clearly, but they
account for the succinct and apparently unimportant elements in
Saint Cyprian's practical recommendations.

The *Banquet of the Ten Virgins* by Methodius of Olympus,
written at the end of the third century, didn't introduce the theme
of virginity into Christian thought; and it wasn't Methodius who
signaled the crucial differences between Christian virginity and
pagan self-restraint. But that dialogue constitutes the first great
elaboration of a systematic and developed conception of virginity.
It attests, well before the development of monastic institutions,

to the existence of a collective practice—at least within the circles of women—and it offers evidence of the very high spiritual value virginity was given. Of course, one doesn't find in this text the description of those methods and behaviors emphasized by the fourth-century authors—from Basil of Ancyra to John Chrysostom, and from Ambrose to Cassian—to show how one can maintain a purity of body and soul, establishing what can be called a technology of virginity. But at the transition point of Alexandrine and Neoplatonic spirituality of the third century and the forms of institutional asceticism of the fourth, Methodius formulates some of the basic themes of the positive practice of virginity. The literary form of the *Banquet* allows not only for a juxtaposition of different discourses, but also for their succession in a continuous and ascending movement, and an indication of the decisive moment through the naming of a "victor." One can pick out the various points of view and the existence of key elements within the flexible unity of the dialogue. For, despite many repetitions, something more is involved than just a succession of homilies, one after the other, exhorting to chastity.

In the first discourse, spoken by Marcella, virginity is linked to a threefold movement of ascension. First of all is a personal ascension, which is described in a strictly platonic style: virginity directs the chariot of souls "upward from the earth," "until, having lightly bounded above the world, they take their stand truly on the vault of heaven."[28] At the end of this ascension, contemplation of the Incorruptible is given to the soul. A historical ascension that, since the origin of the world, has brought mankind closer to heaven: this is the series of customs and laws; when the world was empty and it needed to be filled, men "married their own sisters" until Abraham "received circumcision," which shows that one must separate from one's own flesh, and men had several wives, until it was said to them that they were like "rutting stallions" and that their "fountain" should be kept to each one of them; then they were taught continence, and now at last virginity, the "greatest and most exalted lesson" that makes them despise the flesh and rest in the "peaceful haven of incorruptibility."[29] Finally, Marcella's discourse evokes, in her historico-theological economy of salvation, the cleavage separating the two final moments of the previously described series. Before there was Christ, it was God who—somewhat like a father entrusting his children to increasingly severe teachers—had guided men to continence. But in order to advance to a virginity enabling us—who were created in the image of God—to resemble him and carry this resemblance to its completion, the Incarnation was necessary: the Word needed to take on human flesh so that we might be offered a "divine model of life."[30] Thus the first discourse braids together, within a single figure of ascension, the three movements (grace of salvation, gradual transformation of the law, individual effort of ascent) that place virginity—and Christian virginity, completely distinct from self-restraint—at that apex of perfection where man comes as close as possible to resembling God.

The second and third discourses, Theophila's and Thaleia's, are paired, and together they constitute a discussion of the value of marriage. But we are very far removed, in form and content, from the ancient *ei gamêton* [should one marry?] debate. Theophila talks about the value of marriage, while accepting the idea that man is rising by degrees toward virginity. But for her this is because the time has not come "when the light has completely separated from the darkness"; the right number of human beings has not yet been reached. Marriage, even though it is less precious than virginity, is useful and must still be practiced. But looking at the matter more closely, this rightfulness of marriage is not merely a makeshift concession or temporary solution. The arguments that Methodius places in Theophila's mouth give an entirely positive meaning to marriage: we are still, she says, under the injunction to "increase and multiply." Now, this multiplication, which causes flesh to be born from flesh, should be seen as an act of creation, of demiurgy.[31] Methodius's text underscores three aspects of this demiurgy in turn. It is a procreation of the body by the body: the "foamy and lumpy" seed that will fertilize the female field is formed from all the male members.[32] But it is also a collaboration of man with God, on the model of Adam "offering his rib to the divine creator for him to remove." Finally, it is an activity of God in the body itself, as Theophila explains in her long comparison of the human body with the workshop of the divine modeler, who shapes the wax-like embryos "starting from moist tiny seed," and constructs in this way "the image, totally rational and endowed with a soul, that we are of Him." In the forming of the embryo, in its gestation, and in the development of the infant after its birth, God plays the role of the supreme artisan. *"Ho aristoteknas."*[33]

One easily recognizes themes similar to those in Clement of Alexandria's *Paedagogus*.[34] Procreation was described as a convergence of God's power and the act of his creature. Can one assign a direct influence of Clement on Methodius? For the moment, this isn't the question. In any case, these themes bringing a theology of Creation into play—through medical considerations more or less directly inspired by the Stoics—were clearly common in the third century. It's interesting to see them appearing in the beginning of the *Banquet:* in Theophila's discourse, which will not be less appreciated than any of the others delivered by this troupe of saintly women,[35] but which will be "outstripped" by an ascending movement that the next discourse, Thaleia's, commences by suggesting that they go beyond the immediate meaning of the Genesis narrative.

Thaleia's discourse is a corrective response to Theophila's, offering a spiritual interpretation transcending her literal one. It's not that the literal is false,[36] but it is insufficient, in part because the Bible presents something different than a mere "archetype of the intercourse of the sexes";[37] and above all because, while one is right to see in Genesis "God's unalterable decrees that harmoniously ensure the perfect government of the world"—and still ensure it today—we must not forget that we have now entered another age of the world where the old laws of nature have been replaced by a new disposition.[38] It's the text of this new disposition that must be followed. Methodius finds it in the first Epistle to the Corinthians. Genesis should be interpreted on the basis of that epistle. But Methodius refuses to see in the relation between Adam and Eve simply a foreshadowing, or even the model, of what is now the union of Christ with the Church.[39] He interprets the Incarnation as a veritable re-Creation, a reshaping of Adam. The latter was not yet "dry" or "hardened" when, leaving the hands of the one who molded him, he encountered the sin that washed over him and made him lose his form. So God fashioned him anew, deposited him in the womb of a virgin and joined him

to the Word. In this manner Christ recapitulated and assumed
the nature of Adam. But by that very fact, the order of corruption
is done away with, the form of unions and childbirth is renewed:
"The Lord, the Incorruption that conquered death, harmonizes
the resurrection with the flesh, not suffering it again to be inherited by corruption."[40]

So Methodius returns to the Genesis text, of which he had, in
the previous discourse, suggested a literal, and naturalistic, interpretation. And he applies it to the domain of spiritual significations:
first to the collective plane of the Church with Christ, then to the
individual plane of one righteous being among the righteous—
Saint Paul, who thus finds himself taken into the interpretation he
founded. Methodius thus makes what had been said about Adam
"ricochet" onto Christ. The terms of the analysis are important:
they mark not the eradication of what the order of nature had
shown, but its transposition. The sleep into which the first man
was plunged—that trance that represented, as we've seen, the climax of sexual pleasure—has now become the voluntary death of
Christ, his Passion (*Pathos*). The Church was made from his flesh
and his bones and, as a wife purified by the good, she receives "the
spiritual and blessed seed" into her womb.[41] Christ's rapture is
continuously renewed: each time he descends from heaven to be
joined to his wife, he empties himself and offers his side so that all
those coming to baptism can be born.[42] But what comes to pass
for the whole Church also happens to the soul of the most perfect
individuals: one is fertilized by Christ, to whom the Church and
souls are the virgin wife. In this way, Saint Paul received "into his
womb the seeds of life." He "labored in childbirth" and would
"engender" new Christians.[43]

In view of these unions and fertility that are the spiritual form
of virginity, marriage is therefore no longer that necessity of nature
spoken of by the preceding discourse, which had cited the need to
populate the world. "Increase and multiply" has acquired a different meaning.[44] And if marriage has a place, this is as a concession
made to those who are too weak: think for example of those sick
persons who must be fed, even when the day of fasting has arrived.
Let marriage be left for the weak, then. Which means, Methodius
concludes, still according to Corinthians, that virginity cannot be

obligatory: he who is capable and is honor-bound to "preserve" his flesh "virgin," "does better"; whereas he who is unable, and "dedicates it to lawful marriage" without secret corruption only "does well."[45]

Hence the first three discourses of the *Banquet* establish the time of virginity within a historico-theological framework; it is neither more nor less than an age of the world begun by restaging the initial act of creation through the Incarnation. Understood in this way, virginity is something altogether different than a prohibition concerning a particular aspect of human behavior. A fundamental part of the relationship between God and his creature, virginity is constituted of the lifesaving restoration of an original relation now transposed into the order of acts, procreations, kinships, and spiritual bonds. Methodius's next four discourses can be seen as forming an ensemble in turn: they tell of this new age—what it means for human existence (the discourses of Theopatra and Thalloussa), then what it means in terms of divine rewards (sixth and seventh discourses of Agathe and Procilla); they follow the path of virginity from the soul that practices it to the salvation that crowns it—what Methodius calls the new turn toward Paradise.[46]

Theopatra, the fourth orator, introduces the important notion of purity, *hagneia*. It is important in that it is distinct from virginity. Indeed, in relation to the historico-theological significance of virginity established earlier, purity is its human form: the mode of existence of creatures that have chosen the way of salvation when the age of virginity came with the Savior. But relative to the traditional sense of virginity as physical integrity, purity has an obviously broader meaning. First of all, it shouldn't be seen simply as the result of a voluntary abstinence: it comes from on high. It is a gift of God, who in this way offers man the possibility of guarding against corruption: "Wherefore God—pitying us who were in such a situation, able neither to stand nor to rise—sent down from heaven the best and most glorious help: purity."[47] Purity is a treasure that man in return should cultivate and "practice very especially."[48] This purity must be practiced not merely at a particular age in life, but throughout one's existence—from the first to the third watch: "It is good from childhood to submit the neck to the divine yoke."[49] It should also be practiced in one's being, in the body and the soul alike, in the order of sexual relations as in that of all the other aberrations.[50] Finally, it must be practiced not merely as an abstinence from evil, but as a positive connection with God: a way of dedicating oneself to him.[51] Thus Thallousa describes virginity as a seal laid on the body and the soul: on the mouth, which forbids itself any foolish speech so that it only sings hymns to God; on the eyes that turn their gaze away from "the charms of the body" and "unseemly sights" and focus only on the things above; on the hands that shun "dishonorable dealing"; on the feet that don't loiter about but run straight under the commands that have been given. On thought, lastly: "I think no evil, offering all thoughts to God . . . I meditate on the law of the Lord day and night."[52]

Then comes the moment of reward: after this life, the transformation of souls that take on "the unbegotten and incorporeal Beauty [. . .] which is unchangeable, and grows not old and has need of nothing."[53] They can become the temple of Christ here below; but they are also ready for the moment when Christ will return: "our souls—with our bodies, having put them on again—shall go to meet Him in the clouds, bearing our lamps [. . .] like stars radiating the ethereal splendor."[54] And in the sky, explains Procilla in a discourse on the Song of Songs, Christ will gather his betrothed: "The spouse must be betrothed to the Bridegroom, and called by His name. And, moreover, she must be undefiled and unpolluted, as a garden sealed, in which all the odors of the fragrance of heaven are grown, that Christ alone may come and gather them, blooming with incorporeal seeds."[55]

The last three discourses constitute the summit of the ascent. The most important is the eighth, Thecla's. It will win the prize, in spite of the excellence of all the others. One mustn't forget that in fact Thecla was celebrated as the companion of Saint Paul, nor that the *Acta Pauli et Theclae* was a text regularly referred to by the Encratists and all those among Tatian's disciples who preached strict abstinence. Methodius's use of Thecla as one of his characters signals a desire to emphasize the Paulinian nature of his intervention, and to involve this figure of the first virgin-martyr in a eulogy of virginity that would not be a precept of absolute and unconditional continence. So it's a matter of having Thecla herself, the model of Christian virgins invoked by Encratism, reveal a different understanding of virginity. As for the fact that this "capital" discourse in the strict sense is the eighth one, the reason is easy to discover. Methodius's eschatology attached a very special significance, in fact, to the number eight. Based on the seven days of Genesis, and on the calendar of Leviticus, with the seven holidays of the seventh month, whose observance is a permanent law for the descendants of Israel,[56] Methodius reasoned that the world was destined to last seven millennia: the first five being those of obscurity and the Law; the sixth, which corresponds to creation of man, was that of the coming of Christ; the seventh that of Rest, the Resurrection, and the Feast of Tabernacles. As for the eighth millennium, it will be that of Eternity.[57] Thecla's discourse, in the eighth position, crowns all the others—it is placed at the end of time, so to speak: it reveals Eternity. It is both the culmination and foundation of everything that's been said.

Thecla reviews, in terms more Platonic than ever, the description of the movement of souls—souls that, if they're able to avoid the world's defilements, rise up to the spheres of the Incorruptible. She evokes the wings of those souls that "are strengthened by the sap of purity," and whose flight is all the lighter "as they are accustomed daily to flying far from human preoccupations."[58] She also evokes "those who have lost their wings and fallen into pleasures" where "they wallow,"[59] incapable of any honorable childbirth. To the rising souls Thecla, like those who spoke before her, promises access to incorruptibility: they "ascend into the supramundane life and see from afar what others do not see, the very pastures of immortality, bearing in abundance flowers of inconceivable beauty!"[60] And in this movement, they manifest that resemblance to God that Platonic philosophy had always promised to souls broken free of the world of appearances. By giving virginity this very broad meaning of a purified, "peak" existence,[61] Methodius is able to pair it with God. *Parthenia* = *partheia*.

So nothing new in Thecla's discourse thus far, compared to the previous orators, even if the repeated recourse to Platonic themes assumes a particular significance in this contribution that is more decisive than the others.[62] One expression stands out, however, as

early as the first lines. I'm referring to the comparison—a common one, which in its philosophical usage was more Stoic than
Platonic—of life with a theater. But while, as a trite metaphor, this
served mostly to designate the fleeting illusions of existence or the
theatrical character of a life in which we are an actor whose role
is decided ahead of time,[63] and while Plotinus evokes something
like a pure dramatic spectacle—with changes of scenery and cos-
tumes, cries and laments, murders and wars—as he speaks of the
myriad of scenes in which "the outer man whimpers, complains,
and performs his role,"[64] Methodius, for his part, speaks of the
drama of truth.[65] That drama is acted out in the ascension toward
incorruptible reality. Those who remain attached to pleasure are
dismissed. Taking part all the way to its end are those that seek
"the treasures up above." Virginity is a condition—or rather, as a
general form of existence, it is the precondition in order for this
drama of truth to reach Truth itself. Rather than a stage play, it's
a liturgy in which the souls that "have truly and faithfully lived as
virgins for Christ" process toward heaven and meet the choir of
angels "who have positioned themselves in front" of the cortege;
they sing "the welcoming words," "conduct" them to the pastures
of immortality, and give them "the prize of their victory."[66] Then,
everything they had only glimpsed, as in a dream, in shadowy
forms, they now see clearly: "wonderful and glorious and blessed
things of beauty."[67] Justice itself, Continence itself, Love itself, and
Truth and Wisdom. In sum, the eighth discourse—the crowning
discourse (*discours coryphée*)—reiterates the movement evoked by
the preceding discourses. But while the earlier discourses promised incorruptibility, immortality, eternal bliss, it is truth that is
announced here: the virgins make it to the heavenly fields and in
return God illuminates them.

So it's in this sense that Thecla's discourse completes all the
others. But it also grounds them in the sense that the treasure of
truth it will now reveal concerns virginity itself. Doubtless this is
how we should understand the two arguments that make up the
body of Thecla's discourse, and whose presence at this point may
seem strange: an exegesis of the Book of Revelation and considerations on astral determinism. In one case, it's a matter of taking
up virginity again from the perspective of the end of time and as

a form of time's fulfillment; in the other, it's a matter of looking down on virginity from the top of the world, from the highest celestial spheres.

The passage from Revelation is the one that describes "the great wonder that appeared in heaven": the woman travailing in childbirth, clothed with suns, and the dragon that casts a third of the stars down to earth. An undoubtedly traditional interpretation saw this as a representation of the virgin mother, the birth of Christ, the battle of the serpent against woman and the promise of its defeat by Christ.[68] Methodius was fiercely opposed to this interpretation.[69] Arguing against it, he points to a textual impossibility: Revelation speaks of the ascension toward heaven, far from the serpent's attacks and from the infant born of woman. And Christ descended from heaven to fight the Enemy. He also cites a rule of method: Revelation is a prophetic text; it shouldn't be related to the Incarnation, which occurred before it was written. It must concern only "the present and the future." In short, Methodius replaces the interpretation based on the past descent of the Spirit with an interpretation based on the current and future ascension toward God. Actually, what he proposes through Thecla's mouth is not an original exegesis. In fact, he proposes seeing in the woman—attired as the fiancée who will be escorted to the king's bed—an image of the Church (this being a common theme in the third century).[70] The infant born from her is thus the soul of the Christian, who comes into spiritual life through baptism. But why is this infant represented as a male? Because Christians form "a people of men," because they have renounced the "effeminate passions," because they "become manly through fervor." They bear "the form and likeness of the Word." The true Christian is reborn as a Christ. So this figure of the woman in labor should be read as an image of the virginal fertility of the Church giving birth to souls whose virginity is sealed by the sign of Christ.[71]

As for the dragon, it is quite obviously Satan—not as the enemy of Christ, but as the enemy of human souls, attempting to take them by surprise. The dragon's seven heads confront the seven virtues, and the ten horns are attacking the ten commandments: the sharp horns of adultery, falsification, greed, theft, Methodius says, but going no further with his enumeration. So we shouldn't see a remembrance of Christ's victory in this passage of Revelation, but rather, in the hortatory mode, a call to battle: "Do not, therefore, lose courage on account of the schemes and slanders of the Beast, but bravely prepare for the battle, armed with the helmet of salvation, and the breastplate, and the greaves. For you will bring upon him an immense consternation when you attack him with great advantage and courage; nor will he at all resist, seeing his adversaries set in array by one more Powerful."[72]

From the millennial viewpoint, the age of virginity is therefore the age of the ascent of souls toward incorruptible heaven. In this vision, virginity itself has two aspects: that of a spiritual kinship in which the Church plays a central role—as a virgin impregnated by the Lord, it raises virgin souls, who are lifted by their virginity up to heaven; and that of a spiritual combat in which the soul must fight off the Enemy's constant attacks. The last part of Thecla's discourse allows this same age to be viewed from a spatial perspective of sorts: from above the world and its order. It is there, in fact, that Methodius places a discussion whose structures and elements are clearly philosophical. It's a matter of refuting the claim that the stars decide the destiny of men. Let's leave aside the problem of understanding the points at issue in this long debate. If it has its place in this *Banquet* devoted to virginity, this is because it enables Methodius to maintain that God is not responsible for evil—that he and all the celestial beings remaining under the law of his government are "far removed from evil, and incapable of human actions which spring from the sense of pleasure and pain," that the existence of laws that compel and forbid is not contradictory (which would be the case if destiny were sealed once and for all), that there is a difference between the righteous and the unrighteous, "a gulf between the unruly and the temperate," that "good is the enemy of evil, and evil is different from good"; that "meanness is reprehensible" and that "God cherishes and glorifies virtue." All these principles are recalled to make room, in the world where we exist, for liberty whose absence would make chastity worthless: "To do good or evil is in our power, and not decided by the stars. For there are two motions in us, the lust of the flesh and that of the soul, differing from each other, whence they have received two names, that of virtue and that of vice."[73]

The spiritual kinship and the combat that Thecla spoke of earlier may characterize this age of virginity, announced by the Scripture and defined for the sequence of millennia, but it still leaves room for man's freedom and for the distinction, in terms of merit, between those whom God will save and those who will be lost.

The last two orators of the *Banquet* form the accompaniment for Thecla and her grand discourse. The ninth is delivered in the language of paraenesis: an exhortation of the soul to prepare for the feast that the seventh millennium holds in store. How is one to "adorn oneself with the fruits of virtue"? And "shade one's brow with the boughs of purity"? And "adorn one's tabernacle"? To answer these questions Methodius refers to a text of Leviticus.[74] First gather "fine ripened fruits"—that is, those that grew on the tree of life in paradise, from which man turned away; today it means those Christians who have been "cultivated in the Gospel orchard." Next "the plumes of the palm tree": here it's a matter of purifying the mind, of ridding the soul of the dust and dirt of passion. Then willow branches, signifying justice. And finally, chaste-tree branches, which of course symbolize chastity, the crowning virtue.[75] However, an important qualification: this chastity is not to be identified with celibacy because it can be practiced "by those who live chastely with their wives," though they don't reach the top or even the main branches of the tree like those who constrain themselves to practice a complete virginity. Nor is it to be equated with the refusal of fornication, or with the pure and simple abstinence from sexual relations: virginity demands that even desires and lusts be rooted out. As a virtue and indeed the pinnacle of all the virtues, as a preparation for the completion of the ages, virginity must be not a rejection of the body, but a labor of the soul upon itself.

Finally Domnina, the last speaker, has the task of distinguishing this labor of virginity from the past obligations that God had imposed on men, one after the other. The law of paradise, symbolized by the fig tree from which Adam turned aside. The law of Noah, symbolized by the vine, which promised man the end of his sorrows and the return of joy. The law of Moses, symbolized by the olive tree, whose oil lights the lamps. Now, if man turned aside from these successive laws, this was because Satan was able to manipulate him by making false copies of these plants and their fruits. Only virginity cannot be imitated, and hence Satan can't make use of it to defeat man. But in this final discourse there is one important element: it's that virginity does not differ from the laws of Adam, Noah, and Moses, as one law among others, because it is not a law. And it stands in contrast to law in general, of which the fig tree, the vine, and the olive tree represent three forms. On one side, the Law; on the other, the virginity that succeeds it.[76] Now, this idea that virginity takes over from the Law is doubly important. First because it appears that, in Methodius's mystical doctrine, virginity is not the object of a prescription. It is a mode of relation between God and man; it marks that moment in the history of the world and in the movement of salvation where God and his creature no longer communicate through the Law and obedience to the Law. Second, because virginity is not simply a way of submitting to what was commanded: it is an exercise of the soul upon itself,[77] which carries it as far as the immortalization of the body.[78] It is a relation of the soul to itself in which the unending life of the body is at stake.

# 2

# On the Arts of Virginity

One mustn't imagine too sharp a disjunction between the first texts on virginity and the great flowering of virginity treatises of the fourth century. They prepared the ground for it: by disengaging the virginity principle from the prescriptions relating to continence, by giving it a special status as well as a positive and intense spiritual significance, and by developing a number of virginity themes which the later authors, from Gregory of Nyssa to Augustine, would only have to take up and enrich or rework. Yet the question of virginity, in the fourth century, is embedded in a context that will modify it in important ways: the development of asceticism, the organization of monasticism, the implementation of techniques for the government of oneself and others, the creation of a complex regimen of truth for souls to practice. This modification can be broadly characterized by recalling a passage from Gregory of Nyssa: "In other sciences men have devised certain practical methods for cultivating the particular subject; and so, I take it, virginity is the practical method in the science of the divine life."[1] Virginity—already regarded as a privileged state, laden with particular spiritual values and capable of creating an incorruptible relation to God, immortality, and the heavenly realities—tends to become not just a carefully ordered way of life, but a type of relation to oneself that has its procedures, its techniques, its instruments. From Tertullian to Methodius, virginity-continence became a positive state of virginity. It is this state that will be elaborated in the fourth century into an "art of virginity."

I

A first point has to do with the relationship between this *tekhnê* of virginity and the pagan practice of continence. This is a question that one might think was "outdated" in this period, but it draws its meaning and its topicality from the fact that ascetic existence defines itself as the "philosophical life." In the preface to his *Treatise on Virginity*, Gregory of Nyssa explains the plan his text will follow. After underscoring the negative aspects of ordinary life, he indicates that, following "the right method," he will describe "the philosophical life."[2] So one shouldn't be surprised to find an explicit intention to separate Christian virginity as clearly as possible from pagan continence, combined with the reutilization of a number of themes by which the latter was justified. He writes, in a general way, and subject to a few specific modulations, a critique of the virginity that was connected in the pagan world with status or with religious functions; a reference, in the form of examples, to the recognition given to the virtue of women; and a reiteration of the debates on marriage and the tranquility of the soul.

Some Christian authors simply deny that the pagans ever esteemed virginity. This is what Athanasius maintains: "It's only among us Christians that it is honored."[3] More cautiously, and in line with a historico-religious ranking order, Chrysostom recognizes that the Greeks "admired and venerated" virginity. He thus places them above the Jews, who are said to have rejected it—as is proved by their antipathy to Christ born of a virgin—but below God's Church, to which it owes all its zeal.[4] But it's the Latin Fathers who, on account of their milieu,[5] tend to take these practices of pagan continence into consideration. In any case, Saint Jerome devotes the whole conclusion of the *Adversus Jovinium* to pagan references: examples of the virgins who were honored in Greece and Rome; recollections of the heroic widows who stayed faithful to the memory of their husbands and went so far as to sacrifice themselves on their tombs; the celebrity of certain Roman nobles renowned for their chastity; reflections by moralists like Theophrastus, who recommended abstaining from marriage. And, with more emphasis than exactness, Saint Jerome invokes the opinion of Aristotle, Plutarch, and "our Seneca" on this theme.[6] It is true that he doesn't fail to note the difference between Christian virginity, which is associated with different justifications, and the continence of the pagans, which can't have any sanctifying value. "For celibacy does not avail anything without good works [. . .] and vestal virgins and Juno's widows might upon these terms be numbered with the saints."[7] In general, moreover, the Christian authors are much more discreet than Saint Jerome in this evocation of what the ancients considered to be virtues or values. They prefer to stress how far the latter remain from Christian sanctification. Most authors express the principle of this difference in the form of a simple prohibition (of marriage or sexual relations) to which the pagans give the status of virginity. Be it a definitive or provisional prohibition, or an absolute prescription, or a counsel of prudence—it's all essentially in the form of a rejection or an abstinence that pagan virginity presents itself to the minds of Christian authors who do not recognize it as theirs. At the beginning of *De virginibus*, Saint Ambrose indicates this clearly. If the virginity of pagans is not that of Christians, this is because it takes the form of an external rule for those men or women on whom it is imposed. The vestal is compelled to remain virgin, but for a stated time period: a matter of time that promises to the decency of youth the indecency of old age.[8] Further, if she respects her binding agreement, it's because she has a taste for honor, an expectation of advantages, a fear of being dismissed and punished. So she doesn't offer her virginity, she sells it. Is that better or different than prostitution?[9] We see the same idea under an apparently inverse formulation in Saint John Chrysostom. The virginity of the Greeks cannot count on any reward: "For the Greeks such a virtue is sterile."[10] But if the virgins of paganism cannot expect anything in the afterlife, this is because here below their renunciation is not inspired "by the love of God." Those complying with an order or law "cannot hope for any privilege."[11]

And yet, despite their concern with distinguishing pagan continence from Christian virginity, the fourth-century authors borrowed certain relatively important elements from the rules of life inspired by the pagans' moral notions. They even transposed certain ones directly. Two in particular: the critique of married life and the praise of independent life.

The critique of marriage is a common trope of ancient morals, a trope that the ascetic authors of the fourth century reutilized without many modifications. The hassles of marriage—*molestiae nuptiarum*—were tirelessly described, and in a very repetitive form, by all those who discussed the domestic question in all the philosophical schools: should one marry or not? Theophrastus, whom Saint Jerome cites at length, is just one example of these banalities, from which one sees three or four main themes emerge. There is incompatibility between the philosophical life and married existence: "one can't love a woman and books at the same time"; there are women's intrinsic faults—their jealousy, their greediness, their fickleness; there is the trouble they bring to the soul and to their husband's existence; there are money worries ("looking after them when you're poor is really difficult; putting up with them when you're rich is a torment") or the need for surveillance; finally, there is the relatively small value of the care they may provide or even of the offspring one can expect from them, when you compare them to the friends you can surround yourself with or to the heirs you can choose with full knowledge of the consequences.[12]

Christian texts dealing with virginity were all but obliged to include a passage laying out the problems of marriage. One finds it, with varying degrees of prolixity, in the treatise *Peri parthenias* of Gregory of Nyssa (III, 2–7), in that of John Chrysostom (chapter XLIV in particular plus the long series of chapters LI–LXII), in the *Peri tês en parthenia alêthous aphtorias* [On the Integrity of Virginity] of Basil of Ancyra (chap. XXIII), in *Homily* VII (15–16) of Eusebius of Emesa, in the *De virginibus* of Saint Ambrose (I, 6), in Saint Jerome's *Adversus Helvidium* (chap. XX), in his Letter 22, to Eustochium, and in his *Adversus Jovinium*. Among all these texts, Gregory of Nyssa's can serve as an example, since it is constructed according to the exact rhetoric of the pagan diatribes on the advantages and drawbacks of marriage. Without saying so explicitly, Gregory of Nyssa takes up the three main arguments on which the defenders of married life relied: the happiness of life in a couple, the satisfaction of having children, and the advantage of having a family supporting one in times of illness or in old age. Happiness of the shared life? It is constantly threatened by envy, replies Gregory of Nyssa, if it exists at all, and death may destroy it at any moment. In any case, aging, old age, and time wreck it little by little: beauty's passing "like a wave to end up in nothingness" will leave behind it "no trace, no memory, no remainder of its present flower." The happiness of a life in common—undermined within by the fear of change, which prevents one from truly enjoying present blessings—is therefore only an appearance. Children? But there are the pains of childbirth and the accidents that often accompany it. There are the deaths in childhood, and those offspring that do survive are often a source of permanent worry. Sadness is the shared lot of those who have no children and those who do, of those who mourn dead children and those who regret the descendants that survive. As for old age, when the spouses should be a help to one another, think rather of the widowhood that sometimes strikes in youth and leaves the wives without support and without resources.[13]

The praise of life outside of marriage is just as traditional as these reminders of the *molestiae nuptiarum*, of which it is the flip side. Christian authors sometimes represented the independent life using accents close to those employed by the philosophers of antiquity when they promise bachelors a life of tranquility and calm. Chrysostom, for example, contrasts the life of marriage with an existence "free of dangers" and "without the troubles of business and politics,"[14] a life in which a man would depend only on himself.[15] He describes it, or at least some of its aspects, in terms of human wisdom and philosophical happiness:

"Her modest house [that of the single woman] has been delivered from confusion, and all crying has been banished from her presence. As in a calm harbor, silence rules all within, and another form of detachment more perfect than silence possesses her soul [. . .] What expression could suggest the joy of a soul so disposed [. . .] I do not know what to say, for embarrassment checks me at this point. I cannot understand why almost all mankind, when it could easily and without strain find enjoyment, does not believe this state but enjoys instead fretting and distraction and anxiety!"[16]

So the Christian inducement to virginity, at least in a certain number of texts, involves praise of an "independent" life, invoking the same advantages that the ancient philosophers claimed for it: no external constraints, "one's feet" are "nimble, and unfettered," there are no shackles on one's ankles.[17] No worries about all the appearances that are thought to be the chief benefits of marriage—children, family renown, glory, a future position.[18] No more of those passions that trouble the soul when it is agitated by external circumstances—"anger, violence, oaths, insults, hypocrisy."[19] Lastly and above all, the space for the soul to dwell with itself, making it possible to gather one's thoughts without attachment to external objects: "He whose life is contained in himself either escapes these experiences [those of marriage] altogether or can bear them easily, possessing a collected mind which is not distracted from itself."[20] It is this kind of life that Gregory of Nyssa thought he found in the Prophet Elias or John the Baptist—remaining "apart from all the ordinary events of life" and residing in "a cloudless calm of soul."[21]

There is something paradoxical in this description of virginity as a state of tranquility, in the recourse to the philosophical vocabulary of the serene existence. It seems, at first sight, to be in contradiction with what the same authors are apt to say about the unremitting struggles of virginity and its connection with martyrdom.[22] It also seems to suggest that there are more dangers, hence more trials, hence more merit, in the existence of married people. This is an objection that Chrysostom himself brings up: "Is it not that success in the midst of such great constraint [that of marriage] means a greater compensation? [. . .] Because you endure greater hardship from marriage."[23] This idea led Clement of Alexandria to give marriage a definite value, making it the rival of virginity in merit.[24] But Chrysostom dismisses the objection by stressing that the dangers of marriage cannot be counted toward salvation, since one's exposure to them was entirely voluntary.[25]

This reference to the theme of the tranquil life, which the philosophers had elaborated in an earlier time, has its importance. Doubtless it was necessary, in this period of the development of monasticism and the ascetic institutions, to consider the appeal that the evocation of these traditionally recognized values would exert. What's more, the theme of the tranquil life occupies a doubly privileged position: it is at the meeting point of a traditional understanding of the conditions necessary for true knowledge and true happiness, and the Christian idea of radical detachment from this world; but it's also at the heart of a problem that is internal to Christianity and that concerns the status of contemplative life, the methods for attaining it, and the merits that accrue to it. The fact is that, with different accents, virtually all the Christian authors will preserve the principle that the life of virginity, beyond everyday concerns, freed from the world's preoccupations, is a "tranquil" life. In his *Commentary of Psalm 132*, Saint Augustine evokes three kinds of life in reference to the three figures of Noah, Daniel, and Job. The first symbolizes the activity of those who govern the Church and are responsible for the harvest; the third symbolizes the faithful who serve God zealously. And the second represents the existence of those who have decided against living with a wife in favor of leading the monastic existence. Noah is associated with a figure of two men in the fields; Job with that of two women who work at the mill. Daniel is associated with two men lying in bed, men who "love repose," who "don't mix with crowds" or get involved with the "tumult of the human race" but "serve God in tranquility."[26]

But Saint Augustine immediately indicates how this tranquility of life without marriage should be understood. Daniel, a figure of chastity, was "tranquil," he was "safe," but among the lions. The latter represent the desires that assail the heart and the temptations that lay siege to it. Daniel was called *vir desideriorum*. The tranquility of his state is very different from the calm of the philosophical life in the old sense: this tranquility is inseparable from a permanent confrontation with the Enemy. And it should be understood in two senses: detachment from everything worldly that might be a source of disturbance, and confidence in the grace of God to provide victory in this struggle. In fact, the continuity of the theme of *tranquillitas*, of *otium*, marks the transition from a negative economy of abstinence and continence to a conception of virginity as a complex, positive, and agonistic experience.

II

The state of virginity conceived as an art is regularly presented by fourth-century authors as the result of a free and individual choice. But a choice that, through its meaning and its effects, falls within the general history of salvation of the human race.

Virginity is a free choice in three ways. First, it can't be practiced by everyone. Only those who are strong enough can do it: "virginity is for the few," says Saint Ambrose, "and marriage for everyone."[27] It can't be done on command or through some constraint. In a homily devoted to virginity and addressed to fathers, the unknown author advises parents not to do anything to thwart children who wish to pledge themselves to virginity. He urges them "to persuade them to do it," but he doesn't want the children to be constrained to follow that path.[28] This principle of choice without constraint is so important that Saint Augustine would find support for it using Mary as an example: since in her case the Incarnation willed by God was the matter at hand, "she might have been bidden to continue a virgin, that in her the Son of God would receive the form of a slave," and yet her virginity was the result of a "vow," a "choice out of love" and not a "necessity to obey."[29] A free choice then, in the sense that it is not prescribed by any law such as the commandments to honor God or not to commit adultery: "the Savior has not imposed virginity either in the law of nature or in the Gospels";[30] "the Savior does not give continence the obligatory character of a precept; it leaves that choice to our souls."[31] The insistence on the non-obligatory character of virginity finds several justifications in the texts—apart from the argument that some people do need to marry so that virgins can be born.[32] Above all, this provided a means of opposing all forms of dualism or all the gnostic currents that made abstaining from sexual relations a strict obligation, consequently leaving no room either for marriage or for procreation.[33] It was also a matter of asserting the positive value of virginity. This is an argument that recurs often: if virginity were obligatory, what special merit would there be in observing it? A person who doesn't rob or kill doesn't deserve any honor: "To abstain from what has been forbidden is by no means the mark of a noble and generous soul. Perfect virtue does not consist in not doing those things for which we would think ourselves wicked before everyone. It consists in excelling in what does not entail reproach for those who do not choose it."[34] Virginity is much more valuable than the mere observance of a prohibition. Finally, in a more general way, it was a matter of emphasizing that virginity does not belong to an economy of Law—the economy that had characterized the ancient alliance—but to a new form of relation between God and men.

And there we touch on the other aspect of virginity, the one that concerns the salvation of mankind and the present age of the world. This is the paradox, in fact: virginity can only be a free and individual act, but this act involves some of the drama that unfolded between humans and God and is not yet over. Virginity derives its meaning from that past and has its effects in the movement that is still to come. A choice, and not a law; but a present figure of the world or rather an aspect of its transformation. We have already seen these themes taking shape in the texts of the third century. Cyprian and especially Methodius of Olympus had clearly formulated some of its basic elements.

But it does appear that the development of monasticism reinforced them, that it favored the elaboration of several of them, while modifying certain accents. In any case, the monastic institution was a locus, or at least an occasion, for reflection on this triple aspect of virginity: a state radically different from that of marriage, integrated into life in the world, and demanding a practice, an art, a particular technique in order to produce its positive effects; an object of a free individual choice that no precept could impose, either on everyone in the form of a law, or on some in the form of a commandment; a form of life in which the undertaking of individual salvation is deeply involved with the economy of human redemption.

The role of virginity in the history of salvation is defined, by the authors of the fourth century, first of all in terms of the original paradisiacal state and the relations between man and woman before and after the fall. Obviously, there is no question here of reviewing in detail the long exegetical discussions that, from Origen to Augustine, were focused on the first two chapters of Genesis—on verse 27 for the Origen and on verses 18–24 for the Augustine. I would just like to indicate how the question of the relations between the paradisiacal virginity and the differentiation of the sexes in the Creation was treated.

Many of the dualist-inspired movements denied that the dif-

ferentiation of the sexes was the work of God. However, it was
seen as such by the authors recognized by the Church: madness,
says Saint Augustine, to claim to be Christian and be so blind to
the Scripture as to think that "the difference of the sexes is the
work of the devil and not of God."[35] Even before the forming of
Eve was recounted in the second chapter of Genesis, the sacred
text indicated with the first mention of man's creation (1:26–27)
that God had created them "man and woman." So this passage
gave unequivocal authority to the view that the difference of the
sexes is present since the Creation. But it immediately raises a difficulty in that it comes directly after the affirmation that man was
created in the image and likeness of God. How could the one and
undivided God create man in his likeness and at the same time
bearing this duality of the sexes? Philo had answered this question
by distinguishing in the human creature what was in the likeness
of the Creator from what was the mark of the creature: "as long as
he was single, he resembled, as to his creation, both the world and
God"; but he also bore "the characteristics of the nature of each—
not all of them, but such as a mortal constitution was capable of
admitting."[36] It's in this direction that Christian exegesis oriented
itself. Thus, Origen sees in this duality the mark of all that is created: "Because all things made by God are joined together, as
heaven and earth, as sun and moon, the Scripture wanted to show
that man is likewise a work of God and it was not brought forth
without harmony of the appropriate conjunction."[37] Jerome will
place still more distance between the resemblance to God and the
duality of the sexes: he points out that since "it breaks the unity,"
the number two is not good; moreover, the only day at the end of
which God didn't say his work was good is precisely the second;
in this way the Genesis narrative indicates the negative meaning
of the number two.[38] In any case, for Gregory of Nyssa or John
Chrysostom, and later for Augustine, the image of God and man
should be sought in the soul and not in the duality of the sexes.[39]
An important argument for the doctrine of virginity: inasmuch as
the latter is in fact an ascension that makes one resemble God, it is
not simply, in its spiritual signification, a renunciation of the other
sex. It is a going back beyond this differentiation, beyond even the
creative act that established it, toward the divine unity.

But if the paradisaical state already includes this duality of the sexes, what are its meaning and function? Are we to imagine that there were sexual relations in paradise before the fall, hence in a state of perfect innocence? The reply is universally negative. Either it is assumed, like Origen following Philo, that it was the sexual act, incapable of being innocent, that caused the fall,[40] or that sexual relations occurred after the fall and as its consequence.[41] But this nonexistence of sexual relations in paradise doesn't have the same reason or the same meaning for everyone. The game of exegesis is delimited by two texts: that of the first chapter of Genesis (1:28), where in blessing man and woman God tells them to increase, multiply, and fill the earth; and that of the second chapter, where God decides to give man a woman so that he might have a helpmate similar to him.

This idea of a helper obviously supports the affirmation that the role of Eve was to be a companion, not a spouse. According to Gregory of Nyssa, this "help" should be understood as participation in the contemplation of the face of God which, before the fall, was Adam's sole desire.[42] It is also suggested, it seems, by a passage of the treatise *On Virginity* of Chrysostom, explaining that woman becomes an obstacle for the spiritual life of man through a reversal of the role that was hers before the fall.[43] But if such is the paradisiacal function of the woman, two questions arise. What might be the meaning of the precept "Increase and multiply"? Must one suppose, like certain adversaries that Gregory of Nyssa criticizes without naming,[44] that the human race could grow only after the fall and that the latter therefore has something good about it, since "without it the human race would have continued to consist of the first couple"? Gregory of Nyssa asserts that there is no marriage between angels, and yet "their armies constitute infinite legions": this is because there exists, for this angelic nature, a mode of multiplication that for us humans cannot be conceived or formulated. However, it is certain that there is one, and such must be the power of multiplication given to man in the angelic existence that was his when he left the hands of the Creator.

Now comes the second question: Why was it that God, while giving the first couple an angelic mode of reproduction, endowed

it with a sexual reproduction which the angels do very well without? The answer lies in God's foreknowledge: he knew that man
would deviate from the righteous path and lose his angelic value.
That being the case, the world could not have been populated
or completed. So he devised in advance a way for us to "transmit
life to one another," but according to a mode that suits what we
have become, now that we have lost the resemblance to God: a
reproduction like that of "the brutes and beings without intelligence."[45] In sum, man was already indefinitely reproducible in
the Garden of Eden, but in a completely different way from the
union of the sexes; and yet he was marked with a sexual differentiation, which foreshadowed a coming fall without determining it,
and constituted a reserve reproductive capacity that would be activated by the fall.[46] These strange speculations on paradisiacal sex
show how, in the spirituality of this epoch, the distinction of the
sexes (created by God) is dissociated from their union (which can
come into play only after the fall and the separation from God),
and how reproduction is split into an angelic multiplication and
an animal birth.

We should turn now to the other side of the speculation, relating not to the origin and the fall, but to the present world and the
completion of the ages. The practice of virginity appears at first to
be a return, beyond the fall, to the paradisiacal state when man left
the hands of God and still bore his likeness; thus Gregory of Nyssa
speaks of "restoring the divine image from the foulness which the
flesh wraps round it to its primitive state so that we become that
which the first man was at the moment when he first breathed."[47]
Christians who practice virginity go back in time, as it were, and
reclaim the state of primitive perfection.[48] They re-establish it in
their soul where they rediscover, like a lost drachma, the mark of
divinity. They also re-establish it by detaching themselves from
the corruption of life on earth, and hence by escaping that death
which was punishment for the fall and which our first [ances-
tors] did not know—either because they were created immortal,
or because before the fall God in his prescience had not allowed
death to transform the mortality he had bestowed on them into an
event. "After weaning ourselves from this life of the flesh, which
has its inevitable follower, death, we should search for a manner

of life which does not bring death in its train; now the life of virginity is such a life."[49] Thus, to choose the state of virginity and hold to it rigorously must be regarded as something very different from a simple abstinence that would free one from troubles, passions, worries, and in general from the evils of existence when one is devoted, or simply gives in, to life's pleasures. It is much more than the practice of a virtue that will merit its subsequent reward—even if it is promised finer rewards than other virtues.[50] Virginity is thought of as an actual mutation of existence. It brings about in the individual being—body and soul—a "revolution" that, by restoring it to an original state, frees it from its earthly limits, from the law of death and time and gives it access* here and now to the life that will never end. Virginity opens the door to angelic existence. It elevates those who nonetheless still dwell among us to a state of incorruption and immortality: "It makes one rise up to heaven," says Eusebius of Emesa, "and already live in the company of angels here on earth."[51] Or further, it brings down to earth the principle of heavenly existence. "Though virgins cannot yet ascend to heaven as the angels can because their flesh holds them back, even in this world they have much consolation since they receive the Master of the heavens when they are holy in body and spirit. Do you grasp the value of virginity? that it makes those who spend time on earth live like the angels living in heaven? It does not allow those endowed with bodies to be inferior to the incorporeal powers and spurs all men to rival the angels."[52] And, contrasting virgins who, because of their chastity, pass from the world to heaven, with the fallen angels who, because of their "intemperance," have fallen into the world, Ambrose affirms that "he who has preserved his chastity is an angel."[53]

And it is not just in a metaphorical sense, or to designate a certain attitude of the soul, that the angelic nature of virginity is invoked. It is substantial. It passes through matter. It operates throughout the world and transfigures things. Here on earth it is not simply waiting for the other world: it really carries the latter into effect on earth. Thus Chrysostom describes the life of Elijah, Elisha, and John the Baptist, "those genuine lovers of virginity":

---

* *"fait accéder à"* [trans. note]; manuscript: *"succéder à"* [French editor's note].

"If they had wives and children, they would not have lived in the desert so easily [. . .] Released from all these ties, they passed their lives on earth as if they were in heaven. They had no need of walls or a roof or a bed or a table or the like. They had heaven for a ceiling, the ground for a bed, the desert for a table. And the very thing that seems to others to be a cause of hunger, the barrenness of the desert, was for these holy men a place of plenty. [. . .] Plentiful and sweet drink was supplied them from streams, rivers, and pools of water. An angel laid out for one of them a wondrous and fabulous table [. . .] And John, [. . .] neither food nor wine nor olive oil sustained his physical being, but grasshoppers and wild honey did. Do you behold the angels upon earth? Do you comprehend the power of virginity?"[54]

But there is more to virginity than this "spatial" overlap of heaven and earth. The virginity of individuals also has its place in the economy of the ages. The very numerous and very long expositions of this idea can be lumped into a few main themes.

The history of the world is divided into two phases. That of the still-empty world, and that of the full world. The world was empty on the day after the Creation and it was the proliferation of the creatures, sexual for the animals, non-sexual for the humans, that would complete it and bring it to its point of culmination. The fall had two negative consequences: it prevented the non-carnal multiplication of men, and it condemned them to die. Sexual reproduction ends up having an ambiguous relationship with death. Like death it is the consequence of the fall, but it constantly repairs death's ravages: "Since sin had come on the scene through the act of disobedience, and the sentence had the effect of making them liable to death, for the future, God in his inventiveness arranged for the continuance of the human race according to his wisdom by allowing for the propagation of the race through intercourse."[55] This is why the Old Testament shows us patriarchs who are married and the heads of large families, and why virginity—with the exception of a few singular figures[56]—is not especially honored. Under the law of death, marriage was a precept. But henceforth it's no longer that law which reigns over the world. We are now in the age of the "full," "completed" world, the age when, as Chrysostom says, the human race leaves "early childhood" and reaches maturity.[57] For such was the wisdom of God. As long as men, still too close to their birth and their sin, were willful it would have been impossible for them to follow a prescription like that of virginity. So the Lord had them do "their apprenticeship" under the law of marriage. But the time of perfection has come, when virginity must combine with a world that is coming to an end. This combination was made possible, is now necessary, and is paradoxically fertile.

It is possible because Christ assumed a human form in the womb of a virgin, lived a life of perfect virginity himself, and caused men to be reborn through the spiritual generation of baptism. He didn't just offer them a model of virtue, he gave them the power to subdue the rebellions of the flesh, and he created the possibility for the flesh itself to be resurrected in glory. After and through the Incarnation, virginity became possible as the restitution of angelic life within this world, despite the constraints of the flesh.[58]

It is necessary as well, because "the time is short."[59] The moment of Christ's return is not far away. One might draw negative consequences from this proximity, whose promise was one of the important aspects of fourth-century spirituality. Why concern oneself with the world, seeing that it is ending? Why care about future generations when the future is coming to a close? Why not immediately turn our thoughts to those realities that are beyond our reach, yet so close to us? Up to now, we have been preoccupied with "childish things"; the time has come "to abandon earthly things, which in reality are childish playthings, and place before our minds heaven and the splendor of life there and all of its glory."[60] Some object to the practice of virginity by saying that the human race could then totally disappear, a concern that makes no sense today: in a time when the apocatastasis will occur, let us recall that at the Creation of the world, when man led a joyful existence, "there were no cities, crafts, or houses."[61] And one is thus brought back to the idea of a positive role that virginity can and must play in the ending of the world. A passage from Gregory of Nyssa is very explicit on this point.[62] Virginity is barren. But this barrenness has to do with only carnal birth, which is connected with death in two ways: first because death is

its consequence, and next because it stands for the end of posterity, the passing away of human beings, one after the other. But as
a rejection of generation, virginity is a rejection of death, a way
of breaking this indefinite succession, which commenced in the
world when death appeared there and now continues from generation to generation—that is, from death to death. "Through virginity a boundary line is drawn for death, checking its advance";
those who have chosen virginity "have made themselves, in fact, a
frontier between life and death, and a barrier, too, which thwarts
it." The series that opened with the fall finds itself interrupted.
The power of death can no longer bring its activity to bear, and so
this physical barrenness should not be seen as a slow progression
toward death, but a triumph over it and the advent of a world in
which it will no longer have a place.

Virginity is therefore both an element of a deathless world
and an embryo of that world: a piece of that world here on earth
and access to the heavenly reality that it constitutes. But it is also
conceived, in relation to these realities, as a way of forming and
developing spiritual relationships: it is a form of union, a mode of
kinship, a principle of fertility and begetting. This is one of the
most characteristic traits of the Christian mystique of virginity, a
trait that carries it very far from the old conception of continence.

The virgin is a fiancée and a wife. This theme is quite ancient
in Christianity. Tertullian formulates it several times. In the *Resurrection of the Flesh*, he quickly evokes the voluntary eunuchs and
the virgins "married to Christ."[63] In the treatise addressed *To His
Wife*, he praises the widows who are "enrolled in the militias of
Christ" and who instead of remarriage prefer "to be wedded to
God. With him they live; with him they converse, by day and by
night; to the Lord they assign their prayers as dowries [. . .] Wives
of God while on earth, they are already counted as belonging to
the angelic family."[64] The idea also appears in the next-to-last
chapter of *On the Veiling of Virgins*. Wear the full garb of woman,
to preserve the standing of virgin. Tertullian not only approves of
the wearing of the veil, which was the traditional mark of marriage, but he wants it to be the norm even for unmarried women:
it will be the sign of marriage with Christ. A sign with a dual function: to hide, as must be hidden those who belong only to their

husbands; and to manifest the fact of this belonging, as it must be manifested. "Hide some of your inward consciousness, in order to exhibit the truth to God alone. And yet you do not belie yourself in appearing as a bride. For wedded you are to Christ: to him you have surrendered your flesh; to him you have espoused your maturity. Walk in accordance with the will of your Espoused. Christ is he who bids the wives and future wives of others veil themselves; and of course, he desires the practice that much more when it comes to his own."[65] But Tertullian's purpose with this whole text, as we've seen, is not to give virginity a special status; on the contrary, it's a matter of entering it into a general discipline among the different forms of continence and chastity.[66]

Later, though, the status of wife of Christ will be reserved for virginity alone, not only as a privilege, but as an experience defined by a particular content. With two possible meanings, however: the virgin promised to Christ is the entire Virgin Church, or it is the individual soul of one who has renounced the world. The Hymn that concludes Methodius's *Banquet* is significant in this regard. The company of virgins sing the chorus, each on her own account and for all the others: "I keep myself pure for You, O Bridegroom, and holding a lighted torch I go to meet You!" But they are also the attendants of the Virgin Church, and their song heralds the coming of Christ who will marry her: "O blessed spouse of God, we attendants of the Bride honor You, O undefiled virgin Church of snow-white form, dark haired, chaste, spotless, beloved."[67] It seems that the theme of the individual soul, which, in the experience of virginity, becomes the bride of Christ, separates off from the church theme without the latter disappearing—far from it—and without ending the symbolic references back and forth between the two. In any case, the virgin as the Lord's fiancée is constantly present in the authors of the fourth century, whether in Gregory of Nyssa—"she lives with the incorruptible Spouse";[68] Basil of Ancyra;[69] Eusebius of Emesa—"virgins are not the servants of men; they are the wives of Christ";[70] Ambrose—"among the candidates to the heavenly realm, you have advanced as if to marry the king . . .";[71] or Chrysostom—"there is no spouse that is similar or equal to him; no one approaches him even a little."[72] Historians are well aware of the scope that this theme will take on

throughout the development of Christian doctrine, and of how it
will dominate an entire aspect of it.

I would only like to note here, in a very schematic way, some
of the directions it will take and which are already indicated in the
twentieth chapter of Gregory of Nyssa's treatise on the two marriages. There are two possible but utterly incompatible unions:
one is carnal marriage, the other spiritual marriage. The first
should be understood as physical union with a human being, but
also, in a general way, as attachment to the world of which marriage strictly speaking is at the same time a component, a cause,
and a symbol. The marriage that affords access to spiritual realities and forms the link with them can come about only through
a renunciation of this first type of marriage. And by calling "virginity" that renunciation in its two forms, particular and general,
Gregory of Nyssa can say that virginity is a "collaborator and pro-
vider"[73] of the spiritual marriage. Basil of Ancyra gives a more
figurative turn to the same idea: the virgin who is betrothed to
the Lord is often subjected to the solicitations of those who are
only his servants; but she can't be accepted unless she rejects all
these advances, which are so many insults to her fiancé.[74] In short,
the marriage with Christ is exclusive of any other, whether it's a
matter of no other marriage in the strict sense or, symbolically, of
severing ties with the world.

These spiritual nuptials are not designated as such merely
from the fact that a union is involved. Like all marriages, they
are part of a system of exchanges that constitute for each of the
two spouses both the expected reward and the necessary sacrifice.
What can the soul contribute when it offers itself as the Bride?
Youth? Then this will be the rejuvenation, "the renewal of the
spirit," brought about by conversion. Wealth? This won't be
earthly goods but "heavenly treasures." Good birth? This will not
be the birth that fate determined, but the one that is acquired by
virtue. Finally, strength and good health? It will be those acquired
by strength of mind and weakening of the body.[75]

One has to understand that this union is sustained by an
enthusiasm which, while it mustn't be at all physical, is desire and
love nonetheless; and it leads to a possession and to the real presence of one being in the other: "When 'Christ is all, and in all'

(Col. 3:11) it is equally reasonable that he who is enamored of wisdom should hold the object of his passionate desire, who is the true wisdom; and that the soul which cleaves to the incorruptible Bridegroom should have the fruition of her love for the true wisdom, which is God."[76] While Gregory of Nyssa evokes this theme of spiritual desire as a principle of the soul's ascent, Chrysostom develops the other aspect of the same theme, the attraction that draws the Bridegroom to the beauty of the virgin soul: "For the gaze of the virgin is so beautiful and comely that it has as a lover not men but the incorporeal powers and their master." So great is this interior beauty that it transfigures the body itself and illuminates it, producing the inverse form of physical desire, respect: "Such is the modesty surrounding the virgin that the intemperate, ashamed and blushing, check their frenzy when they look at her attentively [. . .] Like a costly perfume, the fragrance of the virginal soul flowing round the senses gives proof of the excellence stored within."[77] Finally, this union, which is the content of the state of virginity, is fertile—with a fertility free of pain, the richness of which is evoked in another passage by Gregory of Nyssa: "Conception is no more an iniquity, nor child-bearing a sin; and births shall be no more of bloods, or of the will of man, or of the will of the flesh, but of God alone. This is always happening whenever any one in a lively heart conceives all the integrity of the spirit."[78]

I'm aware that this sketch may appear much too schematic or too loose. By focusing on a few important traits of the virginity mystique in the fourth century, I meant to show that the very intense valorization of a total, original, and definitive abstinence from sexual relations didn't have the structure of a prohibition; it doesn't simply constitute the expansion of a restrictive economy of the body's pleasures. Christian virginity is something very different from a radical or more extreme expression of a recommended continence which was a familiar feature of moral philosophy in antiquity and which the first Christian centuries had inherited.

It's true that one sees the theme of virginity, in the strict sense, emerge little by little from a prescription of sexual abstinence that is recommended to everyone with a varying intensity, without being obligatory for anyone. But if it emerges from that, it also differentiates itself from it. Because the continence principle does have the negative form of a rule or at least a general recommendation, whereas virginity, as Methodius of Olympus's dialogue already shows, designates a positive and complex experience, which is reserved for a few and takes the form of a choice. A choice that doesn't involve just one aspect of human behavior but all of life, and which is capable of transfiguring it. From continence to virginity, a negative and general recommendation is turned into a positive and particular experience.

The virginity mystique is connected with a conception of the history of the world and the metahistory of salvation. An important change relative to an ancient perspective: in effect, the latter linked sexual relations, desire, and procreation to the natural world, of which they were a component. Clement of Alexandria remained faithful to this vision by establishing a whole set of close relations between procreation and Creation. But with the theme of paradisiacal virginity, one sees a break assert itself between Creation and procreation—a break enabling sexual activity to play a role in the history of the world: its purpose is to prevent death from completely triumphing; it has to populate the earth, before disappearing in its turn when, with the Incarnation, the time of redemption has come. The age of virginity, which is also that of the world's completion, brings to an end a time when the Law, death, and the union of the sexes were linked to one another. And the practice of virginity thus assumes a completely different meaning from that of the relations between individual abstinence and the mechanisms of nature. Finally, the mystique of virginity [introduced into the domain of acts]* a caesura that projects in the form of spiritual figures a set of movements, unions, ties, and generations that correspond term by term to sexual desires, acts, and relations.

The valorization of virginity is therefore something very different and much more than the pure and simple disqualification or prohibition of sexual relations. It involves a substantial valorization of the individual's relation to their own sexual conduct, since it makes this relation a positive experience, which has a historical,

---

* Manuscript: These words are crossed out.

metahistorical, and spiritual meaning. To make things quite clear: it is not a matter of saying that there was a positive valorization of the sexual act in Christianity. But the negative value that was clearly attributed to it is part of an ensemble that gives the relation of the subject to their sexual activity an importance which Greek or Roman morality would never have dreamed of. The central place of sex in Western subjectivity is clearly marked by the formation of this mystique of virginity.

One sees, then, that in the fourth century the themes of virginity as a spiritual experience, in such authors as Gregory of Nyssa, Chrysostom, or Ambrose, are very close in their essentials to those developed by Methodius of Olympus, even if they differ from them, or diverge from each other, on many points of exegesis. But the most noticeable, and the most important, difference relates to what Gregory of Nyssa called "the art and the science"[79]—that is, virginity as a form, a technique, a deliberate and diligent construction of the relation to oneself. The fourth-century authors were not the first to say that the practice of virginity requires effort, that it is not simply an abstinence decided once and for all but a constant labor. But they gave this principle a privileged status, in three ways. First, they treated it extensively. Basil of Ancyra recalls in reference to it that "the heavenly kingdom belongs to the strong."[80] Chrysostom emphasizes that many "recoil from the thought of those exhausting efforts it demands";[81] he recognizes "the difficulty of the undertaking," "the strain of the fight, the heavy burden of this war."[82] On that basis, the traditional opposition between the drawbacks of marriage and the tranquility of the state of virginity is elaborated. All through Chrysostom's treatise one can find a chiasmal opposition: marriage is presented as a cause of troubles and worries, whereas virginity brings a calm clarity to the soul; but virginity is a hard, unending struggle, while marriage is an easy path—harbor and respite, which the virgin, always on the high seas, braving the storms, cannot know.[83] The harshness of the state of virginity is then compared, according to two metaphors that run through all the ascetic literature of the epoch, to the soldier's battles and the gymnast's exercises. Virgins are a city under siege: they need "eyes always open, much patience, strong defenses, external walls and barriers, watchful and high-minded guards"; night and day their thoughts must be on a war footing; everywhere one must find them "fortified."[84] Or further, the virgin is an athlete who has to face a rival: there are "two choices, either to leave with a crown or, having fallen, to retire with dishonor."[85]

Virginity is clearly situated among the ascetic practices in this way, and comes under the same principle as all the others: it cannot be brought to fruition without the intervention of a director. Methodius of Olympus only evoked a circle of women with one of them victorious over the others—though all of them excelled—by her doctrine and her example. Cyprian for his part exhorted, gave advice, and, with his views, assisted those who had chosen this path. He stressed the importance of a discipline that he saw as an "observance" of the Scripture on which the whole religion was based. Various homilies also emphasize the role of the father and mother in regard to those of their children who had embraced the state of virginity.[86] Gregory of Nyssa devotes the whole last chapter of his treatise *On Virginity* to the need to learn the rules of this state from a mentor.

He gives several reasons for this that are all based on the general principle that in this art error is more serious than in any other, since the object it aims for is ourselves and by going wrong in this domain one harms the soul and exposes oneself to death.[87] That one can't rely on oneself is explained first by the fact that the state of virginity and the rules to be observed are not inscribed in nature. In a way, says Gregory, it's a matter of learning a "foreign language." In relation to man who follows nature, virginity as a type of life (*diagôgê*) has the character of a "novelty."[88] But Gregory goes further: virginity is not simply positioned as a break with nature, it is something of an art, like medicine, for example. It would be impossible, and foolish and dangerous, to learn the latter by oneself. It has gradually revealed itself through experiments, and the observations of forerunners serve as precepts for the future. But looking at this more closely, one sees that Gregory is not using medicine merely as a term of comparison. He recalls that philosophy is an art that heals souls—it's a cure for "every passion that afflicts the soul." And, as a little earlier he has designated the state of virginity as a divine philosophical path, it should be understood that this art is, in the strict sense and at least in certain of its aspects, a way of taking care of one's own soul.[89] A young soul could not practice it alone without exposing itself to errors: the result of ignorance, but also of the lack of a principle of moderation;[90] left to its own devices, the soul flirts with danger from the very fact of its enthusiasm: "Some in their enthusiasm for the stricter life have shown a dexterous alacrity; but, as if in the very moment of their choice they had already touched perfection, their pride has had a shocking fall, and they have foolishly deluded themselves concerning that beauty to which their own mind inclined them."[91] Thus, in this passage that introduces the last chapter of Gregory's treatise on virginity, one re-encounters several of the arguments that served to justify the practice of direction in general, as we have seen.

As for the director's role, Gregory of Nyssa contrasts it positively with written lessons, insisting that in the art of virginity, one must be guided by "practice."[92] Actually, the text is extremely elliptical about the instruction that helps one learn this difficult state. It speaks mainly about the role of example giver.[93] But it does so in two senses: on the one hand, it's a matter of a model, a "canon" for our lives. Gregory presents him as a coryphée whose attendants imitate his gestures; but on the other hand, he also speaks of him as a beacon, a goal on which one keeps one's eyes fixed, because it's in him that one can see what the state of virginity is when it has finally "reached the port of divine will": those who've arrived there "keep their soul tranquil in peace and serenity." They remain fearless far from the tumult of the waves; their life's brilliance forms signals of fire, as it were.[94] So here one re-encounters the theme of virginal tranquility, magnified and carried to its completion. But in fact the role of the director, in the labor that's done, the exercises and battles that pervade this state and sustain it, doesn't appear with any clarity, nor do the techniques he employs, the rules or advice that he gives.

# 3

# Virginity and Self-Knowledge

This direction of virginal life is explicit, however, in other texts. I will take examples of this from two texts. One is Eastern, independent of the monastic institutions and addressed to women: it's the treatise *On the Integrity of Virginity* which figured among the works of Basil of Caesarea, and which since the beginning of this century is attributed to Basil of Ancyra. As for the second example, I will borrow it from the chapters that Cassian, in the *Institutes* and the *Conferences*, devotes to the problems of purity in monastic existence. Very different, then, in their context and their inspiration, they nonetheless both testify to the development of the "techniques of the self" during the fourth century and to the place these techniques occupy in the practice of virginity.

I

Basil of Ancyra's text has been dated to the middle of the fourth century—before 358 in any case. It evokes its own context as early as the first lines, by referring to the development of ascetic practices (abandonment of goods, fasts, austerities like sleeping on the ground). But it distinguishes itself, with an insistence that was frequent in that period, from the literature of praise: it presents itself as a practical text. Which doesn't mean that it has no stake in the themes that one finds in the spirituality of the fourth century. The figure of the Bridegroom Christ, suggested in the first words of the text, keeps returning throughout.[1] The idea of this marriage, with the beauty of the Bride, the love she has for her Lord, the faithfulness that is demanded of her, the desire she must have to please him, is treated extensively.[2] One also finds the affirmation that through virginity the soul is made incorruptible and that it can thus lead the life of the angels here on earth.[3] Reference is also made to two ages, that of marriage inaugurated by Adam, and that of the future world whose seeds were sown by Christ in the form of virginal purity.[4] From this standpoint the treatise of Basil of Ancyra is in direct continuity with the major spiritual texts on virginity.

But the fact remains that its objective is to establish the means in relation to a goal:[5] it's not a matter of teaching those who have already acquired knowledge of the good, but of showing those who feel the love of it how to attain this goodness which they desire. A book of living, therefore, that doesn't define a systematic body of rules: no reference is made to monastic institutions. There is just an indication, in the first lines, that the work is intended for those who, thanks to the bishop Letoius (whom Basil is addressing), have experienced a love of the good, but nothing suggests that this refers to an established community.[6] Only the unfolding of the text shows, without any justification or supplementary explanation, that it constitutes life prescriptions for women. So in this regard it is close to the practical works written, in the second half of the century, by Evagrius Ponticus, by Pseudo-Athanasius, or by Ambrose. It differs from them, however, in that Basil relies on a whole collection of medical knowledge that he evokes with a certain detail, and consequently he has far less to say about rules of comportment (although he does mention them) than about techniques, procedures, and ways of doing and being that concern the soul and the body in their relations. More than one's dress and the company one keeps, it is sensations, desires, images, and memories that form the object of the book. It is more a question of one's relationship with oneself than of the right attitude to have toward others or of one's behavior in their midst. And when Basil stresses the necessary renunciation of all adornments and all forms of elegance, he has recourse, next to the argument we're familiar with (a woman can be pleasing to God only as God has made her[7]), [to another argument]: all of this body care induces sensations, images, and desires in the soul, not only of the spectators, but of the woman who indulges in it.

The art of virginity, according to Basil of Ancyra, presents two aspects. First, it comprises what could be called a technology of separation or rupture.

An interruption first of natural desire. Basil explains the attraction of the sexes by a general principle that holds in the same way among human beings and among the animals. In order to populate the earth, God made use of "prototypical germs" to which he gave the possibility of reproducing themselves by separating a "segment" from the body of the males; this segment constitutes the female with which the masculine individual tries to reunite. To this tendency toward reunification, Basil gives two forms in turn: mutual attraction, which seems to place male and female in a symmetrical position (ontologically, these are two parts of the same individual); and the male's drive toward the female, which, through a "physiological" dissymmetry, places the principle of attraction on one side, and the force of movement on the other. The female is like the magnet; the male like the metal. The woman is passive, since it's toward her that the male directs itself; but she is also a principle of movement, since she is the site of the pleasure that attracts—which ensures moreover that the greater strength on the masculine side is softened and mitigated by the desire to protect. In any case, in this natural dynamic (to describe it, Basil makes only a very distant allusion to the Scripture, the scheme of reference is borrowed from natural history), one sees that the feminine part is in a privileged "strategic" position. Locus of attraction, but herself immobile, the woman can interrupt this movement that is inscribed in nature from the beginning. Such is the role of the virgin: to be the point of rupture in this general process of attraction.

But why would such a rupture be necessary since, if one is to believe Basil, this attraction results only from the will of God? Because souls that in themselves are equal and identical in nature, hence without sexual differentiation,[8] are affected by the movements of the body to which they are connected. They receive, as it were, the impregnation of their corporeal sex, becoming masculine or feminine, and they can accede to the love of the incorporeal

God only by breaking off these affections. Basil gives two forms to this rupture, both of which, although each in a different way, are based on the idea of a certain equivalence between pleasure as a principle of attraction between the sexes, and pleasure as a general form of darkening or weighing down of the soul by the body. Basil first explains that pleasure (*hedônê*) is generically unique, that consequently it's necessary to dominate not only the pleasure that drives us to the union of the sexes, but also all the others as well. And since the flow of pleasure doesn't cease to come and go, to become agitated and bring its disturbance through the five senses and even to tangible objects, and from these, turning back on the soul, it is necessary—and this will be a crucial component of the art of virginity—to watch these entrances and exits and channels, to stay vigilant at the gate of the senses. A whole economy of these pleasure flows must be constructed by focusing one's attention on the boundaries of the body and the outside world, on these organs of perception and what they may perceive. An economy of the gaze, which mustn't be directed haphazardly to everything the eyes can capture; an economy of hearing, which mustn't attend to everything that is said, but to what it would be useful to learn. What is recommended, in short, is a selective closing off of the body to the external world, in response to a danger intrinsic to the pleasure urges that disturb and in a certain way "sexualize" the soul. Now, among these senses that need to be closed at least partially, there is one to which Basil gives a central importance. It's the sense of touch. For two reasons, he says: The sense of touch is more powerful than the others for giving rise to the pleasures of sex. It is also important for tasting (which Basil seems to consider a kind of touching), and food and drink are among the most important factors for stimulating the sexual pleasures. Second and foremost, the sense of touch functions as the general form of all the senses. In each of them, it is touch that imprints the soul with the image of the external things whose different kinds touch the body; it is what makes them spread through the body and trouble the soul. The sense of touch constitutes the general medium, as it were, of the whole corporeal sensitivity. It is more or less present, more or less active, more or less determinant in every form of sensation. So if one intends to control the movement of the pleasures that stream through all the sensory channels, one should pay the most attention to touch. "Avoid contacts": a precept that must be understood in the precise sense of the word. Basil cites several applications of this: avoid embraces, contacts between men and women, even brothers and sisters, while those taking place between two persons of the same sex are without danger.[9] But it should also be understood in a more general way: reduce the strength of the body, weaken its responses, make sure that its impulses don't move the soul too forcefully, due to its excessive vigor. And more generally still: avoid the contact of the body as a whole (as the site of all contact) with the soul. This theme of separation between body and soul, their reciprocal isolation, returns in different forms throughout the text: image of the soul that must carefully close its windows, instead of being like the prostitutes who keep theirs wide open and always show themselves there;[10] of the master of the house who keeps his door locked shut when the soldiers try to get in to find lodging;[11] of water and oil that must stay separated to avoid being troubled.[12] Let the soul and the body remain carefully separated, therefore: by keeping them both "in their place, in their role, and in accordance with their use," one will make peace reign between them.[13]

But for Basil these different procedures of separation—of the senses with respect to sensible things, of the body with respect to the world, and of the soul with respect to the body—are only one side of the art of virginity. A whole other aspect concerns the soul itself and the work it must do on itself. That the purity of the body is nothing without that of the soul is a very traditional theme to which Basil gives several forms. That of the dual purity: one must bring as much attention to bear on the movements of the soul as on those of the body: "if through fasting we cut off the passions of the body, but leave the soul agitated by its own weaknesses, by envy, hypocrisy, and the movements of the other passions, we will not make the body's abstinence useful to virtue. And if we cleanse the soul of its passions, but we give the body over to the passions of the belly and other raptures, even without the disorder of inde-cency, we cannot make our life perfect in virtue."[14] That of the fundamental purity of the soul, which constitutes the primary and determining element compared to the integrity of the body: "For if the soul is free of corruption, the body also is preserved without corruption; but if the soul has been corrupted by bad thoughts, even if the body still appears to be without corruption, no purity will be found in its absence of corruption, since it is corrupted by impure thoughts."[15] Finally, regarding physical castration, Basil puts forward the principle of the sinful intention. Not only is there no merit in physically making oneself a voluntary eunuch, but such a one is to be considered a sinner because he refuses to ensure the virginity of his own soul and hence he consents to the desire without allowing himself the act: "the removal of parts denounces the adultery of the one who mutilates himself," "therefore, if he has disarmed himself by cutting off the instrument of adultery, so that people think he doesn't fornicate with his body, but he fornicates in his intention."[16]

So a specific effort of purification is necessary, in addition to all the abstentions, separations, and closures required by the purification of the body. Basil first raises the question of the persistence of images: objects that strike the senses may very well disappear, but their image remains in the soul. They are like those flaming javelins that carry fire to the target where they stay stuck, or they imprint a trace that remains, as if on wax. Therefore, since it's not possible to keep the eyes of the body always closed, one must take care not to retain such images. It wouldn't serve any purpose to fast if one continued to cultivate those thoughts. What soul could be called virgin if it kept the one that it loves in an embrace "with the incorporeal hands of thought"? The body, which is always mingled with the soul and which follows its movements, would thus be corrupted by it and would accompany it in its dreams.[17] So it's necessary to work constantly to erase such images and replace them, on the wax of the soul, with meditations on holy things with their figures or "characters."[18]

But one must also consider that acts can be committed in the soul. An act is not necessarily done by the body. However, here Basil is not referring to a juridical conception that would make the complete intention equivalent to the implementation of the idea itself. He is utilizing a physiology of the soul according to which thoughts will be inscribed on the soul's "table," where they will not be erased, even if forgetfulness or inattention shrouds them in darkness. Every thought is an act, and remains an act in the soul, inasmuch as its pattern subsists there. Basil resorts to a comparison with the signs of writing: one who learns them inscribes them in one's soul and doesn't need to actually write in order for the words to remain there. Without this inscription, how could one write what one desires to write? In the same way, thoughts are entered like so many marks in the soul. And when death comes, and the soul is set free, then all this abbreviated writing of thoughts, which had remained veiled, will appear in the light of day. And none of the acts of thought, even the most secret ones, will escape the eyes of the one who sees all. The soul that wishes to remain virgin must continually watch over even the most secret activity of its thought.

Finally, purity of the soul cannot be ensured without a constant vigilance concerning what it harbors within it that may be deceptive. It always runs the risk of being fooled, of being taken by surprise. This may happen through the interplay of resemblances and contrary natures that hide beneath analogous forms. Basil takes up the Greek adage that vices are closely akin to virtues and reinterprets it in terms of the devil's tricks: at the door of each virtue, the devil has placed a door of vice that looks just like it. You think you're knocking on the first one and it's the other one that opens. So those who meant to be courageous reveal themselves to be fearful.[19] But there can also be deception through proximity: the soul believes it loves the Lord and becomes enamored of his servants; or it begins by loving the beauty of a soul, but as the latter is manifested through the bodies that one looks at, the voices one listens to, the soul "comes to love, instead of the soul that speaks, that by which it speaks"[20]—somewhat as if, instead of loving a musician, one fell in love with their instrument.

We have seen how important these three points—persistence of images, spontaneous movements of thought, and illusions and resemblances—were in spiritual direction. Basil gives a justification, a model, and a sanction for this degree of vigilance in regard to these points, by emphasizing the principle of total visibility of the soul. A visibility that is "materialized" by the table where all movements produced in the soul are inscribed in durable marks, but a visibility that is actualized in three ways: in the future, death will deliver the soul's truth and reveal it on the day of eternal light;

but God can always see into the depths of our soul—no movement, no matter how secret, can elude him;[21] and the guardian
angel is also always watching over the soul: for the [virgin*] he is
always the guide that will lead the soul to the Bridegroom.[22] And
beyond him, one must think of the armies of all the angels and the
spirits of all the fathers. They are all watching everything, everywhere. Down to its least folds, therefore, the soul is not only visible but actually seen. This gaze, or rather these countless gazes,
are not its own. The soul will ensure its virginity if, to the extent
possible, it strives to see itself and watch over everything that takes
place within it, in the same manner as all the other gazes that scan
its secrets without obstruction. During the period when Basil of
Ancyra is writing, the monastic institutions are in full development;
but in a more general way, a whole regulated, carefully designed,
and controlled practice of asceticism has spread. It is hard to say
whom exactly the treatise he addresses to Letoius is meant for. But
the advice he gives and the unsystematic prescriptions he proposes
focus on the same essential points as the spiritual direction and
examination of conscience that will appear in slightly later texts.
Through this treatise, one sees the practice of virginity, which had
been extricated from the principle of continence and defined as a
positive spiritual experience, being organized as a *type of relation
to the self* that concerns not just the body, but also the relations of
the body and the soul, the opening of the senses, the movement
of pleasures through the body, the agitation of thoughts. One also
sees it open onto a *domain of internal knowledge* where it is a question of sensation, of images and their persistence, of everything
in the soul that can escape others or oneself through the effect of
delusion or the subtlety of the process. Finally, one sees it being
inscribed in a *relation to the power of the other* and to the gaze that
marks the individual's subjugation and an objectification of their
inner being.

By pointing to these processes in connection with Basil of
Ancyra's text, I'm not suggesting that they appear there for the
first time, nor certainly that this is where the transformation that
gave rise to them occurred. I have taken a bit of time with the text

* Manuscript: "virginity"

only because it attests to the existence, in the middle of the fourth century and in an ill-defined pastoral practice, of a rather well-developed technique of the self. I have also focused on it because one sees a whole domain (involving the body and the soul, sensations, images, and thoughts) being constituted in which it is considered necessary to intervene in order for the exclusion of sexual relations to take on the positive meaning expected of it—the essential practical correlate of that abstinence. It is evident that while the practice doesn't involve either the totality of the body or the soul, it is operative in both, from the grasping of an object by the senses to the most secret impulses of the heart.

## II

Cassian's analysis is very different from that of Basil of Ancyra. Its frame of reference is constituted by monastic practice—the cenobium for the text of the *Institutes*, which is concerned with beginners for the most part; and the monastic life for the *Conferences*, which talk about much more advanced spiritual experiences. In any case, Cassian's views, the rules and prescriptions he puts forward, apply to a form of life in which the renunciation of every form of sexual relations has already been carried out. So at his level there is no longer any reason to consider the privileges of the state of virginity over that of marriage; it's a question of elaborating on the implications of the choice that was made. Cassian rarely employs the word *virginity*. It appears twice in the *Conferences*, and in both instances in contrast with marriage: regarding Elijah and Jeremiah who "might without blame have taken advantage of lawful matrimony, yet they preferred to remain virgins";[23] and in reference to the foolish virgins and the wise virgins, who are all called virgins because they have no spouses, but the first practice only the virginity of the body.[24] The term used is "chastity"—*castitas*—which in Cassian covers most of the questions or themes that Gregory of Nyssa, Basil of Ancyra, Chrysostom, and in a general way the Greek Fathers connected to the practice of virginity and the interior rules of that state.

Just as his predecessors had done for virginity, Cassian distinguishes chastity from continence. In the *Institutes*, he bases this distinction on the traditional usage of the Greek words and at the same time he takes note of the hierarchy of values between the two terms: "We do not deny that there are also continent men in the communities: such a thing can easily be done, we know. In reality, they are two very different things, to be continent—that is *enkratês*—and to be chaste and, so to speak, to pass to that state of integrity or incorruption that is called *hagnos*, a virtue that is scarcely attributed to any but those who remain virgins in their flesh and in their minds, as were [. . .] Jeremiah and Daniel."[25] Between the two notions, there is the difference of the positive and the negative. On the one hand, external abstinence in regard to sex, on the other a motivation of the heart: "Purity of the flesh resides less in the deprivation of women than in the integrity of the heart that keeps the holiness of the heart free of corruption through the fear of God or the love of chastity."[26]

In the *Conferences*, Cassian returns to this distinction and comments more extensively. He gives it the same fundamental value: continence is a refusal, a rejection (*districtio*); chastity, a positive force that uplifts and that is sustained by "the delectation it takes in its own purity."[27] Thus, the pagans are capable only of continence. Socrates was not chaste, though he refrained from consummating the love he felt for boys: he did violence to his "bad desire" and to the "delight of his vice," without banishing them from his heart.[28] Yet this opposition is not exempt from a certain ambiguity. Cassian describes the reign of continence, in fact, as a moment that must last for as long as the slightest traces of the carnal passions remain: "So long as there remains an attraction to voluptuousness, one is not chaste but only continent [. . .] So long as we feel the rebellions of the flesh, let us recognize [. . .] that we are still under the miserable scepter of continence, tired out from continual battles, whose outcome necessarily remains in doubt."[29] Compared to these stresses of continence, chastity appears to be an end state in which one would no longer have to combat "the urges of carnal concupiscence";[30] then, and only then, the soul can become "the dwelling place of the Lord," which is never in "the battles of continence," but in "the peace of chastity."[31] Now, Cassian emphasizes throughout his work—and it's precisely the theme of the twenty-second *Conference* on chastity—the fact that the struggle against the assaults of the flesh can never be considered finished. "We also have a body, which is a poor beast of burden."[32] Not only do the attacks resume when one believes them defeated, but, as will be seen, their menace has a positive value for virtue: sometimes they are the blessing of God, who does not want us to doze off in the tranquility of the soul. So that chastity as a spiritually different state than continence constitutes an ideal point toward which one must advance indefinitely, without being sure that it is completely attainable.[33] But Cassian also depicts it in relation to continence (a negative attitude of refusal) as a positive force that overlays the latter, sustains it, animates it, and transforms simple abstinence into a movement of ascension toward God: "One cannot control or banish the desire for present things, if in the place of harmful penchants, that one aspires to do away with, one doesn't put salutary ones [. . .] We want to rid our heart of the lusts of the flesh: for all its incontinence, let us hand the place over to spiritual joys."[34]

Hence chastity is to be conceived in terms of a state and in terms of a combat: a tranquility that nothing can trouble any longer—but it's already no longer "a human virtue or an earthly one; it seems to be, rather, the privilege of heaven, the particular gift of the angels";[35] and also a force of confrontation that demands ardor and passion if one is to triumph, plus a desire that is not completely unrelated to the very desire that it strives to combat. To attain chastity, says Cassian in a remarkable text, "let everyone be passionate [. . .] with the same love that is seen in the miser devoured by greed, the ambitious man driven by his thirst for honors, in the man consumed by his passion for a feminine beauty, when, in the grip of an excessive impatience, they seek to satisfy their desire."[36]

In spite of his many points in common with the major theorists of virginity of the fourth century, the distinction that Cassian establishes between continence and chastity reveals a rather different landscape. It is dominated by the notions of *purity of heart* and *spiritual combat*, which are especially meaningful in the monastic life from which Cassian, following Evagrius, draws his inspiration.

1. *Purity of heart.* Cassian never makes use of the vocabulary of marriage, which was so constant from Methodius of Olympus to Chrysostom, to designate the state of virginity in its plenitude.

It's true that he sometimes uses terms that come close. Among the main ones, there are four that we can note. Cassian speaks of the union that joins the soul with God;[37] of the "fusion" that makes it "melt" into him;[38] of the Lord's sovereign entry into it;[39] of a movement by which he grasps the soul and takes possession of it.[40] However, it's not the sexual union of two individuals that serves as an implicit or explicit model for this experience, but the act of understanding (*connaissance*) considered as a relation between gaze, object, and light. For Cassian, the soul joined to God is not the bride-to-be finally reunited with the Bridegroom. Rather, it is the gaze that is not distracted from the point on which it has fastened, that remains so firmly attached in this way that it no longer sees anything else. When he speaks of the soul that melts into God, Cassian is not thinking of the bride absorbed in the spiritual union, but of the act of contemplation that is at one with, the same thing as, what is contemplated. As for the presence of God in the soul he takes possession of in its entirety, Cassian is not picturing the presence of the Lord on the marriage bed, but the descent into the soul of the beam of light that illuminates it, leaving no part of it in the shadows.

Recall that the monastic life whose art and discipline Cassian defines has contemplation as its goal. One who renounces the world seeks to attain that "principal good" which is established "in theory, that is, in contemplation." When the soul has entered that state, it will have "no other food than the knowledge of God and the joy of his beauty." The knowledge relation underlies the soul's relation to God. And even at the moment when the relation becomes a junction, a fusion, a possession, it's still in the form of knowledge, or more exactly according to the model of the gaze and the light, that Cassian theorizes it. Consequently, for him chastity doesn't have the same role that virginity has in the authors I spoke of previously. For them, it was a matter of preserving integrity that would allow the soul to reach the Bridegroom without ever experiencing any defilement. For Cassian, the role of chastity is to ensure a "purity of heart" or a "purity of mind" that makes the knowledge relation possible: such that there is no cloudiness in one's gaze, nothing shadowy escaping the light, no stain to mar the transparency. In sum, Cassian, like Evagrius,

replaces the series virginity-integrity-spiritual nuptials that one
finds clearly developed in authors like Basil of Ancyra with the
series chastity–purity of heart–contemplation.

The relation of chastity is developed, then, according to two
axes. First, chastity appears as an essential prerequisite of spiritual
science. No one can hope to arrive at the latter if one doesn't start
by practicing the chastity that results in purity of heart. From the
beginning of the *Institutes*, Cassian, in explaining the meaning of
monastic dress, shows that the girdle (which signifies the desire
to destroy all the seeds of lust) attests to the ascetic's ardor "for
spiritual progress and the science of divine things that purity of
heart gives."[41] But it's in the fourteenth *Conference*, that of Abbot
Nesteros, that Cassian gives this theme its full scope. Spiritual
knowledge demands purity of heart and chastity in the very general sense that it is incompatible with agitation of thought, the
disorderly movement of the imagination, and any concern with
the things of the world: "If you would prepare in your heart a
holy tabernacle of spiritual knowledge, purge yourselves from the
stain of all sins, and rid yourselves of the cares of this world. For
it is an impossibility for the soul which is taken up even to a small
extent with worldly troubles, to gain the gift of knowledge or to
become an author of spiritual interpretation, diligent in the reading of holy things."[42] But much more precisely, chastity as control
of the carnal passions in the strict sense is indispensable to spiritual science. The latter, like a perfume, cannot subsist in a soiled
container: "A jar once permeated by evil smells will more easily
contaminate the most fragrant myrrh than receive from it some
sweetness of capacity to please. Purity is corrupted more speed-
ily than corruption is made pure [. . .] So then if you are anxious
to win the incorruptible fragrance of Scripture, begin by turning
your effort to winning the cleanness of chastity from the Lord."[43]
Finally, it needs to be understood that the chastity of the body
is the first form of a series of "chastities" the mind must take on
in order to advance toward spiritual knowledge without ever losing sight of it. One must renounce fornication of the body if one
means to understand the Scriptures, but it's also necessary to stay
well away from that "fornication" constituted by pagan ceremonies, the soothsayers, the omens, and from that other fornication

which is the observance of the Judaic type of law, and from that other one still, that consists of heresy, and finally from the one that makes thought stray—however little—from God, on whom it should always stay focused. And as these different fornications are excluded and the mind becomes chaste in a more and more spiritual sense, the meaning of Scripture will emerge from its mysteries and will appear with increasingly spiritual values.[44] The practice of chastity and the comprehension of the Word grow in spirituality simultaneously. Cassian goes so far as to say, in the *Institutes*, that chastity, in its perfect form, suffices for understanding the Scripture. He speaks of Theodore, who owed his knowledge of the Text not so much to a "studious reading"—he understood just a few words of Greek—as "to purity of heart alone."[45] But this purity of heart is connected to knowledge according to a very different orientation: reflexively, involving the soul itself, its folds and its depths. In relation to this knowledge, purity is not simply a condition, it is at the same time an effect. No purity of heart if the soul doesn't watch attentively over itself, on the lookout for the impulses produced within it and blotting out everything that might divert it from its contemplation. But conversely, it's very much owing to purity that the interior gaze can penetrate into the heart's secrets, shining the light there and dispelling its obscurity: "Thus penetrating with pure eyes of the mind to the foul darkness of vices, we may be able to disclose them and drag them forth to light; and may succeed in explaining their occasions and natures."[46] Now, what needs to be noted in Cassian's analysis here is that the light brought into the heart doesn't illuminate it all at once, ridding it of all the impurities it may contain. Rather, it penetrates the darkness, revealing what may be hidden there. But what hides is impurity, and it is this impurity that one must gradually free oneself from through an attentive examination, a vigilance that never relents, a constant remorse and one's admission of that state. So that, through a circularity that is at the center of this asceticism of self-knowledge, the purer one is, the more light one has for knowing oneself better; the better one knows oneself, the more one recognizes how impure one is; the more one recognizes oneself as sullied, the more important it is to shine the light on one's deepest recesses and dispel the darkness of the soul. Evoking the great spiritual masters, those who never get entangled in "hollow debates" but have the experience and practice of virtue, Cassian says that purity "has taught them this above all: to recognize more and more that they are burdened with sin (for their compunction for their faults increases day by day in proportion as their purity of soul advances), and to sigh continually from the bottom of their heart because they see that they cannot possibly avoid the spots and blemishes of those faults which are ingrained in them through the countless triflings of the thoughts."[47]

In a passage of the *Conference* on prayer, the soul is compared to a feather: sins weigh it down, purity on the contrary gives it an ontological lightness that allows the slightest breeze to lift it toward the ether.[48] This is a way of emphasizing the fundamental relationship chastity has with light. But you can see that this relationship, in the practice of asceticism, assumes complex forms. Chastity is the condition of access for a comprehension of the Scripture, an opening to a spiritual meaning, a righteous direction of the mind, a steadiness of the soul's gaze in the contemplation of God. But this contemplation cannot be approached without a knowledge of ourselves with all our impurities; and in its turn, where would this knowledge draw its light and its strength if not from the Word of God, which shines into us and reveals us as we are without our being able to see it by ourselves? In this way it makes us "yield to our investigation and explanation (*indagini nostrae atque expositioni*)," and "thus breaking the gates of our ignorance, and cutting asunder the bars" of vices which shut us out from the true science, will lead us to the substance of our secrets, and reveal to us who have been illuminated, according to the Apostle's word, "the hidden things of darkness, and make manifest the thoughts of the heart."[49] So one must think of a twofold process of an illumination of the mysteries of the heart which is both the condition and the effect of the knowledge of God, and a progression toward the spiritual science that cannot be accomplished without the self-knowledge that it makes possible. And at the pivot point of these two processes, there is chastity.

2. *Spiritual combat.* The reference to spiritual combat is not absent from the fourth-century treatises on virginity. Discreet in

Gregory of Nyssa, it is much more frequent in John Chrysostom. It allows for a relation between the effort required by the profession of virginity and the theme of the martyr who goes through trials, triumphs, and receives the crown.[50] In Cassian, the notion of combat doesn't just have a reference value, it commands a part of the analysis.[51] After an exposition of the rules of monastic life, the whole second part of the *Institutes of the Coenobia* presents itself as a treatise on spiritual combat.[52] A battle that, as Cassian stresses over and over, evoking a text from the Epistle to Timothy (2:15), must be conducted in the proper way and according to the rules—a *legitimate* battle.[53] He is saying that the life of the monk, at least as long as he has not attained the tranquility of the contemplative life, as long as it is still an active life, must unfold as an unbroken combat whose weapons and tactics must be learned. The *Institutes* form the manual of this apprenticeship. It delivers its general rules, it specifies its particular forms according to the different adversaries that must be fought, and it underscores the need to adapt to the particular situations and forces of each battle. A general discipline that must include a principle of "discernment."[54]

What type of combat is involved? There is an array of terms that Cassian employs: *colluctatio*, *agon*, *certamen*, *pugna*, *bellum*. The first two words refer to the fight of an athlete who encounters a rival and, in order to defeat him, must have followed a training regimen, qualified, and employed the sanctioned moves against the rival that authorize him to finally receive the crown. But the other terms are borrowed from the vocabulary of warfare: rout the enemy, foil the stratagems, rebuff the assault of his troops. On the one hand, the spiritual struggle references the athletic model, on the other the military model. Actually, there is no discontinuity from the first to the second. A long passage of this chapter 5, which, in laying out the rules of the first battle to be waged (against gluttony), outlines the general method of struggle, is characteristic of this dual reference. It begins with a set of allusions to the practice of athletics and games: the training of the competitors, an examination after which the candidates are accepted, the method employed by the javelin throwers, the preparation and practice of the boxers, and so on.[55] But Cassian gradually transitions to the theme of the battle between enemies.

The soldier replaces the athlete: against him "troops," "cohorts of adversaries," that he must force back beyond the territory; there are enemies on the outside, but also enemies within who weaken him through "internecine struggles."[56] The intertwining of these two metaphors brings out two essential components of spiritual combat. First, as an athletic trial, this combat involves exercise, training, a will to surpass oneself, to work upon oneself, and the verification and measurement of one's own forces. Asceticism in the strict sense of the term. But as a war against an adversary (and moreover a tireless enemy, capable of every ruse, instead of a rival in an honest game), the struggle is waged against another. Insofar as it is athletic, the combat requires a certain way of relating to oneself. Insofar as it is warlike, it is a relation to an irreducible element of otherness.

What is this other, and against whom must the combat be waged? The second part of the *Institutes* (chapters 5–12) lists the eight necessary forms of combat and the eight adversaries: gluttony, fornication, avarice, anger, dejection, acedia, vainglory, pride. One will recognize this as an early draft of an enumeration that will become that of the seven capital sins.[57] But just as we shouldn't blend together capital sins and mortal sins, we shouldn't see in the eight adversaries designated by Cassian a kind of code of acts not to be committed, or laws whose violation will be punished. There is nothing structural or juridical in the exposition. It helps to recall that Cassian's list derives directly from Evagrius, and that the latter did not intend to draw up a table of faults or prohibitions; he sought to establish a typology of thoughts. "Eight," he said, "are the generic thoughts."[58] And those thoughts, insofar as they agitate the soul, disturb its tranquility, or muddy its gaze, are introduced there by the demons: *daimoniôdeis logismoi*. That such thoughts assail us is not our doing, therefore, but that of the demons. It is up to us, however, whether they linger or give rise to passions.[59]

Cassian doesn't employ the term "demon" but rather "spirit" (*spiritus*) to designate the eight adversaries into which the spiritual combat is subdivided: spirit of gluttony, spirit of fornication, spirit of avarice, and so on. His use of the great demonology, which was so important in Egyptian monasticism, is rather discreet. It's in the more speculative texts of the *Conferences* that he gives, not the general system of that demonology, [but] the indications necessary for understanding what these spirits are, what the origin and modes of action of these "adverse powers" are.[60] One musn't think that they penetrate the soul itself and take up residence there. Doubtless between them and the human soul there is a kinship and a similarity of nature, but the soul is impenetrable. The spirits can establish themselves only nearby, which is to say in a body, and more easily in a weakened body that accommodates them. Based on this material insertion, they create impulses which, in their turn, induce thoughts, images, memories, and so on. Insidiously, these thoughts develop in the soul all the more dangerously as their origin is hidden, so that everyone is likely to imagine that they come from within themselves. But that is not all: the demon can see how the soul reacts to such insinuations. Not that its gaze can penetrate the soul's interior, but by being alert in the body, it can observe, according to the movements that are produced there, the way in which the soul accepts or rejects the suggestions it makes. So it can pursue them, intensify them, modify them; it can also completely change its attacks, trying, after one "kind" of thoughts, a different kind altogether. So there is a complex game between the soul and its adversary, where thoughts are transmitted, repeated, accepted, retried though the intermediary of the body that sends and receives impulses. In these the Enemy detects signals that guide its action, and it's in them as well that the soul must recognize the signs of the adversary's presence. Spiritual combat is thus, by definition, a confrontation with the Other, a dynamic of impulses that pass from the soul to the body and vice versa, and finally, a task of decipherment in order to grasp what is lurking under the surface appearances of oneself.

As for the end of the combat, while it is defined ideally by the tranquility of the soul, its reality is ambiguous. Cassian does mention the possibility of reaching a state where the Enemy's assaults, after all its defeats, will have ceased. And he cites certain holy figures who arrived at this summit. But as we've seen,[61] such a state can never be considered either a vested right or an unassailable position. Many have fallen who thought they were out of harm's way and because they thought so. More exactly, because they believed that this protection was due to their own efforts, to their exercises, their progress, and their strength. In fact, though, their self-confidence is what exposed them, their security is what made them vulnerable. Those against whom the Enemy can no longer do anything are those who know that they can do nothing against the Enemy if God doesn't come to their aid: "Wherefore it is well for us both to be certified by actual experience, and also to be instructed by countless passages of Scripture, that we cannot possibly overcome such mighty foes in our own strength, and unless supported by the aid of God alone; and that we ought always to refer the whole of our victory each day to God Himself."[62] Consequently, the assaults of bad thoughts can be seen in a very different light: if they subsided, or even if they were always mild, the soul would soon fall asleep in its self-confidence or pride itself on being out of the Enemy's reach. Then the Enemy's power could defeat it by surprise, leaving it no possibility of resisting. So there is a positive value in the permanence and the intensity of the combat. Therefore, in this perpetual and pressing threat of evil, one must see a blessing. A result of God's beneficence. The conflict that rages in us is implanted "by the action and arrangement of the Lord [. . .] And in a way this conflict is useful to us, and calls and urges us on to a higher state: and if it ceased, most surely there would ensue on the other hand a peace that is fraught with danger."[63] Cassian is led in this way to complain about those who are chaste by nature: their lukewarmness endangers them. "Free from the needs of the flesh, they fancy that they have no need either of the trouble of bodily abstinence, or of contrition of heart; and being rendered slack by this freedom from anxiety, they make no efforts either truly to seek or to acquire perfection of heart or even purity from spiritual faults."[64] A basic paradox of spiritual combat: it can come to its conclusion only if it continues; if it ceases, it risks leading one to defeat. Its pains, its labor, its miseries are an indispensable blessing. Its reward in the form of tranquility would thus be a formidable danger. One cannot wage it without entrusting oneself entirely to God, and whoever would take refuge in his strength, without fighting with all one's own, would be abandoned by him.[65]

In this way the essential role of the notion of temptation

appears. Here again, it wasn't monastic spirituality that introduced the complex idea it constitutes. But monasticism certainly assigned it a very important function and organized some of the most decisive elements of its technology around it. Temptation is not in any way a juridical category: it is neither a transgression, nor the beginning of a transgression, nor even the intention to commit one. First, it is a *dynamic element* in the relations between the exterior and the interior of the soul. It is the insinuation into the soul of a thought that comes to it from a power other than itself. There is a temptation only because this thought is already present in the soul, a thought belonging to the soul; but in the soul it is the trace of a movement that comes from elsewhere, the effect of an alien will, which in the soul consists of a path laid down by an other. Next, it is a *dramatic episode* in the conflict, a battle or a phase of the battle that can be won or lost: the temptation can bring the desire along with it, or on the contrary give rise to the fervent will to neutralize it and distance oneself from it. Finally, it is *the object of a necessary analysis:* for if temptation is indeed an attack against the soul, whether violent or imperceptible, frontal or insidious, this attack may come from the devil (not without God providing that the Enemy can thereby lose his grip on the soul) or it may come from God (not without God seeking in this way to test the soul, to exercise and strengthen it, hence to save it). There is always at the heart of the temptation a secret to be uncovered: Satan may conceal himself under the guise of the good, by employing the evil ruses of illusion, but God, his will, and his beneficence are always present in the dangers that the soul risks, even if the soul in its blindness does not perceive this presence.

In actual fact, and it's an important fact, in the formation of the Christian ethic Christianity did not develop the technologies of the soul or the self around the category of sin, even in its broader or internalized sense, but around the notion of temptation, which is at the same time a dynamic element in the self's relations with the exterior, a tactical element of withdrawal or rejection, of generation or expulsion, an element of analysis that demands, in the reflection of oneself on oneself, a recognition of the other and of the interior figures that mask it.

The theme of chastity is thus caught between the principle of

a purity of heart that links it to the objective of divine contemplation and the task of knowing, and the principle of a spiritual combat that links it, through the notion of temptation, to the need to
detect the Other in the secrets of the soul.


Cassian analyzed the battle of chastity in the sixth chapter of
the *Institutes* ("On the Spirit of Fornication"), and in several of the
*Conferences:* the fourth one on "The Lust of the Flesh and of the
Spirit," the fifth on the "Eight Principal Vices," and the twenty-
second on "Nocturnal Illusions." It appears in the second position
on a list of the eight combats,[66] in the form of a struggle against
the spirit of fornication. As for this fornication, it is itself divided
into three subcategories.[67] A classification that is very juridical in
appearance if one compares it to the catalogues of sins that one
will find later, when the medieval Church has organized the sacrament of penance on the model of a juridiction. But it's clear that
the specifics set out by Cassian have a different meaning.

Let's start by examining fornication's place among the other
spirits of evil.

1. Cassian completes the classification of the eight spirits of
evil with internal regroupings. He establishes pairs of vices that
have special relations (of "alliance") and "commonality" between
them:[68] pride and vainglory, indolence and acedia, avarice and
anger. Fornication is paired with gluttony. For several reasons:
because they are two "natural" vices that are innate in us and that
consequently it is difficult to eradicate; because they are both vices
that involve the body's participation, in order not only to form but
to accomplish their objective; and because, finally, there are quite
direct causal links between them: the excess of food is what arouses
in the body the desire for fornication.[69] And, either because it is
strongly associated in this way with gluttony, or on the contrary
due to its own nature, the spirit of fornication plays a privileged
role, compared to the other vices it is in league with.

First of all, regarding the causal chain, Cassian underscores
the fact that the vices are not independent of each other, even if
each of them can be attacked, more specifically, through one of
the others.[70] A causal vector links them together: it begins with

gluttony, which originates with the body and kindles fornication; then this first pair engenders avarice, understood as attachment to earthly goods; which gives rise to rivalries, disputes, and anger; from which is produced the dejection of sadness, which provokes disgust with the whole monastic life and the listlessness of acedia. Such a concatenation assumes that one will never be able to vanquish a vice without triumphing over the one on which it depends. "If we always overcome the earlier ones, the later ones will be checked; and through the extermination of those that lead the way, the rest of our passions will die down without difficulty."[71] At the origin of the others, the gluttony-fornication pair, like "a tall spreading tree,"[72] must be uprooted—whence the ascetic importance of fasting as a means of defeating gluttony and cutting off fornication. It's where the ascetic exercise has its basis, because it is the beginning of the causal chain.

The spirit of fornication is also in a singular dialectical position in relation to the last vices listed, and pride in particular. Actually, for Cassian, pride and vainglory don't belong to the causal chain of the other vices. Far from being engendered by those, they are produced by the victory that one wins over them:[73] "carnal" pride toward others through the show that one makes of one's fasts, one's chastity, one's poverty, and the like, and "spiritual" pride that makes one think that this progress is due solely to one's own merits.[74] A vice connected with the defeat of vices, precipitating a fall all the heavier as it comes from on high. And fornication, the most shameful of all the vices, the most humiliating, is the consequence of pride—a punishment but also a temptation, a test that God sends to the presumptuous to remind them that the weakness of the flesh always threatens them if grace does not come to one's rescue. "Because one has long enjoyed purity of heart and body, as a natural consequence [. . .] deep inside oneself, one glorifies oneself to a certain extent [. . .] but, for one's good, the Lord acts as if he has abandoned him: the purity that gave him so much assurance begins to be clouded; in the midst of spiritual prosperity, he sees himself falter."[75] In the great cycle of combats, at the moment when the soul no longer has to struggle against itself, the goads of the flesh are felt anew, marking the necessary incompletion of this struggle and threatening it with a perpetual recommencement.

Finally, relative to the other vices fornication has a certain

ontological privilege, which confers a particular ascetic importance on it. Like gluttony, it has its roots in the body. Impossible
to vanquish it without subjecting it to austerities. Whereas anger
or dejection are combated "by the soul's industry alone," it cannot
be rooted out without "corporeal mortification, vigils, fasts, work
that breaks the body."[76] Which doesn't exclude, on the contrary,
the struggle that one must conduct against oneself, since fornication can spring from thoughts, images, memories: "The demon
through his subtle cunning has insinuated in our heart the memory
of woman, starting with our mother, our sisters, our relatives or
certain pious women, we must as quickly as possible rid ourselves
of this memory, for fear that if we delay too long, the tempter
will seize the occasion to make us think of other women before
we realize it."[77] However, fornication presents a major difference
from gluttony. The combat against the latter must be waged with
moderation since one cannot give up all nourishment: One must
exercise "the control necessary for life [. . .] lest the body should
be injured by our fault and unable to fulfill its spiritual and necessary duties."[78] We have to keep this natural penchant for nourishment at a distance, cope with it, not try to root it out: it has a
natural legitimacy; to totally deny it, fatally so, that is, would be
to "burden one's soul with a crime."[79] On the other hand, there is
no limit in the struggle against the spirit of fornication; everything
that leads us in that direction must be extirpated, and no natural
inclination can justify, in this domain, the satisfaction of an urge.
So it's a matter of completely doing away with a penchant whose
elimination does not cause the death of our body. Fornication is
the only one of the eight vices that is at the same time innate,
corporeal in origin, and that must be entirely destroyed like those
vices of the soul—avarice and pride. A radical mortification, consequently, which lets us live in our body while liberating us from
the flesh. "Leave the body while remaining in the body."[80] It's to
that beyond-nature, in earthly existence, that the struggle against
fornication gives us access. It "pulls us out of the earthly mire."
It allows us to live in this world a life that is not of this world.
Because it is the most radical, this mortification brings us, already
here below, the highest promise: "in the fragile flesh" it confers
"the citizenship which the saints have the promise of possessing
once they are delivered from carnal corruptibility."[81]

So one can see how fornication, while being one of the eight components of the table of the vices, is in a special position relative to the others: the head of the causal chain, at the origin of the falls and the combat, one of the most difficult and most decisive points of the ascetic struggle.

2. In the fifth *Conference*, Cassian divides the vice of fornication into three types. The first consists in the "intercourse of the two sexes" (*commixtio sexus utriusque*); the second is accomplished "without contact with a woman" (*absque femineo tactu*)—which got Onan his condemnation; the third is "conceived in heart and mind."[82] Almost term by term, the same distinction is reiterated in the twelfth *Conference:* carnal intercourse (*carnalis commixtio*), to which Cassian here gives the name *fornicatio* in the restricted sense; then impurity, *immundita*, which is produced without contact with a woman, when one is sleeping or keeping vigil, and is due to "the carelessness of a mind without circumspection";[83] finally, the *libido* that develops in the "recesses of the soul" and without there being any "corporeal passion" (*sine passion corporis*).[84] This specification is important because it is the only thing that enables us to understand what Cassian means by the general term *fornication*, to which moreover he does not give any overall definition. But it is important above all for the use he makes of these three categories, which is so different from that found in many earlier texts.

There existed a traditional trilogy of these sins of the flesh: adultery, fornication (which translated the Greek word *porneia* and designated extramarital sexual relations), and the corruption of children. It is these categories, in any case, that one finds in the *Didache:* "You will not commit adultery, you will not commit fornication, you will not seduce young boys."[85] They are the categories that one also finds in the letter of Barnabas: "Do not commit fornication or adultery; do not corrupt children."[86] It often happened subsequently that only the first two terms were retained—fornication designating all the sexual faults in general and adultery those that violate the obligation of faithfulness in marriage.[87] But in any case, it was completely customary to combine this enumeration with precepts concerning lustfulness in thought or in one's gaze, or everything that might lead to the consummation of a forbidden sexual act: "Be not a lustful one; for lust leads the way to fornication; neither a filthy talker, nor of brazen eye; for out of all these adulteries are engendered."[88]

Cassian's analysis has two particularities: not singling out adultery, which comes under fornication in the narrow sense; and above all focusing his attention only on the two other categories. Nowhere in the different texts where he evokes the chastity struggle does he talk about actual sexual relations. Nowhere are the different possible "sins" considered according to the act committed, the partner with whom one commits it, their age, their sex, the relations of kinship one might have with them. None of the categories that will constitute the great codification of the sins of lust in the Middle Ages appear here. Doubtless, Cassian, addressing monks who had made a vow to refrain from any sexual relation, did not need to revisit this prerequisite explicitly. It must be noted, however, that on an important point of the cenobium, one that had given rise in Basil of Caesarea or in Chrysostom to specific recommendations,[89] Cassian confines himself to brief allusions: "Let no person, especially the younger ones, remain with another, even for a little while, or leave with him or hold hands."[90] It's as if Cassian were interested only in the last two terms of his subdivision (concerning what happens without intercourse and without the body's passion), as if he were passing over fornication as a union of two individuals and attributing importance only to elements whose condemnation was previously only secondary to that of sexual acts as such.

But if Cassian's analyses omit sexual intercourse, if they operate in such a solitary world and on such an interior stage, the reason is not simply negative. It's that the main focus of the combat is on a target that is not in the domain of acts or relations: it involves a different reality from that of sexual relations between two individuals. A passage of the twelfth *Conference* allows us to grasp the nature of that reality. There Cassian characterizes the six stages that mark one's progress in chastity. Now, since with this characterization it's not a matter of showing chastity itself, but of pointing out the negative signs by which one recognizes that it is progressing—the different traces of impurity that are disappearing one by one—the passage offers an indication of what is to be fought in chastity's combat.

The first stage of this progress: The monk, when he is awake, is not "broken" by an "attack of the flesh"—*impugnatione carnali non eliditur*. Hence no more invasion of the soul by impulses that overwhelm the will.

The second stage: If "voluptuous thoughts" (*voluptariare cogitationes*) are produced in the mind, he doesn't "dwell" on them. He doesn't think about what he finds himself thinking involuntarily and in spite of himself.[91]

The third stage has been reached when a perception of something in the outside world is not capable of arousing concupiscence: one can make eye contact with a woman without any lustful desire.

At the fourth stage, one no longer experiences, during wakefulness, even the most innocent impulse of the flesh. Does Cassian mean to say that no further impulse is produced in the flesh? And that one is then totally in control of one's body? Probably not, since elsewhere he often stresses the persistence of the body's involuntary impulses. The word he uses—*perferre*—relates no doubt to the fact that these impulses are not likely to affect the soul and it does not have to endure them.

The fifth stage: "When the subject of a conference or the necessary follow-up to a reading leads to the idea of human generation, the mind does not let itself be touched by the most subtle consent to the voluptuous act, but considers it with a calm and a pure gaze, a necessary ministry allotted to the human race, and is no more affected by its memory than if he thought of brickmaking or the practice of some other trade."

Finally, one has reached the last stage when "the seduction of feminine phantoms causes no illusion during sleep. Although we do not believe this deception is sinful, it is the indication of a lust that still hides in the marrow."[92]

In this designation of the different traits of the spirit of fornication fading away as chastity progresses, there is, then, no relation with another individual, no act, and not even the intention to commit one. No fornication in the narrow sense of the term. Absent from this microcosm of solitude are the two major elements around which the sexual ethic turned, not only for the ancient philosophers, but for a Christian like Clement of Alexandria—

at least in book 2 of the *Paedagogus:* the joining together of two
individuals (*sunousia*) and the pleasure of the act (*aphrodisia*). The
elements brought into play are the movements of the body and
those of the soul, the images, perceptions, dream figures, the
spontaneous flow of thoughts, the consent of the will, wakefulness
and sleep. And two poles emerge that mustn't be seen as coinciding with the body and the soul: the involuntary pole of the physical impulses, or of the perceptions that intrude, or the memories
and images that supervene and propagate in the mind, invade, call
to, and invite the will; and the pole of the will itself, which accepts
or spurns, turns away or lets itself be captivated, lingers, consents.
On one side, then, a mechanics of the body and of thought, cir-
cumventing the soul, takes on impurity and can even lead to pollution; and on the other, a game that thought plays with itself. Here
one again finds the two forms of "fornication" in the broad sense
that Cassian had defined next to the intercourse of the sexes and
for which he has reserved his whole analysis: the *immunditia* that,
in wakefulness and sleep, surprises a soul inept at monitoring itself
and leads it, without any contact with the other, to pollution; and
the *libido* that does what it does in the depths of the soul and about
which Cassian recalls the kinship of the words *libido* and *libet*.[93]

The work of spiritual combat and the progress of chastity
whose six stages Cassian describes can be understood, then, as a
task of dissociation. One is very far from the economy of pleasures and their strict limitation; far, too, from the idea of a radical
separation between the soul and the body. Such combat calls for
a perpetual labor upon the movement of thought (which either
prolongs and echoes, or induces, the movements of the body),
upon thought's most rudimentary forms, upon the elements that
may trigger such things—a labor to ensure that the subject is
never involved in waywardness, even through the most obscure
and seemingly most "involuntary" form of will. The six degrees
through which chastity progresses represent six stages that must
nullify the involvement of the will. Undo one's involvement in
the body's impulses—this is the first degree. Then undo one's
imaginative involvement (not dwelling on what is in the mind).
Then undo the sensory involvement (no longer feeling the body's
impulses). Then undo the representative involvement (no longer

thinking of objects as objects of possible desire). And finally, undo the oneiric involvement (the desire there may be in dream images, involuntary though they are). To this involvement, in which the willful act or explicit will to commit an act constitute the most visible form, but one so reprehensible that it must be excluded when the ascetic work begins, to this involvement of the subject all the more daunting for being produced in the least voluntary part of him, Cassian gives the name *concupiscence*. It's against concupiscence that the spiritual combat is directed, with the effort of dissociation, of disinvolvement, that this requires.

This explains the fact that, over the whole length of this struggle against the spirit of "fornication" and for chastity, the basic problem, and basically the only problem, is that of pollution—from its voluntary aspects or the indulgences that invite it to its involuntary forms in sleep or dreams. So great a problem that Cassian will make the absence of erotic dreams or nocturnal pollution the sign that one has arrived at the highest stage of chastity. He comes back to this theme often: the proof "that we have attained this purity will be that no image deceives us when we are resting or relaxed in sleep,"[94] or again: "This is integrity's end and definitive proof: that no voluptuous arousal comes to us during our sleep, and that we are not conscious of the pollutions to which nature constrains us."[95] The whole twenty-second *Conference* is devoted to the question of the "nighttime pollutions," and the need to "exert all our strength to be delivered from them." And several times Cassian evokes such holy figures as Serenus who had reached such a high degree of virtue that they were never exposed to inconveniences of this sort.[96]

One could say that, in a code of life where renunciation of any sexual relation was fundamental, it is completely logical for this theme to become this important. One might also recall the value accorded, in groups inspired more or less directly by Pythagoreanism, to the phenomena of sleep and dreams as revealers of the quality of existence, and to the purifications that are meant to guarantee its serenity. Finally and above all, it has to be understood that nocturnal pollution presented a problem in terms of ritual purity; and it's precisely this problem that occasions the twenty-second *Conference:* Can one approach the "holy altars" and [participate

in]* the "saving banquet," when one has fouled oneself during the
night?[97] But if all these reasons may explain the existence of this
preoccupation for theorists of monastic life, they can't account
for the central place that the question of voluntary-involuntary
pollution occupied in the entire analysis of the chastity battles.
Pollution is not just the object of a more intense prohibition than
the others, or one more difficult to observe. It is an "analyzer" of
concupiscence, insofar as it is possible, for the whole course of
whatever enables it, prepares it, incites it, and triggers it, to determine the voluntary part as opposed to the involuntary part amid
the images, perceptions, and memories in the soul. The whole
work of the ascetic on himself consists in never engaging his will
in this movement that goes from the body to the soul and from
the soul to the body and on which this will can gain a purchase, to
encourage it to stop, through the action of thought. The first five
stages of chastity's progress constitute the successive and increasingly subtle disengagements of the will in relation to the more and
more tenuous movements that can lead to this pollution.

So there remains the last stage, the one that saintliness can
attain: the absence of those "utterly" involuntary pollutions that
take place during sleep. Cassian does remark, however, that not all
such pollutions are necessarily involuntary. For them, too much
food or impure thoughts during the day are a kind of acquies-
cence, if not of preparation. He also makes distinctions as to the
nature of the dream that accompanies the pollution and the degree
of impurity of the images. One taken by surprise in this way would
be wrong to shift the blame onto the body and sleep: "It is the sign
of an evil that was incubating internally, to which the hour of the
night did not give birth, but which, buried in the deepest part of
the soul, the repose of sleep caused to rise to the surface, revealing
the hidden fever of the passions that we have contracted by revel-
ing in unhealthy thoughts for days on end."[98] And finally, there
is pollution without any trace of complicity, without the pleasure
that proves you consent to it, even without the accompaniment of
any dream image. This is the point, no doubt, which the ascetic

---

* Manuscript: "*approcher du*," corrected in 1982 ("*Le combat de la chasteté*") to
"*participer au*."

can arrive at after sufficient striving; pollution is nothing more than a "remainder" which the subject no longer has any part in. "So we must make an effort to restrain the impulses of the soul and the passions of the flesh till the flesh satisfies the demands of nature without giving rise to sensual pleasure, ridding itself of the overabundance of its humors without any unhealthy itching or provoking any combat for chastity."[99] Since what remains here is purely a phenomenon of nature, only the power that is greater than nature can free us from it: its intervention is called grace. This is why non-pollution is the mark of saintliness, the seal of the highest possible chastity, a blessing one can hope for, but not acquire.

For his part, man must do nothing less than remain, in relation to himself, in a state of perpetual vigilance concerning the slightest impulses that may be produced in his body or in his soul. On the alert night and day, the night for the day and the day by thinking of the coming night. "Just as purity and vigilance during the day disposes one to be chaste during the night, nocturnal vigilance strengthens the heart and prepares one's forces to observe chastity during the day."[100] This vigilance is the practice of "discrimination." We have seen that it is at the center of the technology of oneself as it was developed in Evagrius-inspired spirituality.[101] The work of the miller who sorts the grains, of the centurion who divides up the soldiers, of the money changer who weighs the coins to accept or refuse them: it's this kind of work that the monk must constantly do on his own thoughts in order to decide if they carry temptation. It will allow him to sort the thoughts according to their origin, to distinguish them according to their particular quality, and to dissociate the represented object from the pleasure it could evoke. A task of permanent analysis that must be directed at oneself and, through the duty of confession, in relation to others.[102] Neither the overall conception that Cassian has of chastity and "fornication," nor the way he analyzes them, nor the different elements he brings forth and interrelates (pollution, *libido*, concupiscence), can be understood without reference to the technologies of the self by which he characterizes monastic life and the spiritual combat it involves.

.  .  .

Should we see a strengthening of the "prohibitions," an increased valorization of complete continence, a growing disqualification of the sexual act, from Tertullian to Cassian? The problem must undoubtedly not be framed in those terms.

The organization of the monastic institution and the dimorphism that was thus established between the life of monks and that of laypersons introduced important changes into the problem of the renunciation of sexual relations. Correlatively, they led to the development of very complex technologies of the self. In this way there appeared, in the practice of renunciation, a code of living and a mode of analysis that, despite visible continuities, exhibit important differences from the past. In Tertullian the state of virginity implied an external and internal attitude of renunciation of the world, complemented by rules of apparel, conduct, and lifestyle. In the great mystique of virginity that developed starting in the third century the rigor of renunciation (on the theme, already present in Tertullian, of the union with Christ) turns the negative form of continence into the promise of spiritual marriage. In Cassian who, once again, is much more a witness than an inventor, there occurs a kind of dividing in two or drawing back that brings out all of the depth of an interior scene.

But this doesn't involve the interiorization of a catalogue of prohibitions, replacing prohibition of the act with prohibition of the intention. It's a matter of opening up a domain (whose importance was already underscored by Gregory of Nyssa or especially Basil of Ancyra) which is that of thought, with its irregular and spontaneous flow, its images, its memories, its perceptions, with its impulses and impressions that are communicated from the body to the soul and from the soul to the body. What is involved, then, is not a code of permitted and forbidden acts, but a whole technique for monitoring, analyzing, and diagnosing thought, its origins, its qualities, its dangers, its powers of seduction, and all the dark forces that may hide beneath the appearance it presents. And if the objective, finally, is indeed to expel all that is impure or an inducer of impurity, it can be attained only by a vigilance that never disarms, a suspicion that must be directed everywhere and at every moment against oneself. The question must always be raised in a manner that will ferret out all the secret forms of "fornication" that may be hiding in the deepest recesses of the soul.

In this asceticism of chastity one can recognize a process of "subjectification" that pushes a sexual ethic centered on acts far into the background. But two things need to be emphasized straightaway. This subjectification is inseparable from a knowledge process that makes the obligation to tell the truth about oneself a necessary and permanent condition of this ethic. If there is a subjectification, it implies an indefinite objectification of oneself by oneself—indefinite in the sense that, never acquired once and for all, it has no end in time; and in the sense that one must always push one's examination of thoughts as far as possible, however tenuous and innocent they may appear. Further, this subjectification in the form of a quest for the truth about oneself is carried out through complex relations with others. And in several ways: because it's a matter of ridding oneself of the power of the Other, of the Enemy that hides beneath the appearances of oneself; because it's a matter of waging against this Other a ceaseless battle which can't be won without the help of the Almighty, who is more powerful than he; and because the testimony of others, submission to their counsel, and permanent obedience to the directors are indispensable to this combat.

The subjectification of the sexual ethic, the indefinite production of the truth about oneself, the construction of relations of combat and dependence with the other are parts of a whole. These elements were gradually formulated in the Christianity of the first centuries, but they were bound together, transformed, and systematized by the technologies of the self that were developed in monastic life.

# PART III

*Being Married*

# 1

# The Duty of Spouses

In ancient Christianity one doesn't find treatises on marriage like one finds treatises on virginity; married life as such is not the object of an elaboration that would make it a specific practice and a "profession" endowed with a special spiritual significance. There is no art, no *tekhnê*, of married life, if an exception is made of the chapter of the *Paedagogus* studied previously and about which we noted how close it was to ancient morality. Which is not to say, of course, that there are no reflections on the very principle of marriage, on its legitimacy or its acceptability: all the debates around Encratism, all the polemics with the gnostics and the dualist movements, are traversed by this question of marriage; the [third] *Stroma* of Clement of Alexandria, as we've seen, offers evidence of the breadth of these debates, which in various forms continued into the following epochs. But while the question of the "right" to marriage and of its relative value compared to strict continence and celibacy is raised very early, it doesn't lead to the constitution of an art of matrimonial existence. It is significant, for example, that Tertullian brings up the problem of the principle of marriage in *Adversus Marcionem*—that is, in a text of theoretical dispute against a gnostic adversary—and that he gives advice concerning married life only through texts relating to ways of living outside of marriage, to virginity, or to widowhood (*De virginibus velandis, Ad uxorem, Exhortatio ad castitatem*).

Primarily at the end of the fourth century, one sees the development of reflections and texts designed to guide married Chris-

tians in their life of marriage and in the relations they maintain
as spouses. Much more clearly than before, marriage appears as
a Christian calling and relations between spouses also become a
domain of analysis and exercise, on the same level as the relations
of oneself to oneself in ascetic existence, although with much less
intensity. This evolution can be linked to several phenomena.

One should see it, first of all, as a consequence of the extreme
valorization of monastic life and the radical renunciation of the
world, both as an effect of these and as a counterweight to them.
Facing the forms of intense asceticism that risked displacing
Christianity's center of gravity outside of urban communities, far
from public life, toward limited groups of the elect, there was,
in the second half of the fourth century, an effort, particularly
noticeable in the East where monasticism had developed, to reinforce the religious meaning of everyday life, and thus counter the
dimorphism that risked taking hold in the forms of Christian life.
It was no longer enough to say that continence was not precept-
based and that it was not indispensable for salvation; it was also
necessary to make these values appear accessible to those living
the social life, and along with the values, the rules to which they
should submit. John Chrysostom often comes back to the idea
that there shouldn't be any basic difference between the life of the
monastic and that of the married man: "For ought the man who
lives in the world to have any advantage over the monk, save only
the living with a wife? In this point he has allowance, but in others
none, but it is his duty to do all things equally with the monk."[1]

This text is revealing of a movement that makes a set of values,
preoccupations, and practices that had attained a particular scope
in the ascetic life flow back toward life in the Christian world. A
new rigorism? Perhaps. But in any case, it should be read both as
a propagation of the monastic ideal and as an effort to limit the
latter's effects to a certain extent: under its influence, it was a matter of giving a religious intensity to a life that didn't demand such
ruptures. At the end of the fourth century, several great pastors
were witnesses of this transfer and its agents at the same time.
Trained in the ascetic discipline, having practiced monasticism for
a time, they had been able, once they were placed at the head
of a church, to develop a pastoral practice inspired by this first

experience. This was the case of Basil of Caesarea, Gregory of Nazianzus, Gregory of Nyssa, and Chrysostom himself. Under quite different conditions, Saint Jerome and Saint Augustine, in the West, played a similar role up to a point: they promoted the development of a pastoral whose objective was to adapt some of the ascetic values of monastic existence, such as the practices of direction of individuals, to life in the world.

Now, this phenomenon cannot be separated from the new relations being established in the same period between Christianity and empire. An institution at first recognized, then made official, the Christian Church occupies more and more easily and visibly functions of organization, management, control, and regulation of society. And for its part, the imperial bureaucracy always sought to increase its hold on individuals, over and above the traditional structures.[2] At the intersection of these two processes, one sees a paradoxical effect being produced: practices and values that had been developed or intensified in modes of living in explicit rupture with the world and civil society came into play, though not without attenuation and modification, in institutional forms sustained or supported by the state organization and the general political structures. A double pressure was produced in this way: one part coming from the reinforcement of the ascetic ideal, outside the traditional forms of social life and even in opposition to them; the other coming from the mutual support that the ecclesiastical institutions and the state structures are prone to give each other.[3] The life of individuals, in what it may have that's private, quotidian, and singular, thus became an object, if not of a takeover, at least of a concern and a vigilance that were doubtless unlike those of the Hellenistic city-states or those exercised by the first Christian communities.

That there is something new in this it would be hard to contest. It's not the case, however, that it produced a sudden rupture. One of the most striking traits of this pastoral of everyday life is that, on several important points, it is continuous with the philosophical morality that one finds in Plutarch, Musonius, Seneca, or Epictetus. So that, even where the explicit references to pagan authors have all but disappeared—they are noticeably less numerous and less positive, for example, in Chrysostom than in

Clement of Alexandria two centuries earlier—one can note the continued presence or resurgence of themes characteristic of Hellenistic philosophy. But, firstly, these themes are reinscribed in a particular theological context, they are connected with values and practices whose asceticism, however attenuated it may be, still refers, more or less directly, to the general requirement of dying to the world; [secondly], they center on authority relations of the pastoral type. For these reasons, the elements shared by the philosophical morality of antiquity and the Christian ethic had different effects. To which it must be added that the spread of Christianity, its establishment as a state religion and the importance of the ecclesiastical institutions—after all, Christianity was the first religion to be organized into a Church—gave it a much greater penetrative capacity than the philosophy of antiquity, even in its popular forms. Here again, one mustn't force things. Christianity, especially in its everyday moral exigencies, did not become a code of living recognized and practiced by everyone; it has not been that, moreover, throughout its history. But it carried a requirement of universality, and it relied on an institutional backing that made it something more than a general principle (as the Stoic ethic may have been, for example): a possibility of indefinite generalization actually put into practice.

In this ethic, marriage—relations between spouses, the constitution and maintenance of the family around the couple—is doubtless one of the essential components. The main reason for this is that between the ascetic existence and life in the world the most salient difference had to do with marriage. "You certainly deceive yourself and are badly mistaken if you think there is one set of requirements for the person in the world and another for the monk. The difference between them is that one is married and the other is not; in all other respects they will have to render the same account."[4] So it will be a matter of defining, in regard to this difference itself and there where the most is at stake—sexual relations between spouses—the set of rules and practices that must be applied so that the least ascetic of these two forms of life is not divested of any religious value or deprived of the hope of salvation. But moreover, the development of the imperial administration and the gradual fading of the traditional powers gave the family, understood as the matrimonial family unit, a more and more important role: they made it appear as the basic component of society and the primary point of articulation between the moral conduct of individuals and the system of universal laws. So that one arrives at this result that can seem paradoxical at first glance: between the intensification of asceticism and the extension of the state structures, the family unit, relations between spouses, the everyday life of the couple, even down to its sexual activity, become important concerns. Weren't they already concerns in the *Republic* and the *Laws*, or in Aristotle's *Politics*? Yes, certainly. But in a different way. What an examination of the Christian texts devoted to this problem toward the end of the fourth century and the beginning of the fifth shows is that, contrary to what was happening among the classical Greeks, and also contrary to what current interpretations suggest, sexual relations between spouses did not become important insofar as they can and must be procreative.

I am saving Saint Augustine's conception for a final chapter. Both because it constitutes the most rigorous theoretical framework that makes room for an asceticism of chastity and a morality of marriage at the same time; and because, having served as a constant reference for the sexual ethic of Western Christianity, it will be the starting point for the next study. In the present chapter I will study the art of matrimonial living that can be found at the end of the fourth century in the homiletic literature, which was one of the main instruments of pastoral activity. And to avoid spreading myself thin in this immense literature, I will take the homilies of Chrysostom as my privileged reference. Not without making it clear that he belongs, with the accents that are peculiar to him, to a whole current. Many of the ideas that he formulates concerning marriage also appear in close contemporaries like Gregory of Nyssa or more distant ones like Saint Jerome. Some have their starting point in Origen. So I won't be referring to a Chrysostom founder of a new ethic of marriage, but to a Chrysostom as a witness and example of a pastoral of married life that was already highly developed in the period in which he wrote. Let me add that Chrysostom knew and practiced the monastic life before returning to Antioch; that the texts he wrote during the years following his return are strongly marked by these ascetic practices—such as *Adversus oppugnatores vitae monasticae* [Against the Opponents of the Monastic Life]; that he wrote his treatise *On Virginity*, around 382, under that inspiration; that having exercised various pastoral responsibilities, from the diaconate at Antioch to the episcopate at Constantinople, most of his work (from 386 on) is devoted to preaching and to homilies. And that, finally, he very often gave advice on how to conduct oneself in the state of marriage: certain of his homilies—namely the twentieth on the Epistle to the Ephesians, the nineteenth on the first Epistle to the Corinthians, the tenth on the Epistle to the Colossians, the fourth of those commenting on the text *Vidi Dominum*, and lastly the three he delivered at Constantinople right at the beginning of the fifth century, usually called *Three Homilies on Marriage*[5]— constitute veritable brief treatises on the matrimonial state. A lot of very concrete questions are considered: how to raise children with a view to their marriage, how to choose a wife, how the wedding ceremony should unfold, how to behave with one's wife from day to day, what principle sexual relations should come under, and so on.

These texts are often counterposed to *On Virginity*, and to the disparaging formulas it employs against marriage: a long description of its drawbacks, a constant affirmation of the superiority of virginity, the theme that time having "come to its end," "it is no longer the moment to consider marriage."[6] Here the problem is not to assess the consistency of Chrysostom's thought. I will remind you only in a preliminary way of a number of propositions that one finds clearly formulated in that text that is otherwise so ascetic: that marriage cannot be regarded as a bad thing in itself (in which case virginity would not merit being honored); that God, even if he desires that one abstain from it, does not at all prohibit it; that the good marriage involves relations of friendship that ensure its peacefulness; that the wife has duties in regard to her husband which even the legitimate concerns of mortification do not exempt her from.[7] Despite the shifts of accent and even the new thematic that Chrysostom will develop in his pastoral of marriage, one has the pivotal propositions that allow him to link the text without contradiction to his statements extolling the definitive renunciation of marriage.

Nevertheless, one can note two great axes of tension in this pastoral. The first is characterized by the coexistence, in the conception of the marriage bond, of a complex theology of the relations between the Church and Christ, and a wisdom whose precepts are very close to those encountered in several moralists of pagan antiquity.

This tension is clearly evident in certain passages such as that of the third *Homily* on marriage, which speaks of the life force that draws together a young man and a young woman, and of the firmness of the bond that forms between them. Until then, birth and a long habit of shared living had bonded the children to their parents.[8] And then all of a sudden, placed in each other's presence, a boy and a girl, forgetting those attachments, feel a stronger tie forming, in spite of all the years of family existence. In this there is something like a replay of what occurred in early childhood, when the infant learned to acknowledge its parents: "Thus the two spouses, without anyone moving them closer, exhorting them, instructing them in their duties, only have to see one another to be united."[9] And, as if they themselves recognized the imperious character and the high value of this sudden bond, the parents don't experience "any regret, or rancor, or pain" as a result; far from it, they give thanks. And referring to the Epistle to the Ephesians, Chrysostom adds: "Paul remarking on all this, considering that the two spouses leave their parents to attach themselves to each other and that such a long experience then has less influence than this fortuitous decision, reflecting more and more that this isn't a human occurrence [. . .], Paul, consequently, wrote: *This is a great mystery.*"[10] A mystery of which one of the *Homilies* on the Epistle to the Ephesians clearly indicates the three visible forms. It has to do with a force that is stronger than all the other forces in nature: more imperious, more tyrannical than those connecting other men or making us desire things: *epithumia* that paradoxically joins two ordinarily incompatible qualities: duration and vivacity.[11] And further, it is a force that, though it appears suddenly, was hidden deep inside us; it is "lurking in our nature," and we're not conscious of it.[12] Finally, to designate the nature of this connection, Chrysostom employs two terms at once, that one finds either together or separately in many of his texts: *sundesmos*, the tie, the chain that binds together two individuals through constraint or at least obligation (Chrysostom often uses the word *desmos* in connection with the theme of servitude); and *sumplokê*, the intertwining, the blending, that joins two substances and two bodies and tends to form a new entity.

How could a force that prevails over nature itself have managed to slip into our own nature without our knowledge? In this love that draws a man and a woman together to constitute a lasting union, in this "mystery" that Saint Paul spoke of, Chrysostom sees the mark of God's will.

Of his will, first of all, as the Creator.[13] It's from man and his very flesh that he fashioned woman. Issuing from the same substance, Adam and Eve were substantially unifiable. And their descendants are still of the same substance. "No foreign essence can penetrate into ours." Down through the generations, humanity has remained bound to itself, and limited to its own substance. In this relation to the original unity, from whence the human race came without ever leaving, incest plays two roles. Unavoidable at the beginning of time, it is valorized ontologically, since it brings back all individuals to the identity of one and the same substance. By allowing "a man to marry his own sister, or rather his daughter, or again his own flesh,"[14] God constructed mankind like a tree; and he gave it the same beauty as the great trees have: for all the branches, a single root. As scattered as men are today, by this root they remain united and combined. Blessèd incest that makes us all relatives. But its prohibition today is not at odds with this first principle. Rather, it only follows from the latter and multiplies its benefits. Chrysostom explains that by preventing men from marrying their sisters and their daughters, by obliging them to turn this force they have from their common origin to the exterior, God ensures that their affection is not concentrated on one object. The primitive kinship tie is, as it were, reactualized with those who are not our immediate relations. Not being able to marry our sisters forces us to form ties with strangers; that is, to renew our ties with unknown relatives.[15]

But the force that connects men and women is not just the

trace of an origin. It is also the figure of another union: that which binds Christ and the Church. Redemption in the process of being realized, and no longer Creation. After having brought up the connection that establishes itself so abruptly between a man and a woman, breaking the long attachment to their parents, Chrysostom goes on to say that it's in the same way that Christ "left his father and descended to the Church":[16] "You know what sort of mystery marriage is, what great things it symbolizes."[17] This idea comes from Origen.[18] It makes marriage the figure representing the tie that Christ establishes with the Church in a perceptible way: he is the Bridegroom, he is the soul and he is the head; he's the one who commands,[19] whereas she is the betrothed; she is the body of his soul and the member of his body; she must obey him. He has come all the way to her, out of love, while men hated him, abhorred him, insulted him.[20] He accepted her with all the flaws she might have, all the impurities she carried; but it was to watch over her, teach her, enlighten her, and save her finally. As a perfect husband, he sacrificed himself for her, enduring every suffering and lacerated a thousand times.[21] But in return, Christ's tie with the Church serves as a model for every marriage: it's the same obedience that should connect the woman to the man; the same preeminence of him over her; the same task of education, and the same acceptance of sacrifice to save her. The marriage tie owes its value to the fact that it reproduces, in its own way, the form of love that attaches Christ and the Church to one another. "The home is a little church."[22]

A double theological foundation of the tie between husband and wife: on Creation on the one hand and Redemption on the other, on the substantial unity of the flesh on one side and Incarnation on the other, on the origin of time and the approach of its end. This allows Chrysostom to approximate the value of marriage to that of virginity. Or more exactly not to conceive of marriage simply as an inability to lead the life of absolute continence. It becomes possible then to give marriage a directly positive value, even if it is not as high as that of a life of continence. Virginity restores the paradisiacal state by realizing an angelic life on earth. The marriage tie does so to a lesser degree for sure, but it recalls Creation's unity of substance. Virginity makes the soul the bride of Christ; marriage for its part is the image of the union of the Church with the Savior. So it should not be surprising to see Chrysostom, who is made by *On Virginity* to look very much like a marriage hater, promise married people merits and rewards that are also quite considerable. A life of marriage, if it obeys the precepts, "is scarcely inferior to monastic life; such spouses will have little cause to envy the unmarried."[23] Or further: if you use marriage in the right manner, "you will occupy the first place in the kingdom of heaven, and you will enjoy all the benefits."[24]

This spiritual promotion of marriage calls forth a whole range of reflections on married life; it authorizes an art of relations between husband and wife that is on a par with the *tekhnê* of virginal existence and, without hoping ever to match its high standing, achieves a certain balance with it. Now what characterizes these rules of married life is their close similarity to those found in the moralists of the imperial era, or in Clement of Alexandria, whose extensive borrowings from those pagan authors we've already noted. In this sense, one has the impression that the theological justification of marriage, while making it possible to avoid the excesses of Encratism and especially the consequences of the dualism implied in the rejection of any conjugality, made it possible to give a foundation to a whole ethic of marriage that was already common; and hence to continue the movement (already noticeable in Clement of Alexandria) to adjust the pagan morality of marriage to Christianity. And in fact (except on one major point that will have to be analyzed at length later), the early theology of conjugality centers, in John Chrysostom, on precepts of married life that are strikingly close to those that Musonius, or Seneca, or Epictetus, or Clement of Alexandria had made familiar. Certain accents are altered, most of the expositions are more extensive, and the values of charity are emphasized. But one finds the same basic themes as before.

> • A principle of natural inequality. By creating man first and giving him woman "as a helpmate," according to the Genesis text, God made it clear that the man ranks higher, and that he is meant to command. He is the head: "Let us take as our fundamental position that the husband occupies

the place of the head, and the wife that of the body [. . .] Paul assigns each one their place; to one, authority and protection, to the other, submission."[25]

• A principle of complementarity, giving a positive content to this inequality, which can then be made to function as a principle of order in marital life, and ensure good harmony whereas marriage might be conflictual otherwise: "Given that two kinds of affairs share out our life, public affairs and private affairs, the Lord divided the tasks between the man and the woman: to the latter he allotted the government of the house, to the former all the affairs of the state." The man throws the javelin; the woman works the distaff. The one participates in the public deliberations; the other makes her views prevail in the home. He manages the public funds; she raises the children who are in their way a "precious treasure." God was thus able to avoid "giving the two aptitudes to the same creature, so that one of the two sexes would not be eclipsed by the other and appear useless; and he didn't want to give an equal share to the two sexes, for fear that this equality would cause conflicts and that the wives would raise their claims to the point of disputing the first rank with the men; but reconciling the need for peace with the conventions of hierarchy, he divided our life into two parts, giving the husband the most substantial and serious one and assigning the wife the smallest and most humble one; so that the necessities of existence cause us to honor her, without the inferiority of her ministry allowing her to enter into rebellion against her husband."[26]

For this complementarity to work as it should, it's not advisable to marry a woman richer than oneself. Because a man who weds a wealthy woman gets himself a "sovereign"; if he chooses a poorer one, on the other hand, he finds an "assistant, an ally in her [. . .] The embarrassment due to her poverty motivates the wife to offer all sorts of care and attention to her husband, makes her obedient and submissive, and eliminates all the causes of disputes."[27]

• Principle of the duty to teach connected with the respect of modesty. Since he is the head, the husband must guide the wife, serve as her instructor, and train her in the virtues. "Let him, from that very evening on which he first receives her into the bridal chamber, teach her temperance, gentleness, and how to live, casting down the love of money at once from the outset, and from the very threshold. Let him discipline her in wisdom, and advise her never to have bits of gold hanging at her ears, and down her cheeks, and laid round about her neck."[28] "During that time therefore, during which shame, like a sort of bridle laid upon the soul, suffers her not to make any murmur, nor to complain, lay down all thy laws [. . .] When is there then another time so advantageous for molding a wife, as that during which she reverences her husband, and is still timid, and still shy? Then lay down all thy laws for her, and willing or unwilling, she will certainly obey them."[29] If it is the right and duty of the husband to instruct his wife, there is one area, however, where ignorance has to be respected: it's in everything relating to modesty. A counsel of prudence that the ancient moralists also gave:[30] "Encourage her bashfulness for a considerable length of time, and do not destroy it suddenly [. . .] Do not break off this reserve too hastily, as unchaste husbands do, but encourage it for a long time. For this will be a great advantage to you."[31]

• Principle of permanence of the bond and reciprocity of the obligations. The marriage bond is established once and for all and, barring adultery,[32] it cannot be broken. The civil laws don't rule in that way, but "God's law" affirms it, says Chrysostom, who on this point again follows the conceptions of authors like Musonius.[33] "Many people imagine that one makes oneself an adulterer only by seducing a woman who is under the authority of a husband. And I maintain that any married man who has culpable and illicit relations with a woman, be she a prostitute, a servant, any unmarried person, commits an adultery. Indeed, it is not just the dishonored person, it's also the author of her dishonor whose quality constitutes the adultery."[34] And further: "If your woman has come to you, if she has left her father, it is not in order for you to mistreat her, for you to replace her with a vile courtesan."[35] One can understand that this intangible bond, one that is even defiled by an episodic relation with a slave girl, cannot be undone entirely by death. Chrysostom has the same position of prudent disapproval of remarriage as most Christian authors, and as several neo-Stoic authors. It is not absolutely forbidden (especially if one is young) to remarry.[36] But it's best to "await death, remain faithful to one's commitments, stay continent, live close to one's children, and in this way merit a more bountiful share in God's goodness."[37]

• Principle of an emotional tie that constitutes both the goal and the necessary condition of the good marriage. If a man has to choose the woman he will marry so carefully (a large part of the third *Homily* on marriage is devoted to defining the principles of this choice), it's because one has to be able to love her: by taking the right one, "we will benefit by never needing to repudiate her, but also by loving her with a deep tenderness."[38] In a passage of the short treatise *Against Remarriage* (which is thought to date from the same period as the one on virginity), he proposes a very down-to-earth interpretation of marriage, making it one of the points in its favor: a man loves what he has authority over, and especially what he is the first and sole master of, as with clothes and belongings. The same must certainly be true in the case of a wife ("who is more prized by a husband than anything else"). When one is sure he is the first and exclusive possessor, he receives her with "eagerness," "affection," and "good will."[39] It's obviously another tone that one finds in the later homilies—and particularly in that imagined speech addressed to a young wife by an ideal Christian husband. There the affection is not framed in a relation of possession and mastery, but in

a certain form of soul-to-soul relation, which has several
aspects: recognition of the wife's qualities of soul; desire to
win her affection; wanting to have the same way of thinking as her—and the definitive union can be established
only in the life to come. And since that is the final objective of the marriage, life here below counts for little and
the husband is ready to sacrifice his own life to that end:
"I gave up everything, and went on till I fell in with the
excellence of thy soul, which I value above all gold [. . .]
I courted thee, and I love thee, and prefer thee to my
own soul. For the present life is nothing. And I pray, and
beseech, and do all I can, that we may be counted worthy so to live this present life, as that we may be able also
there in the world to come to be united to one another in
perfect security [. . .] I value thy affection above all things,
and nothing is so bitter or so painful to me, as ever to be at
variance with thee. Yes, though it should be my lot to lose
my all, and to become poorer than Irus, and undergo the
most extreme hazards, and suffer any pain whatsoever, all
will be tolerable and endurable, so long as thy feelings are
true towards me."[40] And the text ends, in a very characteristic way, with a formula that is exactly opposite to the one
with which an analogous speech in Xenophon opened. In
the latter, the husband was pictured as telling the wife that
if he had chosen her and if her parents had given her to
him, this was with a view to their good home and their
future children.[41] In Chrysostom the husband wishes to
have children only when this meeting of souls, prefiguring
their union in the hereafter, will be realized: "I will want
to have children when you have tenderness for me."[42]
According to Chrysostom, respecting these principles
must constitute the basis of a rule of matrimonial life, of a
"knowing-how to be married." In this way, tranquility of
the soul will be ensured, whereas outside loves, especially
those with prostitutes, are necessarily poisoned. With
such women "everything is bitterness and shame": expenditures, humiliations, magic spells and potions; "If you're
looking for pleasure, avoid the courtesans." By contrast, at
home, with your wife, "you find pleasure, security, relax-

ation, respect, consideration and good conscience [. . .] When you have a source of clear water at hand, why go off to a muddy swamp?"[43] This peace of soul correlates with the good order and prosperity of the household: "When a general has organized his army in a solid way, no enemy dares to attack it: the same is true here. When the wife, children, servants, all work toward the same goal, a perfect harmony reigns in the home [. . .] Therefore, let us take good care of our wives, our children, our servants."[44] The bond between spouses constitutes, for the general order of the household, a model that the children and servants will make use of in turn. So that if this bond is strong, and if it is supported by love, moderation, respect, and recognized authority, the whole family will benefit: "What sort of persons, think you, must the children of such parents be? What the servants of such masters? What all others who come near them? Will they too not eventually be loaded with blessings out of number? For generally the servants also have their characters formed after their master's, and are fashioned after their humors, love the same objects, which they have been taught to love, speak the same language, and engage with them in the same pursuits."[45] The household, organized on the basis of and around a marital tie itself based on such ethical rules, can constitute the shelter a man needs from the agitations of an external world. "A marriage lived according to the rules is not a matter of little importance; and a thousand misfortunes are in store for those who don't use it as they should [. . .] Indeed, the husband who conforms to the marital laws will find in his house, in his wife, a consolation, a refuge from the evils, public or other, that could strike him. Contrariwise, one who treats this one matter lightly and thoughtlessly, when the public place would be without storms, will see only dangerous reefs and rocks when he returns home."[46]

*Kalon ho gamos*, the treatise *On Virginity* already said. So beautiful and so important that Chrysostom (who moreover encourages parents not to oppose their children if they want to renounce the world) considers that adolescents must be prepared for marriage. Part of the nineteenth *Homily* on the First Epistle to Timothy is devoted to this theme. "The daughters ought to go forth from their father's house to marriage, like an athlete leaves the palestra, trained and exercised."[47] This preparation is what should be given to souls and bodies "difficult to tame" and that require "governors, teachers, directors, attendants, and tutors."[48] The main part of this preparation will consist in preventing boys and girls from having sexual relations before marriage. And for two reasons: because "one who is full of reserve before marriage will be more so after; and one who frequented courtesans before marriage will do the same when he is married"; but also because, by being reserved like this for this marriage relation which will be the first, each of the spouses will have "a keener affection" for the other.[49] Preparation for love through chastity; but it would be imprudent for it to last longer: "Let us marry them early."[50] Or, as Chrysostom puts it elsewhere: "Seeing how this furnace burns, let us strive [. . .] to engage them according to God's law, in the ties of marriage."[51]

One sees, then, that when Chrysostom, tempering certain aspects of his first writings, places virginity opposite the properly regulated conjugal family, and when he makes it a place of private tranquility as opposed to the public agitations, capable of leading to the good that is desired, there is nothing, in its principle, that is specifically Christian. All these themes were already formulated. Doubtless one must not overlook the fact that Chrysostom reinscribes them in specifically Christian references: he relates the "natural" hierarchy between man and woman to the Creation; in the virtues of marriage, he sees the promise of future rewards— "thereby, we will be able to please the Lord, spend the whole present life virtuously, and obtain finally the good things promised to those who love God";[52] and for him the prosperity of a well-regulated marital life is the result of a blessing from God.[53]

However, there is a difference—it is major—that keeps us from placing Chrysostom and all those in the fourth century who make the same analyses as he in a simple continuity with Clement of Alexandria and a fortiori the moralists of antiquity. It is the question of sexual relations within marriage. And more exactly the refusal to make procreation one of the essential ends of marriage, together with the affirmation that sexual relations between spouses are objects of obligation.

Marriage doesn't have procreation as its end. Actually, Chrysostom doesn't say things this way. One finds three series of formulations. In some of these, enumerating the ends for which God established marriage, he chooses to make no mention of procreation. Why, he asks in the third *Homily* on marriage, did God give men this institution? "So that we might avoid fornications, so that we might repress our concupiscence, so that we might make ourselves agreeable to God by contenting ourselves with our own wife."[54] This is the thesis of *On Virginity:* "So marriage was granted for the sake of procreation, but an even greater reason was to quench the fiery passion of our nature. Paul attests to this when he says: 'But to void immorality, every man should have his own wife.' He does not say: for the sake of procreation. Again, he asks us to engage in marriage not to father many children."[55] But the *Homilies* on marriage don't really say anything different: "There are two reasons for which marriage was instituted: it's so that we will be continent, and so that we will be fathers. But of these two motives, the most important is that of continence",[56] and after explaining the reasons for this importance and the motives that caused God to institute marriage, he concludes that the latter has only one end: preventing fornication. Thus, at the end of the analysis, procreation has disappeared. Finally, one also finds in Chrysostom the refusal to establish a theological correlation between marriage and procreation. Marriage can be perfectly valuable without occasioning any birth, and besides, without the will of God it would not by itself be capable of populating the earth. God could easily see to that without going through marriage or the coupling of bodies.[57]

This dissociation is important if one recalls the insistence with which the link between marriage and *paidopoiia*, the making of children, was underscored in all of Hellenic culture: one remembers Pseudo-Demosthenes saying that spouses are made for providing a legitimate progeny and that the state of marriage is recognized by the fact of procreating children of one's own; one also remembers all the philosophers making procreation the fundamental end of marriage.[58] Chrysostom's position is surprising, considering that Clement of Alexandria had taken up this ancient theme as something obvious,[59] but also when one considers that very early, and in a general way in Christianity starting with Augustine, procreation will reappear at the forefront of the theology of marriage and the sexual ethic. It will be defined, next to the marriage sacrament and to fidelity, as one of the treasures of marriage and as primary legitimate finality of the sexual act between spouses. Is Chrysostom an exception? Does he simply mark an episode, a moment of hesitation which the doctrine and the practice will not retain? An exception, certainly not: from Origen to him, marriage had been considered not as a function of its procreative ends, but in its hierarchical position relative to virginity and voluntary celibacy. The question of continence, not that of children, was the main focus of the debate. Chrysostom should be seen as belonging to this whole current of thought of which Saint Jerome is the exponent in Western Christianity, and the problem that occupied it is the following: how does one establish a pastoral of marital relations (which can no longer be dispensed with on behalf of a one-sided valorization of asceticism) that is based on a morality of continence? And if this current itself constitutes an episode, it's an important one, for it was there that the matter of sexual relations in marriage was rethought; and as a result, the proposition that procreation is an end of marriage doesn't have the same meaning in Saint Augustine and his successors as it had in previous authors, whether they were pagan like Musonius or Christian like Clement of Alexandria.

Chrysostom dissociates marriage from creation based on the general history of man, his fall, and his salvation. He asserts in fact that procreation is announced in Genesis at the same moment as man's creation—"Increase and multiply,"[60] hence before woman's, before the fall, before the death and sorrow that punishes it. It is earlier, therefore, than the institution of marriage. So what can this God-given precept mean to the unmarried man? We know that Gregory of Nyssa sees it as heralding a generation that would be carried out in the angelic mode and would make it possible to populate paradise the way heaven is populated by angels. Chrysostom sees it rather as an announcement and a promise: the declaration, as early as man's creation, of a possibility that would be realized later.[61] This would be after the fall. Because of the fall? Not directly at least, but in an indirect way, since the fall leads to death, and the production of offspring is given to man as a compensation. It should be noted, further, that this was not in order to fill an earth that death would have soon depopulated, but to give man the image, with the thought of future generations, either of an immortality he had lost through sin, or of a resurrection that would save him. Procreation as an image of the lost immortality is evoked in the first of the three *Homilies* on marriage: "When there was no hope of resurrection [. . .], God gave men this consolation of paternity so that those who would die might go on living in images full of life."[62] The eighteenth *Homily* on Genesis makes procreation a figure of the promise that after death would come life: at the very moment he was imposing "the terrible punishment of death" on men, God showed how much he loved mankind— how much he was *philanthropos*—by granting it "the succession of children as *an image of resurrection.*"[63] Procreation in the physical sense of the term thus makes sense only in relation to these two references that are both situated at the gates of time. And it has no other role than to produce images of it that clearly had no reason for being before the fall, and will no longer have any once the resurrection has come. Procreation will have served its purpose. And the precept "increase and multiply," which had been formulated as soon as man was fashioned by God, and which consequently dominates time, must take on a new meaning: henceforth we should apply ourselves to spiritual productions, more beautiful than those of the body.[64]

As for marriage, if it is also connected to the fall, it's not in the same way. Whereas "multiplication" is ontologically based in the creative act, and it is therefore already present in the earthly paradise, at least as a possibility, and the fall is what gave it its material reality—as well as its image function in relation to the spiritual realities—marriage was completely absent from a human condition that had not yet experienced the fall. The text of *On Virginity* is quite explicit on this point: "Fashioned by God, man lived in Paradise, and there was no reason for marriage."[65] Yet God had created woman before the fall so that she would be man's companion. But companion in the sense of helper, assistant (*boêthos*), not wife: "Even then marriage did not seem necessary. Indeed, one saw no trace of it, they both did without it."[66] Marriage appears with the fall, with "the decay of death, ruin, pain, and a toilsome life."[67] In this sense, one can say that it is the consequence of the fall, like carnal procreation. But while the latter is a consolation, marriage is a way of setting a limit to the desires of the body: a barrier against the excesses which the fall unleashed. The *Homilies* on marriage don't modify anything essential in what *On Virginity* had laid out, a dozen years earlier, concerning the "metahistorical moment" of marriage, its role in Hebrew law, and the function it still has to serve today. At most they slightly lessen the emphasis that Chrysostom had placed on the "condescension" of God, bestowing marriage like the food one gives to infants too weak to tolerate an adult diet, like a bitter medicine one has to swallow when one is gripped by illness.[68] Marriage is presented above all as limit and law. "It was from the day that concupiscence came into play that marriage was introduced, putting a stop to incontinence, and causing man to be satisfied with a wife."[69] Whereas procreation was a prior possibility become a consolation after the fall, marriage is a law that has its reason for being in the rebellion, after the fall, of the body against the soul, and whose end is to subdue the body's desires. It is thus a "habit of servitude." In this way, one re-encounters the odd formulation that figures in the treatise *Against Remarriage*. There it is said that marriage cannot be called that from the fact of the sexual union, for then every fornication would merit receiving that name; what characterizes marriage is that the woman contents herself with one man only.[70] In its essence, marriage is limitation.

This definition of the role of marriage is important. Instead of situating the matrimonial bond in a general, natural, or social economy of procreation, it situates it (in this day and age at least, since the earth is populated and the ages have come) in an individual economy of *epithumia*, of desire or concupiscence. In this sense it connects the ethic of marriage to the preoccupation with asceticism and even the strictest form of continence. Next to virginity or rather beneath it, marriage is a way of dealing with the question of concupiscence. The latter is at the core of both the morality of marriage and the ascetic procedures of those who have renounced any matrimonial tie. Concupiscence is the object shared by the rules of the state of marriage and the *tekhnê* of virginity as a practice.

What distinguishes the rules of marriage from these "techniques," however, is not just that they are more tolerant and they permit with one person what the state of virginity disallows with any person at all. It is also that they have a juridical character. And in several ways. Whereas virginity, as we've seen, is recommended but not precept-based, and it cannot be obligatory, marriage is an obligation for all those who cannot attain the perfection of the virginal state. Marriage is in itself a law. But it also creates obligations. And obligations that refer to what is precisely marriage's reason for being—namely the economy of concupiscence. For if one marries in order to "limit to a single person" one's desire, one binds oneself in effect to this singleness of the relation; but one also commits oneself vis-à-vis the spouse to allow them to satisfy their own desire with one person only. Since the economy of concupiscence is the goal shared by the two spouses when they marry, it is imperative that each of them play the role expected of them by the other, to reach this goal. So the "limitation" of concupiscence that is the end of every marriage necessarily entails a mutual acceptance of the sexual act if each of two spouses is to find in marriage the moderate asceticism which they were seeking. In a way that may seem paradoxical, the rapprochement between marriage and virginity, the definition of a theme which they share— the economy of concupiscence—even though they don't give it the same solution, leads to sexual relations being posited as a strict obligation for each of the two spouses. But with certain provisos attached, of course, and in a regulatory framework.

At the beginning of the nineteenth *Homily* on the First Epistle to the Corinthians, John Chrysostom sets out the reciprocal obligations of spouses as regards sexual relations. He gives a commentary on Saint Paul's statement: "Let the husband pay the wife what is due to her; in like manner the wife the husband" (7:3).[71] Chrysostom presents these obligations essentially as the duty not to introduce into marriage an abstinence and practices of renunciation that are appropriate only to the asceticism of a path devoted to continence. Once marriage is chosen as a form of life, it is not permitted to one of the marriage partners to try to lead the other mode of existence. Either strict chastity, or marriage. Doubtless the symmetry between these types of existence is not perfect, for if it is not allowed for chastity to make an exception in any form whatsoever, by contrast certain abstinences do find a place in marriage. Ritual abstinences with an obligatory character.[72] Voluntary abstinences also, but these should always be decided by common agreement, and not result from the decision of just one of the spouses. And in any case, they should never be definitive; "if you want to abstain together with your spouse, let it be for a short time."[73]

As for the nature or form of the required acts, given the recommendations of modesty and reserve that Chrysostom often makes, he doesn't give any indication here. No precept concerning possible procreation, no indications about opportune moments, or about forbidden sexual acts. In the fourth *Homily* on the Epistle to the Romans, Chrysostom engages in lengthy considerations regarding the sins of sodomy, role reversals between men and women, and overturning the laws of nature, yet it seems that he is not referring to these marriage practices, but for the most part to male passivity and male prostitution, or to sexual relations between women. In any case, neither in this homily nor in the one commenting on the First Epistle to the Corinthians does he appear to be imposing on spouses a particular type of sexual relation that is justifiable because it is capable of being reproductive. It's not the morphology of the relation that is determinant for him, but a principle of formal and juridical equality. Whereas in all the other areas there is a difference and hierarchy between the man and the woman, whereas the wife ought to fear her husband and obey him, in the area of sexual relations on the other hand, there should not be any inequality. "Let man have the advantage in all other matters, but in matters of continence, no"; on this point, one should not distinguish "the more or the less: their right is the same."[74] Here Chrysostom is obviously employing a political and juridical vocabulary. He rejects *pleonexia* ("more power," "more authority" on one side than on the other); he posits the principle of *isotimia* (equality of privileges). The obligations he assigns to spouses constitute, therefore, a kind of political equality as far as sexual relations are concerned: the rights of one determine the duties of the other.

However, Chrysostom doesn't base this system of obligations only on a symmetry in the power of decision and a community of will. Its form is that of a political equality. It is grounded in an idea of property. Referring to Saint Paul's text, according to which the husband's body doesn't belong to him but to the wife and vice versa, he makes the obligation not to refuse oneself to the other the consequence of a mutual appropriation of bodies that would be brought about in marriage. An appropriation that can create two situations, depending on whether the accent is placed on the fact that there is property, or on the fact that this appropriation involves the bodies of human beings. In the latter case, one is led to the model of slavery; but for many reasons— among others, that the *"isotimia"* of marriage implied an equality of free individuals[75]—this theme of slavery remains relatively allusive[76] and metaphorical. On the other hand, the idea of an appropriation leads to that of a debt: one whose body has become another's property owes them something—namely the use of their body. Chrysostom notes that to designate this obligation Saint Paul employs the expression *opheilomenê timên* and that *opheilê* relates to debt. The duty between spouses is a debt. And it's this juridico-economic theme that causes Chrysostom to speak of fraud in reference to those who shirk this duty. Doubtless it should be noted that the explanation he gives is strangely weak: "you don't steal from me," he says, "if I consent to your taking an object that belongs to me, but taking by force from someone who doesn't consent is to steal." One might expect that from such a principle it would follow that each marriage partner would have the freedom to refuse themselves to the other. But if one recalls that marriage has effected a transfer of property, one sees that, for Chrysostom, the one who refuses oneself to the other does them violence: they take or retake by force that of which marriage had made them the owner. This is why, quite logically, he gives as an example of this kind of fraud women who, without the consent of their husband, decide to practice chastity. They commit a grave sin against "justice."[77]

The model of property and debt is very important in Chrysostom. He uses it several times, weaving together the theme of marriage's economic exchanges and the principle of this property transfer of the body. Sometimes he brings out the double merger that, in marriage, makes a single being of two bodies, and a single possession of two fortunes. "You are just one being, one life, and you still speak of thine and mine! [. . .] God made common to us things more necessary than riches."[78] Sometimes, too, he makes the point that if the husband can consider his wife's dowry as his own, his wife is justified in thinking that her husband's body belongs to her. "Is it not strange that the dowry she brings to you is the object of your solicitude, and that you carefully avoid distraction from that, and that those treasures, much more precious than a dowry, by which I mean continence and chastity, and your own person [. . .] you squander and corrupt them?" To this analogy, wife's dowry/husband's body, Chrysostom immediately adds a remark that is even better at showing how inadequate such a comparison is to his own conception of the double mutual possession: "If you manage to meddle with your wife's dowry, it's your father-in-law that you must answer to; but if you sully chastity, it's to God that you must give account, God who instituted marriage and from whom you have your wife."[79] The fact is that once producing offspring is no longer on marriage's horizon, the link between a physical union and the circulation of possessions can be handled only by a questionable analogy. Chrysostom's recourse to the latter shows, however, his desire to emphasize the presence of a formal and juridical type of obligation. For him, there is a right that is internal to marriage, is absolutely symmetrical as concerns both spouses, and derives from the mutual ownership of bodies.

But why does Chrysostom conceive of marriage as a transfer of property, rather than as a union, fusion, constitution of a single being—a theme that he evokes several times but that would not be capable of establishing a juridical type of bond? Precisely because the body subsequent to the fall is the site of the excesses of concupiscence; and because, when one marries in order to set a limit to those excesses, one asks that the other ensure this limitation. Each becomes the master and possessor of the other's body, insofar as they can control its concupiscence. And by refusing, one makes oneself responsible for the troubles that the other's concupiscence may produce. Chrysostom describes those troubles in two ways. Domestic disorder, discord, disarray in the household. We've seen that the good organization of people and things rested on the couple entity. Chrysostom shows that it partly depends on the respect for justice in sexual relations. "Great evils are born" when it is transgressed, "fornications, adulteries; domestic troubles are its consequences"; a husband frustrated in his rights "stirs up quarrels and causes his wife a thousand problems."[80] But more deeply, one who refuses the equilibrium of justice in marital relations makes oneself guilty of the trouble in the other's soul, in their desires, their temptations, and their difficulties controlling them. Because marriage has put one in the position of contributing to one's spouse's salvation. At the bottom of this appropriation of bodies, there is this transfer: here it's no longer the objective of a shared progeny that justifies the "debt of bodies" contracted implicitly by the spouses when they marry, but rather each one's responsibility vis-à-vis the sins of the other. So the "fruit" of which it is a question is spiritual: it is each one's salvation through the other. A salvational chiasmus. On this precise point, Chrysostom can employ the word *agape* in the double sense of marital love and charity.

One has to recognize that on this theme the treatise *On Virginity* doesn't express exactly the same positions as the later homilies. Chrysostom does already insist on the wife's obligation not to evade her marital duty, even for reasons of continence: "The wife practicing continence against her husband's wishes is deprived of the rewards for continence. She is also responsible for his adultery and is more responsible than he. Why? Because she pushed him to the abyss of debauchery by depriving him of legitimate intercourse."[81] But he gives an extremely limited meaning to this obligation: a concession to a physical need that calls for indulgence and that should not meet with a unilateral refusal;[82] but it is not a question of giving a spiritual value to this concession: "Not by living dutifully with him as a wife will she be able to save her husband, but by pointing out to him life according to the Gospel; something that many women have done, moreover, without being married."[83] The help that spouses can contribute to each

other doesn't involve that, even if it must still be respected: "I do
not say she is of no help altogether in spiritual matters (indeed
no!), but I do assert that she successfully accomplishes this not
when she is involved with marital concerns but when she progresses to the virtue of the holy men while adhering to her feminine nature."[84] The sexual relationship between spouses, in this
treatise where the life of marriage is presented in a negative light,
appears as something that must subsist, nonetheless, when one is
sufficiently detached from marriage and is with one's wife "as not
having one."[85] By contrast, in the later homilies this fulfillment of
duty is not an unavoidable remainder that must still be observed
between spouses when they have shed all the other aspects of married life; it has a twofold value: spiritual, since it manifests a bond
of charity, and moral, since it ensures a good understanding that
has an impact on the whole order of the household. When marriage is thought of as a vocation, a state that deserves and calls for
a specific *tekhnê*, then the marital relation is no longer a residual
constraint that one doesn't have the right to get out of; it is part of
the labor for mutual salvation.

Once again, Chrysostom is not taken here as the inventor of
this way of analyzing marital relations and the state of marriage.
He is the witness of a thought that has many of the elements that
are already found in Origen. And just as Origen supplied some of
the basic principles that would later be cited by the institutions
of monastic life, he also very clearly formulated some of the principles of the Christian ethic and spirituality of marriage, before
the latter in its concrete forms gave rise to reflection and specific
prescriptions.[86]

Chrysostom's homilies, in any case, manifest the existence of
a pastoral of married life in which sexual relations are strongly
linked to this notion of *opheilê*, of *debitum*—of duty-debt—which
in Christianity will become a fundamental category for thinking,
justifying, codifying, and distributing marital relations according
to a system of rules. During the Middle Ages, a huge juridical edifice will be constructed making spouses appear as legal subjects in
complex relations of debts, demands, acceptances, and refusals. At
least as much as the great sexual prohibitions, this code will contribute to the juridification of sexual practice, and at the same time

will give the religious institution access to the most secret relations between marriage partners. Now, what needs to be underscored if one intends to explore the history of this strange notion is that it does not derive from the idea that marriage has procreation as its end—except in a secondary, lateral way, and because, after the fact, it could use this as a pre-established support. On the contrary, it was when Christian thought detached marriage from this end, so readily acknowledged since pagan antiquity, that this notion of duty-debt began to take form in a clear way. The eschatological theme of an end of time when it's no longer necessary to think of progeny is no doubt fundamental. But by itself it could not have constituted the support for this notion if marriage had not been inflected by monasticism, the life of virginity and the art of conducting oneself within it, and the Church with its ever more numerous and deeper connections with the state and imperial society had not developed a pastoral of marital existence, for shepherding it and showing spouses how to conduct themselves within it. And this art of matrimonial life organized itself around the same question as that of the life of continence: how to manage, combat, and vanquish concupiscence, in a struggle that is integral to life itself. In a way that is paradoxical only at first sight, *epithumia*, desire, concupiscence, is what constitutes the "raw material" which the arts of monastic life and married life have to process. With this difference: in the one case, one must act with oneself alone and in the form of a spiritual combat with one's own "thoughts" (in the broad sense of the word), in order to give it no possible outlet (the involuntary pollution during dreams constituting the "purest" form of this impurity, as it were, to which God alone can put a definitive end), and, in the other case, there does exist a legitimate, although "joint," outlet but it has to be seen that this legitimacy stems from the fact that each one thereby enables the other to escape the temptations of their own concupiscence. This is to say that the theme is still and always that of the relationship with oneself; with the nuance that, in the case of marriage, this relationship is not managed apart from one's relation to the other. One must bear in mind, however, that in the case of monastic virginity, there is a form of relation to the other that is just as indispensable: the bond of spiritual direction.

The symmetry between the art of monastic life and the art of matrimonial existence should not be overestimated. The differences are legion, of course. And on the specific theme of concupiscence, it has to be noted that monastic asceticism will give rise to practices of constant self-monitoring, of decipherment of one's own secrets, of an indefinite search in the depths of one's heart, of an elucidation of those things that may be a delusion, an error, and a deception on the part of oneself; whereas the precepts of matrimonial life will take the form of a "juridiction" much more than of a "veridiction," and that the theme of debt will give rise to an endless work of codification and a long reflection of jurisprudence. The dimorphism is already apparent in texts like those of Chrysostom. It will become more and more so, profoundly marking the way sexual behaviors are thought of and regulated in the West: in terms of truth (but in the form of a secret deep inside oneself to be elucidated indefinitely if one intends to be "saved"), and in terms of law (but as much in the form of a law of debt and of obligations as in that of prohibition and transgression). This dimorphism is still far from having disappeared, or at least from having exhausted its effects. But it seems to me that at its origin one must not continue to find the juxtaposition in Christianity of an ancient law of marriage and the more recent forms of a complete renunciation of the world. It was the movement to constitute, in the exercise of pastoral power, a *tekhnê* of marital life—inferior to that of monastic life, but not unrelated to it—that led at the same time to making the concupiscence of each spouse (and not the sharing of progeny) the essential form of the marital relation and to organizing between these two solitudes an intersection of responsibilities and a linkage through debt. Even in the dual form of marriage, the basic problem is what to do with one's own concupiscence; hence it is the relation of oneself to oneself. And the internal law of marital sex was first organized as a way of managing through the other this fundamental self-to-self relation.

# 2

# The Good and
# the Goods of Marriage

Virginity is superior to marriage, without marriage being a bad thing or virginity an obligation: Saint Augustine received this general thesis from a tradition that was already clearly formed before him. It runs through his whole oeuvre; he develops it in the two groups of texts he devoted to the problems of marriage and of virginity: in the first years of his bishopric, when he felt the need to discuss both the Manichean-inspired arguments (in *De continentia*, around 396) and the propositions of Jovinian (in *De bono coniugali*, 401, or *De sancta virginitate*, 401); then at the time of his anti-Pelagian polemics, fifteen years or so later, when he bases himself on the superiority of strict and total continence, acknowledged by his current adversaries, particularly Julian of Eclanum, to argue that concupiscence is an evil.[1]

A passage of *De sancta virginitate* clearly situates the general principle, at least in a negative way. It's the same one, with perhaps different emphases and polemical edges, that one can find in Gregory of Nyssa, in John Chrysostom, or in Jerome's *Adversus Jovinianum*. "Some, by aiming for virginity, have thought marriage hateful even as adultery: but others, by defending marriage, would have the excellence of perpetual continence to deserve nothing more than married chastity; as though either the good of Susanna be the lowering of Mary: or the greater good of Mary ought to be the condemnation of Susanna."[2] Against these two errors, Augustine asserts that marriage and virginity are not to be differentiated from each other as evil is from good, or assimilated as two equivalent goods; they are to be evaluated and separated as a lesser good compared to a greater good. Two heights in the same landscape, but one of which is higher than the other. "Whoever therefore shall be willing to abide without marriage, let them not flee from marriage as a pitfall of sin; but let them surmount it as a hill of the lesser good, in order that they may rest in the mountain of the greater, chastity."[3] From this general conception of two unequal goods, Augustine draws conclusions that as such are in line with the already constructed doctrine. Let me quickly indicate them in order to better define Saint Augustine's own particular development of these themes.

- Since marriage is not an evil, it cannot be prohibited in any way; nor can virginity be imposed, despite its excellence. The apostle's phrase, "if you are free of the marriage bond, do not seek a wife,"[4] should not be understood as a prohibition, but rather as a counsel. How could virginity be called "holy" if it were nothing more than the observance of a law decreed for everyone, and if it were not freely chosen by those who lawfully could have married: "one can seek a wife, therefore, but it is better not to."[5]

- One must not understand this superiority of virginity as the advantage it might give in the life of this world. It brings a certain "tranquility," whereas marriage is necessarily in the service of the "present age"? This is true perhaps, although one has to bear in mind the different battles of the life of continence. But one would be wrong to avoid marriage only to keep from being "strained by earthly cares"[6] which virginity is free of. If it is preferable to flee the disadvantages of marriage, this is not because they disturb the soul's repose, but because they divert it from what its object should be; "they compel one to think less of the things of God than is enough for the obtaining of that glory, which shall not come to all."[7] Doubtless it is possible to find, in the marriage bond, the possibility of a "marital holiness"; but it is "less, because of that portion of cares which are concerned with worldly pleasure. Whatever attention of the soul, therefore, is expended on these things by which she would have to please a husband, the unmarried Christian woman ought in a certain way to gather and concentrate on that earnest purpose by which she is to please the Lord. Assuredly she is by so much the more blessed by how much the more she pleases Him."[8]

• If the privilege of virginity is tied to this possibility of concentrating and directing the *intentio animi*, this is because its end consists in establishing a certain relation with God, which is incompatible with the state of marriage. The absence of corruption that characterizes the life of the angels, which will reward the elect and will enable one to see God face-to-face, is what the life of virginity aims for: "virginal chastity and freedom through pious continence from all sexual intercourse is the portion of Angels, and a practice, in corruptible flesh, of perpetual incorruption." By presenting in their flesh "something that is no longer of the flesh,"[9] those who devote themselves to a perfect continence prefigure in a certain way a hereafter in which marriage will no longer exist.

• In this other life, virginity, which has more merits, will receive richer rewards. Like Cyprian or Athanasius, Augustine[10] takes up the parable of the sower in the Gospel of Saint Matthew (some produced a hundred times what was sown, others sixty, and others only thirty), and he applies it to the merits and rewards of virginity compared to marriage. Moreover, he proposes several possible interpretations of the parable: that virginity produces a hundredfold, widowhood sixty, and marriage thirty; or martyrdom a hundred, virginity sixty, and marriage thirty; or again, martyrdom plus virginity a hundred, virginity and martyrdom separately, sixty. Doubtless Augustine doesn't wish to attach too much importance to these symbolic calculations: "The gifts are more in number than to allow of being distributed under those different degrees." But one has to recognize a diversity between them: men would be brash indeed to attempt to set God's choices in the matter. "Yet it is plain both that those differences are

many, and that the better are profitable not for the present
time, but for eternity."[11]

None of these points can be regarded as specific to Saint
Augustine. However, substantial differences appear immediately
in the use he makes of these themes.

In a word, one can say that, in speaking of marriage or virginity,
Athanasius, Gregory of Nyssa, Basil of Ancyra, and Chrysostom
were mainly interested in defining modes of living, in describ-
ing each one's struggles, dangers, and rewards, in assessing their
relative value, in marking their respective place in the Christian
community. Further, in this comparison of *tekhnai*, it was evident
that the strong point, or element of reference, was constituted by
virginity as the most perfect state to which one might accede in
this earthly existence. Even Chrysostom, who, in the same period
as Augustine, outlined a rule of marital life, doesn't avoid relating it to the difficult art of continence, which for him retains not
only its ethical and ontological superiority, of course, but also a
methodological privilege: he defines good marriage practice as the
least bad management possible of a desire against which married
people don't have the strength or the courage to undertake a radical struggle.

The texts of Saint Augustine don't follow exactly the same
direction.

First, there is a shift of accent toward marriage. Once again,
though, Augustine never considers marriage to be equivalent,
let alone preferable, to an authentically practiced virginity. It is,
and will always remain, of lesser value. But Augustine focuses on
this "lesser" and rethinks its meaning up to a certain point. On
one hand, he tries to define what value there is in marriage that
is directly positive: the place it has, and perhaps has always had,
in Creation; the basis it finds in the ecclesiastical community; so
that the "lesser" value of marriage is not to be understood as the
diminution, the partial devaluation, of the high value of virginity. Marriage has its own distinct value, even if it is not the highest. Further, he concentrates most of his "technical" reflection on
marriage, the rules to be observed therein or the right conduct
to have. Which is not to say that one doesn't find numerous and
precise indications on the practice of chastity—in the sermons[12]

or again in certain anti-Pelagian[13] polemics more than in *De sancta virginitate*, where praise of chastity, against the disciples of Jovinian, takes precedence over the art and manner of living in continence. But it is apropos of marriage—in *De bono coniugali*, later in *De nuptiis et concupiscentia*, or in *Contra Julianum*—that Augustine develops a *tekhnê* and rules of conduct appropriate to a [form] of life. Up to a certain point, one can speak of an inversion of methodological priority in favor of marriage and the *tekhnê*, the art of conducting oneself in a manner proper to the matrimonial state.

But for Augustine the main concern is undoubtedly beyond the scope of the comparative definition of two types of existence. And what distinguishes him from his predecessors and contemporaries is his overall objective: defining the general framework that enables one to conceptualize both the practice of virginity and that of marriage, their respective positivity and their difference of value. Through the hierarchy that separates virginity and marriage, through the different behaviors required of them, what Augustine constructs is the general theory they both are seen as deriving from. In a word: in going beyond the comparison of the virgin and the spouses, the continent Christians and the marriage partners, which had largely been developed prior to him, Augustine makes manifest, not a third figure, or a composite figure, but the fundamental element underpinning the other two: the subject of desire.

Before analyzing the constitution of a theory of concupiscence in the next chapter, we'll look more closely at the first aspect I've mentioned above—the shift of accent toward marriage and the definition of a positive "good" that, while not allowing marriage to outshine virginity, establishes it as worthy in its own right. This shift is shown, in Augustine, in a conception of the Church as a spiritual body, in the exegesis of biblical texts dealing with the Creation and existence before the fall, and finally, in the elaboration of a system of rules capable of actualizing the good that is peculiar to marriage in the life of spouses and in their relations.

I

It isn't necessary to be virgin, or renounce marriage, or practice an absolute continence to belong to the Christian community, even if the Church reserves a special place for virginity. Augustine repeats this after so many others, strongly emphasizing the idea that, as valuable as marriage is, as holy as virginity may be, what surpasses both is that they are joined in a single community and they coexist in the oneness of the Church. The whole is finer even than the finest of its components: "The faithful as a body [. . .] form the members of Christ and the temple of the Holy Spirit, wherein assuredly the faithful of both sexes are understood. Thus, there are married women, there are unmarried women also; but distinct in their merit, and as members preferred to members, while yet neither are separated from the body [. . .] Because certain several created things were better than other several things, but all of them together better than any several."[14] But if the coexistence of virginity and marriage is finer than virginity alone, this is because it's not enough to say that marriage too is a good, but attenuated and somewhat lesser: for this implies that it is a kind of subtraction from the excellence of virginity. One must assume that between them there is something other than a simple juxtaposition: a correlation that has meaning and value—a correlation whereby marriage finds a supplement in virginity, and the latter finds a complement in marriage. The modes of living may very well be distinct in the communities of Christians, but in the community which the Church constitutes there must be a necessary linkage of marriage and virginity.

From Origen or Methodius of Olympus to Chrysostom or Jerome, virginity was never dissociated from certain modalities of spiritual union. It was defined by the refusal of any "marriage," be it the institutional one that connects an individual to another human being, or the general one that attaches them to the world of the flesh. But this renunciation had a bond with Christ as its correlative—at the same time its effect and its condition, its reward and its warrant. The virgin soul was the fiancée and the bride of Christ; and countless spiritual fruits would spring from this union.

In Saint Augustine, the relations between virginity, marriage, and spiritual fertility are much more complex. Both because they assume other forms than simply the virginity–betrothal-to-Christ correlation; and especially because they are involved in all the relations of God to his Church, of the Church to Christ, of Christ to the faithful, and of each of the latter to the whole community. Going beyond the characterization that isolates virgins compared to the other faithful, beyond the differences of status that mark married people, those not yet married, those who are widowed, those who lead a life of continence, those who have pledged themselves to it through vows, beyond the question of forms and rules of life, Saint Augustine brings out, through everything that ought to constitute the Church as a unique spiritual reality, relations that assume both virginity and marriage, betrothal and integrity, maternity or paternity, and absolute chastity. It is not a matter, then, of characteristics that might affect individuals and that designate them as virgins, or spouses, or parents, but of a tight fabric of spiritual ties where each of the elements is at the same time, in relation to others, virgin and spouse, parent and child. So that virginity and marriage, at this level, are not set against each other as two alternative ways of living but are joined together as permanent and simultaneous aspects of relations that form the Church as a spiritual unity. Conceived in this way, and in the form of fertile virginity or virginal marriage, there is no difference of value between virginity and marriage. But it's against the background of this conception of the spiritual relations between God and man that Saint Augustine will establish and explain the hierarchy that must be respected between virginity and marriage understood in the carnal sense.

The whole first part of *De sancta virginitate* is informative on this point, especially if one consults the huge group of sermons on the theme of the Virgin Church[15] for clarification. An immense web of spiritual relations and kinships beyond those of blood are represented; marriage and virginity, virginity and motherhood are never separated; their reciprocal implication is constantly recalled by such expressions as *"virginali connubio spiritualiter conjugatus,"* *"virginum sponsus,"* and *"virginitas fecunditatem non impedit [. . .] fecunditas virginitatem non adimit."*[16]

In a summary way, the numerous and tangled relations mentioned in this passage can be outlined as follows.

So Christ is the son of a virgin;[17] he was born to her, physically, corporeally; and not simply to preserve an integrity which a man "could have violated," but as the fruit of a virginity that, voluntarily, had been dedicated to the union with God;[18] a virgin himself, he is the husband of the Church, virgin itself, which is bonded to him in a spiritual union; but he is also, and more especially, in this Church, the Bridegroom of the virgins who are joined to him by virgin wedding vows.[19] Mary, the eternally virgin mother of Christ, is not virgin simply of body, but also spiritually, since she is pledged to God and has given birth to Christ as he willed, thus serving as model for all the souls that, dedicating their will to God, cause God to be born in themselves.[20] Now, all those who do God's will are, already on earth, the brothers of Christ, who came here to show that will and the right path to follow; therefore, the Virgin is also the sister of Christ.[21] But she must be considered Christ's daughter as well, for all who believe in him are his children and deserve to be called, as Saint Matthew says, "the bridegroom's children."[22] As for the Church, it is "the virgin of Christ," united to him in a spiritual way;[23] corporeally, it can be said to be virgin only because of some of its members, whereas it is not if one considers those of the faithful who have married.[24] As Christ's virgin bride, the Church is the mother of Christians since it is she who causes them to be born to the Spirit by receiving them into baptism;[25] but as the community of saints constitutes the mystical body of Christ, by forming them, by giving birth to them, the Church is also in a sense the mother of Christ, as are those "who do the will of the Father"; "the Church, in the Saints who shall possess the kingdom of God, in the Spirit indeed, is altogether the mother of Christ."[26] And it should be added that any pious soul individually is a daughter of Christ, since it was given birth to out of the latter's nuptials with the Church, and a sister of Christ, since like him it does God's will,[27] and the mother of Christ, since it gives birth to him within itself, being in the image of Mary who does what the Father wills.[28]

So Saint Augustine describes a web of spiritual relations that reproduce and reverse themselves, making each of the four elements of the ensemble—Christ, Mary, the Church, the souls—virgins and spouses, progenitors and children. Marriage, fertility, and virginity don't define the position or the intrinsic quality of any one of them, but make it possible to describe the different relations that each maintains simultaneously with all the others.

So one can say that, in the system of spiritual relations, marriage and virginity cannot be dissociated (and their non-dissociation is manifested by their fertility), but neither of these two terms can be regarded as superior or inferior to the other one. Now, from this reciprocal implication of marriage and virginity in spiritual relations, Saint Augustine doesn't draw the conclusion of a sameness of spiritual value between corporeal virginity and the marriage tie. On the contrary, he counters the Jovinianists, and later Julian of Eclanum, with the principle of a strict hierarchy. The reason is that actually, for him, physical virginity may well represent spiritual virginity, but virgins are in fact the manifestation in the world of virginal relations that produce spiritual fruits. Virginity of body cannot truly exist and deserve the name virginity unless it is sustained and motivated by virginity of heart or of mind: "It is itself honored not because it is virginity, but because it has been dedicated to God, and, although it is kept in the flesh, yet is it kept by religion and devotion of the mind. And by this means even virginity of the flesh is spiritual, sealed and preserved as it is by continence and piety. For, even as no one makes an immodest use of the body unless the sin has been before conceived in the mind, so no one keeps modesty in the body, unless chastity has been before implanted in the mind."[29] On this condition, physical virginity will bring forth the things it is capable of and which are promised to it; in itself, it will give birth to Christ. By its example, it will give rise to this same Christ in the heart of others, and in the Church it will give birth to new offspring for Christ by calling souls to convert.

On the other hand, what marriage produces are not spiritual fruits. From the physical union of a man and a woman only human beings are born, not Christians. They can become members of Christ and children of God only through the spiritual operation of the sacrament: "They who in married life give birth to children after the flesh, give birth not to Christ, but to Adam."[30] It's possible, therefore, to say that women who have refused marriage and dedicated themselves to God have taken on one aspect of the role of Mary, both virgin and the mother of Christ: virginity, corporeal as well as spiritual. But it is not possible to say symmetrically that women who have married and had children have taken up the

physical and spiritual motherhood of Mary, for the Virgin gave
birth to Christ through God's intervention. Through the operation of nature, the married woman gives birth to human beings
that are not Christian. And only this virginity of heart that connects her to Christ in the Church and makes her offer her children
to God allows her to be spiritually a mother: "the Church giving them birth, through this, that in a spiritual manner she is the
mother of the members of Christ, of whom also after a spiritual
manner she is the virgin. And unto this holy birth mothers who
have not borne Christians in the flesh are workers together, that
they may become what they could not give birth to in the flesh:
they only contribute, however, wherein they themselves become
virgins and mothers of Christ, that is to say, in faith which works
through love."[31] Hence there is not a symmetry between virginity
and carnal fertility. Or further, transposed and manifested in the
flesh, the connection of virginity and spiritual nuptials is undone,
and marriage, procreation according to the body, cannot be considered as an inheritance of Mary's motherhood, whereas the
chastity of those who have vowed to forgo marriage here below is,
like the Virgin, dedicated to God. So married women would not
be justified in saying to virgins: "You are virgins, we are mothers:
for what is wanting to you in children, let your virginity, that has
been preserved, be a consolation: for us, let the gain of children
make up for our lost virginity."[32]

So in a way, Augustine has expanded, and multiplied, themes
that existed prior to him: that of virginity as a union with the Bridegroom and that of the Church as Christ's bride. He has woven a
whole set of relations that join together, in a spiritual manner, vir-
ginities that are spiritual as well; he has described the myriad fruits
of these nuptials that, while not being corporeal, are nevertheless
something different than a pure symbol. He has placed marriage
and virginity inseparably at the level of relations that constitute
the spiritual unity of the Church. Whatever the inferior place that
marriage must occupy in life on earth, there is a figure of spiritual
marriage that cannot be dissociated from virginity. Which shows
that it is not at all the very form of marriage that constitutes a
lesser good, but rather whatever led it, in the story of our fall, to
be what it is in this world.

Hence the question: What are marriage's connections with the fall? Is one to think that before the fall there was just one form of spiritual union—which virginity in its own way would reproduce in this world? Mustn't one suppose that marriage, with the physical union that it includes, existed already? And that it was not introduced, but modified by the fall?

II

Like Origen, most Christian exegetes had denied that there were sexual relations in paradise and that the first couple may have procreated physically before the fall following carnal intercourse. Gregory of Nyssa conceded that the humans had received the right to and the possibility of multiplying as soon as their Creation: not, however, as the result of a sexual act, but of an intervention that is not known to us—any more than is the action that populated heaven with angels and caused the countless beings to proliferate. Why, then, was the difference of the sexes marked as early as Creation and the order given to the man and the woman to multiply? The answer, according to Gregory of Nyssa, is that God in his prescience knew that man would fall: a means was given to him in advance by which he could perpetuate his kind beyond the death that was to be his condemnation.[33] In this type of exegesis, one sees that the sexual act is part of the fall and its consequences. It belongs to a bloc that includes the first sin, death, and procreation. It depends on the initial disobedience, which determined its realization (in the existence of the first couple) and even its possibility (in God's foresight). It is linked to procreation, which is its end and its reason for being. It is linked to death, since it is one of the forms of that corruption which deprives men of their immortality. Finally, it is inseparable from desire, *epithumia:* indeed, desire is what provoked the fall—desire in general, the desire for pleasure and not the sexual appetite;[34] the taste for the earth's pleasures instead of for the contemplation of God—is what introduces corruption and death; the desire to perpetuate oneself is what impels men to procreate. The sexual act belongs, therefore, either as a consequence or as a means, to a group of four elements that lead to it or call for it.

In this interpretation, which was traditional in his time, Augustine will bring about a displacement and a dissociation. He will move, if not sexual intercourse then at least its lawful possibility back from the fallen world to paradisiacal existence as it left the hands of the Creator. But this could be accepted only provided that the sexual relation was freed from everything that constituted the stigmata of the fallen existence. Augustine was able to complete this metahistorical requalification of the marital relation, with all the dissociations it implies, only in stages.

*De Genesi contra Manichaeos*, written shortly after his baptism, is still close to the theses of Gregory of Nyssa or of Chrysostom. Paradisaical man, with his body of fresh clay, is described there as being endowed with celestial qualities that make him incorruptible, free him of any physical need, spare him all the disorderly urges of the soul, and make him inaccessible to concupiscence.[35] Augustine then encounters the same problem as his predecessors. What meaning should be given, in this existence without sin, without death, and without lust, to these affirmations of Genesis: that God created man and woman (1:27), that he told them to increase and multiply (1:28), and that the Creator gave the woman as a helper to the man (2:18)? How does one avoid relating this theme of helper to that of the birth of a progeny that would derive from the difference of the sexes? And consequently, how does one not make allowance for sexual procreation in the immortal existence without corruption that obtained in paradise?

Augustine, like his predecessors, appeals to the resources of spiritual interpretation. Formally, however, his position is ambiguous; or, to be more precise myself, it permits two interpretations, since it says that these Genesis texts can also be understood *spiritualiter*, which authorizes one, at least by default, to interpret them *carnaliter*. But, in fact, Augustine develops only the spiritual meaning. The "help" that the woman should bring to the man is interpreted as a relationship of command and submission. Hence the relation that is based on the differentiation of the man and the woman doesn't go by way of sex itself. *Casta conjunctio*. As for increase and multiply, Augustine interprets this as referring to spiritual fruits: "intelligible and immortal joys," says the first text of *De Genesi contra Manichaeos*,[36] or "good works of divine praise,"[37] says the second.

Clearly, the most difficult aspect of such an interpretation is the exact meaning to be given to the theme of the help which the man gets from the woman. Why is the contemplation of God not sufficient for Adam to produce the countless fruits of joy? Why did he need someone else in order to sing God's praises? In *De catechizandis rudibus*, Augustine proposes an interpretation through the relations of glorification and imitation. If God can draw glory from man, this is, of course, not due to the fact that man was molded in clay, but to the fact that he resembles him; and resembles him not only because he was made in God's image but because, with his reason, he freely imitates God's wisdom. In the same way, a man in turn is glorified by a woman if the woman follows him, imitates him, and reproduces the example of wisdom that he gives her. And God is glorified all the more as his image in turn becomes a model.[38] As in *De Genesi contra Manichaeos*, Augustine doesn't absolutely rule out the carnal and material interpretation that conjectured sexual relations before the fall. He doesn't imagine it directly, but in presenting the spiritual interpretation he is careful to note that what it excludes is the idea that before the fall the woman may have been a helper as concerns "carnal concupiscence": how could she have been a helper in this sense when both of their bodies were not yet corruptible? It is clear that in this exegesis, a place for sexual relations free of concupiscence remains open, as well as for a proliferation that would not be a compensation for the mortality of the body. But Augustine doesn't say a word about this possibility. He never refers to it. However, on the basis of later texts, it appears retrospectively that here the textual silence hollows out a space, as it were, for other possible interpretations.

The beginning of *De bono coniugali* is unusual in that it offers a set of these interpretations without saying which one is correct. It's plain to see, however, that the very content of the book and its analysis of the good of marriage imply a preference for one of the hypotheses, which Augustine still chooses to consider as equally plausible for the purpose of exegesis, without the need of further scrutiny: no detailed examination of each one, no definitive opinion about this one or that one. So the passage is presented as the indication of the different and "numerous" interpretations that have been given concerning the increase and multiplication which the first couple were ordered to undertake before the fall. The hypothesis of physical but non-sexual procreation is close to the interpretation suggested by Gregory of Nyssa—but he was referring to the enigmatic multiplication of angelic spirits. Augustine considers three models of non-sexual procreation, all three of which concern bodies—and bodies in this earthly world: God's creation of the first man and the first woman; the formation of Christ's body in the womb of the Virgin; and lastly, an example that should speak to unbelievers themselves, the reproduction of the bees. These three procreations were or still are accomplished *sine concubitu*, and through a beneficent act (*munus*) of God. Following the lesson of these examples, one may suppose, then, with some believers, that God could enable the first couple to physically procreate without sexual intercourse.

The second interpretation is well known. It's the one that understands this multiplication in a "mystical and figurative" sense; the multiplication that was proposed—prescribed and promised at the same time—actually represented the progress of the spirit and abundance of virtue. In this case, there would not have been real childbirth before the fall; the latter having brought death, progeny would have been given to man so that he might perpetuate himself in spite of everything. This is the interpretation that we've encountered in Gregory of Nyssa.

The third hypothesis, which Saint Augustine cites as being supported by some, is undoubtedly less common. The Creation would have given man an animal body, not a spiritual one; thus he would have been subject to dying; but if sin had not intervened, this mortality would never have become a death; humans would have directly rejoined their spiritual destiny; in sum, they would have gone immediately from the earthly paradise where they had the world at their disposal to the heavenly paradise where they contemplate God face-to-face. Mortals escaping death, animals of reason and innocence, men would have been perfectly capable of having children, and conceiving them in the animal manner; that is, through sexual intercourse—*etiam per concubitum*—until, according to the Word, the earth would be filled with a progeny that would not have been destined to replace the ancestors but to live side by side with them. In this interpretation the sexual relation, in the strictest physical and animal sense, therefore becomes entirely possible in paradise. It is neither the consequence nor the cause of the fall; it is inscribed in human nature by the creative act itself. Is it therefore cleared of sin, and of concupiscence? And is it likewise exempted from death?

One might think so, after a cursory review, since the increase of human beings would take place without the intervention of death, and continue up to an adequate peopling of the earth. A deathless procreation, a multiplication that no loss would restrain. However, it should be noted that before his exposition of the three interpretative possibilities, Augustine proposes something that doesn't seem to be one of the views that can be held and have been held in fact, but rather a general principle: through sin, men took on death as their condition, and there cannot be any sexual union (*concubitis*) except between mortal bodies. Now, it's this general principle that one finds in the three interpretations, taking into account a specific modulation for the third one: there, too, the *concubitis* is connected with the possibility of death, with mortality, which forms part of human nature as it was created; it thus existed, as a possibility, prior to sin, which simply introduced the actual condition of death for the human race. In such an interpretation, before the emergence of sin, corruption, and death, before the links that connect them to each other, mortality and the sexual relation were originally and simultaneously present, both of them implied in the animality of the created being.

It is this third interpretation that is finally taken up and developed in *De Genesi ad litteram* (the writing of which begins shortly after *De bono coniugali*, but will be finished much later), then in the fourteenth book of *The City of God*, and in the anti-Pelagian texts that are roughly contemporary with it. The third chapter of book 9 of *De Genesi ad litteram* comments on the passage, or rather the phrase of Scripture (Genesis 2:18) where God says in speaking of the man: "I will make him a helper suitable for him." Once again it is the nature of this help that poses the problem of the possible existence of sexual relations in paradise. In book 3, chapter 21 of the same text, Saint Augustine had commented on "Increase and multiply." "Although" this order, he explained, "seems" to have been realizable only through *concubitis*, one can

imagine "another mode" of multiplication: it would not involve
the concupiscence of corruption, and would result from a feeling of piety. What this question fails to address is the question
of whether this "other mode" excludes *concubitis* (and hence one
of those mysterious interventions to which the Lord could have
and still can have recourse) or whether it involved a *concubitis* having the particular feature, surprising for those who are familiar
only with fallen man, of not being accompanied by concupiscence,
but an altogether different urge of the soul.[39] This uncertainty is
resolved—such a thing was doubtless possible—in book 9 of *De
Genesi*.

What might be the nature of the help which God destined
the woman to provide? Five times in the course of this [book],*
the same reply is given: "for engendering children" (III,5), "for
procreation" (V,9), "for generation" (VI,12), "for the gestation
of children" (VIII,13), "for producing offspring" (XI,19). Which
means that here Augustine completely abandons the idea that this
help was of a spiritual kind and was meant to contribute to the joys
of contemplation or prayer.[40] Now, since nothing in the Genesis
verse in question directly authorizes this affirmation, Saint Augustine bases it on reasoning. Or rather on two reasonings. One goes
by way of elimination.[41] What might the woman have been good
for in paradise? For working the ground? Assuredly not, because
work was not necessary then, and in any case a second man would
have been more effective. To make it so that the man was not
alone, that he might live and speak with someone (*conviveri* and
*colloqui*)? Not for that either, because one knows very well that a
man's best companion is another man and that if a certain inequality was necessary for the tranquility of this companionship, a pact
between these two men based on the preeminence of the first one
created would have sufficed. Not for company, not for labor; the
woman's help must have had to do with children, then.

The other reasoning consists in showing the advantages of
progeny for the first humans and a peopling of the entire earth.[42]
It should be noted that Augustine doesn't make direct use of the
text "Increase and multiply" to make paradisaical procreation the

* Manuscript: "chapter."

simple application of this precept. He tries to show that before the fall, apart from death, and independently of the concern for replacing those who disappear, the proliferation of the human race was a thing to be sought after. Indeed, by multiplying, humanity would increase the beauty of the earth. And how would the multiplication of righteous men not have been, before the fall, a very great embellishment if one considers four things: that the animal species themselves add to the beauty of the lower world, that even corrupt men are still better than the animals, that a mankind of numerous sinners, maintained in peace by the example of a few decent men, is something beautiful in itself, and finally that the men born of the first parents without the sin of the latter would be both immortal and righteous? So proliferation is in itself (and not in compensation for death) a good. And what better means to form this *societas* on the surface of the earth than the birth of successive generations "starting from just one man"?

Through this multiplication out of a single trunk, humanity can cover the surface of the earth to the extent God intended, and maintain the unity by which the Creator meant to distinguish it at its very origin. The fourteenth book of *The City of God*, devoted to the consequences of the original sin and concupiscence, opens precisely with this theme. The unity-multiplicity of the human race and humanity as a *societas*, held together by resemblance and kinship in peaceful relations, appear to be the end that God was pursuing as early as the Creation, before any sin and any fall and any death: "God, desiring not only that the human race might be able by their similarity of nature to associate with one another, but also that they might be bound together in harmony and peace by the ties of relationship, was pleased to derive all men from one individual, and created humanity with such a nature that the members of the race should not have died."[43]

Summarizing, the three basic scriptural elements on this subject being the creation of two distinct sexes, the prescription of growth and multiplication, and the addition of the woman as a helper for the man, it seems that the earlier exegetes focused most of their effort on the first two. They wanted to avoid not only the presence of the sexual act, but even its possibility before the fall. For this they had to postpone "till later" the use of a differentiation of the sexes whose significance and effects needed to remain virtual up to the moment of sin. They were obliged to give multiplication a spiritual meaning; and consequently, the third element had to be left vague: the woman's help remained a theme with no precise content. For Augustine, on the other hand, it is this element that gives direction to the analysis. By attempting to narrow as much as possible the meaning to be given to this help, by attempting to define the man-woman relation, apart from any sin and prior to the fall, by trying to establish the likely form and purpose of their association, Augustine, through successive eliminations, is led to attribute a "physical," "corporeal," "carnal" signification to the order given to the first couple to multiply, and an immediately actualizable value to the originary differentiation of the sexes. From the fact that the assistant given to the man was that "other" which the woman is—not only a being who resembles him, not only someone inferior to him, but someone whose resemblance-inferiority takes the form of sexual difference— Augustine deduces that this otherness had the function of founding and developing *societas* spread over the entire earth—that is, a multiplicity of individuals interconnected by an identity of nature and a kinship of origin. The multiplicity of successive births was not introduced into the history of the world to compensate for the limits of death, but rather, according to Augustine, by the originary privilege given to a "society" as an adornment and a beauty added to the world. It was for the sake of man's relations with his fellows that the woman was joined to him as a helper. For planting the seeds of humankind, the seeds of the race of his countless future companions, a man needs the fertility of a plot of ground.[44]

The "marriage" of the first couple implied for Augustine something different than a spiritual relation; it assumed at least the possibility of a physical union, which was indicated by the originary differentiation of the sexes and which promised the physical procreation of progeny. Sexual relations and generation no longer belong in an unequivocal and necessary way to the economy of the fall. They already have a place, with the couple formed by the first humans willed by God, in the order of a Creation not yet corrupted by the fall.

Augustine will never renounce this thesis. One finds it fully set out in the fourteenth book of *The City of God*. God created the first humans, "male and female"; he inscribed "their sex in the flesh"; and this was "in order to engender children and thereby to increase, multiply, fill the earth"; he thus created them "as we see and recognize today the diversity of the sexes among men."[45] One also finds it in the anti-Pelagian writings, without the different polemical contexts, or the need to reply to objections, ever modifying it in its essentials: "And the diversity of the sexes relates to the organs of those who engender, and their union relates to the procreation of children, and fecundity itself relates to the blessing of marriage."[46]

But if the union of the sexes had a rightful place in paradise, with the first couple, to what system of rules should it be subjected in today's world?

### III

Whether or not it was the first great Christian systematization of marital life and its internal relations, *De bono coniugali* has remained in any case the basic reference concerning the moral theology of marriage for medieval and modern Christianity.[47] Its authority has been cited to maintain the two-part theory of the goods and the ends of marriage. The goods of marriage that ensure its value, which is next to but beneath continence: offspring, the faith that unites marriage partners, the sacrament that marks them in a permanent way. The ends of marriage, which codes the "use" of marriage, make it possible to define the prohibited and permitted sexual relations: procreation and the remedy for concupiscence.

This theoretical edifice is very well known. Obviously, it would be completely incorrect to say that its basic elements are not found in Saint Augustine—one re-encounters them in numerous passages of his work.[48] It is also erroneous to claim that they don't correspond to the text of *De bono coniugali*. The end of this treatise, which summarizes the whole, is quite explicit: "Marriage is therefore a good among all the peoples and in all of humanity because it is the basis for begetting children and for the pact of a chaste fidelity, but, so far as pertains unto the People of God, it adds the sanctity of the Sacrament [. . .] All these are goods, on account of which marriage is a good: children, faith, sacrament."[49] And in another passage, Augustine does speak of the two ends that will later be cited regularly: *liberorum procreandorum causa* and *infirmitatis invicem excipiendae causa*.[50] Of course, this schematic formulation doesn't really take into account either the development of the texts, or the substantial revisions that Augustine contributed to the Christian understanding of marriage, to the analysis of it that can be brought to bear, and finally to the system of rules that should govern the conduct of spouses.

As we've seen, Augustine gives marriage a double backing: that of the origin, since it is part of the Creation; and that of the Church, since it is one of the spiritual forms that constitutes it. It is thus a good—*aliquid boni*.[51] A good *in* itself, which means that it is not a good only by comparison (better than the evil of fornication); however, marriage is not a good *by* itself. Referring to a traditional philosophical difference, Augustine distinguishes between what is desirable by itself, and what is desirable for something other than itself, that is, for one of those ends that don't need to relate to any other. He draws up the following table. An end for itself: wisdom (*sapientia*); a good that relates to that end: the knowledge (*doctrina*) that isn't desired for itself but for attaining wisdom. An end for itself: health (*salus*); goods that relate to it: drinking, eating, sleeping. As for marriage, which, like knowledge, food, and sleep, is not its own end, what good does it relate to? To friendship, which, just like health and wisdom, is desirable for itself.[52]

All of *De bono coniugali* is placed under the aegis of this notion that appears already in the first lines of the text: friendship is an end that exerts a considerable force on man, because of his very nature: the individual in fact is an "element," a "part" of the human race, and he is, in himself, as a man, a social being.[53] Friendship binds him to this whole which he belongs to by nature; and marriage is desirable as what makes it possible to form, multiply, and firmly establish these ties of friendship.

This theme is nothing very new. It is completely familiar to ancient philosophy. And it is also present in many Christian authors; we encountered a version of it in Chrysostom's homilies. Yet it's on the basis of this conception of *societas* and *amicitia* that

Augustine fashions his theory of marriage and marital relations, and introduces a number of decisive elements into it—essentially on three points: on the role of marriage in the general economy of salvation; on the nature of the marriage bond; and on the principle of regulation of sexual relations between spouses.

1.  When Chrysostom, in texts exactly contemporary with *De bono coniugali*, saw in marriage a way of establishing a social tie between men, he was designating a usefulness that could be called episodic. Marriage had its role to play between the fall and salvation: after the fall, to repair the ravages of death or console men for them; before salvation, whose imminent arrival makes the multiplication of humans useless henceforth. For him, the value of marriage belonged to a time which is that of law and death. A time that is coming to an end.

*De bono coniugali* articulates the periods of human history and the necessity of *societas* in a different way. In a word: it frees the latter of its episodic function and its temporary status. It makes it a constant and no longer a moment; but the drama of the relationship between God and man brings crucial modifications to this constant.

As we've already seen, if the human being was created "man and woman," this was for the sake of a *societas* whose necessity was inscribed in the very nature of individuals destined to belong to the human race. The *societas* did not wait for the punishment of death to become necessary and to make marriage a good. But is it still written into our present? In the time of the Incarnation, does it have enough of a future to recommend marriage? Isn't its natural role a thing of the past? *De bono coniugali* does in fact speak of the moment when the proliferation of the human race will no longer be required: "For knowledge shall be destroyed [. . .] Thus also this mortal begetting, on account of which marriage takes place, shall be destroyed: but freedom from all sexual intercourse is both an angelic exercise here, and something that continues forever."[54] A formulation like this one is quite close, even in its wording, to those of Chrysostom, Gregory of Nyssa, or Basil of Ancyra. But a distinction must be made between two different ideas in the theme of the "age of continence." The idea evoked in the text just quoted: indeed, it's a matter of the end of time, when in fact physical relations will no longer have their place because the heavenly city will admit of only spiritual relations. And the idea that is expressed several times in other passages,[55] where it's a question of the current situation of the human race, Augustine characterizes it as a fact and a task. As things stand, the earth is already abundantly populated. This was done, and is still being done, by a large number of people, married or not, who did not practice continence; in this way they offer a great "resource of successions." The task consists in forming saintly friendships from among all these humans, and in constituting in this manner, little by little, throughout all the nations, a "vast spiritual kinship," a "pure and holy society." The present is to be thought of less with a sense of urgency than by taking the long view; less as an imminent ending than as an equilibrium to be slowly moved forward. *De bono coniugali* does not announce the entry into an age of virginity, where marriage, necessary heretofore, will have to be abandoned; it shows instead, while of course maintaining the horizon of the end of time, the existence of a period, ours, in which the proliferation of the human race, thanks to physical unions, will be the necessary material, as it were, for the multiplication of spiritual kinships. Virginity and marriage can thus be brought together, each in its place, on the principle that the whole of which they are related parts is even more excellent than the finer of the two.

In this way Augustine profoundly alters the periodization that was rather generally recognized before him: a moment of paradisiacal virginity, in the innocence preceding the fall; then a time of marriage and fecundity, under the law of death; then a return to virginity, when salvation comes and time ends. The overview that emerges in *De bono coniugali* is quite different: it doesn't alternate virginity and marriage in a cycle; it notes instead the different ways of constituting the *societas*, which in any case is the "end" of the human race. There was at first the possibility, in paradise, of a *societas* that was spiritual and corporeal at the same time; then came the time when men propagated the race, some "defeated by passion" (*victi libidine*), others—the Patriarchs—"led by piety." The latter, if they had permission, remained continent; but if they married and "sought sons of their marriage, this was for the sake of Christ; in order to distinguish his race after the flesh from all nations."[56] Today the distribution is different: the division is no longer between impious proliferation and holy procreation, but between those dedicated to spiritual relations and those who, unable to achieve continence, continue to populate the earth. All of them prepare the future city: the first by multiplying spiritual relations; the others by yielding to the law of marriage that symbolically projects the coming unity of the heavenly society.[57] Finally, the fourth age is that of this city itself. There, the multiplicity will no longer be that of the proliferation of human beings, issued from their sexual unions; and the unity will no longer be that of couples constrained to practice a single marriage. The multitude of souls will join together and be of one heart and one spirit in the unity of God. All relations, of a spiritual kind thenceforth, will converge toward him alone; and in this manner, after the "peregrinations" here below, the *societas* for which the human race was destined will attain its final reality in the unity of the heavenly city. Hence Augustine no longer relates the value of marriage to that absolute good, virginity, which characterized the initial state of humanity and the last point in time; he relates it to *societas* as the universal and constant end. And if marriage has not always had the same form, or the same role, or the same obligations, if it has not always stood in contrast to virginity in the same manner, this is because before and after the fall, before and after the Savior's coming, the human race has not advanced in the same manner toward the future city.

2. The privilege given to *societas* enables a characterization of marriage centered on the notion of the *bond*. Before anything else, marriage is an association, and as such, a basic element of society. Now, should it be understood that it owes its value to the natural act of procreation that it permits in rightful forms, or to a juridical structure that binds the spouses in regard to each other? Is the marriage bond the condition of a kinship or the result of a *pactum*? The analysis of *De bono coniugali* is more complex than simply a choice between these two terms.

One mustn't minimize the role of procreation and descendants in the Augustinian problematic of marriage. We'll see its importance further on. And it's a fact that if there were no off-spring, hence no succession in the generations, the human race could not be held together, in its contemporary and successive elements, by a *connexio societatis*.[58] Considering the whole human race and its destiny, the necessity of marriage cannot be conceived without progeny. But taken in itself, and as a joining of two per-sons in a relation, the marriage bond can't be considered as being dependent on progeny and procreation. By itself, marriage consti-tutes society's first link, and this bond is not less strong than that of birth, as the Creator showed "by drawing the woman from the man" and "by signifying the strength of their union by the side he extracted from the one to form the other."[59] Even before any pro-creation, marriage is by itself a good, in that it establishes between the husband and the wife a relation that has the threefold charac-teristic of being "natural," of joining two different sexes,[60] and of forming a combination of friendship and kinship into a basic ele-ment of society.[61] It follows, then, that if procreation furthers this bond—and that, with certain restrictions, it is good that this is the case—it is nonetheless not a requisite condition and its absence doesn't compromise the marriage. And Augustine supports this with two examples in point. Marriage between old people exists, even if it's not possible for them to procreate, or their children are already dead; in any case the bond subsists, independent of progeny.[62] In like manner, the marriage cannot be undone when, undertaken for the sake of having children, it has remained sterile in spite of the spouses.[63]

*De bono coniugali* regularly gives the name *pactum* or *foedus* to this relation, words whose juridical connotations are evident.[64] Looking at things more closely, Augustine develops his analy-sis in two registers. He refers, in fact, to the theme of a bond that receives an institutional sanction, either through legal rules or through divine law; sometimes civil law is invoked as being indicative of the right form of the marriage tie: thus, Roman law manifests the exclusive character of this tie, since it forbids the husband to take a second wife as long as the first one is still liv-ing;[65] other times the religious laws uphold just principles which the rules of society don't take into account; thus they disallow—unlike the civil laws—the remarriage of a husband whose wife has committed adultery.[66] But Augustine also brings the *pactum* into play in another register, that of the relations between souls and between bodies: an attachment of souls that constitutes an *ordo caritas* between spouses, independent of physical ardor, and often even with an inverse intensity relative to the latter; but also a physical attachment, in the sense that each of the marriage partners reserves their body for the other. In the famous passage of the First Epistle to the Corinthians—"the wife's body is not in her power, but in that of her husband, and similarly the husband's body" (7:4)—one sees in general the affirmation of the right of each spouse to have physical relations with the other; but Augustine, at least in one of his two mentions of it, ascribes a somewhat negative signification to it; it would express the prohibition against violating the marital pact, as that happens "when, moved by his own passion, or that of another, the husband has relations with a different woman, or another man's wife."[67] Non-betrayal, rather than possession: such ties are of the order of *fides*.

This order is not unrelated to the law, of course, and often converges with it,[68] but it can still not be reduced to it—as is immediately shown by the example of *fides* given by Augustine: whether, in an affair, it's a matter of a fistful of straw or a heap of gold, the faith that guarantees truthfulness is exactly the same and has the same value. It should be understood that *fides* sustains the agreement, that it is manifested in the exactness with which it is observed, but it is not of the same nature as it. And as far as the sins that may be committed against it are concerned, it has different effects from the agreement as a thing protected by the laws. Using three examples, Augustine shows clearly that for him *fides* is not the same as the *pactum*—at least if the latter is understood in a purely juridical sense. These examples are instances of *adultery*, which is both a category of law and a breach of *fides*. It would seem at first glance that the condemnation of adultery manifests a match between the juridical connection and the attachment of fidelity. But each of the examples cited by Augustine shows the extent to which they are different.

• Let's imagine a wife who has left her husband for a lover: a rupture of fidelity. But for her now, and for her morality, does it make any difference whether or not she stays faithful to her lover? From the viewpoint of the juridical *pactum*, it makes no difference since the only pact that existed—the one connecting her to her husband—was broken. And yet one can say that, while she was dishonest, she is less so if she stays attached to her accomplice than if she again changes partners. But she is more honest if the one for whom she abandons him is her husband to whom she returns. As one sees, *fides* modulates the sin according to degrees that the violation of the *pactum* doesn't recognize.

• Picture now a man and a woman living together; they don't seek to have any children—without doing anything criminal to prevent a birth. They have made the commitment of fidelity and will honor it till one of them dies. To this union that no juridical document sanctions—and is therefore cohabitation—one can give the name "marriage" as long as the fidelity is respected. Thus, from the standpoint of morality *fides* alone can have the same effects as having had a *pactum* recognized by the law.

• Lastly, think of a man and woman who aren't married. They have a transitory liaison. For his part, the man is only waiting for an occasion to find a rich and honorable woman. But the woman intends to remain faithful to her lover; and once she's dropped, she practices continence. One can't say that she hasn't sinned since she's had relations outside of marriage. But could one call her adulterous? And if, during the entire time of her relationship, she didn't do anything to keep from having children, isn't she better than "a good number of matrons," who are not adulterous but use marriage only to satisfy their concupiscence?

These examples[69] show very clearly the non-coincidence of *fides* with something that would be a purely juridical bond. Even where it seems to have the same form and the same consequences—speaking of adultery—it brings in elements that are irreducible simply to a legal obligation. Positive obligations: the attachments of the soul, the commitments with regard to oneself, the respect that one owes to the other; but modulations of the sin, which make it possible to rank behaviors, relative to one another, which the form of the law would lump together.

This time, Augustine doesn't make this a trait peculiar to Christian marriage. It can constitute a good of marriage among "all peoples" and "all men."[70] On the other hand, what belongs only to the union of Christians is the fact that it is a "sacrament." The meaning this word takes in *De bono coniugali* is not easy to grasp, perhaps, because Augustine is obviously not talking about the "sacrament of marriage" as it will be understood much later in medieval Christianity, and yet he likens it to the "sacrament of ordination" that is conferred on a cleric. But the very manner in which the comparison is made, plus a quotation that Augustine borrows from the first Epistle to the Corinthians, helps one grasp what makes Christian marriage a *sacramentum*. The scriptural text says that "a wife must not separate from her husband, but if she does she must remain unmarried or reconcile with him" (1 Cor. 7:10–11). For Augustine this passage illustrates the sacrament and not the fidelity—to which Saint Paul must be referring when he speaks of the power that each of the spouses exercises over the other's body. This is because fidelity assumes reciprocity (hence the word *pactum* that is applied to it, even if this means giving it a non-juridical value). When one of the two spouses breaks this bond, how can the mere duty of fidelity still hold? Whereas if the wife is separated from her husband—Augustine is obviously not thinking of an adulterous wife, but of one who has left her husband after the latter's adultery, or one who has been repudiated by him—the sacrament takes away her right to enter into another union. With the exclusive bond that it establishes with another person, and them only, marriage continues to obligate each of the spouses, even when the other, on their own initiative, has broken it. It's a matter of a personal stamp in a way. This is the meaning of the parallel drawn between marriage and ordination. The latter is invoked by Augustine only in one of its aspects: once consecrated, someone who has received the sacrament of the order may well not have received any flock, or could have been relieved of his office, but he remains ordained and the sacrament stamps him for all time.[71] Now where might this mark come from? Certainly not from a juridical tie that is not apt to impose on an individual a constraint that persists once it has been undone. And certainly not from a fidelity that implies a reciprocity of intentions. But from a seal that is applied by God and that binds an individual to their state of marriage, for as long a time as God himself has not called the spouse back to him. "In the City of our God, where, even from the first union of the two, the man and the woman, marriage bears a certain sacramental character, it can no way be dissolved but by the death of one of them."[72] In sum, the marriage bond as it is described in *De bono coniugali* differs from a juridical connection in two ways: by its "fidelity" and by its "sacrament." Both of these can be called "goods" of marriage in that they are not limited to ensuring what each spouse can seek for themselves, but they bring each one into a *societas*. A society where their soul and their body are connected to one another by the attachment of fidelity. A society in which God causes them to participate individually and definitively through the indelible seal of marriage that he places on them.

3.  We should return now to that question of progeny which seems to become quite secondary once the essence of Christian marriage is defined by the bond of fidelity and the mark of the sacrament. Augustine says explicitly and repeatedly that progeny is one of the three "goods" of marriage—one of the elements that, while leaving marriage beneath continence, allows one to recognize that it is good, if not by itself, at least in itself.

Yet the formulations of *De bono coniugali*, like subsequent texts, give this third good a particular position. On the one hand, Augustine says—and shows by his analyses—that it is, in fact, less important than the others. "In our marriage the holiness of the sacrament has more value than the fertility of the womb."[73] It is less constitutive of marriage than the other two goods, since the absence or disappearance of offspring doesn't undo the marriage and conversely the intention to make children cannot be what transforms a liaison into a marriage.[74] But on the other hand, there's an abundance of statements saying that procreation is the

goal, and even the only goal of marriage. In all the nations marriage has the same goal: the procreation of children;[75] generation
is the reason weddings were instituted.[76]

The explanation is to be sought no doubt in those two notions
of a "good" and an "end" of marriage. If one recalls the general
theory of goods,[77] one easily understands how progeny can be
regarded as a good of marriage next to the sacrament and fidelity. Remember that marriage is a desirable end, but as a means to
another end, which is valuable in itself: friendship or the connection that naturally attaches humans to each other as parts of the
same humankind. Procreation is a way of connecting individuals
and thus of producing or developing the *societas*. But it must be
emphasized straightaway that progeny don't establish this connection in marriage as *sacramentum* or *fides*. These are properties of the
marital bond; they are integral to it. Progeny can be only an effect
of marriage, one of its consequences. And the marriage tie, which
in itself forms a component of society, finds in its offspring a means
of developing beyond itself the relations necessary to this society.
Progeny is an "objective" which marriage takes as an end that it
also attains just by being a permanent bond between individuals.
But it should be added that, without this procreation, the marriage
tie alone would not suffice for the development of a society on the
scale of the human race: the first couple would have remained the
only one in the world. One can say, then, that *proles* is in itself a
good of marriage, since it links individuals; that it is not an indispensable condition for this, since marriage can exist without it; that
it is an objective of marriage, since it is a means for marriage to
attain its end, society; that progeny is even its "sole" objective, as
opposed to the sacrament and to fidelity (which are themselves an
intrinsic part of the marital bond), and seeing that it is indispensable for joining individuals together in one human race.

But the role of procreation in marriage is further complicated
from the fact that it can't be dissociated from the status of sexual
relations. Not only because those relations are indispensable to
*proles*, of course, but because determining progeny as the goal
serves as a regulatory principle for sexual relations: "The continuity of society is guaranteed by the children, the only worthy fruit,
not of the union (*concubitus*) of man and wife, but of their car-

nal intercourse."[78] For Augustine, the necessity of *proles* is clearly what explains that the "conjunction" of two individuals in marriage coincides with an act between a man and a woman. But it would be a mistake to reduce Augustine's analysis to nothing more than the subjection of the sexual relation to the possibility and the obligation of having children. Far from finding in his texts a unitary bloc constituted by marriage, sexual relations, and procreation (which was the case in certain moralists of the Hellenistic and Roman epoch, or in Clement of Alexandria), one can note a number of dissociations and incongruities.

I'll focus first on the way *De bono coniugali* spins the question of the impurity of sexual relations.[79] Leviticus's prescriptions had often been used by the Christian authors to show that every physical relation harbored something evil or sinful within it, since it called for purification rituals, even for lawfully married spouses. Augustine replies to this with two arguments. One of them has a general scope: what is impure is not of itself a sin: women's periods are impure, and corpses are as well; where is the sin? The other argument is specific to the sexual relation: semen, certainly, is impure. But it is impure like everything that is still raw, incomplete, combined with elements that will have to disappear in order for the definitive and complete form to appear. So that, understood in this way, the prescriptions of Leviticus don't refer to the impurity of the sexual act itself, but rather to the semen; they concern only that which the semen must shed before serving its purpose; finally, they have a symbolic value: they show man that he needs to "cleanse himself of this formless life, by assuming the form of the doctrine and the science."[80] Thus Augustine, while justifying the ritual practices, avoids giving a negative character to the sexual act itself. He continues to frame it in terms of its natural usefulness to the development of humankind: "what food is to the conservation of the man, sexual intercourse (*concubitus*) is to the health of the race."[81]

That the sexual act is not bad in itself doesn't mean that it is acceptable in all its forms and in every case. Augustine brings several sorts of limitations to bear. Some already belonged to the ancient morality. The others are more specific to Christian doctrine, prescribing "temperance" and rejection of every form of "excess." But how is temperance defined? It means staying within the bounds of "natural use."[82] And for Augustine as for ancient tradition, this natural use is the sexual act if it has the form that may lead to procreation. But with respect to this natural use, two types of sin can be committed, between which Augustine doesn't establish a very clear division, though he does posit a big moral difference between them. On the one hand, there is simple quantitative "excess": it is the excess one indulges in by going "beyond the necessity of propagation": things done and pleasures taken that are not simply those required by the "natural" sexual act, but which accompany it or prepare it. On the other, there are the acts contrary to nature, which are exemplified by the use of a part of the wife's body that is not meant for that.[83] The first of these faults are rather minor. The second kind, however, are very serious. While maintaining this hierarchy, Augustine condemns them with a formula that one might find in the philosophers of antiquity: "Marital honor is chastity in procreation."[84]

But he also brings into play other principles for regulating the sexual act. The very ones that Chrysostom pointed to during the same period. They open up the possibility of legitimizing sexual acts between spouses that don't have any procreative end: provided that each of the partners is intent only on helping the other avoid greater sins—those they commit either outside marriage, or against the rules of nature. Here it's no longer a question of the "natural" end of marriage, but of the consequence of the personal tie it establishes and the type of obligations it entails. This concern for the other's concupiscence, with a view to the help they need for their salvation, forms the basis of marital duty. It is significant that Saint Paul's text about the wife's body being in the power of the husband and vice versa is not construed by Augustine as the expression of a right of possession of which the sexual act would be the direct consequence.[85] If one of them can demand the body of the other, and if the latter cannot withhold it from them, this is not because they are its sovereign owner, it's that for them it's a matter of not running the risk of falling into sin: "They owe one another a mutual servitude of support for each other's weakness, in order to shun forbidden relations."[86] In sum, each one owes this service, this servitude, not as a function of the partner's power over one's body, but of one's weakness in regard to one's own body.

From this principle, Augustine draws certain general consequences that were already well known: no one can dedicate oneself to perpetual continence without the other's consent. Augustine establishes the hierarchy that will have so much importance subsequently and will give rise to so many difficulties: marital sex for the purpose of procreation is completely exempt from sin; having sex "to satisfy concupiscence" constitutes a venial sin; as for acts that are committed outside or against the marriage ties (fornication or adultery), or those within marriage that are against nature, they are mortal sins. But Augustine goes much further in the codification of sexual relations between spouses. The problem is that the very idea of a venial sin being attached to having sex when this is done only to satisfy concupiscence is not clear. For isn't marital duty designed to make sure that even independently of procreation, one can give the other's concupiscence enough to satisfy it without falling into sins that may be serious? So a distinction must be brought in between the one demanding that they be rendered the marital duty and the one rendering it. The latter, insofar as they consent in order to keep their partner from falling into a serious sin, doesn't commit any sin, even a venial one, since they are only applying a rule deriving from the state of marriage.[87] But the one demanding it? Augustine's position seems less clear. On the one hand, he speaks of a venial sin[88] by those who are "under the yoke of concupiscence," hence, it seems, by those who demand the duty for any other end than procreation. But on the other hand, he cites the tolerance granted by the Apostle to those who insist too strongly that the duty be done:[89] consequently, those are the ones who would commit a venial sin. Should we understand, then, that those who demand the duty with the intention of avoiding the risk of a mortal sin would not be committing any sin at all, but would be just as innocent as those rendering the duty?—something that seems difficult in itself, but which constitutes the only solution compatible with the idea of the venial sin incurred by those who demand it with too much insistence. As for the two spouses who by mutual agreement demand the marital duty of one another, Augustine's text is tricky to interpret. It comes right after the statement absolving of any sin the spouse who renders the duty to keep the other from sinning: "But if both are set under such lust, they do what is plainly not a matter of marriage. However, if in their intercourse they love what is honest more than what is dishonest, that is, what is a matter of marriage more than what is not a matter of marriage, this is allowed to them on the authority of the Apostle as a matter of pardon."[90] It seems possible to understand that the marital act, if it is performed on both sides on account of the concupiscence of each of the two, deviates from the strict rules of marriage, and consequently can become a serious matter. Yet it can remain within veniality's limits of indulgence on one condition: that one keeps to what is honest (that is, to acts delimited by the intention to procreate, although this intention may not be present) or in a general way to what is not "a matter of marriage," which is to say the possible birth of offspring and the fulfillment of one's duty.

In fact, here *De bono coniugali* is providing the rudiments of a jurisprudence of sexual relations between spouses that, especially in the second half of the Middle Ages and up until the eighteenth century, will assume a considerable importance. It will help to constitute an extremely complex code of marital sexuality. A whole ensemble of social and cultural conditions will be necessary for its development. This will also require that certain notions that *De bono coniugali* effectively contains be reshaped or at least completely formulated. These notions pertain to the way marriage qualitatively transmutes sexual relations and the pleasure they produce. Two series of passages in particular are significant. First, there are those concerning moderation of the *libido*. At the beginning of the treatise, it is said that "the marriage bond transforms the evil of concupiscence into a good." And this transformation is explained by the effect of internal moderation that would result from the intention to procreate, even where the sensuality is most intense: "The marriage bond [. . .] compresses sensuality in its transports when, at the moment of union of the man and the woman, it brings a sort of modesty into their passion and tempers them with parental affection. There is interposed a certain gravity of glowing pleasure, when in that wherein husband and wife cleave to one another, they have in mind that they be father and mother."[91] Later, Augustine further accentuates this idea that the right use of marriage constitutes a brake for concupiscence; he goes so far as to say that, well tempered, pleasure in marriage can be something not involving *libido* at all. It's the same with *concubitus* as with food: "both are not without carnal delight (*delectatio carnalis*), which yet being modified, and by restraint of temperance reduced to its natural satisfaction, cannot be regarded as lust (*libido*)."[92]

In the *Retractationes*,[93] Augustine will revisit this passage, asserting that he wasn't talking about an erasure of *libido* through marriage, but that he meant that use of the *libido*, if it is good and correct, is not itself a *libido*. This clarification or correction is very much in line with the theory of concupiscence that he must have developed in the interim. But it doesn't seem that it is actually present in *De bono coniugali*. The principle according to which there is no sexual relation without concupiscence since the fall, and that only the use constitutes the moral difference, is not found in the analysis contained in *De bono coniugali*. A second series of texts proves this. They relate to the Patriarchs, whose irregularities with respect to monogamy presented such a problem for Christian exegetes, as we know. When they married, when they procreated, those Patriarchs, according to Augustine, "were not defeated by concupiscence."[94] They experienced a natural pleasure, to be sure, just as today the saints of the new covenant take pleasure in eating bread; but in them there was not a bit of "irrational and criminal concupiscence." For, knowing that procreation was necessary in order for the race of the Lord to be born, and that their descendants would belong to the "prophetic economy" (*dispensatio prophetica*), their desire (*desiderium*) was spiritual. To explain the spiritual form of this desire, Augustine employs a spiritual term: that of sacrament. The prophets' desire was "in keeping with the sacrament of the age."[95] The use of the word here is explained by an earlier passage where the "prophetic sacraments" are the visible marks under which the future salvation had concealed itself before the Savior's coming. The prophets bore these signs. Their conduct itself showed the seal of God's will. Here there's an overlap with the concept of the "sacrament" evoked in the same text in reference to Christian marriage. And it seems that one can say that the marriage of the Patriarchs—and this is its superiority over marriages today—was a "sacrament" in its entirety: the sign in each one of a present and future spiritual kinship.

One can say in broad terms that in the marriage of the prophets, the sacrament erases every trace of concupiscence, whereas in the marriage of today's Christians, it is attenuated, diminished, and modified. But the possibility and the form of this modification remain enigmatic, which obviously makes several elements of the codification that Augustine intends to apply to sexual relations between spouses rather uncertain. An economy of concupiscence in marriage is still lacking. Or, in other words, a definition of the marriage bond and of the rules of living that ought to characterize the marital state cannot be completed without a theory of *libido*. As long as the main focus of the preoccupations and analyses was virginity or continence, rules of abstinence in an economy of purity were sufficient. But when it becomes necessary to define a *tekhnê* of living and of marital relations based on certain principles, a theory of concupiscence and of an economy of desire is what is needed. And Augustine will set that up by supplying a definition of the difference which the fall introduced into the sexual relation; by specifying the forms that characterize *libido* in fallen man; and by drawing a strict distinction between *libido* and the use of *libido*. In this way he will happen to give the basis both of a general conception of desiring man, and of a meticulous juridiction of sexual acts that will have a profound effect on the morality of the Christian West.

# 3

# The Libidinization of Sex

The physical union of the sexes, when it takes place in marriage with procreation as its end, is therefore free of fault, *inculpabalis* as *De bono coniugali* says.[1] Is there more to be said?

We have seen that it had its place, in the creation of the human being, before sin and the fall, even if it didn't have any reality then: it was the work of God who provided it for the constitution of a human race as a "society." In today's marriage, it still has this role, since it is necessary for procreation; and this procreation is one of the ends and goods of marriage. This being the case, can it not be considered a good itself—a good originally placed by God and maintained after the fall? Isn't one tempted to pass from the *bonum conjugale* to a *bonum sexuale*?

A brief evocation, in *The City of God*, of the sexual act in its form and its unfolding reveals the nature of the problem. In that passage Augustine faithfully reiterates the classic description of the sexual climax with its three essential points: a physical paroxysm that one can't control, a tremor of the soul which is overwhelmed by pleasure despite its resistance, a final eclipse of thought that seems to resemble death. "The desire (*libido*) by which the shameful parts of the body are excited" is not satisfied with "taking possession of the whole body and its outward members, but also makes itself felt within, and moves the whole man with a passion in which mental emotion is mingled with bodily appetite, so that the pleasure is the greatest of all bodily pleasures. So possessing indeed is this pleasure, that at the moment in which it is consummated, all mental activity is suspended." The conclusion addresses the situation rather simply: "What friend of wisdom and holy joys (*sapientiae sanctorumque gaudiorum*), who, being married, would not prefer to beget children without this 'desire' (*libido*)?"[2] The formulation is worth noting: the "friends of wisdom" who would wish to be spared this violent infirmity are undoubtedly also the pagans who have tried to practice the virtue that the Christians who seek heavenly joys in addition to the wisdom of their faith practice. Augustine clearly indicates that he is referring to an ancient idea that the sexual act is a physical event with effects so dangerous to the body and the soul that it is better to refrain from it as much as possible. Perhaps he has in mind the passage in *Hortensius* that he cites moreover in *Contra Julianum*:[3] "What injury to health is not produced by sensual pleasure? Where its action is the most intense, it is the most inimical to philosophy. Who can follow a reasoning or think anything at all when under the influence of intense pleasure? The whirlpool of this desire is so great that it strives day and night, without the slightest intermission, so to arouse our senses that they be drawn into the depths. What sensible man would not prefer that nature had given us no such pleasures at all?" One is thus placed before an alternative. Either grant that humanity, perfect on leaving the Creator's hands, already knew this rage of the senses, this weakness of the soul, this little epilepsy that mimics death—things inconsistent with the sovereignty of a creature to which all the others must be subjugated. Or disregard this act's resemblances to a shameful infirmity and see only what has been natural in it from the founding of the human race. Either, already at the origin, the human body manifested an intrinsic weakness, an evil that belonged to its nature, or else today's sensual delights come down to us with an innocence the body owes to its initial state. It is this alternative that Augustine reproaches the Pelagians with having artificially constructed by placing the choice between a Manicheism that denounces the evil inherent in the Creation, and their own thesis that sees relations between a man and a woman after the fall as simply the effect of a natural appetite—*adpetitus naturalis*[4]—which they go out of their way not to designate by the terms *libido* or concupiscence.[5]

Actually, it was not a matter, either for Pelagians in general or

for Julian of Eclanum in particular, of exonerating all sexual relations on the basis of their original nature and of accepting them
in every case. Augustine acknowledges the continence practices of
his opponents.[6] But what is decisive in this debate is determining
the point at which and on behalf of which the boundary between
the acceptable and the unacceptable comes into play. Where is the
dividing line once it's not a question of refusing all sexual acts
because they're considered bad, and when it's not enough to say
that one tolerates them as long as they take place within marriage?

Julian of Eclanum has a known position. His characterization
of the natural appetite at work in sexual relations is very much in
keeping with a whole philosophico-medical tradition: "its genus
is the vital fire; its species, the genital urges; its mode, marital
action; its excess, the intemperance of fornication."[7] And starting
from there, it was easy for him to mark the point of ethical division: by reason of its genus and species, this appetite is the very
work of the Creator fashioning the human body; for this reason it
cannot be a fault; by its mode, it pertains to human volition, and
if the latter follows the mode that is set for it, that is, marriage, it
is innocent; finally, only in regard to its excesses, that is, when the
intention is bad, can one speak of evil. So it is excess that defines
what is blameworthy.

This notion of excess is important. Both because it leaves the
very nature of desire intact, having evil begin only with the "too-
much"; and because it allows a lot of flexibility in determining the
acts that may show that the limit has been "exceeded." Now, this
was one of the most frequent ethical categories in antiquity, set
in opposition to temperance and moderation: it had often been
taken up in the entire Christian morality. And it must be emphasized that Augustine has recourse to it in *De bono coniugali*: carnal
intercourse, *concubitis*, when one uses it as a condition necessary
to generation, is, he says in that text, "without fault." But it falls
within marriage and its goodness only when it respects this limit.
If it comprises something more, if it goes "beyond this necessity,"
it no longer belongs to reason, but to concupiscence (*libido*).[8]
One can suppose, therefore, that the evil begins with excess; that
short of this limit, there is not yet any *libido*, and hence there can
be a naturalness that, when it remains non-excessive, cannot be
called bad.

In the elaboration that Augustine undertakes later, and especially starting at 412–413, he is concerned both with escaping the alternative which the Pelagians were attempting to construct, and with freeing himself from an ethics of non-excess.[9] If the first aspect of his effort is obviously crucial for the development of Christian theology, the second is essential in the history of our morality. By giving marital procreation so much prominence in Creation and among the present-day ends of marriage, he had partly freed the sexual relation from the ethico-religious disqualification of impurity. But by moving the dividing line, and by inscribing a certain form of evil in the sexual act itself, he taxed it with a negativity much more essential than the mere external limit of excess. The enormous discussion with the Pelagians that Augustine will engage in for more than fifteen years introduces us to a moral system and to rules of conduct in which the great categories that were fundamental for antiquity and early Christianity—impurity and excess—will not disappear, of course, but will begin to lose part of their leading and organizing role.

To escape from the Pelagian alternative or, more generally, to pull free of an overall disqualification due to impurity and a purely external demarcation determined by excess, Augustine had to carry out two operations: tracing a dividing line within the sexual act, prior to excess, that could take account of the evil inhering in the act; but also defining the mechanism by which the fall was able to introduce this potential into a natural sexual act which had no acquaintance with it up to that point. In sum, it was necessary to establish the metahistorical event that reshaped the sexual act in its original form so that from then on it would necessarily include this evil that is evident, as it was to the philosophers, when one looks at how it unfolds; to rediscover what can be called the "libidinization" of paradisiacal sex. He also needed to define a theory of concupiscence—of *libido*—as an internal structural element of the sort that we're familiar with today. And it was on this basis that Augustine was able to sketch out a morality of sexual conduct no longer polarized by the theme of virginity and continence, but centered on marriage and the obligatory relations it requires; and this morality, predicated on the notions of consent and use, will relegate the themes of impurity and excess to a somewhat reduced role, in favor of juridical models. It seems

necessary to try to piece together the general outline of this elaboration from what appears in the texts written in the course of the
polemic with the Pelagians and Julian of Eclanum, at least during
this period: the fourteenth book of *The City of God*, *De nuptiis et
concupiscentia*, *Contra duas epistulas Pelagionoram*, *Contra Julianum*,
and the *Opus imperfectum*.

I

In his *Reply to Two Letters of Pelagians*, Augustine explains that
one can imagine the use of sexual relations in paradise only in
four forms: the humans giving in to their desire every time it
presents itself—which is ruled out, for this would make slaves of
God's creatures; the humans restraining their urges and combat-
ing them till the appropriate moment—which is also incompatible
with the paradisiacal bliss; the humans, at the necessary moment,
by their own volition, and according to the anticipations of a just
prudence, bringing forth the desire-*libido* that leads to sexual
intercourse and accompanies it; finally, the humans, in the total
absence of *libido*, making the organs of generation, like any other
member of the body, obey the orders of the will.[10] Only these last
two possibilities can be retained as being reconcilable with the
beauty and goodness of God's work, and even then, the next-to-
last one seems to be a concession that Augustine granted to his
adversaries. For the moment, let's leave aside the meaning of this
concession. Hence Augustine prefers to define the sexual relation
in paradise as an act from which *libido* is excluded, at least insofar
as it is a compelling force.

Now, if this absence is assumed, what would the sexual act
consist in? In a natural and spontaneous unfolding that nothing
would disturb? Not at all. The text says it without any ambiguity:
one must imagine an act whose every element is placed under the
exact and unfailing control of the will. The human beings could,
and in fact did, intend everything that took place therein. The sexual relation without *libido* is completely occupied by the volitional
subject. This idea doesn't appear for the first time in this text.
Augustine has invoked it often. For example, it already appears in
*De Genesi ad litteram*, at least as a hypothesis: "Why not believe

that these first men, before sin, could command the generative organs in order to beget children, just as they command the other members which the soul moves without any difficulty and without the goad of pleasure so as to apply them to some task."[11] The idea is developed more at length in the fourteenth book of *The City of God.* It draws on four groups of references. Concerning what happens in the human body, where the will can command the arms and legs, "all the members formed by rigid bones, like the hands, the fingers, the feet"; but also, Augustine is careful to note, "members that only have flesh and nerves," or even internal organs such as the lungs which one makes voluntary use of to breathe or shout.[12] Concerning what happens in animals, which God has made capable of twitching their skin at the spot where a fly has bitten.[13] Concerning what can be seen in certain persons who can move their ears or scalp at will, mimic bird cries, sweat, weep, lie as if dead and feel nothing from the blows they're given.[14] Finally, concerning the skill of craftsmen in making the movements they need in their trade: "Do we now move our feet and hands when we will to do the things we would by means of these members? Do we meet with no resistance in them, but perceive that they are ready servants of the will, both in our own case and in that of others, and especially of artisans employed in mechanical operations, by which the weakness and clumsiness of nature become, through industrious exercise, wonderfully dexterous? And shall we not believe that [. . .] so also should the members have discharged the function of generation?"[15] Let us not imagine man, in the sexual union of paradise, as a clueless being moved by the urges whose innocence is guaranteed insofar as they are beyond his grasp; but as a skillful artisan who knows how to use his hands. *Ars sexualis.* If sin had left him the time, he would have been, in the Garden, a diligent sower—one without passion. "The field of generation would have been sown by the organ created for this purpose as the ground is sown by the hand."[16] Paradisiacal sex was obedient and reasonable like the fingers of the hand.

Actually, it does appear that Augustine was led in his discussion with Julian to amend the idea of a sexual relation that would have had the same voluntary progression as an action by the hand, and would then have lost the possibility of self-control, as a punishment for the fall. The example of body movements that don't have the form of voluntary acts and haven't been classed among the consequences of the fall, plus Augustine's not wanting to imagine in the days after the Creation a body fundamentally different from ours, inclined him to grant a sexual activity at the origin that may have been set in motion or interrupted at will, that would not therefore have escaped the orders that were given by reason, but which, in that framework, could have had its own pattern of events. This is hypothesis 3 which he conceded to the Pelagians in his reply to their letter, and which he will accept rather easily in the fourth and fifth books of *Contra Julianum:* there very well could have been "carnal urges" before the fall; the senses may have been "stimulated"; but this stimulation was "subject to the empire of the will."[17]

Whether it was a matter of a voluntary act or of a "carnal urge" controlled by the will, in any event sexual relations at Creation did not include that tremor that now overwhelms the body and the soul, characterizing their present-day "libido."[18] The latter consists not in some substantial impurity, not in a certain exaggeration of their violence, but very precisely in the involuntary form of the urge. The decisive point, the one that, as concerns sexual relations, separates the Creation from the fall, and through which consequently the moral line of division should pass, is the one where the involuntary suddenly usurps the place of the voluntary.

At that point, one will find the mark of the original transgression and the fall—or more exactly, of a restructuring of the relations of obedience and control between self and self that hinge on it. The obligation that God had placed men under by forbidding them the fruit was slight. All the more serious, therefore, was their rebellion. And in his beneficence, God didn't want the consequences of this disobedience to be a definitive punishment, or an abandonment of man to spiritual or material forces that would dominate him forever. He meant it to be exactly fitted to the sin, to man's powers, and to the possibility of salvation. He made sure that it would be the reproduction in man of the disobedience that caused him to rebel against God. The punishment-consequence of the fault is not placed between the soul and the body, between matter and mind, but in the subject itself, henceforth in rebellion against itself (body and soul included). Fallen man did not fall under a law or a force that subjugates him entirely; a scission marks his own will that divides, turns back against itself, and escapes from what it may itself will. This is the principle, fundamental in Augustine, of *inoboedentia reciproca*, of disobedience in return. The rebellion in man reproduces the rebellion against God. Can the change brought into the sexual act be understood on the basis of this principle? One might refer to the exegesis that Augustine proposes in the passage in Genesis where it is a question of sex after the act of disobedience and God's punishment, since shortly after the sin was committed, the first humans made a gesture of modesty. "And the eyes of them both were opened, and they knew they were naked; and they sewed fig leaves together, and made themselves aprons."[19] A comparison of the successive interpretations that Augustine offered of this passage is revealing. In *Genesi contra Manichaeos*,[20] the awakening of this modesty is defined as the passage from a "simplicity" which is the same as innocence to a perversity that affects the gaze itself and is conveyed by it. On their nudity, the man and the woman focus "perverse eyes" because, being already and henceforth inhabited by evil, they recognize what now perverts human nature and shames their pride—their "cunning pride"—which is to say, the very principle of the sin into which they have fallen.[21] In the relation of the eyes that have just opened to the sex that must be covered, the latter appears as a general perversion of human nature.

Later, in *De Genesi ad litteram*, Augustine insists on the necessity of not simply giving this opening of the eyes the figurative interpretation of a loss of innocence. It should be understood that, by means of a preexisting gaze, there was the discovery of a physical reality; and this reality was new, owing its existence only to the fall. This "something," a penalty for the sin and a first manifestation of its countless consequences, was obviously not sex, already there and already seen; it was its urges, whose involuntary spontaneity they had never experienced. Such urges are linked to the gaze in two ways: provoked by it and a spectacle for it. "Once they had violated the precept, totally stripped of that interior grace which they had offended through an arrogant act and a prideful love of their own power, they cast their eyes on their bodies (*membra*) and felt a rush of concupiscence that was unknown to them (*eaque motu eo quem non noverant, concupiverunt*)."[22] And they couldn't help but blush from this movement, because it was the same "carnal urge that pushes animals to copulate," because it is the manifestation which now "the law of the members opposes to the law of the spirit"[23] and it is the "consequence of the transgression of the precept."[24] This interpretation of the opening of the eyes as the perception of a new reality is taken up again in the later texts. Book 14 of *The City of God* is explicit on this point. It must not be imagined that the humans before the sin were blind. Hadn't Eve herself seen "that the fruit was good to eat" and pleasant to look at? They were capable, therefore, of seeing their own bodies. But must we accept that they did direct their gazes to their sex? No, for the latter was clothed in a "vestment of grace"—a vestment that, on the one hand, prevented their members from rebelling against their will and to which, on the other hand and consequently, they didn't pay any attention and didn't seek to know what this clothing might conceal.[25] But with the transgression and the withdrawal of grace, the punishment is revealed: it is the "disobedience in return," physical reproduction, in the body and very precisely through the sexual members, against the human will to insurrection by which man had risen up against God. Now, this revolt draws the gaze and the attention to it: "When they were stripped of this grace, that their disobedience by reciprocity (*recioproca inobedientia*) might be punished, there occurred a completely new and shameless movement of their members that made their nakedness indecent, made them observant, and filled them with confusion (*fecit adtentos redditque confuses*)."[26] Under the regime of grace, the inattention of the gaze and the voluntary use of sex were connected, making it so that the latter was visible without ever risking being naked. The fall, on the other hand, connects the eye's attention and the involuntary character of the movement so that sex is naked, but such a degree of shame, such a feeling of humiliation after so deceptive a pride, that one tries to make this pride the sign and effect of the physically invisible rebellion. In short, sex "springs forth," arisen in its insurrection and offered to the gaze.[27] It is for man what man is for God: a rebel. Like Adam,

God's creature, this creature of man, risen up before him and against him, sensed that it should hide itself after its disobedience.

So one can define that "something" which, with the fall, modified the innocent use of sex that would have been possible in paradise. It is not a new organ—the differentiation of the sexes already existed and the transgression did not render it bad;[28] it was not an act—it already had its place, its function, and it still preserves that function. The involuntary form of a movement is what makes the sexual organ the subject of an insurrection and the object of the eye's gaze. Visible and unpredictable erection.

Let us note, of course, the fact that *libido* conceived in this way is characterized essentially by male genitality, its forms and its properties. It is phallic from the origin. Augustine is quite aware of the possible objection and he tries to find the counterpart, in the woman, of the indecent motion that shames the man by pointing out her internal rebellion, and hence her fall from grace. "It was not a visible movement the woman covered, when in the same members she experienced something hidden but comparable to what the man experienced; both of them covered what each one felt at the sight of the other." And perhaps because he sensed what was artificial in this symmetry that had the woman covering what was invisible to her, and no doubt also to preserve the already evoked theme of modesty in regard to mutual desire, Augustine adds in the same passage: "The man and the woman blushed, either each for each, or the one for the other."[29] In any case, the visibility of the male organ is at the center of things.

And it has to be noted, moreover, that this interplay manifests man's entry into the reign of death. Death relative to the grace that God has withdrawn from him; death also in this world, since death now becomes a fatal illness; death, finally, as we'll see, since it is through the indispensable role of sexual union in childbirth that the original sin is passed down from generation to generation. In the involuntary movement of the sex organ and the visibility connected with it, man must recognize death: "For in the first stirring of the disobedient motion which was felt in the flesh of the disobedient soul, and which caused our first parents to cover their shame, one death indeed is experienced, that, namely, which occurs when God forsakes the soul."[30] Before, most exegetes saw

in physical death the explanation if not for the first appearance of
the two sexes, at least for their use. For Augustine, the sexual act
didn't have to wait for the passing away of the generations to be
practiced, but the involuntariness that now haunts it signifies a
spiritual death of which the end of earthly existences, one after the
other, is also a manifestation. The body that escapes man's will is
also a body that dies. The withdrawal of grace both removes this
control and actualizes death.[31]

Augustine gives the name *libido* to that movement which tra-
verses and sweeps along every sexual act, that makes them both
visible and shameful, that ties them to spiritual death as to their
cause, to physical death as to their accompaniment—that movement or, more exactly, its involuntary form and force. *Libido* is
what specifically marks the sexual acts of fallen man; or, using the
words of another vocabulary, *libido* is not an intrinsic aspect of
the sexual act that would be tied to it analytically. It is an element
which the transgression, the fall, and the principle of "reciprocity of disobedience" tied to the act synthetically. By identifying
and defining this element, by locating its point of emergence in
metahistory, Augustine establishes the basic condition for separating that "convulsive bloc," in terms of which the sexual act was
thought, from its intrinsic danger. He opens up a field of analysis
while sketching out the possibility of a "government" of behaviors
on a completely different basis than the alternative between abstinence and a more or less willing acceptance of sexual relations.

## II

So the fall provoked what could be called the libidinization of the
sexual act: either one supposes that the latter would have been
able, without the transgression, to unfold without any *libido;* or
that it would have strictly obeyed the will.

The *libido*, in any case, is manifested today in the form of the
involuntary. It appears in that supplement that emerges beyond
volition, but is only the correlative of a defect, and the effect of a
fall from grace.

This stigma of the involuntary in the sexual act subsequent to
the transgression has two main aspects. First, there are all the dis-

appointments by which the sex organ can frustrate the intentions of the subject. In Adam, the rebellious member had announced itself by an abrupt springing forth; among the men of his line, it is manifested by inopportune failures as well as by unseemly movements. The involuntary of the fallen sex organ is the erection, but it is also impotence. A passage of *The City of God* says it plainly. While the other organs, in their respective functions, are in the service of the mind and can be "moved by the sign of the will," the same is not true of the sex organ: "Even those who delight in this pleasure are not moved to it at their own will, whether they confine themselves to lawful or transgress to unlawful pleasures; but sometimes this lust importunes them in spite of themselves, and sometimes fails them when they desire to feel it, so that though lust rages in the mind, it stirs not in the body. Thus, strangely enough, this emotion not only fails to obey the legitimate desire to beget offspring, but also refuses to serve the passion to climax."[32] Which Augustine translates with a remarkable expression: the *libido* is *sui juris*.[33]

But Augustine also sees the form of the involuntary in the impossibility of separating the sexual act from those movements that one doesn't control and from the force that propels them. However wise one may be, and however just and reasonable is the goal that one has in the union of the sexes, however mindful one shows oneself to be of the law of God and the example of the Patriarchs, one can't ensure that it takes place without the uncontrollable tremors that mark the ineradicable presence of *libido* in the human being. In this world, no right intention, no lawful will can break the link between it and the use of the sexual organ. Even within marriage, the conjugal act "doesn't depend on the will, but on a necessity without which, however, in the begetting of children, it is impossible to arrive at the result that that same will seeks."[34] Which explains that the end of marriage may very well be known by all, its celebration may very well be solemn, the legitimate act of the spouses, "while aspiring to be known, yet blushes to be seen."[35] The distinction between sexual union and movement of the *libido*, which reflection and exegesis enable one to establish in theory, escapes the will, however, and cannot be realized in practice. To those organs meant for procreation from the origin, but troubled since the fall by movements from which they cannot liberate themselves, human beings, notes Augustine, give the name "nature."[36]

"*Natura*," "*sui juris*": Are we to understand, then, that the *libido* stems from a nature that is foreign to the subject itself, that it is imposed on it as an external element, and that the fall dispossessed the subject of its own flesh, as it were, to the point that the latter acts without it? That therefore one couldn't blame it for what is happening in it? Should the *libido* be considered independent of the subject? If it is a nature, how can one not bring God to account—and hence be led either to make it the creation of a bad God like the Manicheans, or else, like the disciples of Pelagius, to not see anything intrinsically bad in it? In sum, if it is *sui juris*, how can this *natura* be imputed to the subject? To answer this question, Augustine had to define on the one hand the relations of the *libido* to the soul (which satisfies the principle of imputability) and on the other to determine the status of the *libido* relative to sin (which makes it possible to establish what can be imputed).

1.  In regard to the first point, Augustine's thought evolved. Very schematically, one can say that up through *Quaestiones ad Simplicianum*,[37] he places the point of origin of the movements of concupiscence in the body above all, in a body smitten by death and dominated by the principle of evil. Their involuntary character is tied to the fact that they are carnal, in the sense that they mark the body's power over the soul. But beginning with the texts that follow—and especially *De Genesi ad litteram*—he attempts to place the principle of concupiscence and the starting point of the involuntary that pervades it in the soul itself. A passage of *The City of God* which immediately precedes his analysis of the sexual movements sets the general framework of the explanation.[38] Augustine recalls the principle that there can't be any fault unless it has been preceded by a bad intention. Now, this volition, the source of all sin, the origin of the first transgression and hence of the fall, consists in a movement of the soul that, turning away from God, fastens on to and takes pleasure in itself. It is this movement, freely carried out by the two first humans, that introduced concupiscence and its involuntary movements into the world. Human

nature is debased as a result. But what meaning should be given to this "debasement"?[39] What had been made by God and had just left his hands was able to be corrupted by man? How can a willful transgression by a free soul have as its consequence involuntary movements in a body whose nature has been determined by God? The explanation that Augustine proposes has to do with the two facets of the creative act. There was creation of a nature, but that was a creation out of nothing. Which means that man owes the fact of not being nothing to God alone; he gets his being from God's omnipotence and it alone, and by turning away from God's will, he turns away from the very thing that causes him to be. Hence, in debased nature, one must not see the corruption of what was made by God, but the degradation of the being that one derives from him, a degradation that becomes more and more pronounced as one abandons him and finds satisfaction in oneself. "Now, nature could not have been depraved by vice had it not been made out of nothing. Consequently, that it is a nature, this is because it is made by God; but that it falls away from Him, this is because it is made out of nothing. But man did not so fall away as to become absolutely nothing; but being turned towards himself, his being became more contracted than it was when he clave to Him who supremely is. Accordingly, to exist in himself, that is, to be his own satisfaction after abandoning God, is not quite to become a nonentity, but to approximate to that."[40]

By turning away from God, and refusing to obey him, man thought he was becoming the master of himself: he believed he was emancipating his being. He is only falling away from a being that only sustains itself through the will of God. The interior rebellion of the body is the consequence of that volition which, by wanting its own being, turns away from what makes it be, makes it fall when it tries to rise, and weakens it when it thinks it is on the verge of self-mastery. The involuntariness of concupiscence is not to be thought of as a nature opposing the subject, or confining it, or dragging it downward. It is not the body freed of all control and escaping the soul; it is above all the diminished being, the lack of being of the subject whose will finds itself willing the opposite of what it willed. A volition turned back against itself, a divided will, through a failure to be what it wanted to be in wanting to be self-willed. In the movement of the *libido* that splits and accompanies the sexual act without being separable from it, one mustn't see the sudden emergence of a nature external to the subject, and which, freed from the latter's control, would invoke its own laws without the subject being able to do anything about that; but rather the scission which, dividing the entire subject, has made it will what it doesn't will. "So a just condemnation followed the transgression, such that man, who by keeping the commandments should have been spiritual even in his flesh, became fleshly even in his spirit; and as in his pride he had sought to be his own satisfaction, God in His justice abandoned him to himself, not to live in the absolute independence he affected, but instead of the liberty he desired, to live dissatisfied with himself in a hard and miserable bondage to him to whom by sinning he had yielded himself, doomed in spite of himself to die in body as he had willingly become dead in spirit."[41]

So one mustn't imagine the line separating the voluntary and the involuntary passing somewhere between the soul and the body, or between nature and the subject. From the origin, it is placed within the subject. Better: one mustn't imagine two regions separated by a border; what is involved is a will whose voluntary deviation from what maintains it in being allows it to exist in the element that tends to destroy it—the involuntary. The comparison with animal sexuality is illuminating. Augustine takes it up in the *Opus imperfectum*. Julian of Eclanum had asserted that animals experience sexual lust, and that there's no denying that this concupiscence is naturally good, or that God is the author of these urges in them: either it must be recognized that this concupiscence is naturally good, or else that God intentionally created evil. Augustine answers by saying that the evil of concupiscence doesn't exist in animals, not because it is voluntary, but because the involuntariness that characterizes it is not in them a rebellion, it doesn't mark a scission between the desires of the flesh and those of the spirit: "Concupiscence of the flesh is a punishment insofar as it exerts its control over man, not insofar as it exerts its control over the animals, because in them the flesh never lusts against the spirit."[42] Sexual acts in animals may have the same form, but they never stem from the same concupiscence. Or rather the specific character of human concupiscence consists in the fact that its resemblance to that of the animals is the result of a rebellion and of a division of the self against the self that are completely foreign to animal nature. The subject was not confined by the fall in an animal "nature" with its own laws. The involuntariness of concupiscence, which takes the form of animal movements, is embedded, due to the fall, in the present structure of the subject.

Here one touches on an important point in the history of the subjectification of sex and the formation of desiring man. Augustine is obviously not the first, either among the Christian authors or generally among the authors of antiquity, to have stamped sexual desire with the seal of the involuntary. This was even, as we've seen, a commonplace. But this involuntariness was defined either as a modality or part of the soul, the urges of which it was a matter of limiting or controlling while preserving the hierarchical privilege of the others, that is, as a "passion"—a *pathos*—which, coming from the body, risked compromising the sovereignty of the soul over itself. Now, Augustine's analysis doesn't make concupiscence a specific disposition in the soul, or a passivity that limits the soul's power, but the very form of the will, which is to say, of that which makes the soul a subject. For him, it is not the involuntary as against the voluntary, but the involuntariness of volition itself: that without which the will cannot will, except precisely with the assistance of grace, which alone can liberate it from that "infirmity" which is the very form of its willing.

One understands, then, why the fact that concupiscence is *sui juris* does not exclude its being imputable to the subject: being "of our will," it is, by that very fact, *sui juris*; and conversely, our will can escape concupiscence only by ceasing to be *sui juris*, and by recognizing that it can will the good only due to the strength of grace. The "autonomy" of concupiscence is the law of the subject when it wills its own will. And the subject's powerlessness is the law of concupiscence. This is the general form of imputability—or rather its general condition.

2.   However, this possibility of imputation needs to be clarified. The preceding analyses do show that concupiscence is not an autonomous power in the soul, nor a force coming from the

outside to pose as its weakness. It is of the soul, in the very precise
sense that it is constitutive of the present form of the latter's volition: it is a "law of sin."[43] But if it characterizes the structure of the
will, it seems very difficult to impute it as one would impute a sin
to the one who has committed it.

Can the will be guilty of being what it is? But if it isn't, how
can it be reproached for something coming from it that is just the
effect of its nature and yet is held to be a sin? The anti-Pelagian
treatises develop this debate very extensively in connection with
original sin and baptism. There is no question of going back over
that long argumentation here; it's only a matter of showing, in
this interplay between the original sin and subsequent sins, the
role that Augustine has concupiscence play and the way he makes
room for the juridical principle of imputability.

Concupiscence is said to be a "sin," but "in a manner of speaking."[44] And what, exactly, is this manner of speaking?

Before baptism, the law of sin can be called, in every soul,
actual sin, meriting therefore the punishment that awaits all those
who haven't been baptized. Augustine gives several explanations
of this actuality. One of them can be termed originary and syn-
chronic: in Adam, "all men exist in the seed state"; works of God,
these seeds don't contain any evil, but they took part in the act
of transgression and, as a consequence, they did not stay clear
of the condemnation. They are born therefore as bearers of that
sin, having taken part in the act and the punishment.[45] Another
schema is that of permanent resurgence. Augustine illustrates it
with the example of the olive tree, which he often cites. An olive
tree may very well have been carefully cultivated by the gardener,
but it will still give rise to wild olive trees whose fruits are as bitter as if nothing had been done.[46] It's the same with mankind: the
baptism may well have regenerated individuals, but those who are
born from it are still under the law of sin. They are still marked by
the operativity of the first transgression.

But one also finds in Augustine another schema, which is
that of successive actualizations and their linkage. In truth, it's
not a matter of a schema distinct and apart from the others, but
rather of their unfolding in time. There cannot be, in fact, any
birth without the sexual union of the parents; and that union, even

when it takes place within marriage and in pursuit of ends that have been set for it, cannot be carried out without the involuntary movements that constituted, as we've seen, the first stigma of the fall. And that concupiscence, a mark of the first transgression still today, transmits to every soul that comes into this world the form that characterizes it, the law of sin that before baptism exists in the soul as an actual sin. This argumentation that Augustine goes back to very often is important in the history of moral theology and of the Christian ethic.

Two main themes emerge from it in fact. One concerns the place of sexual concupiscence. For Augustine, it was not the effective cause of the original fault; it was only the consequence. But through the temporal chain linking all the sexual acts that cause the generations to be born, it is the medium for actualizing the original sin in every man. You'll recall that it was a matter of debate (it would continue to be subsequently) whether the consumption of the forbidden fruit by the first humans should not be understood in a sexual way. Augustine manages to place the sexual act at the center of the economy of the original sin and its consequences, but as a permanent vehicle of its immediacy down through the human generations. Relative to that initial transgression, it is in the position of a consequence that doesn't fade away and of a cause that always renews it. And only at the end of time, when man will have been emancipated from the deathly body that he owes to his own wrongdoing, will that sexual concupiscence by which the first transgression is actualized in each person disappear from the world. Our being the products of our forebears' sex links us, back down through time, to the transgression of the first among them.

But one can also see another theme taking form in Augustine's arguments, one that is perhaps even more important, because it didn't remain tied to Christian theology alone. It became established, for reasons that will need to be examined later, as one of the constants of Western thought concerning sex. This is the theme of a fundamental and durable connection between the form of the sexual act and the structure of the subject. According to the Augustinian schema, if every individual coming into the world is a concupiscent subject, this is because they spring from a sexual relation whose form necessarily includes the shameful part of the involuntariness that bespeaks the punishment of the first transgression. Conversely, if it isn't possible to use marriage, even for the best ends, without bringing into play in the sexual act those movements which we can't control, this is because every man since the fall is born as the subject of a concupiscent will. In sum, the truth of man's subjective being is manifested in the very form to which every sexual act is submitted. This form, consequently, while bearing the mark of a failure, a defeat, an originary event, is not to be attributed to some foreign nature, but in fact to the structure of the subject itself. Whereas in the Platonic conception, desire carries the mark of a division that sends everyone in search of a partner (whether of the same sex or the different one), so that the defect is the lack of the other, here the "defect" is the degradation and the diminished being that are due to the transgression and that are marked in the subject itself by the physically involuntary form of its desire.

The *libido* in the sense in which Augustine often employs this word without any explanation, that is, the sexual form of desire, is thus the transhistorical link that connects the originary transgression of which it is the consequence to the presence of that sin in every individual. And in everyone, moreover, it is how the involuntary form of the sexual act and the "infirm" structure of the subject are bound together.

3.  Concupiscence, as the active presence of the original sin in every man, is therefore "in a certain way" a sin. It is imputable to him and it is reprehensible in him. It is what justifies the damnation of those who die unbaptized.

Then what is the effect of baptism? Certainly not that of erasing concupiscence. It is evident that it continues to exist not only in Christians in general, but in the most saintly ones as well, just as it also subsisted in the Patriarchs themselves, when they were obliged to beget children as God ordered them to.[47] As to what baptism washes away, a crucial passage of *De nuptiis et concupiscentia* explains it quite clearly: it is the *reatus* of the concupiscence— the fact that it can be imputed to the individual who carries it and that for them it constitutes a current culpability: "Carnal concupiscence is remitted, indeed, in baptism; not so that it is put out of existence, but so that it is not to be imputed as sin."[48] It's a juridical type of operation, therefore, which baptism performs on the subject's concupiscence, since the latter is the active presence of the original sin in the subject. It erases what constitutes the current culpability in that presence, but it leaves untouched that which forms the subject's permanent structure. After baptism, concupiscence by itself can no longer be considered an actual sin in the subject. But it remains as the "law of sin"; that is, as what tirelessly drives the subject to commit sin unless he resists it. "In the regenerate it is no longer itself a sin."[49] However, one can continue to call it "sin" for two reasons:[50] because it comes from sin and because, when it wins out, it commits sin. But after ceasing to be itself a sin, it continues to be the thing that connects the original sin (of which it is structurally the effect) to current sins (of which it is genetically the principle).

In what form does it go on existing? As the projection, the shadow cast by the fall, of which it is the analogical consequence, as it were. From the fact that the fall is a deterioration of being, concupiscence is itself weakness and infirmity. In the medical vocabulary commonly used in Christian literature to designate sin, Augustine, when he wishes to bring out the difference between notions, tends to utilize the terms "wound" or "disease" to speak of the act of sinning, and the terms "disposition" (*affectio* or *valitudo*) or "weakness" (*languor*) to speak of concupiscence. A passage of the last pages of *De nuptiis et concupiscentia* shows this word game in practice. "Those wounds (*vulnera*) which are inflicted on the body produce lameness in a limb, or difficulty of motion [. . .] That wound, however, which has the name of sin [here Augustine means the original sin], wounds the very life, which was being righteously lived. [. . .] Whence it came to pass that our nature having then and there been deteriorated (*in deterius commutata*) by that great sin of the first man, not only was made a sinner, but also generates sinners; and yet the very infirmity, under which the virtue of a holy life has drooped and died, is not really nature, but corruption (*non est utique natura, sed vitium*); precisely as a bad state of health (*mala in corpore valetudo*) is not a bodily substance or nature, but disorder; very often, indeed, if not always, the ailing character of parents is in a certain way implanted, and reappears in the bodies of their children."[51]

But the correlative and inseparable aspect of the infirmity that characterizes concupiscence is the force of the movements of that same concupiscence. That whereby it is weak, as the subject's will in regard to himself, and also that by which it is strong, as the presence in the subject of the bad will. The imputability, the *reatus*, that makes concupiscence an actual culpability was erased by baptism, then, but not the active presence of that concupiscence. It acts in some manner (*agita aliquid*) even in one who is regenerated. And what is the form of that activity, if not "the bad and shameful desires."[52] Augustine's basic propositions concerning the presence of concupiscence in the heart of men are too familiar now to need revisiting.

Let's just recall that in this presence he sees the principle of a spiritual combat that can reach its definitive end only on the day we are liberated from the "body of death," which is our body today. But let's also recall that this body of death is not a material element which has held us prisoner since the fall. It characterizes the very way in which we exercise our will, and no sin has been committed by us without us; in every case, our will had a part in it. Let the sinner not try to hide behind the excuse that it wasn't he who acted, but the concupiscence in him; such talk would show only that he doesn't know himself: "For, whereas he is altogether himself, his mind determining and his body executing his own purpose, he yet supposes that he is himself no longer."[53] Finally, let's recall that since concupiscence belongs to the very structure of our fallen will, that the latter by itself can will only in the form of concupiscence, so they don't confront each other as two foreign elements, hostile to one another and juxtaposed by force, but are amalgamated in a nature which is that of the fall, concupiscence could never be defeated in spiritual combat if divine grace did not intervene.

III

The effects and consequences of the Augustinian theory of concupiscence have obviously been considerable. I would just like to underscore an aspect of it that concerns the government of souls and the sexual conduct of spouses in particular. This government involved their "juridification" or rather the insertion of elements that would give a juridical type of formalization to practices, rules, prescriptions, and recommendations that had previously been reflected primarily in the forms of spiritual asceticism and the techniques of purification of the soul. In centering his analysis of concupiscence not on the problem of the pure and the impure, of the soul and the body, of matter and spirit, of passion and self-control, but on that of the voluntary and the involuntary, or more exactly on the very structure of the will, it's clear that he was inscribing it in a system of juridical references. He undertook the task to which Western Christianity would apply itself for so many centuries and to which (or to the impossibility of which) it would owe the great fracture of the Reformation in the sixteenth century, namely positing the sinner as a subject of law; or, as we would say in another vocabulary, positing the subject of desire and the subject of law as existing simultaneously and in a single form. The two most important notions, no doubt, for this juridification were those of consent (*consensus*) and usage (*usus*).

1. *De nuptiis et concupiscentia*[54] had carefully distinguished between the imputability—the *reatus*—of concupiscence and that of sin. The first was established by the operativity of concupiscence as original sin in every individual newly arrived in the world; and it was imputability that was removed by baptism, although concupiscence itself remained intact. Things work differently with sin: once committed, the act disappears, but its *reatus* remains. A distinction in which Julian of Eclanum saw only a dialectic featuring "the reciprocal of all the contraries": the trouble was that he didn't see the possibility that the *reatus* of the cause—concupiscence—would be done away with, without also erasing that of the sin, or that the sin could be incriminated without making the concupiscence from which it stems into a substantial evil in the human being. The answer that Augustine gives him in book 6 of *Contra Julianum*[55] allows one to locate the exact point where the imputability of the sin, compared to the concupiscence, is formed. Even after baptism the concupiscence is there—in act,

since baptism has erased only the juridical aspect that made it reprehensible. But what does "in act" mean? Certainly not that it
is always active, always manifest, and constantly insistent in the
form of pressing desires, for it is sometimes "dormant," lacking
an object that invites covetousness. Just as a timid man is actually
timid, even if he fears nothing because there's nothing to fear, it is
present only as a "quality." But on that basis, it can be in act as an
activity: in the form of a desire that may have been aroused by an
object. It is not yet a sin, that is, an imputable element, since while
having changed in its form—from being a general disposition, it
has become an active desire—it remains that stigma of the original
sin whose *reatus* has been obliterated. But conversely, even as an
activated disposition, it never dominates the soul entirely, it never
compels any act whatsoever. For the latter to take place, there has
to have been a specific act of the will. However strong the pressure
of concupiscence, and precisely insofar as the latter is the form of
the will—however fallen it is from the being it got from God—it
cannot become an act without the very act of the will. There cannot be any sin without this supplement—however minimal and
invisible one might imagine it to be—which means that one *wills*
what concupiscence wants. And that is the meaning of consent. It
is what makes possible the imputation of an act having its origin
in a concupiscence which is not imputable itself. As another passage of *Contra Julianum* says: "The spirit does a good work in not
consenting to evil concupiscence, but does not perfect the good
because it does not destroy the evil desires themselves; and when
the flesh has an evil desire, but does not fulfill it, because the spirit
does not consent to it, the flesh does not fulfill damnable works."[56]

At first glance, this notion of consent may not appear very
different from what can be found in the spirituality that Cassian
promoted in the same period in the West. After all, the ascetic
labor that it prescribed had consent as one of its main themes:
to welcome or not, to accept or reject the desires that presented
themselves to the mind depending on whether they appeared to
be divinely inspired or the devil's work. However, consent there
doesn't have quite the same form or the same mechanisms. For
Cassian, it's a matter of the entry into the soul of elements—ideas,
images, suggested actions—that must be questioned as to their

value and their origin. It's a problem of opening or closing the doors of the soul, of rejecting a possible corruption that may have found its way in, of protecting the soul, therefore, so that it might finally focus the clear gaze of contemplation on the eternal things. In him, consent conforms above all to the model of the threshold: it has an exterior and an interior; it selects, it opens or closes; it welcomes, it expels, so that with this mechanism one is again presented with the traditional form of the division between the pure and the impure.

In Augustine, consent has a different form and a different mode of action. There is a fundamental reason for this: whereas in a spirituality like that of Cassian desire and will are two different agencies, concupiscence for Augustine belongs to the very form of volition. As he sees it, consent is not the acceptance, by the will, of a foreign element; it's a way for the will to will, as a free act, what it wills as concupiscence. In consenting—and one would say the same thing of its opposite, refusing—the will takes itself as an object. When it consents, it doesn't just will what is desired; it doesn't simply want what is wanted in the desire. It wills that will which has the form of concupiscence; it takes itself for an end as a fallen will. It assumes its own condition as concupiscent will. Reciprocally, non-consent doesn't consist in vanquishing desire by expelling the representation of the desired object from the soul, but by not willing as the concupiscence would have it do. Schematically: consent in Cassian, and in others with similar views, focuses essentially on the *object*—the *object* of desire that one drives out as *object* of the representation, so that it does not become an *object* of the will. Consent and refusal in Augustine unfold within the will, in the movement by which it wills itself or doesn't will itself as it is. In that procedure, the subject takes itself as the object of its own will, proposing to will or not to will the concupiscent form of its fallen will. Consent as a necessary element for the constitution of an act imputable as a sin is therefore not simply the transformation of a desire into a real act; it is not even simply the acceptance of that desire in thought, in the form of a received representation. It is the act of the will upon itself—and on its form rather than on its object. When the subject consents, it doesn't open the gates to a desired object, it constitutes itself and confirms itself as a desiring subject: at that moment the movements of its concupiscence become imputable to it. Consent—and this is the reason for the central role it plays in Augustine and will play later—makes it possible to designate the subject of concupiscence as a subject of law.

2. This structure of the subject of law–subject of concupiscence has important effects in the codification of marital relations. People will be able to say, and they'll be right, that Augustine changed very little in the content of the prescriptions that were accepted before him or in his time: prohibition, at risk of a major sin, of sexual relations outside of marriage, in the form either of adultery if at least one of the partners is married, or of fornication if neither of them is; the recommendation not to practice marital relations in certain circumstances—during the time of prayer or certain periods of the year;[57] extremely severe condemnation, as abominable crimes, of any sexual act that would be performed contrary to natural usage—this would occur when the man did not make use of "the female organ meant for procreation";[58] blame for all the "excesses" spouses may indulge in when, while respecting that natural usage, they go beyond what is strictly required by it: minor sins. This general profile of the prohibitions isn't different from the one that was already familiar and that the non-Christian moralists had long presented at least as pressing recommendations.

But Augustine takes up this whole set, systematizes it, and bases it around the notion of usage. *Usus.* This is actually a complex notion that he finds already employed, but to which he gives a much more precise meaning. The *usage of marriage* was taken to mean sexual relations between spouses, both because it was marriage that legitimized an act which was blameworthy outside the law, and because this act consisted in the exercise of a right thus acquired, over the other's body. So the usage of marriage had a meaning that was both institutional and corporeal, juridico-physical: one made use of a right in making use of a body.

Augustine introduces a new dimension into this already-formed notion. In the sexual act between spouses, one doesn't simply use the right of marriage and the body of the other, one makes use of one's own concupiscence. That was the problem, in fact: since the sexual act and procreation after the fall cannot take place without involuntary and hence shameful movements of concupiscence, can one avoid deducing that all marital sex is bad in itself? How can it be said that marriage is a good if the act that legitimizes it is in itself an evil? Either one cannot hold that marriage is positively a good (and not simply a lesser evil compared to fornication); or one cannot maintain that the evil of concupiscence necessarily accompanies every sexual relation without exception. Now, the notion of *usus* is precisely what enables both of these propositions to be preserved, but this requires two disjunctions: in the marital relation, between the movement of *libido* and the act of will; and in this act of will, between the consent that one could call "objective" with respect to this movement itself (and that cannot be accepted, since it is inseparable from the sexual relation) and the consent or non-consent which is subjective with respect to that concupiscence as a form of will. In this sexual encounter one can in fact willingly satisfy the concupiscence—that is, will that fallen form of willing, or intend instead to engender children, intend to keep one's partner from falling into fornication. In the marital relation, while the unfolding of the sexual act is not modifiable in its concupiscent structure, the consent is modifiable; it remains free. *Usus* is thus a certain modality of the dynamic between consent and non-consent. It can set ends that are such that the subject won't will itself as a concupiscent subject at the moment it is committing an act whose conditions of accomplishment involve concupiscence.

This conception comes with a set of consequences.

It opens up the possibility of considering the sexual relation as being unavoidably connected with an evil; that is, with a concupiscence that is the direct result of the first transgression and the first visible punishment it received, but at the same time of seeing a specific act of will in these sexual relations when one engages in them, an act that will be bad or not, a sin or not, depending on whether or not it wills the form of concupiscence. This is the meaning of the famous formulation that will be repeated for more than a millennium: in marital relations, one makes use of an evil in any case; but one can use this evil in a good or a bad manner, and this is where the possibility of sin resides. The importance of this conception becomes clear when one compares it to Julian's propositions. Visibly, they are exactly symmetrical and inverse, with Julian saying: "He who holds to the mode of natural concupiscence uses a good well. He who does not hold to the mode uses this good evilly; lastly, he who from love of holy virginity also despises even the lawful one, refusing what is good so as to arrive at what is better." And Augustine: "He who holds to the mode of natural concupiscence uses an evil well. He who does not hold to the mode uses an evil evilly. But he who [. . .] despises even the lawful mode refrains from the use of evil and attaches himself to what is more perfect."[59] Underneath the term-by-term correspondence of the two formulations one cannot help but recognize a profound dissymmetry. For Julian, as the pleasure taken in sexual relations is a good arranged by God himself in the Creation, it can only be good to have recourse to it provided this is in the forms placed by providence and designed by nature; the sin begins with deviation or excess. The usage he speaks of in his text is therefore the modality of the physical act, its form (and in this, Julian remains well within the framework of a morality of excess). For Augustine, as the evil of concupiscence is "found in human nature," the decisive point is to be situated in the ends pursued, which is to say in the very form of the will; that form is what determines the value of the physical act.[60] And with Augustine one enters into a morality of the juridical subject. In Julian, it is the sin (the excessive act) that determines the evil and makes it appear. In Augustine, the evil is preexistent and fatally inscribed in the sexual encounter; but the sin that derives from it is sufficiently distinct from it that it is never necessitated by it and it constitutes an imputable act.

Thus the idea of a *usage* of concupiscence, which Augustine inserts into his analysis of the sexual act between the justified usage of marriage and the natural usage of the body, allows the individual (that is, each one of the two partners) to be thought of as forming a single subject of desire and of law; it is "one and the same" subject (and not through a juxtaposition of two natures, or through an exile of the soul in a foreign world) which acts in the necessity of desire and in the freedom of good and evil. But it's important to see that, despite this unity of the subject, desire remains an evil and its usage remains independent. It is possible to make an utterly non-concupiscent use of concupiscence, but the latter will not be done away with for all that. It often happens that one makes use of it just for the concupiscence, so that the latter seems to carry the day, but this usage will nonetheless remain a specific and imputable act. Now, through this very irreducibility, one sees very large possibilities open up for juridifying sexual relations between spouses. If the sexual act were naturally a good in itself, the codification of these relations could be implemented as a function of the form that is judged to be "natural," everything else being excess, abuse, violation of the limits, crossing into the counter-natural. In this way, one would remain within a morality of nature. If the sexual relation were defined only by the evil or defilement that it carries with it, the codification would be implemented based on an ideal of complete continence and the value of behaviors would be ranked in relation to the ideal: one would then be in an ethics of purity. Finally, if one supposed that the evil of desire could be absorbed little by little into the exercise of a will that controls and limits it, one would still be reliant on the prescriptions of theological wisdom. But the separation, in the sexual act, between the evil of *libido* and the possibility of using it well or badly enables the sexual behaviors to be codified according to these uses, the ends they give themselves, the circumstances they alter, et cetera. The two ends that are considered legitimate—procreation, preventing the other from sinning—will thus serve as a guiding principle for controlling the unfolding of sexual acts between spouses and for defining what is permitted and forbidden, under what conditions, on what occasions. Augustine, it's true, doesn't develop these possibilities very much. They will be developed, and much later, not just as a logical development, moreover, but when a whole ensemble of other processes in medieval society and the medieval Church will have increased the importance of the juridical type of relations. The fact remains that in the Augustinian analysis one finds the theoretical matrix that will make such developments possible. Marital relations which, under the overall recommendations of moderation, modesty, and respect and under the general finality of procreation, remained a private and secret matter will give rise to endless rules and a devel-

oped casuistry concerned with how to exercise one's rights and
discharge one's duties within it. Medieval Christianity—especially
from the thirteenth century on—will doubtless be the first form of
civilization to develop such verbose prescriptions regarding sexual
relations between marriage partners. To the rules of marriage, to
those concerning the exchange or transfer of goods in that alliance, to the rules of mutual comportment between the partners,
which one finds in most societies in various forms and with very
diverse mechanisms of constraint, it adds this singular feature: a
very precise codification of the moments, the initiatives, the invi-
tations, the acceptances, the refusals, the positions, the gestures,
the caresses, even the words, as we'll see, that can take place in
sexual relations. The great dimorphism that had characterized
ancient life—separating those sexual relations about which one
speaks, one tells, and which are necessarily outside of marriage,
from those of matrimony which are out of view and excluded
from discourse—that great dimorphism disappears. One speaks
as much about the latter as the former, if not more, at least in the
practice of confession. Sex in marriage thus became an object of
juridiction and veridiction.

But in Augustine and in his time, those are still only possibilities. What was more important for then, perhaps, is that with
the idea of concupiscence as an evil, it was possible to combine,
under the same theme of spiritual combat, the exercise of virginity and the practice of marriage. One deals with the same evil in
the two states; the same renunciation of the concupiscent form
of the will is required, the difference being that in marriage non-
consent follows a certain usage that virginity will artfully turn
away from. The two states were defined as rather similar practices with regard to concupiscence, of which there was now a
theory capable of justifying both, with their difference of value
but also their intrinsic connection. And above all one can see that,
in such a conception, the notions of *consensus* and *usus* don't serve
to directly define relations between spouses. They establish their
codification only through the consent (or non-consent) that each
individual gives to their own *libido*. This means that all regulation
of sexual behaviors can be applied on the basis of the relationship that everyone maintains with themselves. The problematiza-

tion of sexual behaviors—whether it's a matter of knowing what they are in truth or of defining what they should be—becomes the problem of the subject. The subject of desire, whose truth can be discovered only by the subject itself in its innermost being. The subject of law, whose imputable actions are defined and separated into good or bad according to the relations it has with itself.

In a word, we can say that the sexual act in the ancient world was thought of as a "paroxysmal bloc," a unified convulsional event where the individual would lose themselves in the pleasure of their interaction with the other, to the point of mimicking death. It was not something calling for analysis. It only needed to be resituated within a general economy of pleasures and forces. This bloc was fragmented, in Christianity, by rules of living, arts of conducting oneself and others, techniques of examination or procedures of confession, by a general doctrine of desire, the fall, transgression, and so on. The unity reconstituted itself, however, in such a way that the diffraction remains and its analysis is possible: it is possible in the form of theory and speculation as well as in the practical form of individual examination, whether by others or by oneself. And in these latest forms, it is not merely [recommended] but obligatory. So there was a reconstitution around what can be called, by contrast with the economy of paroxysmal pleasure, the analytic of the subject of concupiscence. In that analytic, sex, truth, and law are bundled together, by ties that our culture has tended to draw closer rather than loosen.

*Appendices*

## Appendix 1

What is to be demonstrated:

1. There exists a relatively constant prescriptive core in Christianity. This core is ancient. It formed prior to Christianity. It is clearly attested in the pagan authors of the Hellenistic and Roman period.

2. One finds this core again without major modification in the Apologists of the second century. Clement of Alexandria incorporates it into his Platonist-inspired theology, along with a group of precepts deriving from Stoicism.

3. A new definition of the relations between subjectivity and truth will give this ancient prescriptive core a completely new significance, and bring important modifications to the ancient conception of the pleasures and their economy.

4. These modifications involve the analysis of the domain of the *aphrodisia* and the relational mode which the subject is urged to maintain with them more than the division between permitted and forbidden. Hence it is not so much the law and its content that have changed, but experience as a condition of knowledge.

# *Appendix 2*

## I

It appears, then, that the Christianity of the first centuries defined two regular and distinct modalities according to which the individual needed to manifest themselves "in truth" if they were to liberate themselves from evil: on one hand, a great penitential ritual that was unique and comprehensive, that involved the whole of their existence and reshaped their entire life, sometimes in a definitive way; on the other, a continuous practice of examination and vigilance that attempts to apprehend and disclose the deepest stirrings of the soul. On one hand an alethurgy in which the "truth-doing" of gestures, attitudes, tears, mortifications, and forms of life seems to far outweigh the formulations of discourse; on the other an alethurgy in which "truth-telling" seems to impose an all-but-exhaustive verbalization of the secrets of the soul. *Exomologesis* as manifestation of sinful being can be set against *exagoreusis* as enunciation of the movements of thought. This opposition seems to be justified both from the standpoint of the technology appropriate to each of these practices and from that of their institutional context. The technique of exomologesis of the penitent involves the structuring, radical intensification, and highlighting of a set of discontinuities: a break with one's former life, whose forms and marks one abandons; an estrangement from the community, toward which one humbles oneself to show how unworthy one is of remaining a member; a break with one's own body which one abandons to hunger, misery, lack of care; a clash between life and death, since by placing oneself like Lazarus at the threshold of the tomb one contrasts the death of the body—which one accepts—to the eternal life of the soul—which is its recompense. In this interplay of discontinuities, ruptures, and clashes, the truth comes to light in the form of a manifestation. It is not the wrongs committed that appear in their details, with their conditions and their author's share of responsibility; it's the very body of the sinner, the sinful body, as the first transgression has marked it: destined to die, defiled by impurities, troubled by needs it cannot satisfy. And this manifestation is not simply the revealing of a hidden figure: it is a test for the subject, or rather the subject itself. A test in two senses: since by practicing the rigor of this relentlessly and as long as possible (or at least for the set time span), the sinner will "win" his reconciliation: and like a metal subjected to the test of fire, the impurities that were blended with their soul will separate out and be burned up in the fierce struggle of the penitent against himself.

The penitent's exomologesis is a double manifestation (of the renunciation of what one is and of the being of defilement and death that one renounces) as a purifying test of oneself conducted by oneself.

In his long-term remolding of his life as an "art" that is learned and practiced, the monk also subjects himself to the test of self-renunciation. But in a different sense and by other means. Since he has detached himself from the world, he won't have to make the truth of evil appear in the form of discontinuity and rupture, but rather in the form of a triple continuity: a constant watchfulness over oneself, one's thoughts, their spontaneous flow, their insidious movement; the maintenance of a relation of spiritual direction that obliges one to speak and to listen, to confess and to submit; and humility toward everyone plus strict obedience to the community's rules. The manifestation peculiar to *exagoreusis* is expressed through language; it involves a mandatory discourse, frequent and as thorough as possible, addressed to the one charged with directing the conduct of the one confessing: it has as its main object that which hides deep in the soul, and hides there both because it consists in the very first movements of the soul, so tenuous still that they risk escaping one's gaze if the attention wanders, and because one is dealing with the incitements of the Seducer, who disguises himself in deceptive forms. So here *exagoreusis* has the task of telling the truth but as the result of acts of knowledge which in the depths of oneself light up the unperceived and reveal the presence of the Other. Self-renunciation thus takes a very particular form: it's a matter of focusing a continuous attention, as detailed and deep as possible, on oneself. Not, however, in order to know what one is at one's core, not in order to extract the authentic, primitive, and pure form of a subjectivity, but in order to discern the deceptions of the Evil One in the deepest mysteries of the soul, and consequently to refuse to participate through one's will in all the movements that are just so many temptations, and finally, in order to abandon all personal volition in favor of God's wishes and the lessons of one's director.

Schematizing enormously, we can say that the exomologesis specific to the penitential status relates to a "ceasing to be" which, within the confines of life and death, promises the next world through a renunciation of the real; and that the examination-avowal of monastic life aims at a "ceasing to will" which expels the Other in the depths of the soul through the formulation of the true.

Moreover, each of these two practices appears to have its own institutional setting. The penitential dramaturgy finds its place in a community of believers where it's a matter of extending a second lifeline to the one who has fallen, but in such a way that the fallenness can be answered by a hope of forgiveness while the manifest brightness of the satisfaction will match the scandal of the transgression. As for the examination-avowal, it would seem to have its place, rather, in a monastic life where the objective of contemplation makes thought control necessary, where the communitarian existence calls for obedience exercises as a form of askesis, and where the practice of direction must determine the measured and righteous ways of asceticism.

Further on, we'll see what limits ought to be given to this contrast and what correctives should be brought to it. Yet it should be kept in mind even when it is relativized, even when it is related to an ensemble that incorporates its elements. The dimorphism, in Christian societies, between life in the world and life under monastic rules was too constant and too important a phenomenon not to have had decisive consequences in this regard and others as well. And in fact many of the great modifications that the procedures of penance would undergo between the sixth and the sixteenth centuries originated in practices that were emblematic of the monastic milieu; starting in the seventh century, private chargeable penance came out of the monasteries; those regular and systematic examinations of conscience that were practiced in the monasteries were taken up by the *devotio moderna* and spread in secular milieus; and it was again the religious orders that were the main agents of the spread of spiritual direction—that phenomenon which was so prominent in the sixteenth and seventeenth centuries. In the growing importance assumed by the techniques of examination (of oneself and others) and by the procedures of verbalization of transgressions, and in the correlative shrinking of the status of "truth-doing" compared to "truth-telling," the monastic institutions played a decisive role. For more than a millennium, they were, if not the constant, at least the very intense seminary of the art of arts, the *regimen animarum*; they developed it, disseminated it, at times augmented it. It was sometimes copied from them, and people tried to use it in competition with them and to limit their influence. They were a real factor in the substantial upsurge in the penchant for discourse and the will to know (*volonté de savoir*) that characterize the experience of self and others in our societies. And when one will hear it said in the seventeenth century—and in a rather questionable way from a dogmatic standpoint—that confessing is a way of directing consciences, one can say that *exagoreusis* has prevailed over exomologesis—that at least it largely overshadows it.[1]

In any case, the history of the relations between "wrongdoing" and "truth-telling" in the Christian West could not be written without referring to the existence of these two forms, their differences, their tension and the slow movement that ended up privileging one at the expense of the other, when, in the course of the sixteenth century and more so all through the eighteenth, the question of the government of individuals became, from the political viewpoint and the religious viewpoint as well, a major problem.

## II

It would be a mistake, however, to imagine that these were two problems without overlaps and deriving from two radically separate institutional ensembles. Things are more complicated: first, because an examination of the institutions shows how the practices are juxtaposed and intermixed; next, because, looking at the practices themselves, one can recognize not only components but a foundation which they have in common.

1.  It is certain that the monastic status was not compatible with the status of penitent, and all the more so as the monk appeared more and more clearly as leading the penitential life par excellence. "When it's a matter of the monk who has renounced the world and its service, and has pledged to always serve God, why would he be made to do penance? [. . .] For the monk, public penance is of no use because, recovered from his sins, he weeps, and he has made an eternal pact with God."[2]

However, while one doesn't have to become a penitent as well after becoming a monk, some elements of the penitential rites are utilized in the monastic life. Cassian's texts, and especially the *Institutes* which refer to the practices of the cenobium, are very clear on this point: forms specific to public penance are described in that work, and the expression *publice paenitere* reappears several times, without it being a matter of assuming the status of penitent, of course. Thus Pafnutius, who accepts, in a spirit of humility, being wrongfully accused of a serious sin, is subjected to a treatment just like one that could be evoked by Tertullian, Ambrose, or Jerome in regard to public penances: "And when he had immediately left the Church [. . .] he continually shed tears at his prayers, and fasted thrice as often as before, and prostrated himself in the sight of men [. . .] with all humility of mind. But when he had thus submitted himself with all contrition of flesh and spirit for almost a fortnight, so that he came early on the morning of Saturday and Sunday not to receive the Holy Communion but to prostrate himself on the threshold of the Church and humbly ask for pardon."[3] But short of these great manifestations meant to atone for serious sins, one finds a record of other practices, intermediate between the confession of temptation and the solemn and long-lasting exomologesis. Moreover, Cassian lists a series of transgressions that call for a precise penitential act, determined in advance: accidentally breaking an earthenware jar; hesitating even slightly in chanting a psalm; replying roughly, unnecessarily, impertinently; obeying carelessly; preferring reading to working; lingering after the service instead of going back to one's cell; talking with someone from the world outside the presence of the elder, and so on.[4] Cassian employs the expression "public penance" to designate the prescribed sanction, although it seems that this involves only a certain number of elements borrowed from the great dramaturgy of canonical penance: separation from the community, gesture of supplication, attitude of humility[5] ("when all the brethren are assembled for service he must lie on the ground and ask for absolution until the service of the prayers is finished; and will obtain it when by the Abbot's command he is bidden to rise from the ground"[6]).

There we have a sketch of a whole monastic discipline combining the ostentatious manifestations of penitential rites and the control of gestures and thoughts in a continual and unconditional relation of obedience. The importance of this juxtaposition is twofold.

First, it manifests the "penitential" sense which will be given to the monastic institution, more and more insistently. Organizing a disciplined art of contemplation by way of humility, submission to the other, and purification of the heart is the objective that seems to have been given originally to the cenobium.[7] And Cassian doesn't say that the end (*finis*) or the goal (*destinatio*) of monastic existence is to lead the life of penance. Yet one sees a principle of coincidence emerging from his texts. Indeed, on the one hand he gives the notion of penance a narrow meaning, when he speaks of it as the collection of procedures at the end of which the transgressions can be forgiven by God.[8] But he also gives it a very general definition, which refers to the results not only of these practices, but of all the spiritual exercises of monastic life. Penance is thus characterized as a state, the state which the monk must try to attain: "it consists in never again yielding to the sins."[9] This state has its marks, the principal one being that one's heart is freed from what inclines to its sins, and this mark (*indicum*) itself has signs that allow it to be recognized: the very image of faults has been erased from the secrets of the heart, and by "image" one should understand not just the delight that one takes in thinking of it, but also the mere fact of remembering it.[10] Penance is therefore that purity of heart which the examination, the humility, the patience, the obedience, the discretion, and the trust in the elders, as well as the determination not to conceal anything from them, can, with the grace of God, produce in the soul. And since contemplation, which is the purpose of monastic life, is possible only by means of such a purity of heart, one sees that penance, understood not only as a procedure for remission but as a constantly maintained purified state, ends up coinciding in sum with monastic life itself.

That life must be directed toward the avowal of transgressions, penitential manifestations, the discovery of the heart's secrets, and the opening of the soul. A perpetual discourse: "While then we do penance [. . .] the shower of tears which is caused by the confession of our faults is sure to quench the fire of our conscience."[11] But this very thing will make it possible to purify one's thought, down to its deepest recesses, of everything that may give rise to temptation, that constitutes its first stirrings or allows its last traces to subsist. A forgetting, consequently, and a silence of the heart. In this powerful pulsation of confession and forgetting, the monastic life reveals what it is: the penitent life par excellence; penance (exercise) for penitence (state)—it being understood that this state is never anything else than a combat that demands a permanent exercise.

Now, this tendency to think of monastic existence as the very practice of the life of penitence accompanied an institutional evolution whose historical importance was considerable. The cenobitic discipline, the relations of hierarchy and obedience, the rules of life in common and of individual behavior gave more and more space to practices that can be called intermediary (between the great penitential rites and the perpetual examination of thoughts): these were practices, of a juridical and regulatory type moreover, that tend to define a code where specific sanctions are paired with specific infractions. Actually, this development is only sketched out in Cassian, where it is mainly a matter of showing how the smallest offenses are answered by acts of satisfaction that are at the same time harsh, public, and humiliating. Thus, one sees a monk on duty for the week who does public penance for having overlooked three lentils that fell to the floor,[12] and Saint Jerome relates that in the three women's monasteries directed by Paula, speech excesses were sanctioned by exclusion from the common table and standing upright at the refectory door.[13] But a comparison between the *Cenobitic Institutes* and the *Rule of the Master* or that of Saint Benedict shows the increasing importance of these punitive codifications that establish between transgression and penitence a rather different relation from the preceding ones. Firstly, this relation includes a principle of proportionality: "The measure of excommunication or of chastisement should correspond to the degree of fault, which degree is estimated by the Abbot's judgment." It includes a clear distinction that separates public faults from those "whose matter is hidden." The latter must be disclosed to the Abbot only and to a few elders capable of "attending to their own wounds and those of others." Finally, it includes a principle of progressive correction (punishments are less severe if the guilty party is less than fifteen years old; the repeat offense alters the penalty; the Abbot lectures the delinquent and must watch over him in particular).[14]

In a word: the monastic institution, insofar as it presented itself as the place of permanent penitential life, deployed a whole ensemble of procedures designed to ensure the remission of evil—by expelling it, correcting it, or healing it. At one extreme one finds the ritualistic and ostentatious forms of exomologesis; at the other the techniques of examination and confession in the discourse of *exagoreusis;* and between them the methods for punishing according to a code that defines the gravity of the faults and the proportional punishments. Between the manifestation of the true through the "acts and gestures" of the penitential status (a sort of *veri-fication*) and its enunciation in a permanent relation of direction (*veri-diction*), the monastic rule brings into being what will later become, in Western Christianity, the most important form of the relation between the evil and the true, between "wrong-doing" and "truth-telling"—namely *juri-diction*.

2.   Conversely, it would be just as incorrect to see on the side of the laypersons nothing but the solemn forms of public penance. Among them, as well as among the monks, there was a whole gra-

dation of diverse practices going from the canonical forms that marked one's belonging to the order of penitents to the subtle modalities of direction.

First of all, one should note the difference, indicated from the origin, between serious sins that call the purification of baptism into question, and the little daily failings that show how far one still is from complete perfection. The three great "falls" that had occasioned, in the second century, long discussions about penance were idolatry, homicide, and adultery. Subsequently, the system of sins and the distinction between those that necessitated canonical penance and those for which it wasn't necessary became much more complicated. Two axes of distinction emerged: that of the public and the hidden, on the one hand; that of the serious and the minor, on the other. One sees the idea affirmed that the public nature of penance, apart from its functions of humiliation and of the sinner's manifestation, must have the role of responding to the public awareness of the fault; the example must compensate for the scandal. But conversely, if the transgression is secret, and if no one has any reason to be scandalized or to find a bad example in it, the stir of the spectacular exomologesis risks having harmful effects. Hence the idea that the hidden fault must be atoned for rather with a "private" penance: "We must strike back at all those sins that have been committed in front of everyone and more secretly at those that have been committed in a secret way."[15] In the same spirit, Saint Leo, a bit later, will criticize the (perhaps local) practice of publicly reading the list of faults committed by the sinners[16] and will recommend not disclosing the details except in secret confession. The arguments given in the fifth and sixth centuries for non-public forms of penance are interesting, moreover, in that they clearly show a discontent with those solemn routines, a reluctance to yield to such humiliations, and a tendency to postpone till the last period of one's life the acceptance of a penitential status that loses all its content as a result. Whence Saint Leo's counsel of human prudence: while it is good, he says, not to refuse to blush before men when one has committed a fault, yet there are sins that it is best not to make public, because they might serve the enemies of those who confess them in that way.[17] Pomerius will go even further in the *Vita contemplativa* [since] he advises those who are loath to confess their faults to impose their own penance on themselves and to voluntarily withdraw from the communion.[18] In any case, this will be a binary system (public fault—public penance; private fault—private penance) that the theologians of the Carolingian epoch will emphasize, basing themselves on the authority of Saint Augustine.

The other distinction is established between serious sins and minor sins. The former, first defined by the triad idolatry-homicide-adultery, were broadened and systematized in a more or less approximate way as infractions of the Decalogue.[19] And Césaire, the bishop of Arles, gives, through different sermons, a list that can be summarized as follows: sacrilege, apostasy, and superstition; homicide; adultery, concubinage, fornication; bloody or lascivious spectacles; theft; false witness, perjury, and calumny.[20] In contrast to these major sins, there are the minor or everyday faults, those that one risks committing almost unawares, or at least to which one sometimes attributes no importance. It's for minor faults that Saint Cyprian recommends that one go find the priests, that one confess to them "in all sweetness and complicity" and that one lay bare to them one's burden of conscience so that they might supply a remedy.[21] Now, for these faults of lesser importance, resorting to the penitential status is not required. Various means can be brought into play. One can refer to the famous list of the means of remission that Cassian recalled in his twentieth *Conference:* charity, alms, tears, confession, affliction of the heart, life improvements, intercession of saints, conversion of others, pardon of offenses. But above all, it is taken to be the priest's task as a therapist to choose the satisfaction to be accomplished depending on the transgression and the sinner. "Since men sin in such different ways, it stands to reason that they cannot be healed in the same way, some through teaching, others through exhortation, others through tolerance, others through reprimand."[22]

So one can see the role of the priest as a life guide and director of souls taking shape within the lay community. The *ars artium* that undoubtedly developed in a more intense, deliberate, and carefully theorized manner in the monastic milieu didn't remain foreign to the functions of the bishop (or the priest) in relation to the believers he was responsible for. And this was keyed to two principles. The first is that the whole Christian life must be a life of penance. The *metanoia*, that change which accompanies baptism, is not the act of a moment: it must span an entire life, subjecting it to "the perpetual humility of supplication."[23] So the bishop is called upon not just to "grant" penance, to lay on hands, to decide reconciliation, to concern himself with the committed evil, to try to determine its gravity and see to its expulsion; he must also constantly watch over everyone's existence and their everyday life. Hence the second principle: the head of the community—whether he is called bishop or priest—must be like a shepherd with his flock, taking care of [everyone] and [each one] individually, and striving to know them down to the bottom of their soul. As Saint Gregory says, at the beginning of the sixth century, what is most important are not the sins that are visible and known by all, it's the hidden transgressions; there are walls that must be pierced and secret doors that must be opened,[24] and if the pastor is required to carefully examine the external conduct of the faithful, it's in order to discover what abominable and criminal things their heart may contain.[25]

The relation of direction and the practice of examination-confession are therefore not exclusively reserved for the cenobitic institution, even if it is there that they received their most complex elaboration in the third century; and in the context of the persecutions, Saint Cyprian had especially emphasized the general tasks of teaching and the assistance, oversight, and encouragements that were needed by the fallen away.[26] Saint Ambrose also places, unequivocally, the duty of instruction among the primary concerns of the episcopal office: *"episcopi proprium munus docere populum."*[27] But it is significant that at the beginning of the sixth century, Gregory the Great opens his *Regula pastoralis* with an explicit reference to Gregory of Nazianzus, seeming to indicate thereby that the role of the bishop or priest, like that of the abbot or the elder in the monastery, is to direct souls: "The art of conducting souls is the art of arts, the science of sciences. Who does not know that it is incomparably more difficult to heal the wounds of souls than those of bodies";[28] no one can call oneself a physician without knowing the remedies; "and yet there are some who are not afraid to take on the soul-physician's mantle without knowing the rules of that divine science."[29]

In sum, one can approach the analysis of penitential practices, or more precisely that of the relations between wrong-doing and truth-telling, in two ways: according to a "technical" or "praxeological" perspective, which makes two distinct procedures appear, that of exomologesis and that of *exagoreusis;* or according to an institutional perspective, which makes a continuum of practices appear, where these two schemas stand side by side, combine, or project intermediary figures. A duality, therefore, of truth procedures, a duality of forms of alethurgy, or of ways for the Christian to cleanse himself—his body and his soul, his life and his discourse—the locus of emergence of the truth of the evil he wants to cleanse himself of. But also a gradation of instituted practices and rituals, a gradation in the forms of behavior that are imposed on individuals, and that are meant to respond to the evil with a set of conducts going from public and solemn macerations to secret and quasi-perpetual confession.

The two great forms of alethurgy are thus brought into effect, sustained, and drawn closer to each other by an institutional domain that presents a certain unity, despite the difference of status between secular life and regular life. The unity is constituted by the existence of a quite particular form of power. A power that is specific to the Christian Churches and to which it would be very hard, no doubt, to find equivalents in other societies and religions. A power one of whose most important functions is to conduct the life of the faithful as a life of penance, to constantly require, as the price of evil, the deployment of truth procedures—exomologesis or *exagoreusis.*

### III

The idea of a power that would be exercised on men in the same way as the shepherd's authority over his flock appeared long before Christianity. A whole series of very ancient texts and rites make reference to the shepherd and his animals to evoke the power of the gods or the prophets over the peoples they have the task of guiding.

In Egypt, in Mesopotamia, it seems that the theme of the (divine or royal) pastorate was clearly marked, while remaining rather rudimentary. In the coronation ceremony, the pharaohs received the emblems of the shepherd.[30] The term *shepherd* figured on the list of titles of the Babylonian and Assyrian kings, to convey both that they were the [proxies]* of the gods and that they needed to ensure, on the latters' behalf, the well-being of the flock.[31] But among the Hebrews, the thematic of the pastorate is much more ample and complex. It covers a large part of the relations between the Eternal One and his people. Yahweh governs by leading: he walks at the head of the Hebrews when they leave the city, and by his strength, he "guides them toward the pastures of his holiness."[32] The Eternal One is the shepherd par excellence. The shepherd reference characterizes the monarchy of David, in that his reign was legitimized by having been given responsibility for the flock by God;[33] it also characterizes the role of those who, brought to the head of the people, communicated Yahweh's will to him and let themselves be guided by him in guiding the sheep as they should: "You have led my people like a flock by the hand of Moses and Aaron."[34] It also marks the messianic promise; the one who is to come will be the new David: as against all the bad shepherds who have scattered the sheep, the one to come will be the unique pastor, designated to bring back his flock to him.

By contrast, in classical Greece, the theme of pastoral power seems to have occupied a minor place. The Homeric sovereigns were indeed designated as "shepherds of the peoples," but without there being much more than a trace of an ancient titulature. But later the Greeks don't seem to have been inclined to make the relation between the shepherd and his sheep the model of relations that must obtain between the citizens and those who command them. The term *shepherd* is not part of the political vocabulary either in Isocrates or in Demosthenes.[35] Exceptions: the Pythagoreans, where some see an oriental and even a specifically Hebraic influence, others just a popular belief.[36] And of course, Plato in the *Republic*, the *Laws*, and the *Statesman*. In the first two texts, the theme of the shepherd is relatively ancillary: it serves to conduct a moral critique of the arguments of Thrasymachus,[37] or to define the functions of certain subordinate mag-

* Manuscript: mandants.

istrates.[38] On the other hand, it occupies a central position in the *Statesman*. When one determines to define what the "royal" art of commanding consists in, it's to this theme that one turns: isn't the king the shepherd of men? We know that in applying the method of division to this theme, the interlocutors of the *Statesman* fail. And they fail because the particular activity of the shepherd with his flock—feed it, care for it, lead it by the sound of his music, or set up fertile unions—can designate the functions of the baker, the physician, or the gymnast, but it can't specifically characterize one who exercises a political power. Or rather, according to the lesson of the myth, the phases of the world must be distinguished. When the latter turned on its axis in a certain direction, every species was guided by its spirit shepherd; the human flock, for its part, was guided by "the divinity itself": everything in the way of food was furnished to men and they returned to life after death. A meaningful affirmation: "Since the divinity was their shepherd, they had no need of a political constitution."[39] But when the world started to turn in the other direction, the shepherd god having withdrawn, men needed to be led: not, however, by a human shepherd, but by someone able to weave the elements of the city together like the threads of a cloth. He must make a tight web out of all the different individuals. The political man is not a herdsman, he is a weaver. So Plato doesn't exclude the figure of the herdsman altogether, but he divides its role. On the one hand, he relegates it to the past of a mythical history, on the other, to the auxiliary activities of the doctor and the gymnasiarch. But he dismisses it when it's a matter of analyzing the real city and the role of the one who exercises power. Politics in Greece is not a shepherd's affair.

It will take the spread of oriental themes in Hellenistic and Roman culture for the pastorate to appear as the adequate image for representing the highest forms of power: "the task of the shepherd is so elevated," says Philo of Alexandria, "that it is rightly attributed not only to kings, sages, souls of a perfect purity, but even to God almighty."[40] In the political literature of the imperial age, the power of the prince is sometimes likened to that of the shepherd; either to manifest the mutual attachment that must bind the sovereign and his people,[41] or to exalt the preeminence of the one who rules over his subjects as much as the shepherd over his animals.[42]

. . .

Let's forget places and chronologies for a moment. Let's not try
to learn what place and what meaning the shepherd figure might
have in the different cultures where one saw it appear. Let's take
it as a theme that circulates in the Hellenistic and Roman world,
during the period when Christianity will take it over and give it,
for the first time in the history of the West, an institutional form.
What type of power, then, was represented in the figure of the
shepherd?

1. *Gathering.* His power consists in a relation essential to the
multitude; it is exercised on the number (be it innumerable)
rather than the surface area. Others build the edifice of a state,
a city, a palace with solid foundations. He gathers a crowd: "He
who scattered Israel will gather them and watch over his flock
like a shepherd."[43] This gathering has two operative mechanisms. Singleness, because he is the one and only the shepherd
constitutes the unity of the sheep, by "subjecting the peoples" to
his unique will; the sovereign herdsman ensures that "the loyal
men all walk at the same pace."[44] And instantaneous action: it
is his voice, his gesture that creates, at each moment, the flock
out of the multitude: "I will signal for them and gather them
in."[45] With him absent, the animals cannot help but scatter.
Unlike the founder of an empire or the lawgiver, he does not
leave his work behind him.

2. *Guiding.* It is characteristic of the shepherd not to set the
boundaries of a country, nor to conquer new lands. His residence is his route; he crosses the prairie, leads men to the
springs, he makes his way in the desert. Amon, the shepherd
god of the peoples of Egypt, "led the folk over all the paths"; he
"guided the king at all times in each of his excellent undertak-
ings."[46] The shepherd is the master of transhumances. When
the others exercise their power, for the most part they stay
"above," whereas he goes "forward": "O God, when you went
out at the head of your people . . ."[47] Which relates to several
essential differences: his power doesn't have its raison d'être
there where he is; it locates its purpose in an elsewhere and a

later. A power that has the form of a *mission*. It doesn't consist in laying down the law once and for all, but in setting the goal and choosing moment by moment, according to the circumstances, the best path. A power that *indicates*. Finally, rather than bending the peoples to his will, the shepherd shows them the way that he himself is taking; he gives them the example and directs them less by a might that makes things tremble than by a singular and somewhat mysterious force. A power that *draws*.

3. *Nourishing*. "Brilliant companion who participates in God's pastorate, who takes care of the country and nourishes it, shepherd of abundance."[48] The shepherd is not one who levies taxes, or accumulates treasures. His role is to make the animals prosper by giving them more than enough to drink and eat. He makes life abundant, not in the very broad sense where good governments enrich the state, but in the precise sense that he ensures, head by head, the maintenance of all: "Because of your beneficent mouth, O my shepherd, all the people look anxiously to you."[49] He is a nurturing principle. The sophists, and Thrasymachus with them, were mistaken in believing that the shepherd's power was self-seeking, like any other, only concerned "night and day" with utilizing the animals for his benefit—good eating or a profitable market; "what they imagined was not a shepherd." The latter must be concerned only with procuring the best possible conditions for the flock.[50] A curse, too, on the kings of Israel who did not think first and only of their people: "Woe to you shepherds of Israel who only take care of yourselves! Should not shepherds take care of the flock?"[51] The shepherd's relation with his sheep has three characteristics, then: by its desired objective, it must be productive of abundance—or at least of life or survival; by its form it is on the side of zeal, application, potentially of worry and sorrow;[52] finally, its effect is in a sort of overall identification between the plumpness of the flock that one takes nothing from and the wealth of a shepherd who thinks only of them. Power over . . . seems to turn into an attention to . . . that justifies and ends up enveloping all its effects of authority.[53]

4. *Watching over.* The shepherd's attention extends to all; but his art is to cast a particular eye on each one. Where the king saw only indifferently subjugated subjects, as the magistrate of equal citizens, pastoral cratism tries to consider the individuality of each one. Which means first of all that to the extent possible one must take the slightest differences into account: the shepherd of men should never forget that "between them as between acts, there are dissimilarities, besides which nothing human, as it were, remains stable." Which also means that for the shepherd of the multitudes the law, as a general imperative imposed on all in the same way, is assuredly not "the most correct method of government." Which means, finally, that he would be able to play his role only by coming close to each sheep; assessing its age, its nature, its strength and its weakness, its character and its needs, he would have to "prescribe exactly what is suitable to it," to it and it alone.[54] This is doubtless one of the most characteristic traits of the pastoral mode of power: he is responsible for the whole flock, but he must modulate the care to be given to each of the heads that compose it. A power over multiplicities which he unifies and at the same time a power of decomposition that individualizes. *Omnes et singulatim,* according to a formula that will remain in use for a long time, what could be called "the shepherd's paradox," the major challenge which the pastoral of power must constantly face.

5. *Saving.* The ultimate task of the shepherd is to bring back the flock safe and sound. Salvation in this case comprises four essential tasks: ensure that the flock escapes the dangers that threaten it where it is and force it to go in search of a refuge elsewhere, hence determine the opportune departure, wake the sleeping animals, in sum *call out*—"I will bring you out from the peoples and gather you out of the countries where you are scattered."[55] Turn away the enemies that may present themselves on the path, keep them at a distance like guard dogs do, *defend.*[56] Know how to avoid the perils of the route, the fatigues, famine, and diseases, dress the wounds and sustain the weakest ones, in sum *take care of;*[57] finally, rediscovering the right path, make sure that all the animals have returned to the fold, *gather*

them in. The good shepherd must save the whole world, but also the least of the sheep that might be in danger. It is here that the shepherd's paradox becomes a decisive test. For there are cases where to save the whole flock, one must exclude the animal whose illness risks infesting all the others—it is necessary to "make a selection between the elements that are healthy and those that are not, those that are well-bred and those that are not well-bred," give one's care to the former and send back the others, keep only "what is healthy and uncontaminated."[58] But there is the opposite case and it is there perhaps that the singularity of pastoral power distinguishes itself most clearly from the role of the magistrate or the skillful sovereign; the latter always knows that the city, the state, the empire must be saved, even if this one or that one has to perish for the salvation of all. The shepherd, however, is prepared, when a single sheep is threatened, to act for a moment as if the rest of them didn't exist. For the shepherd, each one of the sheep is priceless, its value is never relative. Moses, when he was Jethro's shepherd, had lost one of his lambs. He went looking for it and found it next to a spring ("I didn't know that you had gone off because you were thirsty; you must be tired"); he had brought it back on his shoulders and Yahweh, seeing that, had said: "Since you feel pity for a man's flock, you will be the shepherd of my flock, the shepherd of Israel."[59] Between the salvation of everyone and the salvation of each one, both absolute imperatives, pastoral power multiplies irreconcilable obligations.

6. *Giving account.* The imminence of famine and death, the need for a constant protection, and the concern with salvation dominate relations of the sheep and the shepherd; they don't allow for the latter to ever be innocent of the bad things that happen to them; the least of his faults—negligence, avidity, egoism—risks leading them to their perdition: "If they are driven hard just one day, all the animals will die."[60] A fault the shepherd would immediately pay for himself, for if the flock is lost, it is he himself who will lose; and he will go hungry in his turn if he reduces it to famine: "the shepherds have become stupid . . . therefore they have not prospered and all their flock is scat-

tered."[61] But he will also have to report his failings to the one who handed over his animals for him to lead. Ambivalence of pastoral power: it is total, it has to oversee everything down to details; the shepherd takes responsibility for everything having to do with the flock, his power is undivided in its exercise, its only limit and its only law being the well-being of the animals themselves. But the time comes when the shepherd must report everything. The pastorate is a power that is born in the morning and dies with the evening; a "transit" power not only by its object, but also by the form according to which it is delegated and given back. The shepherd receives the flock only to return it. Even if he is king, he has charge of it only because he was chosen: "You took me from the middle of the mountains, you called me to be the shepherd of men, you entrusted me with the scepter of justice."[62] He will be asked for an accounting of his faults and if he has lost the flock, he will be punished. Yahweh will ask: "Where then is the flock you were entrusted with, the sheep that were our pride?"[63] And seeing that the shepherds have failed, he will tell them: "Because you have scattered my flock and driven them away and have not bestowed care on them, I will bestow punishment on you for the evil you have done."[64] The shepherd's power is caught in a long network of responsibilities where the faults are tied both to immediate sanctions and deferred punishments; he is subjected to a perpetual "accounting"—counting of the animals in his care and given back, a toting up of the living and the dead, a reckoning of mistakes, poor decisions, and instances of negligence.

I realize that I've mixed together, contrary to any method, many disparate things: Plato and the Bible, the gods of Egypt and the kings of Assyria. This is because it was only a matter of showing that in speaking of the gods, kings, prophets, or even of the magistrates as shepherds at the head of their flock, one doesn't just celebrate their power or goodness through the use of a familiar metaphor, one also designates a certain way to exercise power. Or at least one designates an ensemble, without systematicity but not without coherence, particular functions that go with a certain type of authority. Even detached from the political religious contexts

in which it took on its profound value, the image of the shepherd
had its logic.

A considerable double event for the ancient world: Christianity is
the first religion to organize itself as a Church. And that Church
defines the power that it exercises over the faithful—over each and
all of them—as a pastoral power.

Far from being in Christianity a way of representing some
specific aspect of power, the figure of the shepherd covers, on
the contrary, all the forms of ecclesiastical government: all of
them justify themselves by the fact that, through the example of
Christ the Shepherd and under his direction, they have to lead
the human flock (including the least of the sheep) to the eternal pastureland. This is not just a metaphor; it implies the setting in place of institutions and procedures designed to regulate
the "conduct" of men throughout society. The term should be
understood in the sense of the word: a way of directing, a way for
them to behave. Christianity and the Church established a general
power capable of "conducting the conduct" of men: a power very
different from those which the ancient world knew, be it that of
the prince over the empire, of the magistrate over the city, the
father over the "family," the owner over his clientele, the master
with his servants or slaves, the schoolmaster with his disciples.
And if Christianity was able, rather quickly, to insert itself into the
organization of the *romanitas*, this was perhaps in part because it
brought with it such procedures of power: new enough and specific enough not to be immediately incompatible with those that
already existed, effective enough to respond to a whole ensemble
of recently emerged needs. Pastoral power became an institution
that was at the same time global (that concerns in principle all the
members of the community), specialized (since it has particular
objectives and methods), and relatively autonomous (even if it is
linked to other institutions with which it interferes or from which
it draws support).

There is no question here of summarizing this institutional
process even briefly. I only wish to indicate some of the modifications that Christianity brought to the earlier thematic of the

pastorate: those allowing the importance attributed to the confessions of the flesh to be understood. That is, those that tend to make the pastorate a government of men through the manifestation of their individual truth. They have two main aspects which the Latin patrology brings into clear focus.

1. The first concerns the nature and form of the ties that attach the shepherd to the entire flock and to each one of the sheep.

   *a.* In the ancient thematic of the pastorate, the shepherd owes his flock zeal, his attention, his vigilance and vigils, his devotion; a relation of charity, necessary to the flock's survival. In Christianity, it's the very life of the shepherd that must be capable of being offered to the flock for the flock: he defends against the wolves, he gives his existence for it; and it is by his sacrifice that the sheep gain access to eternal life.[65] On the Christlike model, the death of the shepherd, his death in this world at least, is the necessary condition of the salvation of the flock. A sacrificial relation where the shepherd is exchanged against each and all, gaining his own merit in this way by the act that saves the others.[66]

   *b.* Before Christianity, the reciprocity between the shepherd and the flock obeyed a principle of overall causality: fatness of the flock, wealth of the shepherd; poor condition of the livestock, poverty of their master. In the Christian form of the pastorate, the reciprocity is not about causality but identification; and it is established, moreover, point by point; each suffering by each sheep is a pain felt by the shepherd; its progress is his own improvement. The shepherd's compassion is an immediate identity; he feels "deep in his heart, the infirmity of the weak souls"; he considers the "advancement of his brethren as his own" and takes pleasure therein.[67]

   *c.* The Christian shepherd doesn't just have to account for each animal, but for each fault, each fall, each step taken. On the fateful day, he will be rebuked for the sins of the sheep, if he was[n't]* able to prevent those sins by his teaching, his vigilance, his strictness or his charity. Even those who denied, even the *lapsi* will be able to argue that they were not supported, encouraged, supplied with teaching and saving counsel.[68]

*d.* The shepherd's sin is at the center of the relation he maintains with the flock: his own faults lead to the missteps of the sheep (and become all the more serious); and the sins of the flock increase his culpability. The importance consequently for the shepherd to be as pure and flawless as possible: "no impurity ought to pollute him who has undertaken the office of wiping away the stains of pollution in the hearts of others."[69] But the importance, too, of not falling into the sin of pride, into blindness with regard to his own sins, of not ascribing any superiority to himself, and even of keeping his own imperfections always in mind.[70] The servant of all, a sinner among the others, and even more so than the others since he must recognize his weaknesses in the sins of the flock.

*e.* Which means that the shepherd must not derive any pride from being designated as such, no reason for exerting a domination (*potestas*[71]). On the example of Saint Gregory, he should tremble when he sees himself charged with the direction of souls, an apprehension that he must never lose if he wishes to stave off "pride, illicit thoughts, inappropriate and iniquitous thoughts." And it would be a sin, however, to shirk this duty and leave the sheep without a shepherd.[72]

Between the Christian pastor and his flock, the economy specific to sin and salvation, the contagion and multiplication of transgressions, the exchange of sacrifices, vigilance as regards oneself which must never be separated from the solicitude for

---

* Manuscript: "s'il a pu."

others, establish much more numerous, complex, and solid links than those existing in the ancient thematic of the shepherd. And above all, the individuality of the connection plays an essential role: because of the direct communication established between each act of each believer and the merit of the pastor, and the problematization of the pastor himself who is not by some natural or institutional right the "good shepherd," but like all the others a sinner whose faults each sheep must fear.

2. Christianity demands of the pastor a form of knowledge which goes well beyond the skill or experience that tradition attributed to the shepherds of men. At the heart of the pastoral activity, the Church inscribed an imperative of truth, or rather a set of imperatives.

*An imperative of doctrinal rigor.* For want of knowing the truth himself, and being unconditionally attached to it, the pastor will lead the flock to its doom: "it cannot be that the priests, being the first guides, lose the lights of science without those who follow them remaining bent over from the weight of the sin that oppresses them."[73] And he must always make sure that the members of the community remain attached to that truth and by it; for it's the truth that unites them, error that separates them, scatters them far from the path and makes it necessary finally to exclude them; it's the pastor's job to bring back "the bleating errant sheep, whom the heresies of the sectarian spirit will tend to separate."[74]

*An imperative of instruction.* A shepherd of truth, the pastor must supply spiritual nourishment to all in the form of correct doctrine. *"Episcopi proprium munus docere,"* said Saint Ambrose right at the beginning of *De officiis ministrorum.* But this instruction is more complex than a simple lesson. First, because the pastor, whose science is never ready to hand, must learn by teaching:[75] the truth is revealed for him in the zeal and charity of his speech. And then it cannot be a matter of communicating doctrine alone: what he teaches must appear and show its presence in his life, his conduct, his virtue; it must be like a living face of the truth that he preaches.[76] Finally, he cannot teach everyone in the same way: the minds of the auditors are like the strings of the zither, strung differently: one can't play them in the same way; often certain procedures are beneficial to some and harmful to others: one can't instruct men like one does women, the rich like the poor, the cheerful like the sad.[77]

*An imperative of knowledge of individuals.* One who guides the community must be familiar with each person, therefore, and each one must be able to confide in him: when they are set upon by temptation, the weak have to seek refuge in the bosom of their pastor, "like children in the bosom of their mother."[78] But the pastor also has to discover, even against their resistance, the things they are hiding, or hiding from themselves. According to the word of Ezekiel, digging into the wall, and opening the hidden doors;[79] that is, "examine the external conduct" of sinners in order to "discover thereby what they are concealing in their heart that is the most criminal and detestable."[80] The extraction of truths willfully or involuntarily hidden forms part of the shepherd's relation with his flock.

*An imperative of prudence.* As attached as he may be to celestial things, the pastor must not be ignorant or neglectful of the realities: he must "apply himself to examining all things, of making a right and exact discernment of good and evil, know how to study times, places, manners, and persons when it's a matter of saying or doing something."[81] He must be careful not to throw out his words "on the fly,"[82] not to be either too indulgent or too severe,[83] not to do, when he punishes, like those clumsy woodcutters whose axe flies from their hand and strikes their friends.[84] Without losing any of his fidelity to the pure doctrine, without "detaching himself from the contemplation of the highest things," the pastor must not forget the "needs of the neighbor" and he must "stoop to the material necessities of his brethren."[85]

Hence the pastorate is a nexus for the formation and transmission of truth. In the Christian Church, the shepherd's know-how—that familiarity with things, combining anticipation and vigilance—becomes more precise and complex, with rules and methods; for, in the shepherd's relation with the sheep, truth has become a decisive operator, in the dual form of a doctrinal conformity that one must know and spread, and individual secrets that must be uncovered, even if it means punishing and correcting. In any case, they must be reckoned with.

## *Appendix 3*

"Declare your fault in order to destroy your fault," says Saint John Chrysostom, in the second of his *Homilies* on penance.

He recalls that God, after the crime, questioned Cain. Not that God needed his reply to know what the voice of blood proclaimed on earth. He only wanted the murderer to say: Yes, I killed. He was asking him at least to acknowledge: *homôs homologies tauta.*[86] And God will punish him because he refused to acknowledge that, because he claimed "not to know." Two expressions employed by Saint John Chrysostom are worth retaining. Because Cain was not the first to declare his transgression, God declined, not to directly forgive his act, but to "allow him *metanoia*"—that is, the lack of a confession deprived Cain of the very possibility of repentance, of conversion, of turning away (or being turned away) from the committed crime. It was necessary to declare the crime in order to separate oneself from it. Further, and as a consequence, what God will punish is not so much the murder itself as Cain's impudence.[87] An important term, *anaideia:* it relates to the temerity of the evident lie; to the absence of repentance concerning the crime committed; to the contradiction in the fact that Cain is ashamed to admit what he wasn't ashamed to do; to the affront, finally, against God who was offering the criminal the possibility of being pardoned.[88] The indecency of the non-avowal thus shifts the crime against Abel toward an offense against God; in any case the sin against the truth that was owed to God overrides the sin against the blood tie with the brother.

Now, what does the punishment for this impudence consist of? Doubtless, the law of blood called for the death of the culprit. But Cain will stay alive, and this is precisely his punishment. His punishment will be to become the law incarnate on earth—*nomos empsukhos;* he will have to walk through the world like a "living law," a "walking stele," sealed with his own silence, but which makes the voice bellow "louder than a trumpet." *Phônê:* the word is significant. It is the same as the one employed to designate the voice of Abel's blood drying on the furrows. Since there was no confession to silence it, it is still this cry that makes itself heard in Cain's punishment. But with this blood cry, the voice, the *phônê* that resounds in Cain's voice, presents two differences. It doesn't demand death for death; on the contrary, it tells every man in this world: Don't do what I did. And moreover, this voice is not that of the spilled blood and the abandoned dead body; it is a voice that is now joined to Cain. For having avoided the confession that would have brought him relief, he has himself become the law that never falls silent; a person who killed him would be cursed seven times over. Cain was seized by the law; he cannot get free of it; he will travel the world moaning—*stenôn*—endlessly broadcasting the cry of the law, which no discourse of confession (*homologia*) can interrupt.[89]

The patristic tradition often contrasts Cain with two other figures, Eve and David, who both recognized their fault. In the same second *Homily* on penance, Saint John Chrysostom evokes, after Cain's silence, the confessions of David. In fact he draws up, around each of these two figures, two cycles of truth and the transgression that opposes it term by term. Cain knew his sin; David, claims Chrysostom, was not aware of his; and to establish this fact, which is not justified by anything in the Bible, he evokes a "philosophical" conception of passion: the soul must direct the body like the soul directs the chariot; if it is dazzled by some passion, or if it is inebriated, or even if it is just distracted, it no longer knows where it is going, and the chariot tips over in the mud. It was this way with David who, drunk with passion, did not know that he was in the process of sinning. Another difference: it is God who presents himself to Cain, the all-powerful God whom nothing escapes; it is only Nathan who presents himself to David. Nathan is a prophet like David, he has no preeminence over him. One imagines a physician who wants to treat another physician; and David might very well have rebuffed him, saying: "Who are you? Who sent you . . . ? What audacity is pushing you . . . ?" No authority in any case, no coercion, could force David to speak in spite of himself. Better: Cain had to reply to the question that already pointed to his crime: Where is Abel? David, for his part, hears himself being offered a fable: to spare his own flock, a rich man kills one of the sheep of a poor man who had only that one possession. The fable, as one understands it according to Chrysostom, had two functions: a test of the king's judgment, an apologue to decipher to identify the guilty one. So tested, David replies by rendering the sentence himself: "The man who did that deserves death." As for the enigma, it is Nathan who solves it: you are the man who did that; but David immediately accepts the designation and with the admission occupies the place that Nathan assigns him: "I have sinned against the Eternal One." In his two responses, to the test and to the enigma, David stands in contrast to Cain. The latter had negated the law that joined him [to his brother] (I am not his keeper); and when he had ended up recognizing the magnitude of his crime and asked for the death sentence himself, it was not at the right moment—*en kairô*—it was after the fact, once the voice of the blood had denounced him. David, on the other hand, had begun by stating the law, delivering the sentence, and condemning himself without knowing it yet; then, once the truth was discovered, he had placed himself under the sentence that he had just pronounced. Made in this way, David's avowal appears with its two faces—that of the formulated and accepted sentence and that of the admitted fault, and with all the more merit as it was not a matter of reducing the severity of a sentence one had oneself decided in advance. Thus analyzed through David's adultery, or rather the carefully altered version that Saint John Chrysostom gives of it, the avowal appears as being not just the recognition that he's committed a transgression, but the profound adherence to the sentence that condemns him.[90] In accordance with a thematic essential to Christian penance, the sinner who confesses like David is both his own accuser and his own judge: "You have had the greatness of soul to admit your fault . . . You have formulated your own sentence." If the pardon responds immediately to the avowal, this is because the latter is not simply an accurate statement of the facts, it's also because it incorporates the constituent elements of a judicial procedure. Truth-telling, "veridiction,"

involves its effects of remission in a relation to "juridiction"—
a relation that shifts the agency that accuses and the one that
judges onto the subject.

Eve is the other figure who is regularly contrasted with Cain.
In the seventeenth *Homily* on Genesis (5), Chrysostom makes
Eve and Adam into sinners who confess. This confession has
two forms. A verbal form when Adam then Eve, after having
tried for a moment to hide, reply to God who is calling them and
acknowledge that they did eat the forbidden fruit. (Chrysostom
notes that if God asked the man Did you eat? and the woman
Why did you eat?, if therefore he solicited confessions from them,
on the other hand to the serpent, whose sin is unforgivable, he
does not extend this lifeline, and he only says: Since you did that,
you will be damned.) But this verbal confession was preceded by
another, which was not in words, but both in conscience and in
gesture. As soon as they ate the fruit, Adam and Eve felt naked;
they were ashamed and sought to cover themselves. This interpretation of shame as a form of confession is important and it
clarifies what Chrysostom describes, in the nineteenth *Homily*, as
Cain's impudence, his *anaideia*. By giving this modesty the value
of a confession, Chrysostom means first of all that the confession
is not simply a communication to the other of something which
one already knows, but that it is above all an interior discovery.
He also means to say that the confession is a gesture that both
conceals and shows, more exactly that it shows by intending to
hide. This desire to hide authenticates the awareness that one has
done wrong, and the telling gesture shows that one is not afraid
to reveal this awareness to everyone. Hence, at the heart of the
confession there needs to be this game of modesty. Without the
shame of having sinned and thus without the desire to conceal it,
there would be no confession, but only an impudent sin. But if
this shame leads one to hide to the point of not being willing to
confess, and entails that, like Cain, one denies one's own crime,
then this shame becomes impudence.

Because Adam and Eve had this shame that is not ashamed to
confess, their fault is not irremissible. And if their fault resulted
in the fall of men, their modesty, which uncovers in concealing, is
like the first form of what will appear as redemption. As against the

serpent and Cain, who belong to the race of malediction, Adam and Eve, like David, are placed on the genealogical tree of salvation. And by their confession, in this exegesis by Chrysostom, this doubtless fundamental idea in Christianity emerges very clearly: that sin, at the very moment it contravenes God's will or breaks his law, makes an obligation of truth come into effect. The latter has two aspects: one must recognize oneself as the author of the committed act and recognize that this act is evil. It is this obligation of truth that Cain evaded with his "I don't know," which added a truth crime against God to the blood crime against his brother. It is this obligation that Adam, Eve, and David submitted themselves to, thus redeeming the disobedience of the law through obedience to the principle of truth-telling. At the core of the economy of sin, Christianity placed the duty of truth-telling. But the exegeses of John Chrysostom, which are there only as examples and a first indication, make it clear that this duty of truth doesn't simply have an instrumental role in the procedure of forgiveness: a way to obtain it, or to lessen the penalty. The crime scarcely committed, a debt of truth is contracted with God. This debt is so essential, so fundamental, that if one settles it, even the gravest sin can be pardoned; but if one shirks it, not only does the committed transgression remain, but one commits another one that is necessarily more serious, since it is pointed directly at God. It is significant that Saint Ambrose, commenting on the same passage of Genesis (4:9–15) as Saint John Chrysostom, affirms like him that in Cain, God punished the man who didn't tell the truth more than the man who killed his brother. *"Non tam majori crimine parricidii quam sacrilegii."*[91] Where Chrysostom spoke of impudence, Ambrose speaks of sacrilege. Not that there is any difference of severity between them. *Anaideia*, in Chrysostom, designated the violation of the relation of "modesty" which the sin causes the sinners to contract with God; it is this infraction that Ambrose, in the juridical Latin vocabulary, designates as a *sacrilegium*. A little later, Saint Augustine will give Cain's non-avowal an apparently quite different meaning. He also stresses that the question posed by God is nothing more than a test offered to Cain so that he might possibly save himself; for God knew exactly what had been done. But by answering "I don't know" Cain gave in a sense the first figure of the Jews' refusal to hear the Savior. Cain rejects the call to recognize the truth of his crime; the Jews will reject the call to recognize the truth of the Gospel. One mendaciously says that he doesn't know what the voice of blood is crying out and what God recalls. The others mendaciously deny what the blood of Christ is crying and what the Scripture had heralded. *"Fallax ignoratio, falsa negatio."*[92] But by thus shifting the lesson of Cain from the avowal of faults to faith in the Gospel, Saint Augustine doesn't modify anything basic in what the *Homilies* on penance and *De paradiso* were saying. He strongly and explicitly links together what Chrysostom and Ambrose, in the text in question, left implicit: namely that the obligation of truth in relation to transgressions is deeply connected to the obligation of truth in relation to the Revelation. Truth-telling and believing, veridiction in regard to oneself, and faith in the Word are or should be inseparable. The duty of truth, as belief and as confession, is at the center of Christianity. The two traditional meanings of the word "confession" include these two aspects. In a general way, "confession" is the recognition of the duty of truth.

I will leave aside, of course, the problem in Christianity of the duty of truth understood as faith, and consider only the duty of truth understood as an avowal, which produces its effects in an economy of fault and salvation. But the relations between these two aspects will need to be evoked again and again. And this insofar as it must always be emphasized that in Christianity "truth-telling" of the transgression occupies a much more important place, no doubt, and in any case plays a much more complex role than in most religions—and they are numerous—that require the confession of sins. At the very least, compared with the Greek and Roman religions, Christianity imposes on its believers an obligation to "tell the truth" about themselves that is infinitely more imperious in its form and more demanding in its content.

It is through these new rules of "veridiction" that one must try to understand what is said in Christianity about the flesh.

# Appendix 4

But the central problem is elsewhere. It is in the necessity of thinking the possibility of sexual relations prior to the fall outside the category of corruption. Corruption, in effect, as it was utilized by most of Augustine's predecessors, established between the death of individuals and the union of the sexes both a commonality of essence and a reciprocal causality: impure, the sexual act was a form of corruption, just like death, since it is the destruction of the body. So the sexual act could be thought of as one of the effects of that corruption which struck men when death was imposed on them as a punishment. And conversely, one could consider that by bringing impurity into the body, it imperiled incorruptibility and exposed them to destruction. The basic reformulation carried out by Augustine consists in dismantling this global category of corruption by separating, on the one hand, death from mortality and, on the other, the union of the sexes from a corrupted state of the body.

That the first couple would not have died if they hadn't sinned is clearly shown, according to Augustine, in the Genesis text (2:17): "When you eat [of the forbidden fruit], you will surely die." So it is after and because of the transgression that death is produced, but like the intervention of an already formed possibility, which before that event had not yet found the conditions for its realization. In the case where it would be the very possibility of death and not its realization, which would be owing to the transgression, God would not have spoken of a temporal succession, but of a necessary implication: he would have said "If you eat of it, you will die." One must imagine, then, that man, on leaving the hands of the Creator, bore the possibility of death within him: like an absolutely healthy body, which is not infected with any form of disease or aging, can be said to be mortal. But it's in a different sense that one says a sick body risks dying. Such was the state of mankind after the fall: "This life, I do not say just starting with birth, but from the first moment of our conception, is it anything but a kind of nascent illness that leads us fatally to death?"[93] So mortality must be distinguished from death, or rather mortality before the sin must be defined as the ontological condition of man as he was created. Far from marking a defect, it was capable of marking his virtue and his wisdom, as long as it remained in suspension as a general condition and as long as he followed the law of God faithfully. And mortality after the sin should be defined as the effective progression of death throughout a life whose original sin constituted, for all men, a kind of protracted illness. The mortality of the human condition is not the effect of a corruption, even if the day comes when, fatally, all men die from the corruption of their bodies.[94]

Furthermore and symmetrically, Augustine separates the sexual act from corruption, at least the act in its beginning and its originary possibility. A passage of *The City of God* is especially significant on this point. Concerned with maintaining the principle of an uncorrupted paradisiacal existence, many exegetes denied any physical relation between Adam and Eve before their transgression. Humanity before the fall was virgin, therefore, and virginity today was therefore, *mutatis mutandis*, a return to this original status. Now, Augustine accepts both the possibility of a real physical relation and the maintenance of the woman's virginity: "The husband would have fertilized the wife without the spur of a seductive passion, in the serenity of soul and the perfect integrity of body. If experience cannot show it to us, this is not a reason to doubt it; for those parts of the body would not have been aroused by a troubling ardor, but employed according to the needs by a power of self-control. Thus, the seed would have been communicated to the wife while preserving her virginity, like at present the menstrual flow can be produced without any effect on virginity. Because it is by the same path that the one is introduced and the other expelled."[95] Further on, it will be necessary to come back to the meaning of this fertilizing effusion that would have been absolutely voluntary and would have occurred without a rupture of the hymen. What should be stressed here is that the sexual relation is accomplished without physical "corruption." And corruption should be understood both as an attack on the corporeal integrity of the woman and as the violence of a movement that involuntarily overwhelms the body of the man.

The first couple would have been able to remain exempt from all these phenomena that release the body from the soul's mastery, that traverse it with uncontrolled movements, that strike it like a disease and partly destroy it, from all this that announces and prepares the fatality of death. They would have known "an honored marriage" and "a bed without defilement."[96]

But once this general category of corruption that linked the sexual relation to death and impurity has been separated out, the problem is knowing what the relation of the sexes among mortals might be, mortals for whom death was not yet inevitable, and among whom sin had not yet introduced impotence, weakness, the passions, and all the maladies of the body and the soul. In short: the theory of the relations between the sexual act and concupiscence will need to be constructed.

# Notes

FOREWORD

1. Paris, Gallimard, coll. "Bibliothèque des Histoires," 1976.
2. It's said that nearly forty thousand pages containing the preparatory manuscripts (courses, lectures, articles) are housed here,
   as well as Michel Foucault's reading notes. They are distributed
   in a hundred or so boxes labeled NAF 28730.
3. Boxes 87 to 89.
4. Boxes 44 and 51.
5. *L'usage des plaisirs* and *Le souci de soi*, printed respectively on
   April 12 and May 30, 1984. Daniel Defert indicates in his
   "Chronologie" that on June 20 Pierre Nora brought Michel
   Foucault, hospitalized at the Salpêtrière (he will die on the
   25th), a copy of *Le souci de soi* (Michel Foucault, *Œuvres*, edited
   by Frédéric Gros [Paris: Gallimard; "Bibliothèque de la Pléiade," 2015], vol. 1, p. xxxviii).
6. One cannot, however, speak of a "publishing void." In addition to the numerous articles published between 1976 and
   1984 (republished in *Dits et écrits*, edited by Daniel Defert and
   François Ewald [Paris: Gallimard; coll. "Bibliothèque des sciences humaines," 1994, 4 vols.; republished coll. "Quarto,"
   2001, 2 vols.]), one can mention the editing of the recollections
   of a "pseudo-hermaphrodite" (*Herculine Barbin, dite Alexina
   B.* [Paris: Gallimard; coll. "Les vies parallèles," 1978]) and *Le
   désordre des familles* (Paris: Gallimard; coll. "Archives," 1982),
   cowritten with Arlette Farge.
7. *L'usage des plaisirs*, in *Œuvres*, vol. 2, pp. 739–748.
8. M. Senellart, in his notice concerning the *Volonté de savoir*,
   informs us that, moreover, Foucault had considered giving this

volume devoted to modern Christian penance the title *Les aveux de la chair* (*Œuvres*, vol. 2, p. 1504).

9. Ibid., p. 627. In these first investigations, Foucault already took an important step backward historically in order to measure the breadth of these transformations, going back to the twelfth and thirteenth centuries (citing for example the Council of Lateran of 1215, which regulated the sacrament of penance).

10. *Les anormaux*, ed. V. Marchetti and A. Solomoni (Paris: Gallimard, Le Seuil; coll. "Hautes Études," 1999), pp. 155–186.

11. They are found in box 22.

12. "Chronologie," in M. Foucault, *Œuvres*, vol. 2, p. xxvi.

13. *Sécurité, territoire, population*, ed. M. Senellart (Paris: Gallimard, Le Seuil; coll. "Hautes Études," 2004).

14. By this Foucault means a technique of direction of individuals aimed at their salvation.

15. The two lectures will be published under the title *"Omnes et singulatim.* Towards a Critique of Political Reason" (cf., for this text, the edition and presentation of M. Senellart, in M. Foucault, *Œuvres*, vol. 2, pp. 1329–1358 and 1634–1636).

16. *Du gouvernement des vivants*, ed. M. Senellart (Paris: Gallimard, Le Seuil; coll. "Hautes Études," 2012). The content of this course (apart from the first lectures devoted to a reading of Sophocles's *Oedipus the King*) will be rewritten but included in its entirety in the definitive manuscript.

17. Cf. their publication in *L'origine de l'herméneutique de soi*, ed. H.-P. Fruchaud and D. Lorenzini (Paris: Vrin, 2013).

18. The manuscripts of these lectures are located in box 40. I thank H.-P. Fruchaud for entrusting me with his personal transcription of this seminar, which marks a decisive step in the elaboration of *Les aveux de la chair*.

19. A moment of this seminar is found in the text titled "Sexuality and Solitude" (published in the *London Review of Books*, May-June 1980, and included in *Dits et écrits*, text # 295).

20. "Sexualités occidentales. Contribution à l'histoire et à la sociologie de la sexualité," *Communications* 35, May 1982, coedited by Ph. Ariès and A. Béjin.

21. "Le combat de la chasteté," ed. M. Senellart, in M. Foucault, *Œuvres*, vol. 2, pp. 1365–1379 and 1644–1648. With this article,

Foucault "excerpts" a complete chapter of the second part (we have taken account of the minor corrections made by Foucault to his text). Also in April 1983, Michel Foucault considers having *Les aveux de la chair* preceded only by a single work devoted to the ancient experience of the *aphrodisia* (under the title *L'usage des plaisirs*). Cf., on the history of this text, my notice covering *L'usage des plaisirs* and *Le souci de soi* for the "Bibliothèque de la Pléiade," in M. Foucault, *Œuvres*, vol. 2, pp. 1529–1542.

22. *Subjectivité et vérité*, ed. F. Gros (Paris: Gallimard, Le Seuil; coll. "Hautes Études," 2014).

23. *Mal faire, dire vrai. Fonction de l'aveu en justice*, ed. F. Brion and B. Harcourt (Louvain: Presses Universitaires de Louvain, 2012).

24. *Dire vrai sur soi-même*, ed. H.-P. Fruchaud and D. Lorenzini (Paris: Vrin, 2017).

25. Text included in *Dits et écrits*, ed. D. Defert and F. Ewald (Paris: Gallimard, 1994), # 263. Same thing again some six months later with the lecture on "The Cultivation of the Self" at the University of California at Berkeley in April 1983 (*La culture de soi*, ed. H.-P. Fruchaud and D. Lorenzini [Paris: Vrin, 2015]).

26. *L'herméneutique du sujet*, ed. F. Gros (Paris: Gallimard, Le Seuil; coll. "Hautes Études," 2001).

27. On the dossier preserved by Pierre Nora that includes the original typescript of the Éditions Gallimard, a label is affixed, saying "October 1982."

28. *Le gouvernement de soi et des autres*, ed. F. Gros (Paris: Gallimard, Le Seuil; coll. "Hautes Études," 2008); *Le courage de la vérité*, ed. F. Gros (Paris: Gallimard, Le Seuil; coll. "Hautes Études," 2009). Cf. also the series of courses given at Berkeley (University of California) in the autumn of 1983 on *parrêsia: Discours et vérité* (ed. H.-P. Fruchaud and D. Lorenzini [Paris: Vrin, 2016]).

29. It is found in box 84. In addition, one finds in this box a folder containing eleven pages that take up developments present in the main manuscript. Reading it, one understands that they constitute what looks like a piece detached from a much larger ensemble (cf. the first phrase: "But this exclusion leaves room, . . ."; and the last: "In any case, whether the sinner is by himself . . .").

30. The typescript preserved at the Institut Mémoires de l'édition

contemporaine (Imec, Caen) does not include Foucault's corrections.

31. It is contained in boxes 85 and 86.

32. One finds some rare corrections in the third part of the text, but they are not all from the hand of Foucault. When Foucault, who didn't necessarily have his own manuscript in front of him, contributed corrections to the typescript but where we suspected an error of transcription, most often we kept the initial version.

33. With the exception of the square brackets appearing inside quotations: they involve an intervention by Foucault himself to clarify the meaning of the quote, or more traditionally, with three periods—[. . .]—to indicate that passages were intentionally left out.

34. When, however, footnote numbers correspond to propositions that are too general for one to determine the content of these notes, we have simply indicated "[Empty note]."

35. We haven't added translations, however, when Foucault's text gives sufficient indications for understanding the phrase.

36. They are mainly grouped in boxes 21, 22, and 24. One notes each time, and for the ensemble of the Christian Fathers, the consideration of a substantial critical literature, but a systematic return to texts of origin (most often either in the collection of the "Sources chrétiennes" at the Éditions du Cerf, or directly in the *Patrology*, Greek or Latin, of J.-P. Migne).

37. Cf. his remarkable editions of *Le gouvernement des vivants, La volonté de savoir,* "*Omnes et singulatim*. Vers une critique de la pensée politique," and "Le combat de la chasteté."

38. P. Chevallier, *Michel Foucault et le christianisme* (Lyon: ENS Éditions, 2011).

39. Cf. note 36 above.

40. Concerning each Father or each specific practice (baptism, penance, etc.) one finds very long bibliographical lists in these boxes.

41. They are found in box 85. Actually, boxes 85 and 86 do contain the manuscript, having served as the basis for constituting the typescript by Éditions Gallimard, but they don't follow its order: one finds in box 85 chapters 2, 3, and 4 of the first

part and the whole third part. In box 86, one finds chapter 1 of the first part, as well as all of the second part. One also finds there, in the first folder, an introduction and the outline of an introduction, but which evidently correspond to the project of *La chair et le corps*. It's not out of the question that for a time Foucault envisaged taking up materials worked up for *La chair et le corps* to provide a follow-up to the *Aveux de la chair*. Indeed, one reads in the text of the *Aveux* the following statement: "I am saving Saint Augustine's conception for a final chapter. Both because it constitutes the most rigorous framework that makes room for an asceticism of chastity and a morality of marriage at the same time; and because, having served as a constant reference for the sexual ethic of Western Christianity, it will be the starting point of the next study" (cf. infra p. 197).

42. The *incipit* of the *Aveux de la chair* may appear rather abrupt ("The *aphrodisia* regime, defined in terms of marriage, procreation, a disqualification of pleasure, and a respectful and intense bond of sympathy between spouses, was formulated by non-Christian philosophers and directors . . ."), but it isn't certain that Foucault thought of having it preceded by an introduction. Actually, *Le souci de soi* also began in a rather brusque manner: "I will begin with the analysis of a rather singular text . . ." in M. Foucault *Œuvres*, vol. 2, p. 971). The long "Introduction" to *L'usage des plaisirs* seems in fact to apply to all "three volumes, which form a whole" (the "Please insert" of 1984).

PART I. THE FORMATION OF A NEW EXPERIENCE

1. CREATION, PROCREATION

1. Justin, *First Apology*, 29, 1.
2. "*Hêmin metron epithumias hê paidopoiia.*"
3. "*Ho gar deuteros [gamos] euprepês esti moikheia.*"
4. "[. . .] *mekhri kai tôn tês psukhês hêdeôn.*" All these texts are found in the *Supplicatio pro Christianis*, chap. 33. In his article "Ehezweck und zweite Ehe bei Athenagoras" (*Theologische Quartalschrift*, 1929, pp. 85–110), K. von Preysing stresses the similarity between the statements of Athenagoras and the theoretical positions or attitudes of Marcus Aurelius.

5. This is how K. von Preysing concludes his article: *"Wirhoffen dargetan zu haben, dass die zwei Anschauungen des Athenagoras in Bezug auf die Ehe nicht aus der christlichen Umwelt, jedenfalls nicht aus ihr in erster Linie stammen. Stoïsche Beeinflüssung in Bezug auf beide Ansichten dürfte wohl anzunehmen sein"* ["I hope I've shown that the two conceptions of marriage developed by Athenagoras don't come from the Christian world, in any case not primarily. For both, one must suppose a Stoic influence."], ibid., p. 110.

6. Cf. also Justin, *First Apology*, XV, on the condemnation of those who lust after a woman or have the intention of committing adultery.

7. The *Paedagogus* corresponds to that *tekhnê peri bion* [art of living] which is said to be the wisdom that watches over the human flock (II, II, 25, 3).

8. *"Idias leitourgias kai diakonias,"* Clement of Alexandria, *Stromata*, III, XII.

9. [Empty note.]

10. Clement of Alexandria, *Paedagogus*, I, II, 4, 1. [*Christ the Educator*, I, 2, (4).]

11. This is the hypothesis that H.-I. Marrou presents, as a note to this passage of *Le Pédagogue* (I, XII, 102, 4–103, 2), in the Sources Chrétiennes edition (Paris, 1960), pp. 294–295.

12. "The unfailing practical application of the truths taught by the Logos, an accomplishment which we call fidelity," *Paedagogus*, I, XIII, 102, 4.

13. This cohesion between the *kathêkonta*, the *katorthômata*, and the saving value of acts appears clearly in formulations like *"to mentoi tês theosebeias katorthôma di'ergôn to kathêkon ektelei"* (ibid., I, XIII, 102, 3 ["The virtuous act, inspired by religion, thus realizes duty through acts"]); or again: *"kathêkon de akolouthon en biô theô kai Khristô boulêma hen, katorthoumenon aidiô zôê"* (["The duty, consequently, is to have a will united with God and with Christ, which is a right act for eternal life"] ibid., I, XIII, 102, 4).

14. Ibid., II, X, 90, 3, and Musonius Rufus, *Reliquiae*, XIV, [10–11], p. 71 (Hense edition).

15. Ibid., II, X, 92, 2, and Musonius Rufus, ibid., XII, [3–4], p. 64.

16. Ibid., II, X, 97, 2, and Musonius Rufus, ibid., XII, [15–16], p. 63.

17. Ibid., II, X, 100, 1, and Musonius Rufus, ibid., XII, [1–2], p. 65.
18. Democritus and Heraclitus are cited once; Chrysippus under the name of the "Stoics" in general. Plato is cited more, not counting many implicit citations.
19. On the difference between the two teachings: Clement of Alexandria, *Paedagogus*, I, VII, 60, 2. On their continuity: ibid., I, X, 95, 1, and especially I, XI, 96, 3 ("It was through the intervention of Moses that the Logos was Educator") and 97, 1.
20. Diocles, *Du régime*, in Oribase, *Collection médicale. Livres incertains*, ed. Daremberg, vol. III, p. 144.
21. This list is found in Hippocrates, *Epidemics*, VI, VI, 2. There also exist other types of presentation.
22. F. Quatember, *Die christliche Lebenshaltung des Klemens von Alexandrien nach dem* Pädagogus, Vienna, 1946.
23. Clement of Alexandria, *Paedagogus*, II, X, 83.3–88.3.
24. Ibid., II, X, 89.1–97.3.
25. On the theme that the *Logos* presides over the order of the world and over that of bodies and the soul, cf. ibid., I, II, 6, 5–6.
26. "*Zêtoumen de ei gamêteon,*" Clement of Alexandria, *Stromata*, II, XXIII, 137, 3.
27. "*[. . .] sunodos andros kai gunaikos hê prôtê kata nomon epi gnêsiôn teknôn spora,*" ibid., II, XXIII, 137.
28. Ibid., II, XXIII, 143, 1.
29. Ibid.
30. Ibid., II, XXIII, 143, 2.
31. Ibid., II, XXIII, 144, 1.
32. Ibid., II, XXIII, 145, 1–3.
33. Ibid., II, XXIII, 146, 1–4.
34. "*Sunousias de ton kairon,*" Clement of Alexandria, *Paedagogus*, II, X, 83, 1; "*[. . .] Hopênika ho kairos dekhetai ton sporon,*" ibid., II, X, 102, 1.
35. "*[. . .] Epitêrôn men tên eukairian,*" ibid., I, XII, 100, 1.
36. [Empty note.]
37. Musonius Rufus, *Reliquiae*, XII (p. 64): the *aphrodisia* are justified only within marriage and when they have the birth of children as their goal.
38. Ocellus Lucanus: We don't have relations for pleasure, but to have children (*De Universi natura*, IV, 2).

39. In the *Nicomachean Ethics*, I, 8, 16, Aristotle says that the happy existence is characterized by three things: "good birth," "beauty," and the *"euteknia"*: which is balanced between descendants and the future on the one hand, and the good family, good birth, that is, origin, on the other. Euripides, in *Ion*, uses the word in this sense: "Intercede [...] so that through a limpid oracle, the ancient house of Erectheus finally receives a rich posterity" (verses 468–470).

40. In this sense, Clement is only taking up, strictly speaking, the Stoic assertion that the fact of having children [constitutes] "the completion," "the accomplishment" (*teleiôtês*) for an individual.

41. Clement is not unmindful of these advantages. He mentions them in the *Stromata*.

42. The expression is not *heneka tou theou*, but *dia ton theon*.

43. [Clement of Alexandria, *Paedagogus*, I, X, 83.1.]

44. Ibid., I, III, 7, 1. God made man with his hands: *ekheirourgêsen*. This difference between creation of the animals by fiat and the manual fabrication of man is a common theme in that period, cf. Tertullian.

45. "God is rich in mercy for us who do not compare with him in the least way, *têi ousia, ê phusei, ê dunamei*," Clement of Alexandria, *Stromata*, II, XVI, 75, 2. The whole chapter is slanted against the gnostics.

46. *"Kata noun kai logismon,"* ibid., II, XIX, 102, 6.

47. Ibid., II, XIX, 100, 4.

48. An error of the Stoics, who, in speaking of life in conformity with nature, didn't see that they should have spoken of conformity with God (ibid., II, XIX, 101, 1).

49. Clement of Alexandria, *Paedagogus*, I, III, 7, 3.

50. Clement employs the verb *sunergein* to designate God's collaboration in procreation, and *ekheirourgein* for his role in Creation.

51. This formula found in Book I, chapter III, 7, 3, is not applied to generation in particular, but it contributes to defining the relations of God, as Creator, to man, as the creature through which God manifests his love.

52. Ibid., II, X, 95, 3. This "lesson-giving" nature is a Stoic theme. Cf. for example Hierocles: *"dikaia de didaskalos hê phusis"* (Stobaeus, *Florilegium*, ed. Meineke, p. 8). But one sees the shift of meaning carried out by Clement.

53. Clement remarks several times that he sometimes happens to use negative examples: *Paedagogus*, I, I, 2, 2, and I, III, 9, 1.

54. This belief, reported by Archelaus, was apparently borrowed from Pseudo-Democritus (*Geoponica*, XIX, 4; cf. Ovid, *Metamorphoses*, XV, 408–410).

55. Aelian, *Natura animalium*, I, 25.

56. Clement closely follows Aristotle, *History of Animals*, IX, 632b.

57. Cf. for example Lucretius, *De rerum natura*, I, 871, 874, 898, 928; III, 719.

58. Origen evokes the same problem in *Contra Celsum*, IV, 57. He asserts that if there are transformations (cow into bee, donkey into beetle, and horse into wasp) these changes follow "established paths" (*hodoi tetagmenai*).

59. Clement of Alexandria, *Paedagogus*, I, IV, 10, 2.

60. "*Epithumias dikhazousês,*" ibid., I, IV, 10, 3.

61. Aristotle, *History of Animals*, VI, 579b. Cf. also *Generation of Animals*, III, 757a.

62. By contrast to this counter-nature that is manifested naturally in the too-much (*peritton*), Clement uses the word *aperittotês* to characterize the virtuous life (*Paedagogus*, I, XII, 98, 4).

63. Cf. note 53 of the edition of the *Épître du Pseudo-Barnabé* [*Epistle of Barnabas*], by S. Suzanne-Dominique and Fr. Louvel (Paris, 1979).

64. *Paedagogus*, II, X, 83, 4–5; and II, X, 94, 1–4.

65. One finds these explanations in the *Epistle of Barnabas:* " 'You will not eat any hare.' Why? This means: you will not be a corrupter of children and you will not incite people of that sort, because the hare acquires an additional anus every year" (X, 6).

66. Clement of Alexandria, *Paedagogus*, II, X, 88, 3.

67. In fact Clement credits Moses with the threefold prohibition of fornication, adultery, and corruption of children, which is actually the traditional trilogy of the philosophers.

68. This is one of the first examples of the "sexual" interpretation of the story of Sodom.

69. "They assemble themselves like troops in the harlots' houses, like well-fed lusty stallions they run to and fro; everyone neighs after his neighbor's wife." Jeremiah 5:7–8.

70. Clement of Alexandria, *Paedagogus*, II, X, 90, 1. Clement says

that this is the supreme principle, the one that commands all
the others (*arkbikôtaton*).

71. Ibid., II, X, 90, 2.
72. [Ibid., II, X, 90, 3]. On *aidôs* (respectful restraint) as distinct
from *aiskhunê* (shame) and on the fact that the sexual parts call
for the first and not the second, cf. *Paedagogus*, II, VI, 52, 2.
73. Ibid., II, X, 90, 3–4. On this point Clement combines the teaching of Plato and the law of Moses.
74. Cf. ibid., II, X, 90, 4; 91, 1; 92, 2; 92, 3; 95, 3. On the anti-
gnostic theme that the commands of God are good and just, cf.
ibid., I, chapters 8 and 9.
75. Ibid., II, X, 96, 1.
76. The texts that Clement cites are found in book 8 of the *Laws*
(819a—841e).
77. [Clement of Alexandria, *Paedagogus*, II, X, 83, 3.]
78. *Paedagogus*, II, X, 92, 1. Cf. also Philo, *De specialibus legibus*, III,
32–33.
79. Clement employs the word *apokatharma* [ibid., II, X, 92, 1].
80. Soranus, *Traité des maladies des femmes* [*Gynaeciorum*], I, X.
81. Clement uses the word *borexis*, which in the Stoic vocabulary
designates desire as a natural impulse (in contrast to *epithumia*).
82. Soranus, loc. cit., chap. 10. It's also a medical idea that the
woman can conceive only if she desires sexual relations. People
drew from this the conclusion that if a woman conceived after a
rape this meant that in a certain way she had desired it.
83. Ibid.
84. Clement of Alexandria, *Paedagogus*, II, X, 93, 1. The phrase
refers back explicitly to the first chapters on the cooperation of
the creature and the Creator in the birth of men.
85. Democritus, *Fragment* B 32, ed. H. Diels.
86. Galen, *Commentaire aux Épidémies d'Hippocrate* [Commen-
tary on the Epidemics of Hippocrates], III, 3, where he cites
Democritus; cf. also *De utilitate partium*, XIV, 10.
87. Rufus of Ephesus, *Œuvres* [Works], ed. Daremberg, p. 370.
88. Clement of Alexandria, *Paedagogus*, II, X, 89, 2; 90, 2–4; 93, 2;
96, 1.
89. The *"sôphrôn gamos."* Recall that the purpose of the *Paedagogus* is
to introduce others to a temperate life (*"sôphrôn bios,"* I, I, 1, 4).

90. Musonius Rufus, *Reliquiae*, XII, 1–2 and 7.

91. Seneca, *Lettres à Lucilius* [Moral Letters to Lucilius], 82, 8 and 16.

92. Clement of Alexandria, *Paedagogus*, II, X, 99, 6.

93. Ibid., II, X, 100, 1.

94. Luke 20:27–37.

95. Clement of Alexandria, *Paedagogus*, II, X, 100, 3. Here "abandonment of the works of the body" (*katargêsantes ta tês sarkos erga*) doesn't mean abandonment of procreation; this seems to be a reference to the Epistle to the Galatians where the acts of the flesh are listed as indecency, impurity, debauchery, idolatry, wizardry, enmities, quarrels—in short, the principal sins in general (Saint Paul, Epistle to the Galatians 5:19–20).

96. Clement of Alexandria, *Paedagogus*, I, III, 9, 1.

97. "One does not have the right to give in to sensuality or to remain there stupidly waiting for sensual desires, nor to let oneself be affected by desires contrary to reason, nor finally to desire nocturnal emissions" (ibid., II, X, 102, 1). However, in the *Stromata* III and VII, Clement will express a much more demanding conception of the relationship with desires. The *egkrateia* of the pagans consists in not surrendering to the desires; that of the Christians resides in the *mê epithumein:* to defeat not just desires, but the fact of desiring.

98. "*Oukoun aphrodisiôn hêttasthai [. . .]. Speirein de monon . . . ,*" Clement of Alexandria, *Paedagogus*, II, X, 102.

99. Clement of Alexandria, *Stromata*, II, XXIII, 141, 5. For Clement this position is not absolute. Cf. the passage on the possibility of marrying or not marrying.

100. "*Semnôi kai sôphroni paidopoioumenos thelêmati,*" ibid., III, VII (P.G., vol. 8, col. 1161).

101. In *De carne Christi*, for example, Tertullian sees the origin of the fall in the fact that the serpent insinuated itself in the still-virgin body of the woman. Cain would be the offspring of this (XVII, 5).

102. "*Thatton ê prosêkon ên, eti neoi pephukotes,*" Clement of Alexandria, *Stromata*, III, XVII (P.G., vol. 8, col. 1205). On the danger, in general, which young people incur, that desire inflames too early, Clement of Alexandria, *Paedagogus*, I, II, 20, 3–4.

103. *"Pais andrizomenos apeitheia,"* Clement of Alexandria, *Protrepticus*, XI, 111, 1.

104. Clement of Alexandria, *Stromata*, III, XVII (P.G., vol. 8, col. 1205). Clement points out that it would be blasphemy to condemn this *genesis* that God takes part in.

105. Especially starting at 34, 3 (*Paedagogus*, I, VI), where he comments on the first Epistle to the Corinthians 3:2: "I gave you milk, not solid food."

106. *"Sungeneia dia to haima [. . .] Sumpatheia dia tên anatrophên,"* Clement of Alexandria, *Paedagogus*, I, vi, 49, 4.

107. "It does need to be recognized that it [Clement's sexual morality] is extremely rigorous: its precepts often surpass in severity the positions that would become traditional in the Great Church," J.-P. Broudéhoux, *Mariage et famille chez Clément d'Alexandrie* [Marriage and Family in Clement of Alexandria], Paris, 1970, p. 136.

108. One of the principal new prohibitions, the complex and extensive incest regime, would not really be developed before the Early Middle Ages.


2. THE LABORIOUS BAPTISM

1. Acts of the Apostles 2:38.

2. A. Benoît, *Le Baptême chrétien au second siècle*, Paris, 1953, p. 188.

3. *Epistle of Barnabas*, XI, 11.

4. Hermas, *The Shepherd*, *Similitudo IX*, 16, 2–4.

5. On the different meanings of the seal, cf. F. J. Dölger, *Sphragis*, Paderborn, 1911. According to Hermas, it appears as the sign one uses in order to enter a reserved space: *"hina eiselthôsin eis tên basileian tou theou"* (*Similitudo XIX*, 16, 4).

6. Justin, *First Apology*, 61. Note that this second birth is described with the vocabulary that characterizes the virtuous act and wisdom.

7. Irenaeus, *Adversus haereses*, IV, 33, 4.

8. Hermas, *The Shepherd*, *Similitudo IX*, 16, 3–5.

9. Justin, *First Apology*, 61.

10. *Didache*, I–IV. On the content and the form of this cateche-

sis, during the second century, cf. A. Turck, *Évangélisation et catéchèse aux deux premiers siècles*, Paris, 1962.

11. [Justin, *First Apology*, 61, 2.]

12. Thus in the *Excerpta ex Theodoto* (86) [of Clement of Alexandria]: "The faithful soul that has received the 'seal' of Truth, which bears the marks of Christ." On this seal-image-truth relation, cf. F.-J. Poschmann, *Penitentia secunda*, Bonn, 1940.

13. Justin, *First Apology*, 61, 10.

14. Hermas, *The Shepherd, Mandatum IV*, 2, 2. The word *sunesis* is translated as "understanding."

15. Plato, in *Cratylus*, explains that, in *sunesis*, the soul accompanies things as they advance (*sumporeuesthai*, 412a–b).

16. Hermas, *The Shepherd, Mandatum IV*, 2, 2: "*Emprosthen tou kuriou.*"

17. [Ibid.] The word employed by Hermas is *basanizein*, which is used to designate the action of the touchstone or the means utilized to verify that a witness has spoken the truth.

18. "*Non ideo abluimur, ut delinquere desinamus, sed quia desiimus, quoniam jam corde loti sumus,*" Tertullian, *De paenitentia*, VI.

19. [Empty note.]

20. [Tertullian, *De baptismo*, II, 2.]

21. The spiritual powers of water are recalled by Tertullian in *De baptismo*, [III, 2; III, 5; VIII, 74; IX, 1; V, 5].

22. On Christ's baptism as the end of the old law and the beginning of the new, cf. Tertullian, *Adversus Marcionem*.

23. Tertullian, *De baptismo*, I, 1.

24. Tertullian, *De paenitentia*, VI.

25. ". . . *Cum rursus ad suam misericordiam [. . .] irarum pristinarum,*" ibid., II.

26. Ibid., VI.

27. [Ibid., VII.]

28. Ibid.

29. Ibid., VI.

30. Ibid., VI, 9.

31. "*Ceterum ratio ejus, quam cognito Domino discimus, certam formam tenet*" ["Au reste, la règle de la pénitence, que nous connaissons en même temps que le Seigneur, est assujettie à des formules

certaines," trans., E.-A. de Genoude] ["Moreover, the rule of penitence, that we know at the same time as the Lord, is subject to definite formulas"] ibid., II.

32. Ibid., VII.
33. Ibid., II.
34. Ibid.
35. [Tertullian, *De baptismo*, X, 6.]
36. Tertullian, *De paenitentia*, VI.
37. Tertullian, *De baptismo*, XX, 1.
38. Tertullian, *De paenitentia*, VI.
39. In any case these are the four reasons suggested by [A. Turck, "Aux origines du catéchuménat," *Revue des sciences philosophiques et théologiques*, vol. 48, 1964, pp. 20–31].
40. [Empty note.]
41. On this point, cf. M. Dujarier, *Le parrainage des adultes aux trois premiers siècles de l'Église*, Paris, 1962.
42. Hippolytus, *The Apostolic Tradition*, 15–16. The *Canons* attributed to Hippolytus stress examination of the reasons for embracing Christianity, so as to reject those bent on deception: *"examinentur omni cum perseverantia, et quam ob causam suum cultu respuant ne forte intrent illudendi causa"* ["que ceux qui viennent à l'église pour devenir chrétiens soient examinés en toute rigueur (. . .) de peur qu'ils n'entrent par moquerie," translated by R.-G. Coquin] ["let those who come to the Church to become Christians be examined rigorously, (. . .) in case they would enter out of mockery"] (Canon 10).
43. Hippolytus, *The Apostolic Tradition*, 20.
44. Saint John Chrysostom, *Huit catéchèses baptismales*, catéchèse III, 8.
45. F. J. Dölger, *Der Exorzismus im altchristlichen Taufritual: eine religionsgeschichtliche Studie*, Paderborn, 1909.
46. Cf. R. F. Refoulé, "Introduction" to Tertullian's *De baptismo* (Paris, 1976).
47. Hippolytus, *The Apostolic Tradition*, [20].
48. Saint Augustine, Sermon 216, *Ad competentes*, XI.
49. This is the opinion of Dondeyne, "La discipline des scrutins dans l'Église latine avant Charlemagne," *Revue d'histoire ecclésiastique* 28, 1932.

50. On this impossibility of a coexistence of the evil spirit and the Holy Spirit in the same soul, cf. Origen, *Homilies on Numbers*, VI, 3.
51. This comparison is very frequent. Thus Cyril of Jerusalem, *Procatechesis*, section 9.
52. [Saint Ambrose, *Explanatio symboli*, 1.]
53. [Quodvultdeus, *Sermones*, 1–3, "*De symbolo ad cathechumenos.*"]
54. Tertullian, *De baptismo*, XX, 1.
55. [Ibid.]
56. *Canons* of Hippolytus (Canon 3).
57. Cf. infra.
58. Saint Ambrose, *De sacramentis*, III, 12–14.
59. Hermas, *The Shepherd*, Similitude IX, 151. As A. Benoît notes, for Hermas death doesn't occur in baptism: "l'homme est déjà mort avant le baptême par suite de son péché, et, par le baptême, il accède à la vie" ["man is already dead before baptism as a result of his sin, and through baptism he gains entry into life"], *Le Baptême chrétien au second siècle*, p. 133.
60. Saint Paul, *Epistle to the Romans*, 6, 4.
61. Tertullian, *De resurrectione carnis*, XLVII (P.L., vol. 2, col. 862).
62. On the relations between water and death in baptism, cf. P. Lundberg, *La Typologie baptismale dans l'ancienne Église*, Leipzig, 1942. Cf. Saint Ambrose, *De sacramentis*, III, 2: "quand tu te baignes et que tu te relèves, il y a une image de la résurrection" ["when you bathe and you emerge, there is an image of the resurrection"].
63. Saint John Chrysostom, 25th *Homily* on the Gospel of Saint John (3:5), 2 (P.G., vol. 59, col. 151).
64. Gregory of Nyssa, *Oratio catechetica magna* XXXV, 4–6 and 10.
65. Saint Paul, Epistle to the Romans, 6.6.
66. Origen, *Commentary on Saint John*, VI, 44.
67. Saint Ambrose, *De sacramentis*, II, 17.

3. THE SECOND PENANCE

1. Hermas, *The Shepherd*, *Mandatum IV*, 31, 1–6. [*Mandates*, III, The Apostolic Fathers, vol. 1, New York: Cima Publishing Co., 1947, p. 264.]

2. The thesis of the Jubilee, which was accepted at the beginning of the twentieth century, had been criticized by A. D'Alès (*L'Édit de Calliste. Étude sur les origines de la pénitence chrétienne*, Paris, 1914), then by B. Poschmann (*Paenitentia secunda*, Bonn, 1940); it was taken up and reworked by R. Joly, in his edition of the *Shepherd* (1958) in particular.

3. Saint Paul, Epistle to the Hebrews 6:4–6.

4. Clement of Rome, *First Epistle*, LI, 1.

5. *Didache*, IV, 14. The *Epistle of Barnabas*, XIX, 12, takes up the expression and adds "such is the path of light."

6. *Didache*, XIV, 1.

7. Clement of Rome, *First Epistle*, LVI, 2. Cf. also *Didache*, XV, 3: "Correct one another."

8. Clement of Rome, *First Epistle*, LVI, 1.

9. Ibid., II, 4–6.

10. Polycarp, *Epistle to the Philippians*, VI, 1.

11. Cf. expressions like "God has given *metanoias topon* to everyone" (Clement of Rome, *First Epistle*, VII, 5; VII, 5).

12. This idea that had been discussed concerning relapses and baptism given to heretics had been clearly rejected: *"iterandi baptisma tis opinio vana,"* Saint Ambrose, *De paenitentia*, II, II, 7.

13. Note that one sometimes finds the expression, but in a metaphorical and non-ritual sense: Clement of Alexandria, *Quis dives salvetur*, XLII, 14 (P.G., vol. 9, col. 649).

14. Tertullian, *De paenitentia*, VII.

15. Thus Saint Ambrose, *De paenitentia*, II, II.

16. Saint Ambrose, *De Spiritu Sancto*, III, 13.

17. Saint Ambrose, *De paenitentia*, I, VIII, 36.

18. A very frequently evoked analogy. Thus by Saint Ambrose in the letter XLI, 12; or in the *Enarratio in Psalmum 37*, 10–11.

19. Saint Cyprian, letter XV, 2.

20. Saint Ambrose, *De paenitentia*, I, XI, 52; cf. the notation of the same type in letter LV of Saint Cyprian, chaps. 16 and 20.

21. Saint Ambrose, *De paenitentia*, II, VII, 58–59.

22. Saint Ambrose, letter XXV.

23. Saint Leo, letter [108].

24. Saint Ambrose, *De paenitentia*, II, X, [95].

25. [Empty note.]
26. *"Sacerdotibus Dei obtemperans," "operibus justis,"* Saint Cyprian, letter XIX, 1; *"justo tempore,"* letter IV, 4. On the general meaning and the exact meaning of *"paenitentiam agere"* cf. J. Grotz, *Die Entwicklung des Busstufenwesens in der vornizänischen Kirche*, Fribourg, 1955, pp. 75–77.
27. Pacian distinguishes between catechumens, penitents, and Christians in good standing.
28. Cf., for example, Saint Cyprian, letters XV and XVI.
29. On the role of the bishop in these incitements to penance, cf. Pacian [letter III, 16]: the bishop *"ad paenitentiam cogit, objurgat, crimen ostendit, vulnera aperit, supplicia aeterna commemorate"* ["... contraint à la pénitence, réprimande, montre le crime, met à nu les blessures, rappelle les supplices éternels," trans. C. Épitalon and M. Lestienne] ["... constrains him to penance, rebukes him, shows him his crime, lays bare his wounds, tells him of eternal punishments"].
30. On all these points, cf. R. Gryson, "Introduction" to *De paenitentia de Saint Ambroise* (Paris, 1971, p. 37 et seq.) and *Le Prêtre selon saint Ambroise* (Louvain, 1968).
31. Cf. Saint Leo, letter 167.
32. Pacian, letter III, 18: *"Baptismus enim sacramentum est dominicae passionis: paenitentium venia meritum confitentis. Illud omnes adipisci possunt, quia gratiae Dei donum est; id est, gratuita donatio; labor vero iste paucorum est qui post casum resurgunt, qui post vulnera convalescunt, qui lacrymosis vocibus adjuvantur, qui carnis interitu reviviscunt."* ["Le baptême, en effet, est le sacrement de la passion du Seigneur: le pardon des pénitents, le salaire de l'aveu. Celui-là, tous peuvent l'obtenir, car c'est un don gratuit de Dieu, c'est-à-dire un pardon gratuit; mais celui-ci est le fruit de l'effort du petit nombre de ceux qui se relèvent après la chute, qui reprennent force après les blessures, qui se font aider par des cris pleins de larmes, qui revivent par la destruction de la chair," trans. C. Épitalon and M. Lestienne.] ["Baptism is the Sacrament of the Lord's Passion: the pardon of penitents is the earning of him that confesseth. The former all can obtain, because it is the gift of the grace of God, that is, a free gift; but

penitence is the toil of the few, who after falling arise, who after wounds recover, who are helped by tearful prayers, who recover life through the destruction of the flesh."]

33. On this point cf. K. Rahner, ["La doctrine d'Origène sur la pénitence"], in *Recherches de science religieuse* (vol. 38, 1950), p. 86.

34. [Gregory of Nazianzus, *Discourses* XXXIX, 17 (P.G., vol. 36, col. 356a).]

35. *"Cor scrutari et mentem perspicere non possumus,"* Saint Cyprian, letter LVII, 3.

36. Ibid., letter LIX, 15 and 16.

37. Ibid.

38. Ibid., letter LV, 18; cf. also LVII, 3.

39. *"[Libellus] ubi singula placitorum capita conscripta sunt,"* ibid., letter LV, 6.

40. Ibid., letter LV, 13.

41. In letter XXVII, Cyprian refers to a missive of Lucianus concerning "those whose conduct since their transgression was examined." It's also to this examination that letter LXVI, 5, refers: *"communicatio nostra examinatione concessa."*

42. Ibid., letter XXX, 6, addressed by the priests of Rome to Cyprian.

43. Ibid., letter LV, 23.

44. Ibid., letter XXX, 5, addressed to Cyprian.

45. *"Is actus, qui magis graeco vocabulo exprimitur et frequentatur, exomologesis est"* ["Cet acte, que nous nommons le plus ordinairement par un mot grec, c'est l'*exomologèse*," trans. E.-A. de Genoude] ["This act, which we usually name with the Greek word, is exomologesis"]. Tertullian, *De paenitentia,* IX, 2. The term, which one found already in Saint Irenaeus (six times in the verbal form in *Adversus haereses*), is very frequent in Saint Cyprian; it is still found in Pacian at the end of the fourth century.

46. Thus A. D'Alès, *L'Édit de Calliste,* p. 440 et seq.

47. E. Amman, the article "Pénitence" in the *Dictionnaire de théologie catholique,* vol. 12 (1933): under the word *exomologèse* was entered "the ensemble of penitential exercises preparatory to ecclesiastic reconciliation"; B. Poschmann, *Paenitentia secunda*

(Bonn, 1940): *". . . den ganzen Komplex der vom Sünder und von der Kirche zu erfüllenden Bussakte"* [". . . the whole complex of penitential acts that the sinner and the Church must perform"] (p. 419). This was the interpretation of J. Morinus: *"exomologesis est actio exterior paenitentiae"* (*Commentarius historicus de disciplina in administratione sacramenti paenitentiae,* 1682).

48. Saint Cyprian, letter XXII, 2. Cf. J. Grotz, *Die Entwicklung des Busstufenwesens in der vornizänischen Kirche,* p. 82.

49. This is roughly the thesis of E. Göller, "Analekten zur Bussgeschichte des 4. Jahrhunderts," *Römische Quartalschrift* 36, 1928. Cf. R. Gryson says in this regard for the penitential practice in Milan in the fourth century, in *Le Prêtre selon saint Ambroise,* p. 277 et seq.

50. [Saint Cyprian, letter IV, 4.]

51. Saint Cyprian, *De lapsis,* XXVII–XXVIII; on the meaning to be given to this passage cf. J. Grotz, [p. 59].

52. Paulinus, *Vita Ambrosii,* [P.L., vol. 14, col. 27–50].

53. Saint Cyprian, letter XV, 1: *"Ante actam paenitentiam, ante exomologesim gravissimi atque extremi delicti factam ante manum ab episcopo et clero in paenitentium impositam"* ["Avant toute pénitence, avant la confession de la plus grande et de la plus grave des fautes, avant l'imposition des mains par l'évêque et le clergé," trans. canon Bayard] ["Before any penance, before confession of the greatest and gravest sins, before the laying on of hands by the bishop and the clergy"]; XVI, 2: *"Cum in minoribus peccatis agant peccatores paenitentiam justo tempore, et secundum disciplinae ordinem ad exomologesim veniant, et per manus impositionem episcopi et cleri jus communicationis accipiant"* ["Quand il s'agit de moindres fautes, les pécheurs font pénitence, le temps prescrit, et, suivant l'ordre de la discipline, sont admis à la confession, puis par l'imposition des mains de l'évêque et du clergé, rentrent en communion," trans. canon Bayard] ["When it is a matter of lesser sins, the sinners do penance, for the prescribed time, and following the order of the discipline, are admitted to communion, and by the laying on of hands of the bishop and the clergy, enter back into communion."] Cf. also letters IV, 4; XVII, 2.

54. Tertullian, *De pudicitia,* III, 5.

55. Ibid., XIII, 7.

56. Saint Jerome, letter 77, 4–5.

57. Saint Ambrose, *De paenitentia*, II, X (91).

58. Ibid., II, VIII (69).

59. Saint Irenaeus, *Adversus haereses* [I, 6, 3; III, 4, 3].

60. Tertullian, *De paenitentia*, XII.

61. Tertullian, *De paenitentia*, IX, 3–6.

62. "*[. . .]ut probent lapsus sui dolorem, ut ostendant verecundiam, ut monstrent humilitatem, ut exhibeant modestiam,*" letter to Cyprian, XXXVI, 3.

63. "*Quaeso vos, fratres, aequiescite salubribus remediis, consiliis obedite melioribus; cum lacrymis nostris vestras lacrymas jungite, cum nostro gemitu vestros gemitus copulate*" ["Je vous en prie, mes frères, suivez nos conseils, profitez du remède salutaire. Unissez vos larmes à nos larmes, vos gémissements à nos gémissements," trans. abbé Thibaut.] ["I beseech you, my brothers, follow our counsel, take advantage of the remedy of salvation. Join your tears to our tears, add your sorrow to our sorrow."] Saint Cyprian, *De lapsis*, XXXII, 2.

64. Saint Ambrose, *De paenitentia*, I, V, 22.

65. "*Confitentur gemitibus, confitentur ejulationibus, confitentur fletibus, confitentur liberis, non coactis vocibus,*" ibid., I, V, 24.

66. "*Sacco corpus involvere, cinere perfundere, macerare jejunio, moerore conficere, multorum precibus adjuvari*" ["s'envelopper le corps d'un sac, le couvrir de cendre, le consumer par le jeûne, l'accabler de chagrin, et se faire aider par les prières de beaucoup," trans. C. Épitalon and M. Lestienne.] ["to clothe the body with sackcloth, to sprinkle it with ashes, to macerate yourselves by fasting, to wear yourselves out with sorrow, to gain the aid of the prayers of many."] Pacian, *Paraenesis*, XXIV.

67. [Tertullian, *De paenitentia*, X, 1.]

68. On the double meaning of the penitential manifestation, cf. Tertullian: "In humbling a man it exalts him. When it defiles him, he is cleansed. In accusing, it excuses. In condemning, it absolves," *De paenitentia*, IX, 6; Saint Cyprian: "let faithful tears be shed from the eyes, that those very eyes which have looked evilly upon idols may wipe out with tears pleasing to God that which they had unlawfully committed," letter XXXI, 7; Saint Jerome: "What sins would such a penance fail to purge away?

What ingrained stains would such tears be unable to wash out?," letter 77, 4.

69. When Saint Cyprian talks about those who have simply "thought" of sacrificing, he mentions the need for them to confess to the priest, then to do an *"exomologesis conscientiae"* (*De lapsis*, XXVIII). It seems that this involves an admission and a manifestation of repentance addressed, in private and in secret, directly to God.

70. In the middle of the fifth century, Saint Leo condemns the custom of reading in public the list of sins committed by the faithful (letter 168).

71. [Saint Ambrose, letter XXXVII, 45.]

72. Saint John Chrysostom, [2nd *Homily* on penance, 1].

73. Saint Ambrose, *De paradiso*, XIV, 71: *"non tam majori crimine parricidi [. . .] quam sacrilegii."* Cf. also Saint John Chrysostom, 19th *Homily* on Genesis.

74. Saint Ambrose, *Apologia de propheta David*, [VIII, 36–39].

75. Saint John Chrysostom, 17th *Homily* on Genesis.

76. Cf. as an example: Hermas, *The Shepherd, Vision I*, 1, 9 and 3, 1; *Precept IV*, 1, 11; *Precept XII*, 6, 2; *Similitude V*, 7, 4; *Similitude VIII*, 11, 3; *Similitude IX*, 23, 5 and 28, 5; Tertullian, *De paenitentia*, VII, X, 12; Saint Cyprian, letters XXX, 7; XXXI; XXXVI; LV, 7 and 15–17; *De lapsis*, [XXVIII]; Saint Ambrose, *Expositio Evangelii secundum Lucam*, V, 2; X, 66; *Enarratio in Psalmum 36*, 14; *De paradiso*, XIV, 70. For *De paenitentia*, cf. the index of the Gryson edition (Sources chrétiennes).

77. Obviously, this is not the only justification of the penitential confession, but it is constantly evoked.

78. Hermas, *The Shepherd, Mandatum IV*, 12.

79. An endlessly repeated theme. Thus in Tertullian, *De paenitentia*, X.

80. Present in Tertullian, it is given a lot of space in Saint Ambrose and in Saint Augustine.

81. *"Frustra autem velis occulere quem nihil fallas: et sine periculo prodas, quod scias esse jam cognitum"* ["Il serait vain de vouloir dissimuler à Celui que vous ne tromperez sur rien; et vous ne risquez rien à dénoncer ce que vous savez déjà être connu," trans. Dom G. Tissot] ["It would be futile to try and dissemble

to the one whom you will never fool about anything; and you risk nothing by denouncing something you realize is already known"], Saint Ambrose, *Expositio Evangelii secundum Lucam*, VII, 225.

82. *"Mora ergo absolutionis in confitendo est, confessionem sequitur pec-catorum remissio,"* Saint Ambrose, letter XXXVII, 45.

83. *"In judiciis saecularibus [. . .] quaedam tangit judicem miseratio con-fitentis,"* Saint Ambrose, *De Caïn et Abel*, II, 9.

84. Thus Saint Ambrose, *De paenitentia*, II, VII, 53: *"Si te ipse accusaveris, accusatorem nullum timebis."* Cf. also *De paradiso*, XIV, 71.

85. Saint Ambrose, *Expositio Evangelii secundum Lucam*, VII, 225: *"Confitere magis, ut interveniat pro te Christus, quem advocatum habemus aput Patrem"*; cf. Saint Augustine, *Exposition on Psalm 66*, 7.

86. Saint Ambrose, *Apologia de propheta David*, X, 53: *"si autem dix-erimus quia non peccavimus, mendacem facimus Deum."*

87. Origen speaks of the "baptism of martyrdom" that is given in persecution (*Exhortatio ad martyrium*, 30); he says in the same text (39) the blood of martyrdom washes sin away. Tertullian speaks of martyrdom as a *secundum lavacrum* (*De baptismo*, 16) or an *aliud baptisma* (*De pudicitia*, 22). On this subject, cf. E. E. Malone, *Martyrdom and Monastic Profession as a Second Baptism*, Düsseldorf, 1951.

88. Saint Augustine, *Discours sur la seconde partie du Psaume 101*, 3 [Exposition on the second part of Psalm 101, 3]. Later, Saint Gregory will say: "Although we are no longer exposed to per-secutions, we can still find in peace the merit of martyrdom; for while we don't bow our head under the executioner's sword, we carry the spiritual sword in our soul," *Homily on the Gospels*, III, 4 (P.L., vol. 76, col. 1089).

## 4. THE ART OF ARTS

1. Not without a certain disdain: "Go have a look at the ant, idlers! Observe its ways and become wise" (Proverbs 6), Saint John Chrysostom, 17th *Homily* on Saint Matthew, 7 (P.G., vol. 57, col. 263).

2. Cf. J. Hani, "Introduction," in Plutarch, *Consolation à Apollonios*, Paris, 1972.

3. "We must depend on others to discern the diseases of the soul, and not on ourselves; we must not appoint just anyone as overseers [. . .] We must appeal to others: that they may observe, that they may point out our errors," Galen, *Treatise on the Passions of the Soul*, VI, 23.

4. *"Dicam quae accidant mihi; tu morbo nomen invenies [. . .]. Rogo itaque, si quod habes remedium"* ["Je vais t'indiquer ce que j'éprouve: tu trouveras le nom de la maladie (. . .). Ainsi je t'en conjure, si tu connais un remède . . . ," trans. R. Waltz] ["I will indicate to you what I am feeling; you will find the name of the disease (. . .) Thus I beseech you, if you know a remedy . . .], Seneca, *De tranquillitate animae*, I, 4 and 18.

5. *"Non tempestate vexor sed nausea,"* ibid.

6. Cf. I. Hadot, *Seneca und die griechisch-römische Tradition der Seelenleitung*, Berlin, 1969, p. 64 et seq.

7. Regarding these multiple exercises, cf. P. Rabbow, *Seelenführung. Methodik der Exerzitien in der Antike*, Munich, 1954.

8. Example: The debate between Stoics and Epicureans on the problem of knowing if one needed to think of the misfortunes that might arrive (*praemeditatio malorum*) in order to determine how to react to them.

9. The next verses would be from a later date: "Begin with the first and go over them all. If then you find that you have committed wrongs, rebuke yourself; but if you have acted properly, rejoice."

10. On the mnemonic value of this practice and its meaning as a preparation for sleep and dreams, cf. H. Jaeger, "L'examen de conscience dans les religions non chrétiennes et avant le christianisme," *Numen* 6, 1959, pp. 191–194.

11. Seneca, *De tranquillitate animae*, I, 4.

12. Galen, *Treatise on the Passions of the Soul*, VI, 22–24.

13. *"Nec aegroto nec valeo,"* Seneca, *De tranquillitate animae*, I, 2.

14. *"Illum tamen habitum in me maxime deprehendo"* ["Cependant la disposition où je me surprends le plus souvent," trans. R. Waltz] ["The disposition, however, which I most often find myself in"], ibid.

15. *"Facta ac dicta mea remetior,"* Seneca, *De ira*, III, 36.

16. Note [in *De ira*, III] expressions such as *excutere diem, speculator, remetiri acta, scrutari totum diem.*
17. Cf. Epictetus.
18. Seneca, *De ira*, III, 36.
19. Cf. J.-C. Guy, the article "Examen de conscience (chez les Pères de l'Église)" in *Dictionnaire de Spiritualité*, vol. 4.
20. Clement of Alexandria, *Paedagogus* III, I, 1. This passage references the Platonic theme of the three parts of the soul, of which the first, the *logistikon*, is the interior man guided by God.
21. Saint Hilary, P.L., vol. 9, col. 556a–b. Cf. in the same sense: Saint Ambrose, *In Psalmum David CXVIII Expositio*, P.L., vol. 15, col. 1308c.
22. Cf. Epictetus.
23. Clement of Alexandria, *Quis dives salvetur,* XLI.
24. "What a fine guardian I have given to my brother's soul!" [ibid., XLI, 10].
25. [Ibid., XLI, 13.]
26. It should be noted that, even when the techniques of Christian direction will be developed, the model of Christian sacrifice will not be erased for all that. It will be re-encountered constantly, but with a more restricted scope.
27. Cf. Saint Nilus: "*[Philosophia gar estin] êthôn katorthôsis meta doxês tês peri tou ontos gnôseôs alêthous.*" [*Logos askêtikos*, III, P.G., vol. 79, col. 721.]
28. [Saint Basil, *Constitutions monastiques*, P.G., vol. 31, col. 1321a.]
29. [*"Di'ergônphilosophia,"* Gregory of Nazianzus, *Discours* VI (P.G., vol. 35, col. 721), cited by I. Hausherr, *Direction spirituelle en Orient autrefois*, Rome, 1955, p. 57.]
30. [Empty note.]
31. [Gregory of Nazianzus, *Discours* II, 16, cited by I. Hausherr, *Direction spirituelle en Orient autrefois*, p. 57.]
32. Thus, as examples: [note incomplete].
33. J. Cassian, *Institutes*, "Preface," 7–8.
34. J. Cassian, *Conferences*, I, 2. Cf. also in *Conferences*, II, 11 and II, 26, the characterization of the monastic life as *ars* and *disciplina*. Similarly: *Conferences*, XIV, 1; XVIII, 2; X, 8.
35. [Proverbs 11:14 (Septuagint).]
36. The conference distinguishes among three kinds of monk: cen-

obites, anchorites, and sarabaites; but a fourth is added at section 8.

37. [John Cassian, *Conferences*], XVIII, 7.

38. Ibid., 8.

39. "The least one can say is that their faults aren't corrected; they worsen, due to the fact that no one excites them *(a nemine provocata)*," ibid.

40. This was the case with Pafnutius, whose life and lesson are evoked in the third *Conference*.

41. J. Cassian, *Institutes*, V, 4, 2. A bit further up, however, Cassian says, according to the abbot Pinufius, that the cenobites should attach themselves to one teacher in the community, instead of drawing support from several (IV, 40).

42. On this point cf. O. Chadwick, *John Cassian. A Study in Primitive Monasticism*, Cambridge, 1950.

43. Pachomius, dying, declares that he has accepted even the reproaches of little children (*Fragments captés de la vie de Pacôme*, translated by R. Draguet, in *Les pères du désert*, Paris, 1949, pp. 116–117).

44. "J'ai connu des moines qui après de grands travaux sont tombés et arrivés à la folie, pour avoir compté sur leurs œuvres et avoir éludé par de faux raisonnements le commandement de Celui qui a dit : Interroge ton père et il te renseignera," Saint Anthony, P.G., vol. 65, col. 88b [trans. in I. Hausherr, *Direction spirituelle . . .*, p. 16] ["I have known monks who, after great deeds, have lapsed and fallen into madness, for having counted on their works and evaded through false reasoning the commandment of the One who said: Question your father and he will teach you."] The second *Conference*, devoted to *discretio*, cites a series of examples of monks whose insistence on self-direction led to a lapse. The most meaningful of these is that of the monk who, believing he is beyond temptation, directs a disciple too sharply and as punishment falls into a temptation that only the abbey Apollo can rescue him from (section 13).

45. *Institutes*, IV, 30–31; *Conferences*, XX, 1.

46. *Conferences*, II, 3.

47. In the *Rule* of Saint Benedict, it's said of the monks: "*ambulant alieno judicio et imperio*" (chap. 5).

48. J. Cassian, *Institutes*, IV, 8.

49. Ibid., IV, 9.

50. [J. Cassian, *Institutes*, IV, 30.]

51. ["*Nec de majorum sententia judices, cujus officium est obedire,*" Saint Jerome, letter 125 to the monk Rusticus (P.L., vol. 22, col. 1081).]

52. [Saint Basil, *De renuntiatione saeculi*, 4 (P.G., vol. 31, col. 363b), quoted by I. Hausherr, *Direction spirituelle* . . . , pp. 190–191.]

53. J. Cassian, *Institutes*, IV, 10.

54. Dorotheus of Gaza, ["Vie de Dosithée," in *Œuvres spirituelles*, Paris, S.C., 1964, pp. 122–145].

55. J. Cassian, *Institutes*, IV, 24.

56. Ibid., IV, 12.

57. *Conferences*, XVIII, 15.

58. *Institutes*, IV, 27.

59. Saint Nilus, *Logos askêtikos*, chap. XLI (P.G., vol. 79, col. 769d—772a) [trans. in I. Hausherr, *Direction spirituelle* . . . , p. 190].

60. J. Cassian, *Institutes*, IV, 39. Cf. also *Conferences*, II, 10: "The first evidence of humility is when everything done or thought is submitted to the authority of the elders. This is to ensure that one trusts one's own judgment in nothing, that one yields to their authority in everything, that the norms for good and bad are established in accordance with what they have handed down."

61. J. Cassian, *Institutes*, IV, 12.

62. [Ibid., IV, 39.]

63. Cf. The story of Pafnutius, told in *Conference* III, 1. In the cenobium, "disciplined by humility and obedience," he had learned to mortify his own wishes; he had then fled into utter solitude, where he was said to "enjoy each day the delight of meeting with the angels."

64. On the meaning of the Stoic exercises, especially in Marcus Aurelius, cf. P. Hadot, "Théologies et mystiques de la Grèce hellénistique et de la fin de l'Antiquité," *Annuaire de l'École pratique des hautes études*, 5th section, vol. 85, pp. 297–309.

65. J. Cassian, *Conferences*, II, 16.

66. Ibid., II, 2.

67. Ibid., II, 4.
68. This accentuation is more pronounced in the *Conferences*, which is devoted to progress toward contemplation, than in the *Institutes*, which deals mainly with the beginner's entry into the cenobium.
69. Thus the old man Hero [who], after fifty years of desert and abstinence, imagined he could throw himself into a well and his merits would protect him from all harm; the two monks who intended to cross the desert without provisions; the one who wished to imitate Abraham's sacrifice; or that other famous monk from Mesopotamia who "lapsed wretchedly into Judaism and circumcision" or the overly strict master who was gripped by the same temptation as his disciple [(ibid., II, 5–8)].
70. Ibid., II, 2.
71. Ibid., II, 16.
72. Ibid., II, 17.
73. Cf. likewise Saint Jerome.
74. J. Cassian, *Institutes*, II, 5.
75. On how the spirit of evil acts on man's soul, cf. *Conference VII*, chap. 7–20.
76. J. Cassian, *Conferences*, II, 1.
77. *"Discretionis gratiam atque virtutem,"* ibid., II, 26.
78. Ibid., II, 2.
79. Ibid., II, 13.
80. Saint Basil, P.G., vol. 31, col. 985 [trans. I. Hausherr]. On *exagoreusis* in Eastern spirituality, cf. I. Hausherr, *Direction spirituelle . . .* , p. 155 et seq.
81. [Saint John Chrysostom, *Qu'il est dangereux pour l'orateur et pour l'auditeur de parler pour plaire*, 4.]
82. As in Seneca, the "managerial" character of this examination is very pronounced: "Let us examine what is to our advantage and to our detriment [. . .] Let us quit spending unwisely and let us try to put useful funds in the place of harmful expenditures" (ibid.).
83. J. Cassian, *Conferences*, I, 2–4.
84. Evagrius Ponticus, *The Praktikos*, 48. On the *logismoi* in Evagrius, cf. A. Guillaumont, "Introduction" to the *Traité pratique* (Paris, 1971, pp. 56–63).

85. J. Cassian, *Conferences*, XXIII, 5. Similarly, *Conference* VII, 3: "For when we feel the aim of our heart directed towards what we purposed, insensibly the mind returns to its previous wandering thoughts and slips back with a more violent rush, and is taken up with daily distractions."
86. [Ibid., VII, 4.]
87. Ibid., I, 16–17.
88. *Aeikinêtos kai polukinêtos*. By using these Greek words (ibid., VII, 4), Cassian shows that he is borrowing the idea from Eastern Christian spirituality. One finds in Evagrius the characterization of the mind as *planômenos* and *eukinêtos* (chap. 15 and chap. 48 of *The Praktikos*).
89. [J. Cassian, *Conferences*, IX, 4.]
90. Ibid., I, 18.
91. Ibid., VII, 5.
92. Ibid., I, 20.
93. Ibid.
94. Thus Seneca asked himself if he was right to believe that everyone could be educated; or whether every truth was good for anyone without exception (*De ira*, III, 36).
95. The expression is found in John Cassian, *Institutes*, VI, 11, among other places.
96. Ibid., IV, 9.
97. Ibid.
98. Cf. the anecdote about the old man who through excessive reproaches drives a novice to despair. He finds his punishment in the fact that he becomes in turn a victim of the temptation that had beset the young man. (J. Cassian, *Conferences*, II, 13).
99. Interesting in this regard is the advice that Saint Anthony is said to have given to loners: to note down on a tablet, as if they were going to show it to someone, their actions and the movements of their soul (Saint Athanasius, *Vita Antonii*, 55, 9).
100. J. Cassian, *Institutes*, IV, 9.
101. J. Cassian, *Conferences*, II, 10.
102. There is an indirect effect, however, which Theonas himself underscores: the disciple had been convinced by the old man's sermon on gluttony and secret thoughts [(ibid., II, 2)].

103. [J. Cassian, *Conferences*, II, 11.]
104. J. Cassian, *Institutes*, V, 2.

PART II. BEING VIRGIN

1. [Dom David Amand and M.-Ch. Moons, "Une curieuse homélie grecque inédite sur la Virginité," *Revue bénédictine*, 63, 1953,
   pp. 18–69.]
2. Athenagoras, *Legatio*, chap. 33.
3. Tertullian, *De resurrectione carnis*, LXI.
4. Saint [Ambrose], letter 18 (*ad Valentianum*).
5. Saint Cyprian, *De habitu virginum*, 3.
6. [Galen, *Liber de sententiis politiae platonicae*], cited by Adolf Von
   Harnack, *Die Mission und Ausbreitung des Christentums in den
   ersten drei Jahrhunderten*, Leipzig, 1906, [book 2, chap. 5].
7. Thus in the *Didache*: "You will not kill, you will not commit
   adultery, you will not corrupt any children, you will not commit
   any fornication, you will not steal" (II, 2). *Epistle of Barnabas*:
   "Do not commit either fornication or adultery; do not corrupt
   children" (XIX, 4).
8. [Eusebius of Caesarea, *Ecclesiastical History*, IV, 23, 7.]

1. VIRGINITY AND CONTINENCE

1. Further on, we'll come back to this idea that the virginity of
   children has a sacrificial value for the atonement of their parents' sins.
2. On the first theme cf. Tertullian, *De virginibus velandis*, XVI. On
   the second, *Exhortatio ad castitatem*, X.
3. Tertullian, *De virginibus velandis*, XI.
4. Ibid., XIV–XV.
5. Tertullian, *Exhortatio ad castitatem*, X.
6. Tertullian, *De virginibus velandis*, X. Same idea in *Ad uxorem*,
   I, 8: "not to crave after that which you know not [. . .] nothing
   is easier. More glorious is the continence which is aware of its
   own right, which knows what it has seen."
7. Tertullian, *De cultu feminarum* [On the Apparel of Women], I, 2.

8. This is especially noticeable in the passage from *De virginibus velandis*, X, where Tertullian criticizes everything that might be an outward sign of the status of virgin women, noting that there are "so many virgin men," so many "voluntary eunuchs," and God hasn't granted them anything to honor them.

9. Saint Cyprian, *De habitu virginum*, 3.

10. Ibid., 24.

11. "*Disciplina custos infirmitatis,*" Titus Livy, *History of Rome*, XXXIV, 9.

12. Saint Cyprian, *De habitu virginum*, 1.

13. Ibid., 2.

14. Ibid., 3.

15. Ibid., 23.

16. Ibid., 22.

17. Ibid.

18. Ibid., 3.

19. Ibid., 21.

20. Ibid.

21. Ibid.

22. Ibid., 5.

23. "*Continentia vero et pudicitia non in sola carnis integritate consistit, sed etiam in cultus et ornatus honore pariter ac pudore*" ["Mais la pudeur ne consiste pas seulement dans l'intégrité de la chair; elle exige encore la modestie de la parure et des vêtements," trans. Father Thibaut] ["But reserve doesn't consist only of the integrity of the flesh; it also demands a modesty of adornment and apparel"], ibid.

24. Ibid., 17.

25. Ibid., 21.

26. Ibid., 22.

27. Ibid., 5.

28. Methodius of Olympus, the *Banquet*, First discourse, I.

29. Ibid., II and III.

30. "*Theion ektupôma biou,*" [ibid., IV].

31. "*To ek tôn osteôn ostoun kai hê ek tês sarkos sarx [. . .] hupo tou autou tekhnitou dêmiourgêthôsi,*" ibid., Second discourse, I.

32. [Ibid., II.] It's interesting to note that the pleasure peculiar to the sexual relation is compared, as being of the same type, to the

sleep into which God plunged Adam, when from one of his ribs, he drew Eve. A scriptural justification of orgasm.

33. Ibid., VI.

34. Cf. supra, pp. 19–20.

35. It is greeted, moreover, by "a flattering brouhaha," "all the virgins approved her discourse" (Third discourse, VII); and Thaleia recognizes that "no fault could be found with her exposition" (ibid., Third discourse, I).

36. "I admit that given the mode in which you have placed your exposition, Theophila [. . .], it would be imprudent to despise the text as it presents itself," ibid., II.

37. Ibid, I.

38. "*Heterô diatagmati tous prôtous tês phuseôs analusê thesmous,*" ibid., Third discourse, II.

39. This was the original interpretation.

40. Ibid., VII.

41. "*To noêton kai makarion sperma,*" Third discourse, VIII.

42. Note the expressions such as "*Ho Khristos kenôsas heauton,*" or "*proskollêtheis tê heautou gunaiki.*"

43. This last expression is found in Saint Paul, Epistle to the Corinthians 4:15.

44. Methodius of Olympus, the *Banquet,* Third discourse, VIII.

45. Ibid., XIV

46. "*Hê eis ton paradeison apokatastasis,*" Fourth discourse, II.

47. Ibid.

48. "*Diapherontôs askein,*" ibid., VI.

49. Ibid., Fifth discourse, III.

50. Ibid., IV.

51. Methodius employs the term *eukhê* (ibid.), but it's not certain that he's referring to an institutional and ritualized confession.

52. Ibid., Fifth discourse, IV.

53. [Ibid., Sixth discourse, I.]

54. Ibid., IV.

55. Ibid., Seventh discourse, I.

56. This passage of Leviticus, 23: 39–43, is cited in the Ninth discourse of the *Banquet.*

57. One encounters in the *Banquet* many other elements recalling the value of the number eight. For example the final Hymn

contains the seven examples of purity that are found in the Scripture, to which is added the martyrdom of Thecla herself.

58. [Ibid., Eighth discourse, I.]

59. [Ibid., II.]

60. [Ibid.]

61. *"Koruphaiotaton [. . . ] epitêdeuma,"* I.

62. In a general way, Methodius, in his other works, claims an authentic Platonism as opposed to the tendencies inspired by Plato (cf. J. Pargès, *Les Idées morales et religieuses de Méthode d'Olympe*, Paris, 1929).

63. Cf. Epictetus, *Manual*, 17: "Remember that you're an actor in a play that is as its author chooses it to be"; Marcus Aurelius, *Meditations*, XII, 36. Cf. also Cicero, *De finibus*, III, 20.

64. Plotinus, *Enneads*, III, 2, 15.

65. *"To drama tês alêtheias."* Methodius of Olympus, the *Banquet*, Eighth discourse, I. The expression appears again in the next chapters of the same discourse.

66. Note the terms: *parapempein, ta nikêtêria, tois anthesi stephtheisai* (ibid., II).

67. Ibid., III.

68. On the importance of not interpreting annunciatory figures by reference to the past (as the Jews do), see the first and second chapters of the Ninth discourse.

69. The term "squabbler," "quarreler," which he employs to designate the holders of the interpretation he rejects, indicates the existence of a debate about the meaning of this text from Revelation.

70. Christian exegesis had transposed the Hebraic theme of God's alliance with his people into a relation between Christ and the Church. Saint Hippolytus and Origen had thus made the Church the wife of Christ.

71. Origen sometimes saw the wife of Christ as the Church, other times as the soul of the Christian. It seems that Methodius, on the other hand, means to emphasize that the Church—the fiancée and temple of God—is a "power in itself, distinct from its children" and that the soul can be reborn Christian only through the power of its mediation and its maternity. On these ecclesiological debates, cf. F.-X. Arnold.

72. Methodius of Olympus, the *Banquet*, Eighth discourse, XII.
73. Ibid., XVII.
74. Leviticus 23: 39–43.
75. In Greek, the play on words is *agninos—hagneia.*
76. *"Hê parthenia diadexamenê ton nomon,"* Methodius of Olympus, the *Banquet*, Tenth discourse, I.
77. *"Hê ergazomenê tên psukhên askêsis,"* ibid., VI.
78. *"Hê athanatopoios tôn sômatôn hêmôn hagneia,"* ibid.

2. ON THE ARTS OF VIRGINITY

1. *"To tês parthenias epitêdeuma tekhnê tis einai kai dunamis tês theioteras zôês,"* Gregory of Nyssa, *On Virginity*, V, 1.
2. Ibid., Preface, 1.
3. Athanasius, *Apologia ad Constantium*, 33 (P.G., vol. 25, col. 640).
4. Saint John Chrysostom, *On Virginity*, I, 1.
5. This is the opinion of F. de B. Vizmanos, *Las vírgenes cristianas de la Iglesia primitiva*, Salamanca, 1949.
6. Saint Jerome, *Adversus Jovinianum*, I, 41–49.
7. Ibid., I, 11.
8. *"Aetate non perpetuitate praescribitur,"* Saint Ambrose, *De virginibus*, I, IV, 15.
9. Same idea in Saint Ambrose, letter 18 (*ad Valentianum*). This is how he describes the vestals: *"Vix septem vestales capiuntur puellae. En totus numerus, quem infulae vittati capitis, purpuratarum vestium murices, pompa lecticae ministrorum circumfusa comitatu, privilegia maxima, lucra ingentia, praescripta denique pudicitiae tempora coegerunt"* ["Sept vestales, à peine sept jeunes filles enchaînées par force à leur état! Tel est le chiffre de celles que la séduction des bandelettes sacrées, l'éclat des robes de pourpre, le faste d'une litière environnée de tout un cortège d'esclaves, d'immenses privilèges, des revenus considérables, et un terme légalement assigné à leur continence, ont enrôlées dans son rang," trans. Mgr. Baunard] ["But how many virgins have the promised rewards gained for them? Hardly are seven vestal virgins received. See the whole number whom the fillets and chaplets for the head, the dye of the purple robes, the pomp of the litter surrounded by a company of slaves, the greatest privileges,

immense revenues, and a prescribed time of virginity have gathered together."]

10. Saint John Chrysostom, *On Virginity*, IV, 2.
11. Ibid., II, 2. Note however that Chrysostom is much more pointed in his critique of virginity among heretics inspired by dualism. If all marriage is bad, he says, abstinence becomes obligatory and has no merit; but by abstaining based on an error that offends God, with their virginity these heretics commit a sin that will be punished severely.
12. [Theophrastus, *On Marriage*, cited by Saint Jerome, *Adversus Jovinianum*, I, 47.]
13. [Gregory of Nyssa, *De la virginité*, III, 2–7.]
14. Saint John Chrysostom, *On Virginity*, XLIV, 2.
15. "*Kath' heauton ôn ho anêr,*" ibid.
16. Ibid., LXVIII, 1–2. Note the terms: *apêllaktai tarakhês, ataraxia, hê euphrosunê tês outô diakeimenês psukhês, eukolia.*
17. Ibid., [XLIV, 2].
18. Gregory of Nyssa, *On Virginity*, IV, 4.
19. Saint John Chrysostom, *On Virginity*, XLIV, 2.
20. Gregory of Nyssa, *On Virginity*, III, 9.
21. Ibid., VI, 1.
22. Cf. infra, p. [214].
23. Saint John Chrysostom, *On Virginity*, XLV, 1.
24. Clement of Alexandria, *The Stromata*, III.
25. Saint John Chrysostom, [*On Virginity*, XLV].
26. Saint Augustine, *Discours sur le psaume 132*, 4 (P.L., vol. 37, col. 1730).
27. Saint Ambrose, *De virginibus*, I, 7, 35.
28. This text was published by Dom David Amand ("Une curieuse homélie grecque inédite sur la Virginité," loc. cit.).
29. Saint Augustine, *On Virginity*, IV, 4.
30. Basil of Ancyra, *On the Integrity of Virginity*, 55 (P.G., vol. 30, col. 780).
31. Saint John Chrysostom, *On Virginity*, II, 17.
32. Thus Saint Ambrose, *De virginibus*, I, 7; Eusebius of Emesa, *Homily* VI, 6.
33. Thus all the first chapters of Saint John Chrysostom's *De virginitate*.

34. Saint John Chrysostom, *On Virginity*, VIII, 4.
35. Saint Augustine, *De continentia*, IX (23).
36. Philo of Alexandria, *De opificio mundi*, 151.
37. Origen, *Homélies sur la Genèse*, I, 14.
38. Saint Jerome, *Adversus Jovinianum*, I, 16.
39. Saint Augustine, *De Genesi ad litteram*, III, 22.
40. [Philo of Alexandria, *De opificio mundi*, 151 and 167.]
41. This is the opinion of Gregory of Nyssa who, as M. Aubineau notes (Gregory of Nyssa, Paris, 1966, *De la Virginité*, p. 420, note 1), sees the allure of pleasure (*hêdonê*) as the reason for the fall, without this pleasure being specifically sexual pleasure. Neither Chrysostom nor Jerome nor Augustine sees a sexual act as being the first sin.
42. Gregory of Nyssa, *On Virginity*, XII, 4.
43. Saint John Chrysostom, *On Virginity*, XLVI, 5. Thus in the *Homilies on Genesis*, XV, 4, he also mentions this help, but he doesn't assign it any precise function.
44. Gregory of Nyssa, *On the Creation of Man*, XVII, 188 a–b.
45. Ibid., XVII, 189d.
46. There again, Saint John Chrysostom, in the *Homilies on Genesis*, XVII, is less precise than Gregory of Nyssa; but he also grants an angelic existence, as well as the intervention of sexual reproduction after the fall to avoid depopulation owing to the new reign of death.
47. Gregory of Nyssa, *On Virginity*, XII, 4. The term employed here to designate the first man as he was upon leaving the hands of God is *prôtoplastos*.
48. Gregory of Nyssa uses the verb *palindromein*.
49. [Ibid., XIII, 3.]
50. [Empty note.]
51. Eusebius of Emesa, *Homily* VII, 5.
52. Saint John Chrysostom, *On Virginity*, XI, 1–2.
53. *"Castitas enim angelos fecit,"* Saint Ambrose, *De virginibus*, I, 8.
54. Saint John Chrysostom, *On Virginity*, LXXIX, 1–2.
55. Saint John Chrysostom, 17th *Homily* on Genesis, cf. in the same sense Gregory of Nyssa, *De hominis opificio*, XVII.
56. Such as Miriam cited by Gregory of Nyssa, Athanasius, Ambrose; Elijah, cited by Methodius and Gregory of Nyssa.

57. Saint John Chrysostom, *On Virginity*, XVI–XVII, and [note incomplete].

58. [Saint John Chrysostom, *On Virginity*, XI.]

59. Saint Jerome, *Adversus Helvidium*, chap. 20 [quoting Saint Paul, "*Tempus breviatum est,*" 1 Cor. 7:29].

60. Saint John Chrysostom, *On Virginity*, LXXIII, 1.

61. Ibid., XIV, 5.

62. Gregory of Nyssa, *On Virginity*, XIII, 1.

63. Tertullian, *De resurrectione carnis*, LXI.

64. Tertullian, *Ad uxorem*, I, 4.

65. Tertullian, *De velandis virginibus*, XVI.

66. Cf. the lines preceding the passage cited, where Tertullian urges all women to wear the veil.

67. Methodius of Olympus, the *Banquet*, "Chorus and Verse," XX.

68. Gregory of Nyssa, *On Virginity*, III, 8.

69. Basil of Ancyra, *On the Integrity of Virginity*, 27.

70. Eusebius of Emesa, *Homilies*, VI, 16.

71. Saint Ambrose, *De lapsu virginis consecratae*, V, 19.

72. Saint John Chrysostom, *On Virginity*, LX.

73. [Gregory of Nyssa, *On Virginity*, XX, 1.]

74. Basil of Ancyra, *On the Integrity of Virginity*, 37.

75. Gregory of Nyssa, *On Virginity*, XX, 4.

76. [Ibid.]

77. Saint John Chrysostom, *On Virginity*, LXIII, 2–3.

78. Gregory of Nyssa, *On Virginity*, XIII, 3. Cf. also Ambrose, *De virginibus*, I, 6.

79. Gregory of Nyssa, *On Virginity*, IV, 9.

80. Basil of Ancyra, *On the Integrity of Virginity*, 4.

81. Saint John Chrysostom, *On Virginity*, XXII, 2.

82. Ibid., XXVII, 1.

83. Ibid., XXXIV, 1–2.

84. Ibid., XXVII, 1–2; cf. also XXXVII, 4.

85. Ibid., XXXVIII, 1.

86. Thus the homily published by Dom David Amand De Mendieta, loc. cit.

87. Gregory of Nyssa, *On Virginity*, XXIII, 2.

88. Ibid. Those who practice virginity compared to those who don't yet practice it are *alloglôssoi*.

89. Ibid., XXIII, 2.
90. *"Enkrateias metra,"* ibid., XXIII, 1.
91. Ibid., XXIII, 3.
92. *"Hê dia tôn ergôn huphêgêsis,"* ibid., XXIII, 1.
93. He gives examples such as a flame that lights other flames (ibid., XXIII, 5).
94. Ibid., XXIII, 6.

3. VIRGINITY AND SELF-KNOWLEDGE

1. Basil of Ancyra, *On the Integrity of Virginity*, 1.
2. Ibid., 24–29 and 36–39.
3. Ibid., 2 and 51.
4. Ibid., 54 and 55.
5. Ibid., 1.
6. In any case, it also indicates that its advice may be useful to reading groups.
7. *"Areskei de toiautê hoian autos autên plasa iêthelêsen,"* ibid., 17. The same argument was found in Cyprian, cf. supra pp. 147–149.
8. The question of sexual differentiation in souls was an old question. Thus Tertullian [(*On the Veiling of Virgins*, 7–8; *On the Soul*, 27, etc.)].
9. Basil of Ancyra, *On the Integrity of Virginity*, 44–45.
10. Ibid., 15.
11. Ibid.
12. Ibid., 46.
13. Ibid., 47.
14. Ibid.
15. Ibid., 43; cf. ibid., 13.
16. Ibid., 61. Against eunuchism, Basil also invokes, based on physiological considerations, the remnants of desire that haunt the body and are all the more violent as they can't find any means of escape.
17. We'll see, further on, the importance of this question of the image in sleep, of the defilement it produces in the body, and the indulgence it induces.
18. Ibid., 13.
19. Ibid., 36.
20. Ibid.

21. Ibid., 27.
22. Ibid., 28.
23. J. Cassian, *Conferences*, XXI, 4.
24. Ibid., XXII, 6.
25. J. Cassian, *Institutes*, VI, 4.
26. Ibid., VI, 19.
27. *"Propriae puritatis delectation subsistit,"* J. Cassian, *Conferences*, XII, 10.
28. Ibid., XIII, 5.
29. Ibid., XII, 10.
30. Ibid., XII, 11.
31. Ibid.
32. Ibid., XI, 15.
33. As we'll see, only by grace can one attain it, and the temptations themselves are perhaps a form of grace.
34. Ibid., XII, 5.
35. Ibid., XII, 14.
36. Ibid., XII, 4.
37. Ibid., X, 8: *"Deo jugiter inhaerere."*
38. Ibid., IX, 18: *"in illius dilectio resoluta atque rejecta."*
39. Ibid., IX, 19.
40. Ibid., XI, 13: *"Quem semel sua virtute possederit, non partem, sed totam ejus occupet mentem"* ["Lorsqu'il s'est emparé d'une âme, il ne la possède pas en partie seulement, mais tout entier," trans. E. Pichery] ["When he has taken hold of a soul, he doesn't possess it only in part, but in its entirety."]
41. J. Cassian, *Institutes*, I, 11.
42. J. Cassian, *Conferences*, XIV, 9. "It is impossible for the soul that is not pure to obtain the gift of spiritual science" (ibid., XIV, 10).
43. Ibid., XIV, 14 and 16.
44. Ibid., XIV.
45. J. Cassian, *Institutes*, V, 33. In VI, 18, John Cassian gives a more cautious formulation: "It is possible no doubt to find chaste persons who do not possess the grace of science, but it is impossible to possess the spiritual science without a complete chastity." Actually, as the rest of the Theodore example shows, it is the grace of Christ that provides their ignorant chastity with an understanding of the mysteries of the Scripture.

46. Ibid., V, 2.

47. Ibid., XII, 15.

48. J. Cassian, *Conferences*, IX, 4.

49. J. Cassian, *Institutes*, V, 2.

50. Cf. in particular Saint John Chrysostom, *On Virginity*, XXXVIII. See also VII, 17 and 22; IX, 24; LXXXIV.

51. This notion of combat is also central in Pachomius and Evagrius.

52. "After the four books which have been composed on the customs of the monasteries, we now propose [. . .] to engage the struggle against the principal faults," J. Cassian, *Institutes*, V, 1.

53. The expressions concerning the "correctness" of the combat are quite numerous. Some examples: ibid., V, 17 and 18; VI, 5; VII, 20; VIII, 5; IX, 2; XI, 19; XII, 32.

54. Thus, apropos of the struggle against gluttony: "on the manner of fasting a uniform rule cannot easily be observed [. . .] there is a difference of time, manner, and quality of the food in proportion to the difference in physical condition, age, and sex; but there is one and the same rule of restraint to everybody as regards continence of mind, and the virtue of the spirit," ibid., V, 5.

55. Ibid., V, 12.

56. Ibid., V, 19–21.

57. On the history of these lists of capital sins, cf. A. Guillaumont, ["Introduction" to volume 1 of the *Traité pratique d'Évagre le Pontique*, p. 67 et seq.].

58. Evagrius Ponticus, *The Praktikos*, 6.

59. [Ibid.]

60. [J. Cassian, *Conferences*, VIII, 13.]

61. [Cf. supra, pp. 208–209.]

62. Ibid., V, 15.

63. Ibid., IV, 7.

64. Ibid., IV, 17.

65. Regarding all this, cf. [note incomplete].

66. The other seven, again, are gluttony, avarice, anger, [dejection], acedia, vainglory, and pride.

67. Cf. infra, pp. 224–225.

68. Ibid., V, 10.

69. J. Cassian, *Institutes*, V, and *Conferences*, V.

70. *Conferences*, V, 13–14.

71. Ibid., V, 10.

72. [Ibid.]

73. Ibid.

74. J. Cassian, *Institutes*, XII, 2.

75. J. Cassian, *Conferences*, XII, 6. See examples of falling into the spirit of fornication, due to pride and presumption, in *Conferences*, II, 13; and especially in J. Cassian, *Institutes*, XII, 20 and 21, where the sins against the humility that is owed to God are sanctioned by the most humiliating temptations, those of a desire *contra usum naturae* for the filthiness of an "impure passion."

76. J. Cassian, *Conferences*, V, 4.

77. J. Cassian, *Institutes*, VI, 13.

78. Ibid., V, 8.

79. *Conferences*, V, 19.

80. *Institutes*, VI, 6.

81. Ibid.

82. *Conferences*, V, 11.

83. Ibid., XII, 2.

84. Ibid. Cassian bases his tripartition on a passage of [Saint Paul's] Epistle to the Colossians 3:5.

85. *Didache*, II, 2.

86. *Epistle of Barnabas*, XIX, 4. A little higher up (X, 6–8), regarding food prohibitions, the same text interprets the prohibition against eating hyena as a prohibition against adultery, that against eating hare as a prohibition against the seduction of children, that against eating weasel as a condemnation of oral relations.

87. Thus Saint Augustine, Sermon 56, 12.

88. *Didache*, III, 3.

89. Basil of Caesarea, *Exhortation to Renounce the World*, 5: "Avoid all commerce, all relation with the young brothers of your age. Flee them like fire. Numerous, alas, are those that through them the enemy has set alight and delivered over to the eternal flames." Cf. the precautions indicated in *The Long Rules* (34) and the *Brief Rules* (220). See also Saint John Chrysostom, *Contre les détracteurs de la vie monastique* [*Against the Detractors of Monastic Life*] (P.G., vol. 47, col. 319–386).

90. J. Cassian, *Institutes*, II, 15. Those who violate this law commit a grave sin and are suspected of *"conjurationis pravique consilii."* Are these words an allusive way of designating an amorous behavior or do they allude to the danger of privileged relations between members of the same community? Same recommendations in the *Institutes*, IV, 16.

91. Cassian's term for designating the fact that the mind dwells on these thoughts is *immorari*. *Delectatio morosa* will later become one of the important categories in the sexual ethic of the Middle Ages.

92. *Conferences*, XII, 7.

93. Ibid., V, 11 and XII, 2. Cf. supra, pp. 221–224.

94. J. Cassian, *Institutes*, VI, 10.

95. Ibid., VI, 20.

96. J. Cassian, *Conferences*, VII, 1 and XII, 7. Other allusions to this theme in J. Cassian, *Institutes*, II, 13 and III, 5.

97. Ibid., XXII, 5.

98. J. Cassian, *Institutes*, VI, 11.

99. Ibid., VI, 22.

100. Ibid., VI, 23.

101. Cf. supra, pp. 121–124.

102. Cf., in *Conference* XXII, 6, the example of a "consultation" about a monk who every time he presented himself for communion was the victim of a nocturnal illusion, and so did not dare take part in the holy mysteries. After the questioning and discussion, the "spiritual physicians" diagnosed that it was the devil that was sending these illusions to prevent the monk from achieving the communion he desired. To abstain would thus be to fall into the devil's trap. To commune in spite of everything would be to defeat him. Once this decision was made, the devil had no further reason to cause that prohibitive impurity.

PART III. BEING MARRIED

1. THE DUTY OF SPOUSES

1. Saint John Chrysostom, 7th *Homily* on the Epistle to the Hebrews, 4. Cf. also *Against the Opponents of the Monastic Life*, III, 14.v.

2. On this point, cf. [J. Daniélou and] H.-I. Marrou, *Nouvelle histoire de l'Église*, Paris, 1963, vol. 1, p. 268.

3. Cf. concerning this support and the conflicts connected with it, ibid., p. 282 et seq. Cf., on marriage, pp. 362–364.

4. Saint John Chrysostom, *Against the Opponents of the Monastic Life*, III, 14.

5. They are contemporaneous with Saint Augustine's *De bono coniugali* (401).

6. [Saint John Chrysostom, *On Virginity*, LXXIII.]

7. Ibid., I, II, III, XLVII, XLVIII, LIV, LXXXV.

8. Saint John Chrysostom, 3rd *Homily* on marriage, 3.

9. [Ibid.]

10. Ibid.

11. *"Outôs pasês turannidos autê hê agapê turannikôtera,"* Saint John Chrysostom, 20th *Homily* on the Epistle to the Ephesians, 1.

12. *"Emphôleuôn tê phusei, kai lanthanôn hêmas,"* ibid.

13. This theme is developed in particular at the beginning of the 20th *Homily* on the Epistle to the Ephesians, 1.

14. [Ibid.]

15. The incest prohibition explained by the obligation to form ties with external others is not peculiar to Saint John Chrysostom nor to the Christian authors. One finds it in [note incomplete].

16. [Ibid., 4.]

17. [Saint John Chrysostom, 3rd *Homily* on marriage, 3.]

18. [Cf. for example, Origen, *Homilies* on the Song of Songs.]

19. [Saint Paul, Epistle to the Ephesians 5:23.]

20. Saint John Chrysostom, 3rd *Homily* on marriage, 2.

21. Saint John Chrysostom, 20th *Homily* on the Epistle to the Ephesians, 2.

22. [Ibid., 6.]

23. Ibid., 9.

24. Saint John Chrysostom, 7th *Homily* on the Epistle to the Hebrews, 4.

25. [Saint John Chrysostom, 20th *Homily* on the Epistle to the Ephesians, 1.]

26. Cf. Saint John Chrysostom, 3rd *Homily* on marriage, 4. Same theme in the treatise *On the One Marriage*, 4. In a note to this

last text, B. Grillet likens this passage to Xenophon's text: "The deity made provision from the first by shaping the woman's nature for indoor and the man's for outdoor occupations," *Oeconomicus*, VII, 22.

27. Saint John Chrysostom, 3rd *Homily* on marriage, 4.

28. [Saint John Chrysostom, 20th *Homily* on the Epistle to the Ephesians, 7.]

29. Ibid., 8.

30. Cf. chap. "Ischomachus' Household," in *The Use of Pleasure*.

31. Ibid., 7.

32. Saint John Chrysostom, 19th *Homily* on the Epistle to the Corinthians, 2.

33. Cf. supra, first part, p. 8.

34. Saint John Chrysostom, 1st *Homily* on marriage, 4.

35. Ibid.

36. Remarriage with a repudiated woman is an adultery, because the repudiation doesn't destroy the bond, Saint John Chrysostom, 2nd *Homily* on marriage, 3.

37. [Ibid., 4.]

38. [Saint John Chrysostom, 3rd *Homily* on marriage, 2.]

39. *Prothumia, philia, eunoia:* Saint John Chrysostom, *Against Remarriage*, 5.

40. [Saint John Chrysostom, 20th *Homily* on the Epistle to the Ephesians, 8.]

41. [Xenophon, *Oeconomicus*, chap. 7.]

42. Saint John Chrysostom, 20th *Homily* on the Epistle to the Ephesians, 8.

43. Saint John Chrysostom, first *Homily* on marriage, 5. Cf. also in the third of these *Homilies*, 9: "If we direct our efforts in this way, there will be neither divorce, nor suspicion of adultery, nor cause for jealousy, nor fights, nor quarrels, but we will taste all the delights of peace and harmony."

44. Saint John Chrysostom, 20th *Homily* on the Epistle to the Ephesians, 6.

45. Ibid., 9.

46. Saint John Chrysostom, 2nd *Homily* on marriage, 1.

47. [Saint John Chrysostom, 19th *Homily* on the First Epistle to Timothy, 2.] The relation between exercise in preparation for

marriage and the athletic combat of those who have chosen virginity appears clearly in the 5th *Homily* on the First Epistle to the Thessalonians, 3. Before marriage children are like a flammable material. One has to watch over them like "over cloistered virgins," [1st *Homily* on Hannah, 6].

48. [Saint John Chrysostom, 19th *Homily* on the First Epistle to Timothy, 2.]

49. Ibid.

50. [Ibid.]

51. Saint John Chrysostom, 59th *Homily* on Genesis, 3 (P.G., vol. 54, col. 517–518).

52. Saint John Chrysostom, 20th *Homily* on the Epistle to the Ephesians, 9. Cf. also: "Use marriage with moderation, and you will occupy the first place in the Kingdom of Heaven," 7th *Homily* on the Epistle to the Hebrews, 4.

53. [Saint John Chrysostom, 3rd *Homily* on marriage, 9.]

54. Saint John Chrysostom, 3rd *Homily* on marriage, 5. Or further: "Do you see that marriage is not esteemed for itself, but as a means of avoiding fornication, temptations and incontinence?," *On Virginity*, XXXIX.

55. Saint John Chrysostom, *On Virginity*, XIX.

56. Saint John Chrysostom, 1st *Homily* on marriage, 3.

57. Saint John Chrysostom, *On Virginity*, XV. The example of Abraham proves that marriage in itself does not determine procreation.

58. Cf. supra, p. 15.

59. Cf. supra, pp. 15–16.

60. Genesis 1:28.

61. [Empty note.]

62. Saint John Chrysostom, 1st *Homily* on marriage, 3.

63. Saint John Chrysostom, 18th *Homily* on Genesis, 4.

64. [Empty note.]

65. *"Gamou logos oudeis ên"*: Saint John Chrysostom, *On Virginity*, XIV, 3.

66. *"Kai oude houtôs ho gamos anankaios einai edokei,"* ibid. On the question of the meaning to be given to this helper's function which woman had before the fall: [cf. supra, p. 190, and infra, pp. 232–239].

67. [Ibid., XIV, 5.]

68. Ibid., XVI and XVII.
69. Saint John Chrysostom, 1st *Homily* on marriage, 3. On the idea that the law is to sin as the remedy is to illness, cf. *On Virginity*, XVII, 3.
70. *"Dia to stergein heni tên gamoumenên andri,"* Saint John Chrysostom, *Against Remarriage*, 2.
71. Saint John Chrysostom, 19th *Homily* on the Epistle to the Corinthians, 1.
72. Ibid.
73. Ibid.
74. Ibid.
75. On marriage as a tie between two free individuals, cf. [note incomplete].
76. Ibid.
77. *"Meizona tês dikaiôsunês amartian."*
78. Saint John Chrysostom, 19th *Homily* on the Epistle to the Ephesians, 9.
79. Saint John Chrysostom, 1st *Homily* on marriage, 4.
80. [Saint John Chrysostom, 19th *Homily* on the Epistle to the Corinthians, 1.]
81. Saint John Chrysostom, *On Virginity*, XLVIII, 1.
82. Ibid., LXXV: "Concupiscence is a natural instinct which from that fact has the right to a great indulgence, and one of the spouses does not have the power to frustrate the other against their wishes."
83. Ibid., XLVII, 2. In this text, the expression *para to suneinai*—"in the sexual relation"—undoubtedly should not be translated by "in fulfillment of one's marital duties," which is to force and limit its meaning. It refers to all sexual relations, whether the wife is doing her duty or seeking satisfaction.
84. [Ibid., XLVII, 1.] Note the text: *"hotan mê ta tou gamou prattê alla menousa têi phusei gunê."* The wife must remain a woman "by nature," "physically," but it's not "the practice of the things of marriage" that will have a salvational value. It seems that here one has the opposition between the state in which one must remain and the practice that will have a value or not. This is not the opposition that will be so important subsequently in penitential jurisprudence between demanding and assenting to the marital duty.

85. [Ibid., LXXIV–LXXV.] Gregory of Nyssa as well, in his treatise *On Virginity*, speaks of the debt—*ophlêma*, but he indicates that it is something base—*tapeinon* (V) or shallow, sterile—*psukhron* (VIII).

86. Cf., in particular, the fragments on the 1st Epistle to the Corinthians, published in the *Journal of Theological Studies* 9 (1908), where it is a question of debt, and chapter XIV, 24, some *Commentaries on Saint Matthew*, where it is a question of the husband who makes his wife an adulteress by not satisfying her desires.

## 2. THE GOOD AND THE GOODS OF MARRIAGE

1. Many other texts treat the same themes: sermons, treatises that respond to specific pastoral questions (*De bono viduitatis*, 414), or to juridical remarks (such as *De conjugiis adulterinis*, 419, concerning the Pauline privilege).

2. Saint Augustine, *De sancta virginitate*, XX (19).

3. Ibid., XVIII (18).

4. [First Corinthians, 7:27.]

5. Saint Augustine, *De sancta virginitate*, XV (15).

6. [Ibid., XIII (13).]

7. Ibid., XIV (14).

8. Saint Augustine, *De bono viduitatis*, XIX (23).

9. [*De sancta virginitate*, XIII (12).]

10. Ibid., XLIV (45)–XLV (46).

11. Ibid., XLVI (46). Cf. *Quaestiones in Evangelium secundum Matthaeum*, I, IX, where Augustine sets out the second of the interpretations indicated here.

12. In particular the sermons 205–211. Cf. on this point, L. Verheijen, *Nouvelle approche de la Règle de saint Augustin*, Bégrolles-en-Mauges, 1980, pp. 153–200.

13. Thus in *Contra Julianum*, III.

14. Saint Augustine, *De bono viduitatis*, VI (8–9).

15. In particular the sermons [138, 188, 191, 192, 195, 213].

16. Saint Augustine, *De sancta virginitate*, II (2).

17. Ibid.

18. Ibid., IV (4).

19. Ibid., II (2).

20. Ibid., V (5).
21. Ibid.
22. Ibid., VI (6) (Matthew 9:15).
23. Ibid.
24. Ibid.
25. Ibid., II (2); V (5).
26. Ibid., VI (6).
27. Ibid., V (5).
28. Ibid.
29. Ibid., VIII (8).
30. [Ibid., VI (6).]
31. Ibid., VII (7).
32. Ibid.
33. Gregory of Nyssa, *De hominis opificio*, XVII.
34. Gregory of Nyssa doesn't believe the first sin was sexual: it involved only a surrender to pleasure in general. Cf. M. Aubineau, note to the translation of *De sancta virginitate*, p. 420.
35. Saint Augustine, *De Genesi contra Manichaeos*, II, 7 (8) and I, 19 (30).
36. [Ibid., I, 19 (30).]
37. [Ibid, II, 11 (15).]
38. Saint Augustine, *De catechizandis rudibus*, XVIII, 29: *"Fecit illi etiam adjutorium feminam* [. . .] *ut haberet et vir gloriam de femina, cum ei praeiret ad Deum, seque illi praeberet imitandum in sanctitate atque pietate, sicut ipse esset gloria Dei, cum ejus sapientiam sequeretur."* ["Puis, pour l'aider, il a créé la femme [. . .]. Il visait à ce que l'homme se fît de la femme un titre de gloire, quand il s'avancerait devant elle vers Dieu et s'offrirait à son imitation par la sainteté et la piété, tout comme lui-même serait un titre de gloire pour Dieu, quand il imiterait sa sagesse," trans. G. Combès.] ["Then, he made the woman to be a helpmate for him [. . .] and that man might derive glory from the woman as he went before her to God, and presented in himself an example to her for imitation in holiness and piety, just as he himself was to be the glory of God insofar as he followed God's wisdom."]
39. On this passage, cf. the commentary of P. Agaësse and A. Solignac in *Œuvres de saint Augustin*, vol. 49, *De Genesi ad litteram*

(*VIII–XII*), Paris: Desclée de Brouwer, Bibliothèque augustinienne, 1972, pp. [516–530], note 42.

40. Which is not to say that in marriage the woman cannot play any
spiritual role. Here it's a matter of her original purpose.

41. Saint Augustine, *De Genesi ad litteram*, IX, 5, 9.

42. Ibid., IX, 9, 14 and 15.

43. Saint Augustine, *The City of God*, XIV, 1.

44. *"Propter quid aliud secundum ipsum quaesitus est femineus sexus
adjutor, nisi ut serentem genus humanum natura muliebris, tamquam
terrae fecunditas, adjuvaret"* ["Pour quelle autre raison Dieu a-t-
il doté l'homme d'une aide de sexe féminin semblable à lui,
sinon pour que la nature de la femme, comme une terre fertile,
le secondât dans l'ensemencement du genre humain," trans. P.
Agaësse and A. Solignac] ["Why else did God give the man a
helper of the feminine sex, if not in order that the nature of the
woman, like a fertile ground, would assist him in sowing the
human race"], Saint Augustine, *De Genesi ad litteram*, IX, 9, 15.

45. Saint Augustine, *The City of God*, XIV, 22. To the objection that
the Scripture didn't mention any sexual union before the fall,
Augustine replies that the fall intervened too soon after the
Creation; or that God had not yet given the order to the first
couple to have sex.

46. Saint Augustine, *De nuptiis et concupiscentia*, II, 5 (14).

47. [Empty note.]

48. Thus in *De nuptiis et concupiscentia*, I, 1 (1) and I, 21 (23). In *Contra Julianum*, V, 46, one has the "classic" exposition of the "two
ends" and the "three goods."

49. Saint Augustine, *De bono coniugali*, XXIV (32).

50. Ibid., VI (6).

51. Ibid., III (3).

52. *"Propter amicitiam sicut nuptiae vel concubitus,"* ibid., IX (9). On
*"vel concubitus,"* cf. infra, pp. [296–297].

53. *"Homo humani generis pars est et sociale quiddam est humana
natura,"* ibid., I (1).

54. Ibid., VIII (8).

55. Thus in XXIV (32), ibid.: "But at this time, it is better, in every
respect, and more holy not to seek carnal offspring [. . .] and to
submit oneself spiritually to the one husband, Christ."

56. Ibid., XVII (19) and XIX (22).
57. Ibid., XVIII (21).
58. Ibid., I (1).
59. Ibid.
60. *"Naturalis in diverso sexu societas,"* ibid., III (3).
61. *"Amicalis quaedam et germana conjunction,"* ibid., I (1). Note that this conjunction is defined here by the relation of obedience and command.
62. Ibid., III (3).
63. Ibid., VII (7) and XV (17).
64. On this subject, cf.. [note incomplete].
65. *De bono coniugali,* VII (7).
66. Ibid.
67. [Ibid., IV (4).]
68. Note Augustine's expression concerning this principle of non-betrayal: *"Cui* fidei *tantum juris tribuit Apostolus ut eam* potestatem *appellaret."* [Underlined by M. F.] ["L'Apôtre attribue à cette fidélité un tel caractère de justice qu'il l'appelle puissance," trans. G. Combès] ["The Apostle attributes such a quality of justice to this fidelity that he calls it power"], ibid., IV (4).
69. They appear in chapters 4 and 5.
70. *De bono coniugali,* XXIV (32).
71. Ibid., XXIV (32), cf. also VII (6): *"Usque adeo foedus illud initum nuptiale cujusdam sacramenti res est, ut nec ipsa separatione irritum fiat"* (and what follows) ["Le contrat conjugal est à ce point sacré que même la séparation ne peut le rompre," trans. G. Combès] ["The marriage contract is so sacred that even separation cannot break it"].
72. Ibid., XV (17).
73. Ibid., XVIII (21).
74. Ibid., XXIV (32). We have seen on the other hand that a liaison involving a commitment to fidelity, without there being an intention of progeny, can be called *connubium.*
75. Ibid., XVIII (22).
76. Ibid.
77. Presented in XVI (18), cf. supra, pp. [293–294].
78. [*De bono coniugali,* I (1).]
79. Ibid., XX (23).

80. Ibid.
81. Ibid., XVI (18).
82. This moderation has the role of redirecting the pleasure, *redigere* the *delectatio*, *"in usum naturalem,"* ibid., XVI (18).
83. Ibid., XI (12).
84. Ibid.
85. Regarding another citation of this same text and its interpretation as a rule of fidelity, cf. supra, p. [304].
86. *De bono coniugali*, VI (6).
87. Ibid., X (11).
88. Ibid., XI (12).
89. Ibid.
90. [Ibid., X (11).]
91. Ibid., III (3).
92. Ibid., XVI (18).
93. [*Retractationes*, II, 22 (2)].
94. *De bono coniugali*, XIII (15).
95. Ibid., XVII (19).

### 3. THE LIBIDINIZATION OF SEX

1. [Saint Augustine, *De bono coniugali*, X (11).]
2. [Saint Augustine, *The City of God*, XIV, 16.]
3. Saint Augustine, *Contra Julianum*, IV, 72; cf. also ibid., V, 42.
4. Saint Augustine, *De nuptiis et concupiscentia*, II, 7 (17).
5. Augustine often makes this less-than-correct reproach to Julian of Eclanum, in *De nuptiis et concupiscentia* (loc. cit.) and in *Contra Julianum*.
6. Augustine uses this fact to conclude that the Pelagians themselves are obliged to acknowledge the evil of concupiscence in themselves (*Contra Julianum*).
7. [Saint Augustine, *Contra Julianum*, III, 26.]
8. Saint Augustine, *De bono coniugali*, X (11).v.
9. On the discussion of the Pelagian theme of excess, cf. in particular Saint Augustine, *Opus imperfectum*, IV, 24.
10. Saint Augustine, *Contra duas epistulas Pelagionorum*, I, 17 (34).
11. Saint Augustine, *De Genesi ad litteram*, IX, 10 (18).
12. Saint Augustine, *The City of God*, XIV, 24. In *De nuptiis et con-*

*cupiscentia*, II, 31 (53), Augustine also cites the example of the bladder and urine.

13. Saint Augustine, *The City of God*, XIV, 24, 1.

14. Ibid., 24, 2.

15. Ibid., 23, 2.

16. Ibid., 23, 3. Note the re-use of the traditional metaphor of sowing. Clement of Alexandria and many others employed it to convey the necessity of fertilizing the right furrow. Augustine employs it to characterize paradisaical procreation as being voluntary on the man's side, honorable and not unpleasant on the woman's. This is developed in full in *De nuptiis et concupiscentia*, II, 14 (29). The human seeds would have been sown without the slightest shameful passion, the genital organs "obeying in accordance with the will, just as the others [the seeds of grain] are planted by the farmer's hands [. . .]. And then the Creator [. . .] would have acted upon the male seeds in the woman as he pleased—which he still does—just as he acts upon the grain seeds in the earth, making blessed mothers conceive without libidinous pleasure and give birth without arduous labor."

17. Saint Augustine, *Contra Julianum*, IV, 62.

18. For the use of this term, more or less equivalent to *concupiscentia* in Augustine's writings, it should be noted that one finds it employed either in the very general sense of the desire for what one doesn't have (it can have a positive value: concupiscence for spiritual things), or in the sense of a fleshly impulse such as could be manifested under the control of the will in paradise (a much [rarer] use, but attested in *Contra Julianum*, IV, 62), or most often in the sense of an involuntary urge provoked by sexual attraction.

19. Genesis 3:7.

20. Cf. also *De nuptiis et concupiscentia*, I, 6 (7).

21. "Then they saw that they were naked by perverted eyes to which that simplicity signified by the term, nakedness, seemed to be something to be ashamed of. And, so that they might no longer be simple, 'they made aprons for themselves from the leaves of the fig tree,' as if to cover their private parts, that is, to cover their simplicity, of which that cunning pride was ashamed." Saint Augustine, *De Genesi contra Manichaeos*, II, 15, 23.

22. Saint Augustine, *De Genesi ad litteram*, XI, 31 (41).

23. [Saint Augustine, Sermon 162, 12.]

24. Saint Augustine, *De Genesi ad litteram*, XI, 32 (42). Note that according to Saint Augustine, the gesture of modesty should not be seen as evidence of a clear awareness, but as the effect of a "concealed instinct" (*occulto instinctu*).

25. *"Non adtenti, ut cognoscerent quid eis indumento gratiae praestaretur,"* Saint Augustine, *The City of God*, XIV, 17 (39).

26. [Ibid., XIV, 17 (39–40).]

27. In this passage, Augustine doesn't return to this notion in *De Genesi ad litteram* of a concupiscence-inducing gaze. Here the eyes only observe. In the two books *On the Grace of Christ, and on Original Sin*, he especially emphasizes that before the fall there was no reason to feel ashamed: "What God had made was not such that it would cause any confusion to man; nor were the members designed to bring a blush to the creature: that simple nudity was not hurtful to the eyes either of God or of man himself" (II, 34).

28. Cf. in *Contra Julianum*, III, 16, the affirmation that sexual differentiation isn't bad; even if today men were so dominated by concupiscence that their acts would be performed against the laws and rules, "the condition of bodies, as God created them" would remain the same.

29. Ibid., IV, 62. Cf. also V, 23.

30. Saint Augustine, *The City of God*, XIII, 15. Cf. Sermon 179, 4: "Our first parents, after having sinned, made themselves aprons to cover the shameful parts of the body, which give us life and at the same time death"; *Discourse on Psalms* 19:4: "The gates of death" are perhaps to be interpreted "as the body's senses and the eyes that were opened in man after he had tasted the forbidden fruit."

31. Saint Augustine, *The City of God*, XIV, 15, 2.

32. Ibid., XIV, 16; cf. in *De nuptiis et concupiscentia*, II, 35 (59), an allusion to too much quickness or slowness by which the organs disappoint the will.

33. Ibid., I, 6 (7).

34. Ibid., I, 8 (9).

35. Saint Augustine, *The City of God*, XIV, 18. Augustine explains

in this way the fact that children are not allowed to witness the sexual relations of their parents—even though they are relations like those from which they were born (ibid.). Cf. *De gratia Christi et de peccato originali;* the marital relation doesn't occur without an "animal movement *(bestialis motus)* that makes human nature blush," II, 38 (43).

36. Saint Augustine, *De nuptiis et concupiscentia,* I, 6 (7).

37. On this subject, cf. the article of A. Sage, "Le péché originel dans la pensée de saint Augustin," *Revue d'études augustiniennes* 15, 1969.

38. Saint Augustine, *The City of God,* XIV, 13–15.

39. Saint Augustine, *De nuptiis et concupiscentia,* I, 32 (37). He speaks of *mutatio naturae.*

40. Saint Augustine, *The City of God,* XIV, 13, 1.

41. Ibid., XIV, 15, 1.

42. Saint Augustine, *Opus imperfectum,* IV, 38.

43. Saint Augustine, *De nuptiis et concupiscentia,* I, 23 (25).

44. Ibid.

45. Saint Augustine, *Opus imperfectum,* V, 12.

46. Cf. Saint Augustine, *De nuptiis et concupiscentia,* I, 32 (37) and II, 34 (58); *Contra Julianum,* VI, 15.

47. Speaking of Abraham, Augustine says that God restored his lost fertility so that he might engender Isaac, but left his concupiscence as it was in the body. While Julian of Eclanum thought that from the Augustinian thesis he should conclude that God would have restored to Abraham a concupiscence that was declared to be bad, or that Isaac was born free of any concupiscence, *Contra Julianum,* III, 23. Cf. also *Opus imperfectum,* V, 10.

48. Saint Augustine, *De nuptiis et concupiscentia,* I, 25 (28); cf. also *Opus imperfectum,* V, 10.

49. [Saint Augustine, *De nuptiis et concupiscentia,* I, 23 (25).] Cf. the restatement of this thesis in *Contra Julianum,* VI, 60.

50. Saint Augustine, *De nuptiis et concupiscentia,* I, 23 (25).

51. Ibid., II, 34 (57). This passage develops the indications of Book I, 25 (28). Julian of Eclanum had criticized these two texts and Augustine answers him in *Contra Julianum,* VI, 53–56, and in the *Opus imperfectum,* VI, 7.

52. *"Agit autem quid nisi ipsa desideria mala et turpia,"* Saint Augustine, *De nuptiis et concupiscentia,* I, 27 (30).
53. Ibid., I, 28 (31).
54. Ibid., I, 26 (29).
55. Saint Augustine, *Contra Julianum,* VI, 60.
56. Ibid., III, 62.
57. [Empty note.]
58. Saint Augustine, *Opus imperfectum,* V, 17.
59. Saint Augustine, *Contra Julianum,* III, 42.
60. Note that Julian is talking about someone who observes "the lawful mode" (referring to the form of the sexual act); and Augustine about someone who observes "the mode of concupiscence" (referring to the form of the will).

APPENDICES

1. The play of opposition and complementarity between exomolegesis and *exagoreusis* appears clearly in those movements of penitents which were so important, especially in southern Europe starting in the 14th century (cf. I. Magli, *Gli uomini della penitenza,* Bologna, 1967). There the ostentatious demonstrations were combined with an intensive practice of oral confession and direction. Similarly among the French penitents at the end of the 16th century, and in the different movements of the Counter-Reformation where techniques of direction and ascetic demonstrations developed simultaneously.
2. [Faustus of Riez, *Discours aux moines sur la pénitence* (P.L., vol. 58, col. 875–876), quoted in C. Vogel, *Le pécheur et la pénitence dans l'Église ancienne,* Paris, 1966, p. 131.]
3. J. Cassian, *Conferences,* XVIII, 15. Note the expression *"locum paenitentiae suppliciter postulavit"* to say that Pafnutius has requested penance. This is the traditional form for soliciting the status, the place of the penitent.
4. J. Cassian, *Institutes,* IV, 16.
5. In the Latin version that Saint Jerome gives of the rules of Pachomius, one also finds the expressions *"aget paenitentiam publice in collecta, stabitque in vescendi loco,"* Praecepta et Instituta, VI, in Dom A. Boon, *Pachomiana Latina,* Louvain, 1932.

6. J. Cassian, *Institutes*, IV, 16.

7. However, it seems that Syrian monasticism emphasized the penitential aspect of monastic life (cf. A. Voôbus, [*History of Asceticism in the Syrian Orient*, Louvain, 1958]).

8. Cassian is referring to these penitential acts when he writes: *"Dum ergo agimus paenitentiam, et adhuc vitiosorum actuum recordatione mordemur"* (*Conferences*, XX, 7) ["During all the time, then, that the penance lasts and we feel remorse for our wrongful acts."]

9. Ibid., XX, 5 ("it consists in never again yielding to the sins for which we do penance or for which our conscience is pricked").

10. Ibid.

11. Ibid., XX, 7.

12. J. Cassian, *Institutes*, IV, 20.

13. Saint Jerome, Letter 107, 19.

14. *Rule* of Saint Benedict, XXIV, XLIV, XLVI; cf. *Rule of the Master*, XIV.

15. *"Corripienda sunt secretius quae peccantur secretius,"* Saint Augustine, Sermon 72 (P.L., vol. 38, col. 11).

16. Saint Leo, Letter 168.

17. Ibid.

18. Pomerius, *De vita contemplativa*, II, 7 (P.L., vol. 59, col. 451–452).

19. Explaining the three forms of penitence—the one preceding baptism, the one that should characterize one's entire life, and the one that should respond to serious transgressions, Saint Augustine, in Sermon 351 (7), says [of the last form] that it should take place *"pro illis peccatis [. . .] quae legis decalogus continent"* [trans.: "for sins included in the Decalogue"]. In Sermon 352 (8), still speaking of this third form of penitence, he says that it concerns serious wounds: "Perhaps it is an adultery, a murder, a sacrilege; in any case, it's a grave matter and a dangerous, mortal wound, putting salvation in peril."

20. Cf. C. Vogel, *La discipline pénitentielle en Gaule*, Paris, 1952, p. 91. This list of mortal sins should not, of course, be confused with the capital sins that come under a different type of analysis, since it's a matter of defining the root, the "spirit" that may lead to sin. This definition of the eight "bad spirits" came out of the

monastic tradition. One finds it in Evagrius and Cassian. Cf. A. Guillaumont, "Introduction" to the *Traité pratique* [of Evagrius Ponticus].

21. Saint Cyprian, *De lapsis*, XXVIII (P.L., vol. 4, col. 488). Note however that even for minor transgressons Saint Cyprian seems to indicate that one should take a penitent's status for a time, according to the canonical ritual (Letters XVI, 2 and XVII, 2).

22. Pomerius, *De vita contemplativa*, II, 1.

23. Saint Augustine, Sermon 351.

24. Gregory the Great is referring here to a text from Ezekiel that will often be quoted subsequently in connection with spiritual direction and the methods of examination: "I dug into the wall and saw a doorway there" (8:8).

25. Gregory the Great, *Pastoral Care*, Book I, chap. 9.

26. Thus Saint Cyprian, Letters VIII, XXX, XLIII. Or again, concerning the reintegration of backsliders: "Examine the conduct, works, and merits of each one; take account of the nature and quality of the faults . . . Upon a religiously attentive examination, settle the granting of requests that are addressed to us" (Letter XV).

27. Saint Ambrose, *De officiis ministrorum*, I, 1.

28. [Gregory of Nazianzus, *Orations II*, 16.]

29. Gregory the Great, *Pastoral Care*, Book I, chap. 1.

30. H. Frankfort, *La royauté et les dieux*, Paris, 1951, p. 161.

31. C. J. Gadd, *Ideas of Divine Rule in the Ancient East*, London, 1948.

32. Exodus, 15:13.

33. Philippe de Robert reckons that David benefited from the pastoral titulature; other kings were called shepherds only collectively and to designate them as "bad shepherds" (*Le berger d'Israël*, Geneva, 1968, pp. 44–47).

34. Psalms 77:21 [the Psalm says "your" and not "my people"].

35. The fact is all the more striking in Isocrates as the description of the good magistrate in the *Aereopagiticus* attributes to him several functions and virtues that elsewhere belong to the thematic of the shepherd.

36. The first opinion is that of Grube, in his edition of the *Fragments* of Archytas. The second is that of A. Dellate in his *Essai*

*sur la politique pythagoricienne*, Paris and Liège, 1922. The texts of the Pseudo-Archytas cited by Stobaeus bring together *nomos* and *nomeus* and call Zeus *Nomios*.

37. Plato, *Republic*, Book I, 343–345.
38. Plato, *Laws*, Book X: shepherds are set against the "beasts of prey," but are distinct from the masters.
39. Plato, *Statesman*, 271e.
40. Philo of Alexandria, *De agricultura*, 50.
41. Dio Chrysostom, *Orations*, I.
42. Philo of Alexandria reports that for Caligula, "the herdsmen of animals not being themselves bullocks, goats, or sheep," he himself, herdsman of the human race, must then belong to a different, even more superior race; that is, divine and non-human, cited by P. Veyne, *Le pain et le cirque*, Paris, 1976, p. 738. On the metaphor of the prince who is not a cowherd, but a bull in the midst of the herd, cf. Dio Chrysostom, *Orations*, II.
43. Jeremiah 3:10.
44. C. J. Gadd, *Ideas of Divine Rule in the Ancient East*, p. 39.
45. Zechariah 10:8.
46. In S. Morenz, *La religion des Égyptiens*, Paris, 1962, p. 94.
47. Psalms 68:8.
48. R. Labat, *Le caractère religieux de la royauté assyro-babylonienne*, Paris, 1939, p. 352.
49. Cited, ibid., p. 232.
50. Plato, *Republic*, Book I. Cf. *Critias*, 109b: in Atlantis, the gods, like shepherds, were the "feeders" of the human livestock.
51. Ezekiel 34:2.
52. "O Rê, you who stand watch when all men sleep, and seek what is nurturing for your livestock." Egyptian hymn, quoted by S. Morenz, *La religion des Égyptiens*, p. 224.
53. Dio of Prusa speaking of the sovereign-shepherd says that it wasn't for himself, but for the good of men, that he didn't partake in wealth and pleasures, but in *epimeleia* and *phrontides*, *Discourses*, I.
54. Plato, *Statesman*, 294a–295c.
55. Ezekiel 20:34.
56. On the shepherd who stands guard with his dogs, cf. Plato, *Republic*, III, 416a and IV, 440d.

57. Thanks to the shepherd, the animals are neither hungry nor thirsty, "nor will the desert heat or the sun beat down on them" [Isaiah 49:10].
58. Plato, *Laws*, 735a–736c.
59. Rabbinical commentary of Exodus, quoted by Philippe de Robert, *Le berger d'Israël*, p. 47.
60. Genesis 33:13.
61. Jeremiah 10:21.
62. Prayer of Ashurbanipal II to the goddess Ishtar, quoted by Ph. de Robert, loc. cit., p. 14.
63. Jeremiah 13:20.
64. Jeremiah 23:2.
65. Gospel of John 10:11–18.
66. Saint Jerome, Letter 58: *"Aliorum salutem fac lucrum animae tuae."*
67. Gregory the Great, *Pastoral Care*, Book I, chap. [10]. Cf. also Book II, chap. 2: "regard as one's own good and one's own advantage the good and advantage of the neighbor."
68. Saint Cyprian, Letter XLIII, cf. also Letter VIII.
69. Gregory the Great, *Pastoral Care*, Book II, chap. 2.
70. Ibid., Book IV; Saint Ambrose, *De officiis ministrorum*, Book I, chap. 24. Fortunately, God always leaves a few imperfections in the righteous "so that in the midst of the brilliance of the virtues that brings them the admiration of the whole world, the trouble caused them by these imperfections keeps them humble."
71. Ibid. Ambrose is referring here to the first Epistle of Saint Peter, 5:3.
72. Gregory the Great, *Pastoral Care*, Book II, chap. 2; and Book I, chap. 6: "Those who fly from the direction of souls through humility are truly humble when they resist not the Divine decrees."
73. Gregory the Great, ibid., Book I, chap. 10.
74. Saint Cyprian, Letter XLV; cf. also the letter of Denys, bishop of Lydda: "bring back the human race that was fettered by many errors to its true shepherd, Christ's flock that was scattered" (in *Lettres de saint Jérôme*, vol. IV, p. 159, Letter 94).
75. Saint Ambrose, *De officiis ministrorum*, I, 1.
76. Those who don't practice what they teach "destroy with their

corrupt ways that which they strive to establish with their words; they are like shepherds who drink the same clear water, but corrupt it with their dirty feet and only leave the sheep with a muddy water," Saint Gregory the Great, *Pastoral Care*, Book I, chap. 2.

77. Saint Gregory thus sets out in *Pastoral Care* thirty-six distinctions that should be taken into account for proper instruction of the faithful.

78. [Ibid., Book I, chap. 4.]

79. Ezekiel 8:8.

80. Gregory the Great, *Pastoral Care*, Book II, chap. 9.

81. Ibid., Book II, chap. 1.

82. Saint Ambrose, *De officiis ministrorum*, I, 1.

83. Ibid., II, 24.

84. Gregory the Great, *Pastoral Care*, Book II, chap. 10.

85. Ibid., Book II, chap. 1 and Book II, chap. 5.

86. The word employed here is, as we'll see, a term that has both an exact and a complex meaning in the penitential procedure. In the 19th *Homily* on Genesis, 2, the reinterpretation of the biblical text in regard to penitential practices is more explicit still: God, *hiatros* [physician], wanted Cain's transgression to be erased *dia tês homologias tou ptaismatos* [by the recognition of the sin].

87. God condemns the impudence much more than the sin.

88. The element of shame and indecency in the act and in the avowal is at the center of the Christian economy of penance. In the 19th *Homily* on Genesis, 2, Cain is characterized by [three] adjectives: *agnômôn, anaisthêtos, anaiskhuntos* [ungrateful, insensitive, impudent].

89. In the 20th *Homily* on Genesis, 3, Chrysostom points out that Cain made a precise avowal—*meta akribeias*—when he said: I thought my crime too great to be pardoned. But this avowal is not valid because it was not made in time—*en kairô*. This problem of the right moment is also important in the doctrine and practice of penance.

90. In this exegesis of Samuel 2:11, the role that Chrysostom attributes to David's ignorance is capital, since it allows him to render a sentence all the more "pure" and "rigorous" and just, as

he doesn't know that he is being targeted by Nathan's fable and that he is not even aware [of having] committed a sin with Bathsheba: which makes his avowal a discovery. Now, this ignorance of the nature of the act he has committed is added on to the biblical text by Chrysostom. Should one see in this an echo of Greek tragedy? Or more generally the value ascribed to the scenario of someone condemning a guilty individual who turns out to be oneself?

91. [Saint Augustine, *De paradiso*, XIV, 71.]
92. Saint Augustine, *Contra Faustum*, XII, 10.
93. Saint Augustine, *De Genesi ad litteram*, IX, 9, 16–17.
94. When Augustine speaks of the *necessitas mortis*, when he says that all men are *morituri*, he gives a strong and precise meaning to these expressions: it's a matter of distinguishing this inevitable future of fallen men from the status of *homo mortalis* given to our first parents.
95. Saint Augustine, *The City of God*, XIV, 26.
96. [Epistle to the Hebrews 13:4.]

# *Bibliography*

THE BIBLE*

*Old Testament*
Genesis
Exodus
Leviticus
Samuel
Psalms
Proverbs
Isaiah
Jeremiah
Ezekiel
Zechariah

*New Testament*
Gospel according to Saint Matthew
Gospel according to Saint John
Acts of the Apostles
Paul, First Epistle to the Corinthians
Paul, Epistle to the Galatians
Paul, Epistle to the Ephesians
Paul, Epistle to the Colossians
Paul, Epistle to the Hebrews
First Epistle of Saint Peter
Book of Revelation

* Michel Foucault doesn't ever stick with a single translation: he may cite Louis
Segond's translation, that of the *Bible de Jérusalem* (Paris: Éditions du Cerf, 1977),
or that of the translators of patristic treatises.

ANCIENT AUTHORS*

*Abbreviations*

C.U.F. "Collection des Universités de France" ("Collection Budé"), Paris: Les Belles Lettres.

S.C. "Sources chrétiennes," Paris: Éditions du Cerf.

P.G. *Patrologie cursus completus, Series Graeca*, edited by J.-P. Migne, Paris, 1844–1865.

P.L. *Patrologie cursus completus, Series Latina*, edited by J.-P. Migne, Paris, 1844–1865.

B.A. "Bibliothèque augustinienne," Paris: Desclée de Brower.

Œ.C. Saint John Chrysostom, *Oeuvres complètes*, translation into French edited by M. Jeannin, Bar-le-Duc: L. Guérin & Cie, publishers, 1863–1867.

Œ.T. *Oeuvres de Tertullien*, Paris: L. Vivès, 1852.

Saint Ambrose, *Apologia de propheta David*, text translated into French by M. Cordier, S.C., 1977.

———, *De Caïn et Abel*, P.L., volume 14.

———, *Enarrationes in Psalmos Davidicos*, P.L., volume 14.

———, *Explanatio symboli*, edited and translated into French by Dom B. Botte, S.C., 1961.

———, *Expositio Evangelii secundum Lucam*, edited and translated into French by Dom G. Tissot, S.C., 1956–1958.

———, *De lapsu virginis consecratae*, P.L., volume 16.

———, *De officiis ministrorum*, P.L., volume 16.

———, *De paenitentia*, edited and translated into French by R. Gryson, S.C., 1971.

———, *De paradiso*, P.L., volume 14.

———, *De sacramentis*, edited and translated into French by Dom B. Botte, S.C., 1961.

———, *De Spiritu Sancto*, P.L., volume 17.

* We have mentioned here the edition that Foucault uses ordinarily. However, he may very occasionally refer to another source—for example, for Saint Augustine: Mgr Péronne et al., Paris: L. Vivès, 1869–1878; or, for Saint John Chrysostom: Abbé Bareille et al., Paris: L. Vivès, 1865–1873, or again: Abbé Joly, Nancy: Bordes, 1864–1867. It should be added that the citations may have been revised by Foucault based on the Latin or Greek text (further, he doesn't hesitate to refer directly to De Migne's Greek or Latin *Patrologie*).

————, *De virginibus*, P.L., volume 16.

————, *In Psalmum David CXVIII Expositio*, P.L., volume 15.

Saint Anthony, *Apophtègmes des Pères*, P.L., volume 65.

Aristotle, *Éthique à Nicomaque*, edited and translated into French by R.-A. Gauthier and J.-Y. Jolif, Louvain-Paris: Publications universitaires de Louvain, 1958–1959.

————, *Histoire des animaux*, edited and translated into French by P. Louis, C.U.F., 1964–1969.

————, *Génération des animaux*, edited and translated into French by P. Louis, C.U.F., 1961.

Saint Athanasius, *Apologia ad imperatorem Constantium*, P.G., volume 25.

————, *Vita S. Antonii*, P.G., volume 26.

Athenagoras, *Supplicatio pro Christianis (Supplique au sujet des chrétiens)*, edited and translated into French by G. Bardy, S.C., 1943.

————, *Legatio*, edited by W. Schoedel, Oxford: Clarendon Press, 1972.

Saint Augustine, *De bono coniugali*, edited and translated into French by G. Combès, B.A., 1948.

————, *De bono viduitatis*, edited and translated into French by J. Saint-Martin, B.A., 1939.

————, *De catechizandis rudibus*, edited and translated into French by G. Combès and A. Farges, B.A., 1949.

————, *De conjugiis adulterinis*, edited and translated into French by G. Combès, B.A., 1948.

————, *De continentia*, edited and translated into French by J. Saint-Martin, B.A., 1939.

————, *Contra duas epistulas Pelagionorum*, edited and translated into French by F.-J. Thonnard, E. Bleuzen, and A. C. De Veer, B.A., 1974.

————, *Contra Faustum*, P.L., volume 42.

————, *Contra Julianum*, edited and translated into French by the abbé Burleraux, in *Œuvres complètes de saint Augustin*, edited by M. Poujoulat and M. l'abbé Raulx, Bar-le-Duc, 1864–1872, 17 volumes, volume 16, 1872.

————, *La Cité de Dieu*, edited and translated into French by G. Combès, B.A., 1959–1960.

————, *Discours sur les Psaumes*, P.L., volumes 36 and 37.

———, *De Genesi ad litteram*, edited and translated into French by P. Agaesse and A. Solignac, B.A., 1972.

———, *De Genesi contra Manichaeos*, in *Œuvres complètes de saint Augustin*, volume 3, translated into French by M. Péronne et al., Paris: L. Vivès, 1873.

———, *De gratia Christi et peccato originali*, edited and translated into French by J. Plagnieux and F.-J. Thonnard, B.A., 1976.

———, *De nuptiis et concupiscentia*, edited and translated into French by F.-J. Thonnard, E. Bleuzen, and C. De Veer, B.A., 1974.

———, *Opus imperfectum*, P.L., volume 45.

———, *Quaestiones in Evangelium secundum Matthaeum* I, P.L., volume 35.

———, *Retractationes*, edited and translated into French by G. Bardy, B.A., 1950.

———, *De sancta virginitate*, edited and translated into French by J. Saint-Martin, B.A., 1939.

———, *Sermons*, P.L., volume 38.

Barnaby, Pseudo-Barnaby, *Épître*, edited and translated into French by Sister Suzanne-Dominique and Fr. Louvel, in *Les écrits des Pères apostoliques*, Paris: Éditions du Cerf, 1979, volume 3.

Basil of Ancyra, *De l'intégrité de la virginité*, P.G., volume 30; translated into French by A. Vaillant, in Saint Basile, *De virginitate*, Paris, Institut d'études slaves, 1943.

———, *De renuntiatione saeculi*, P.L., volume 31.

Basil of Caesarea, *Constitutions monastiques*, P.G., volume 31.

———, *Exhortation à renoncer au monde*, text in P.L., volume 31.

———, *Grandes règles*, P.G., volume 31.

———, *Règles brèves*, P.G., volume 31.

Saint Benedict, *La Règle*, translated by A. de Vogüé, S.C., 1972.

Cicero, *De finibus*, edited and translated into French by J. Martha, C.U.F, 1928–1930.

Clement of Alexandria, *Excerpta ex Theodoto*, P.G., volume 9.

———, *Le pédagogue*, translated by H.-I. Marrou and M. Harl, S.C., 1960.

———, *Le protreptique*, edited and translated into French by C. Mondésert, S.C., 1949.

———, *Quis dives salvetur*, P.G., volume 9.

————, *Les stromates* (II), edited and translated into French by C. Mondésert, H.-I. Marrou, and O. Staehlin, S.C., 1976.

————, *Les stromates* (III), P.G., volume 9.

Clement of Rome, *Première Épître*, text translated into French by Sister Suzanne-Dominique, in *Les écrits des Pères apostoliques*, Paris: Éditions du Cerf, 1979, volume 1.

Saint Cyprian, *Correspondance*, edited and translated into French by the canon Bayard, C.U.F., 1925.

————, *De habitu virginum*, P.L., volume 4.

————, *De lapsis*, P.L., volume 4.

Cyril of Jerusalem, *Procatéchèse*, edited and translated into French by A. Faivre, Lyon: J.-B. Pélagaud, 1844.

Democritus, In *Die Fragmente der Vorsokratiker*, edited by H. Diels and W. Kranz, Berlin: Weidmann, 1903.

Pseudo-Democritus, In *Geoponica sive Cassiani Bassi scholastici de re rustica eclogae*, edited by H. Beckh, Leipzig: Teubner, 1895.

*Didache*, translated by R.-F. Refoulé, in *Les écrits des Pères apostoliques*, Paris: Éditions du Cerf, 1979, volume 1.

Diocles, *Du régime*, in Oribasius, *Collection médicale. Livres incertains*, volume 3, translated into French by U. Bussemaker and Ch. Daremberg, Paris: J.-B. Baillière, 1858.

Dio Chrysostom [Dio of Prusa], *Discours 1–11*, edited and translated by J. Cohoon, Cambridge, MA: Harvard University Press, Loeb Classical Library, 1932.

Dorotheus of Gaza, *Vie de Dosithée*, in *Œuvres spirituelles*, edited and translated into French by Dom L. Regnault and Dom J. de Préville, S.C., 1964.

Elian, *De natura animalium*, edited and translated into French by M. Dacier, Paris: Impr. Auguste Delalain, 1827.

Epictetus, *Manuel*, edited and translated into French by A. Jagu and J. Souilhé, C.U.F., 1950.

Euripides, *Ion*, edited and translated into French by L. Parmentier and H. Grégoire, C.U.F., 1959.

Eusebius of Caesarea, *Histoire ecclésiastique*, Books 1–4, edited and translated into French by G. Bardy, S.C., 1962.

Eusebius of Emesa, *Homélies*, in *Clavis Patrum Graecorum. Ab Athanasio ad Chrysostomum*, edited by M. Geerard, Turnhout: Brepols, 1974.

Evagrius Pontificus, *Traité pratique*, edited and translated into French by A. and C. Guillaumont, S.C., 1971.

Faustus of Riez, *Discours aux moines sur la pénitence*, P.L., volume 58.

Galen, *Commentaire aux* Épidémies *d'Hippocrate*, in *Opera omnia*, edited by C. G. Kühn, Leipzig: Carl Cnobloch, 1821–1833, volume 17.

————, *De utilitate partium*, in *Opera omnia*, edited by C. G. Kühn, Leipzig: Carl Cnobloch, 1821–1833, volume 4; French translation Ch. Daremberg, *Œuvres anatomiques, physiologiques et médicales de Galien*, Paris: J.-B. Baillière, 1856.

————, *Traité des passions de l'âme et de ses erreurs*, text in the *Opera omnia*, edited by C. G. Kühn, Leipzig: Carl Cnobloch, 1821–1833, volume 5; French translation R. Van der Helst, Paris: Delagrave, 1914.

Saint Gregory the Great, *Homélies sur l'Évangile*, P.L., volume 76.

————, *Le pastoral*, edited and translated into French by M. l'abbé Boutet, Paris: Desclée de Brouwer et Lethielleux, Collection "Pax," 1928.

Gregory of Nazianzus, *Discours 1–3*, edited and translated into French by J. Bernardi, S.C., 1978.

Gregory of Nyssa, *De la création de l'homme*, translated into French by J. Laplace, S.C., 1943.

————, *Oratio catechetica magna*, translated into French by A. Maignan, S.C., 1978.

————, *De la virginité*, edited and translated into French by M. Aubineau, S.C., 1966.

Hermas, *Le pasteur*, edited and translated into French by R. Joly, Paris, S.C., 1968.

Hierocles of Alexandria, Fragments, in Joannes Stobaeus, *Florilegium*, edited by A. Meineke, Leipzig: Teubner, 1856–1864, volume 3.

Saint Hilaire, in P.L., volume 9.

Hippocrates, *Épidémies*, in *Œuvres complètes*, volume 5, text translated by E. Littré, Paris: J.-B. Baillière, 1846.

Saint Hippolytus, *Canons*, edited and translated into French by R.-G. Coquin, in *Patrologia Orientalis*, volume 31/2, Paris: Firmin-Didot, 1866.

————, *Tradition apostolique*, edited and translated into French by Dom B. Botte, S.C., 1946.

Irinaeus of Lyon, *Adversus haereses*, P.L., volume 7.

Isocrates, *Aréopagitique*, edited and translated into French by G. Mathieu, C.U.F., 1942.

John Cassian, *Conférences*, edited and translated into French by E. Pichery, S.C., 1955–1959.

———, *Institutions cénobitiques*, edited and translated into French by J.-C. Guy, S.C., 1965.

Saint John Chrysostom, *Commentaires sur saint Matthieu*, in Œ.C., volume 7.

———, *Contre les ennemis de la vie monastique*, in Œ.C., volume 2.

———, *Homélie Vidi Dominum*, in Œ.C., volume 6.

———, *Homélies* sur Anne, in Œ.C., volume 5.

———, *Homélies* sur l'Épître aux Colossiens, in Œ.C., volume 11.

———, *Homélies* sur la Première Épître aux Corinthiens, in Œ.C., volume 9.

———, *On the First Epistle to the Corinthians, Fragments*, in *Journal of Theological Studies* 9, 1908 (edited by C. Jenkins).

———, *Homélies* sur l'Épître aux Éphésiens, in Œ.C., volume 9.

———, *Homélies* sur l'Épître aux Hébreux, in Œ.C., volume 9.

———, *Homélies* sur la Première Épître aux Thessaloniciens, in Œ.C., volume 11.

———, *Homélies* sur la Première Épître à Timothée, in Œ.C., volume 11.

———, *Homélies* sur l'Évangile de saint Jean, in Œ.C., volume 8.

———, *Homélies* sur la Genèse, in Œ.C., volume 5.

———, *Trois homélies sur le mariage*, in Œ.C., volume 4.

———, *Homélies* sur la pénitence, in Œ.C., volume 5.

———, *Homélies* sur saint Matthieu, in Œ.C., volumes 7 and 8.

———, *Qu'il est dangereux pour l'orateur et pour l'auditeur de parler pour plaire*, in Œ.C., volume 3.

———, *Sur le mariage unique*, edited and translated into French by B. Grillet and P. Ettlinger, S.C., 1968.

———, *Huit catéchèses baptismales*, edited and translated into French by A. Wenger, S.C., 1957.

———, *De la virginité*, edited and translated into French by B. Grillet and H. Musurillo, S.C., 1966.

Saint Jerome, *Adversus Helvidium De perpetua virginitate B. Mariae*, P.L., volume 23.

———, *Adversus Jovinianum*, P.L., volume 23.

———, *Lettres*, edited and translated into French by J. Labourt, C.U.F., 1949–1963.

Justin, *Apologies*, edited and translated into French by L. Pautigny, Paris: A. Picard et fils, 1904.

Saint Leo, *Lettres*, P.L., volume 13.

Lucretius, *De natura rerum*, edited and translated into French by A. Ernout and L. Robin, C.U.F., 1920–1928.

Marcus Aurelius, *Pensées*, edited and translated into French by A.-I. Trannoy, C.U.F., 1925.

Methodius of Olympus, *Le Banquet*, edited and translated into French by H. Musurillo and V.-H. Debidour, S.C., 1963.

Musonius Rufus, *Reliquiae*, edited by O. Hense, Leipzig: Teubner, 1905.

Ocellus Lucanus, *De universi natura*, edited by F. W. A. Mullach, Paris: A. Firmin-Didot, 1860.

Origen, *Commentaire sur saint Jean, livre VI*, edited and translated into French by C. Blanc, S.C., 1970.

———, *Contra Celsum*, edited and translated into French by M. Borret, S.C., 1976.

———, *Exhortatio ad martyrium*, translated into French by G. Bardy, Paris: J. Gabalda, 1932.

———, *Homélies sur le Cantique des cantiques*, translated into French by Dom O. Rousseau, S.C., 1954.

———, *Homélies sur la Genèse*, edited and translated into French by H. de Lubac and L. Doutreleau, S.C., 1976.

———, *Homélies sur les Nombres*, P.G., volume 12.

Ovid, *Métamorphoses*, edited and translated into French by G. Lafaye, C.U.F., 1965.

Pacian of Barcelona, *Lettres*, P.L., volume 13.

———, *Parénèse*, P.L., volume 13, French translation in C. Vogel, *Le pécheur et la pénitence dans l'Église ancienne*, Paris: Éditions du Cerf, 1969.

Pachomius, *Praecepta et Instituta*, in Dom A. Boon, *Pachomiana Latina*, Louvain: Bibliothèque de la *Revue d'histoire ecclésiastique*, 1932.

Paulinus, *Vita Ambrosii*, P.L., volume 14.

Philo of Alexandria, *De opificio mundi*, edited and translated into French by R. Arnaldez, Paris: Éditions du Cerf, 1976.

————, *De specialibus legibus*, translated into French by S. Daniel and A. Mosès, Paris: Éditions du Cerf, 1970–1975.

————, *De agricultura*, translated into French by J. Pouilloux, Paris: Éditions du Cerf, 1961.

Plato, *Cratyle*, edited and translated into French by L. Méridier, C.U.F., 1931.

————, *Les lois*, edited and translated into French by A. Diès and E. des Places, C.U.F., 1951–1956.

————, *Le politique*, edited and translated into French by A. Diès, C.U.F., 1935.

————, *La république*, edited and translated into French by E. Chambry, C.U.F., 1931–1934.

Plotinus, *Ennéades*, edited and translated into French by E. Bréhier, C.U.F., 1924–1938.

Pomerius, *De vita contemplativa*, P.L., volume 59.

Quodvultdeus, *Sermones 1–3*, edited by R. Braun, Turnhout: Brepols, 1953.

————, *Règle du maître*, edited and translated into French by Adalbert de Vogüé, S.C., 1964.

Rufus of Ephesus, *Œuvres*, edited by C. Daremberg and C. E. Ruelle, Paris: Imprimerie nationale, 1879.

Seneca, *De ira*, edited and translated into French by A. Bourgery, C.U.F., 1922.

————, *Lettres à Lucilius*, edited and translated into French by F. Préchac and H. Noblot, C.U.F., 1945–1964.

————, *De tranquillitate animae*, edited and translated into French by R. Waltz, C.U.F., 1927.

Soranus, *Traité des maladies des femmes*, in *Corpus Medicorum Graecorum*, volume 4, Leipzig, 1927; French translation by F. J. Hergott, Nancy: Impr. Berger-Levrault, 1895.

Tertullian, *Adversus Marcionem*, edited and translated into French by A.-E. de Genoude, in *Œ.T.*, volume 1.

————, *De baptismo*, edited and translated into French by F. Refoulé and M. Drouzy, S.C., 1952.

————, *De carne Christi*, trans. A.-E. de Genoude, in *Œ.T.*, volume 1.

————, *De cultu feminarum*, edited and translated into French by M. Turcan, S.C., 1971.

————, *Exhortatio ad castitatem,* translated by A.-E. de Genoude, in *Œ.T.,* volume 3.

————, *De paenitentia,* edited and translated into French by P. de Labriolle, Paris: Picard, 1906.

————, *De pudicitia,* translated into French by P. de Labriolle, Paris: Picard, 1906.

————, *De resurrectione carnis,* translated into French by A.-E. de Genoude, in *Œ.T.,* volume 1.

————, *Ad uxorem,* translated into French by A.-E. de Genoude, in *Œ.T.,* volume 3.

————, *De virginibus velandis,* translated into French by A.-E. de Genoude, in *Œ.T.,* volume 3.

Titus Livius [Livy], *Histoire romaine,* French translation under the direction of M. Nisard, Paris: Firmin Didot frères, 1839.

Xenophon, *Économique,* edited and translated into French by P. Chantraine, C.U.F., 1949.


MODERN AUTHORS

A. D'Alès. *L'Édit de Calliste. Étude sur les origines de la pénitence chrétienne.* Paris: Beauchesne, 1914.

Dom D. Amand and C. Moons. "Une curieuse homélie grecque inédite sur la virginité adressée aux pères de famille." *Revue bénédictine* 63, 1953.

E. Amman. "Pénitence," in *Dictionnaire de théologie catholique,* volume 12. Paris: Letouzey et Ané, 1933.

A. Benoît. *Le baptême chrétien au second siècle. La théologie des Pères.* Paris: PUF, 1953.

J.-P. Broudéhoux. *Mariage et famille chez Clément d'Alexandrie.* Paris: Beauchesne, 1970.

O. Chadwick. *John Cassian. A Study in Primitive Monasticism.* Cambridge, U.K.: Cambridge University Press, 1950.

A. Delatte. *Essai sur la politique pythagoricienne.* Paris and Liège: Bibliothèque de la Faculté de Philosophie et Lettres de l'Université de Liège, 1922.

F. J. Dölger. *Der Exorzismus im altchristlichen Taufritual: eine religionsgeschichtliche Studie.* Paderborn: F. Schöningh, 1909.

————. *Sphragis.* Paderborn: F. Schöningh, 1911.

A. Dondeyne. "La discipline des scrutins dans l'Église latine avant Charlemagne," *Revue d'histoire ecclésiastique* 28, 1932.

R. Draguet. *Les pères du désert.* Paris: Plon, 1949.

M. Dujarier. *Le parrainage des adultes aux trois premiers siècles de l'Église.* Paris: Éditions du Cerf, 1962.

J. Fargès. *Les idées morales et religieuses de Méthode d'Olympe.* Paris: Beauchesne, 1929.

H. Frankfort. *La royauté et les dieux.* Translated by J. Marty and P. Krieger. Paris: Payot, 1951.

C. J. Gadd. *Ideas of Divine Rule in the Ancient East.* London: Oxford University Press, 1948.

E. Göller. "Analekten zur Bussgeschichte des 4. Jahrhunderts." *Römische Quartalschrift* 36, 1928.

J. Grotz. *Die Entwicklung des Busstufenwesens in der vornicänischen Kirche.* Fribourg-en-Brisgau: Herder, 1955.

R. Gryson. *Le prêtre selon saint Ambroise.* Louvain: Éditions Orientalistes, 1968.

J.-C. Guy. "Examen de conscience (chez les Pères de l'Église)." *Dictionnaire de spiritualité*, vol. 4. Paris: Beauchesne, 1961.

I. Hadot. *Seneca und die griechisch-römische Tradition der Seelenleitung.* Berlin: De Gruyter, 1969.

P. Hadot. "Théologies et mystiques de la Grèce hellénistique et de la fin de l'Antiquité." *Annuaire de l'École pratique des hautes études*, 5th section, vol. 85, 1970.

A. Von Harnack. *Die Mission und Ausbreitung des Christentums in den ersten drei Jahrhunderten.* Leipzig: J. C. Hinrichs, 1906.

I. Hausherr. *Direction spirituelle en Orient autrefois.* Rome: Pont. Institutum Orientalium Studiorum, 1955.

H. Jaeger. "L'examen de conscience dans les religions non chrétiennes et avant le christianisme." *Numen* 6, 1959.

R. Labat. *Le caractère religieux de la royauté assyro-babylonienne.* Paris: Librairie d'Amérique et d'Orient, 1939.

P. Lundberg. *La typologie baptismale dans l'ancienne Église.* Leipzig: Éditions A. Lorentz, 1942.

I. Magli. *Gli uomini della penitenzia.* Bologne: Capelli, 1967.

E. E. Malone. *Martyrdom and Monastic Profession as a Second Baptism.* Düsseldorf: Vom christlichen Mysterium, 1951.

H.-I. Marrou and J. Daniélou. *Nouvelle histoire de l'Église.* Paris: Le Seuil, 1963.

S. Morenz. *La religion des Égyptiens.* Translated by L. Jospin. Paris: Payot, 1962.

J. Morinus. *Commentarius historicus de disciplina in administratione sacramenti paenitentiae.* Anvers, 1682.

B. Poschmann. *Paenitentia secunda.* Bonn: P. Hanstein, 1940.

K. Von Preysing. "Ehezweck und zweite Ehe bei Athenagoras." *Theologische Quartalschrift* 110, 1929.

F. Quatember. *Die christliche Lebenshaltung des Klemens von Alexandrien nach dem Pädagogus.* Vienna: Verlag Herder, 1946.

P. Rabbow. *Seelenführung. Methodik der Exerzitien in der Antike.* Munich: Kösel-Verlag, 1954.

K. Rahner. "La doctrine d'Origène sur la pénitence." *Recherches de science religieuse* 37, 1950.

Ph. de Robert. *Le berger d'Israël.* Genève: Labor et Fides, 1968.

A. Sage. "Le péché originel dans la pensée de saint Augustin." *Revue d'études augustiniennes* 15, 1969.

A. Turck. *Évangélisation et catéchèse aux deux premiers siècles.* Paris: Éditions du Cerf, 1962.

———. "Aux origines du catéchuménat." *Revue des sciences philosophiques et théologiques* 48, 1964.

L. Verheijen. *Nouvelle approche de la règle de saint Augustin.* Bégrolles-en-Mauges: Abbaye de Bellefontaine (Vie monastique, VIII), 1980.

P. Veyne. *Le pain et le cirque.* Paris: Le Seuil, 1976.

F. de B. Vizmanos. *Las vírgenes cristianas de la Iglesia primitiva.* Madrid: La Editoral Católica, 1949.

C. Vogel. *La discipline pénitentielle en Gaule.* Paris: Letouzay et Ané, 1952.

———. *Le pécheur et la pénitence dans l'Église ancienne.* Paris: Éditions du Cerf, 1966.

A. Voöbus. *History of Asceticism in the Syrian Orient.* Louvain: Secrétariat du Corpus Scriptorum Christianorum Orientalium, 1958.

# Translator's Note

I would like to thank the editors at Pantheon, Catherine Tung and Caitlin Landuyt, for shepherding this text—Catherine for the first part and Caitlin for the bulk and the follow-up. Their perceptive notations and apt queries, always offered in good humor, guided my revision.